I0822002

WEAVING
THE HISTORY:
MYSTERY OF
A CITY
Sof

KOÇ
UNIVERSITY

Vekam

Weaving the History: Mystery of a City, *Sof*

Prepared for Publication by
Filiz Yenişehirlioğlu, Gözde Çerçioğlu Yücel

Exhibition Curators
Gözde Çerçioğlu Yücel, Filiz Yenişehirlioğlu

Article Authors
Filiz Yenişehirlioğlu, Gözde Çerçioğlu Yücel, Çiğdem Maner, Bengi Çınar Kul, Erman Tamur, Frédéric Hitzel, Semih Çelik, Feyza Akder, Turkish Cultural Foundation (TCF) Cultural Heritage Preservation and Natural Dyes Laboratory (DATU), Halis Akder, Sadık Karamustafa

Translation
Turgut Berkes

Catalog Photographs
Semih Yolaçan

Book Design
Barek

Print
Dumat Ofset
Bahçekapı Mah. 2477 Sokak No:6
Şaşmaz, Etimesgut - Ankara / Turkey
T +90 312 278 82 00
dumat@dumat.com.tr

ISBN: 978-605-9388-13-9

First Printing: 500

Ankara, 2018

This exhibition catalogue is published within the framework of the *Weaving the History: Mystery of a City, Sof* Exhibition at the Rahmi M. Koç Museum Ankara, 12 May-16 September 2018.

This exhibition catalogue is the English translation of the Turkish catalogue printed with the original title Tarihi Dokumak: Bir Kentin Gizemi, Sof.

Koç University VEKAM
Vehbi Koç Ankara Studies Research Center

Pınarbaşı Mahallesi, Şehit Hakan Turan Sokak, No: 9
Keçiören 06290 Ankara / Turkey
T +90 312 355 20 27
F +90 312 356 33 94

vekam.ku.edu.tr

VEKAM Publication No: 44

WEAVING THE HISTORY: MYSTERY OF A CITY

PREPARED FOR PUBLICATION BY

FİLİZ YENİŞEHİRLİOĞLU

GÖZDE ÇERÇİOĞLU YÜCEL

Contents

Preparing an Exhibition...

FİLİZ YENİŞEHİRLİOĞLU
Koç University, VEKAM

Very few are aware of the significance and reputation of the *sof* fabric and the Angora goat, both of which are identified with Ankara in historical documents. From the past to the present, the naturally delicate Angora goat, and the soft, bright and silky *sof* fabric are known to represent Ankara.

Ottoman documents tell us that the *sof* fabric, no more manufactured today, used to be exported to many European countries, and widely utilized in the various countries within the historic boundaries of the Ottoman geography. Until recently, a comprehensive research had not been conducted into authentic samples of this fabric and products made from it, their appearances and other physical properties.

We have been studying this issue for nearly a year and a half here at the Koç University Ankara Studies Research Centre. Research no doubt needs to continue. However, as we believed that better research could be facilitated by building on accrued work, we decided to create and exhibition and a book/catalogue to share what we have compiled.

We kept our scope wide in view of the relatively low public awareness on the subject. We believed it was important to present knowledge of Angora goat breeding, its economy and physical characteristics, as well as the *sof* fabric and its preparatory phases of processing and dyeing the mohair. While we pursued the equipment for spinning the mohair yarn, the combs and looms, used even today, we discovered the continuity in Anatolian civilizations of equipment that have remained unchanged from their earliest samples seen in Hittite Period reliefs or found in archaeological excavations.

Fabric samples attached to absolutely certain dates were very difficult to find. No doubt, historically *sof* fabrics were of different qualities and varieties. The water-resistant fabric used as sailcloth mentioned in archive documents, the textiles woven for underwear and garments, and the material manufactured for use in hosiery most likely were of dissimilar qualities. However, for the now, we have no access to samples of *sof* produced between the 15th and 19th centuries that would demonstrate us their properties, nor are we able to see concretely the physical characteristics of the *sof* manufactured for diverse purposes. In spite of the variety and density archive documents in this matter, there are no samples of fabric known to have reached our day.

The earliest known sample of mohair weaving is not a cloth, but a *velense*[1] floorcovering that belonged to Ottoman Padishah Sultan Süleyman the Magnificent (1520-1566). This sample, preserved at the Topkapı Palace Museum (Inventory no. 13/148), have survived thanks to palace servants who seed to it that deceased sultans' chattels were bundled and stowed. Kaftans and other garments of padishahs and princes found in museums were most likely selected by

---

1 *Velense*, named after Valencia in Spain, was commonly used as a blanket, and it is known that some good samples from the early 16th and early 17th centuries were included in the Topkapı Palace Museum collection (T. N.).

these people, who bundled these garments and objects as a matter of personal choice rather than anything systematic. Similarly, the six Angora goat fleeces that belonged to Sultan Murat IV (1623-1640) may also be evaluated as 17th century samples (Topkapı Palace Museum, Inventory no. 13/482 and 13/483).

Two other pieces of fabric we believe are from the 18th century reside at very diverse locations. Analyses have shown that one among the pieces of fabric, found in a ship that ran aground in Finland while on its way to Queen Catherine, was mohair-based (Vajanto, 2014). Considering that Angora goats were not bred anywhere else than Anatolia until the 19th century, it would not be far off the mark to link the origins of this finding with Ankara mohair. Similarly, a piece of upholstery fabric at the Victoria and Albert Museum (V&A, Inv. no. T.331-1998) has been identified as an English product dated to 1700. There is a high probability that this was woven in England with mohair yarn imported from Ankara.

The fabrics dated to the end of the 19th century, found at the İstanbul Sadberk Hanım Museum, and the fabric samples from 1890 that belong to Prof Dr Zahide İmer are other dated samples and therefore impart important information on 19th century production.

Another fact that complicated the matter was that mohair was exported not only in the manufactured form of *sof*, but also as plain yarn to be woven into fabric in other countries. The woollen fabric was mixed sometimes with silk yarn, too. Specimens like these need to be closely examined at the museums. Today DNA analyses are extensively used to determine the provenance and physical characteristics of the mohair and fabrics.

The final part of the exhibition was reserved for the status of mohair during the Republican era and examples of contemporary mohair products. The formation of the The Mohair Society of Turkey is significant in this regard. The *sof* fabrics found at the Ankara Museum of Ethnography are examples of these products.

In addition, the visual appearance of the Angora goat as symbol on Republican era stamps and banknotes stand witness to how this image has become prevalent in our cultural memory.

We find a most comprehensive source of visual information on the shearing of mohair goats, spinning mohair yarn, and weaving *sof* in the 19th century painting *View of Ankara* kept at the Rijksmuseum in Amsterdam. This work, which has the skyline of the Citadel of Ankara depicted at the background, will be exhibited for the first time in Turkey at the Rahmi M. Koç Museum, Ankara, based at Çengelhan where *sof* trade used to be conducted. In this way we will have transported a work of art that conveys to us a momentary cross-section of 18th century Ankara to a similar location.

Furthermore, a number of documentary films were created for this exhibition with the purpose of better understanding mohair economy and diverse uses of the commodity within the scope of contemporary practices. Edifying maps and interactive screens were prepared. Finally, we created an environment where guests may visually examine and touch the softness of mohair.

We would like to thank on behalf of the Koç University Ankara Studies Research Centre all persons and institutions, particularly the Turkish Ministry of Culture, and the Embassy of the Netherlands, who shared with us the pleasure in our endeavour to create a work that may serve as a reference to further studies, and provided us their knowledge and materials.

Weaving the History: Mystery of a City, *Sof* Exhibition Tracing the 600-year adventure of *Sof*, Mohair and the Angora Goat

GÖZDE ÇERÇİOĞLU YÜCEL
Koç University, VEKAM

Like most people in our country today, I had heard the word *sof* for the first time when I was introduced the idea of an exhibition project on *sof* through Prof. Dr. Filiz Yenişehirlioglu. I have repeatedly encountered situations during the preparation of the exhibition where I discovered that today the word is unknown to most people. In fact, many people who are relatively within the scope of this field, from Angora goat breeders to textile workers, were hearing the word *sof* for the first time, and some of them even thought it was a kind of fabric used for lining and/or would pronounce it as *soft*. I developed a formula over time to describe the word that represents this precious fabric and what we are planning to exhibit: SOF; it is coded as "Samsun, Ordu, Fatsa; and pronounced *sof*; and woven in Ankara!"[1] Starting from this mysterious incantation, a reading (weaving) of Ankara's history required movement on an interconnected tripod, with Ankara as a city of textiles at the centre: the Angora goat, mohair and Ankara *sof*.

First, I learned that the Ankara *sof* was a very special fabric, woven with a yarn, spun from the long and white mohair obtained from the Angora goat, which had existed only in Ankara and vicinity for centuries during the Ottoman period, the only place in the world where it yielded such silky and brilliant fibre. This fabric is valued for the moiré aspect it gains from the quality, the brightness, the finesse and the many arduous processes of the mohair used to weave it. Moreover, it was not just the Ottoman sultans who were preferred this fabric for their palace clothes; the European elite, too, were enamoured with *sof*! The first thing that struck me was how such a precious product has not attracted much attention by anyone other than eminent historic researchers and could remain mysterious without arousing public curiosity. Today, I could not help but wonder how we could relate to this fact if we knew that a fabric that could be produced only in Ankara was a much sought for commodity in world fashion centres. Thus, I immersed myself in the mysterious world of *sof*, which has remained so mysterious in everyday life, to make a *sof* exhibition.

This article will endeavour to focus on the preparations of the exhibition *Weaving the History: Mystery of a City*, which is designed to create awareness of the Ankara *sof*, one of today's forgotten values, starting out from the three-point axis I have mentioned to trace the adventure of the *sof*, the commodity that made Ankara synonymous with mohair weaving for many centuries. In other words, I will try

1 Rhymes in Turkish (T. N.).

to convey to the reader, that the methods applied to reveal information that is rarely transcribed, generated and shared under the roof of an institution and within a restricted circle, that the problems encountered and their solutions, are the very factors that shape the planned activity.

In this context, this article consists of two main sections. The first part will focus on the meaning of the word *sof* and its equivalents in foreign languages, the sources that determine our path during the preparations for the exhibition and tracing the adventure of the Ankara *sof*. In the second part, we shall take up the fabric itself and the garments produced with it, on the path to exhibit such an original and historical fabric like the Ankara *sof*; the problems we have encountered, and the factors that played a part in determining the works and objects to be exhibited and the preparation the exhibition.

The Word *Sof* and its Equivalents in Foreign Languages

According to the Contemporary Turkish Dictionary of the Turkish Language Association, the word *sof* comes from the Arabic word *sûf*, however, it has two meanings. First of these is "a type of stiff wool fabric," while the second is "lining fabric made of raw silk," and the expression "Ankara *sof*" is assigned to this latter meaning (TDK Turkish Dictionary, 2018). However, neither of these quite convey the meaning of the Ankara *sof* fabric as we are dealing with. Because, Ankara *sof* was neither "stiff," nor "of raw silk". On the contrary, it was soft and woven with yarn spun from the sheer mohair of Angora goats. Characteristics shared by sources written on the Ankara *sof* maintain that it was a precious fabric woven from the mohair of the Angora goat, that it is shiny, and that it was unique to Ankara and its vicinity. One of the simplest definitions of is that *sof* is, "a type of precious moiré fabric woven out of unadulterated mohair (Tamur, 2003, p. 236).

We come closer to the most important feature of *sof* when we scrutinize the etymology of the word. It is thought that the word *sof* comes from the Arabic word *sûf*, and that this is related to goat's fleece. On the other hand, Hasbi Ateş (1968) has claimed that the origin of the word *sof* is from Turkish; he has noted: "In the past, mohair fabrics were called *sof*. Elders and the wealthy of the Ottoman Empire used to wear *sof*. *Sof* is a Turkish word. Turkey is the homeland of the Angora goat. (...) Sufi means "one who has/wears *sof*." In the past, they used to wear mohair, especially the clerical elders. (...) let us suffice saying that, derived from *sof=sov* are words such as *savat*, *savaç*, *savayı*, all of which denote "brightness," "brilliance". (p. 5).

The *sof* fabrics, produced in Ankara after going through many phases, were a significant trade commodity, especially in the 16th century. It was exported to various cities, both inside and outside the Ottoman Empire. The *sof* sent from the Empire, from cities such as Istanbul, Aleppo, Bursa, and Damascus, were sold mainly to European countries such as Venice and Poland (Ergenç, 1995, p. 113). As *sof* was a tradable commodity, words developed in various European languages as equivalent terms for the Ankara *sof*. In French and English sources, particularly the word *camlet (camelot)* is used; and that word has become *chamblet* in English, *zambelotti* in Italian, and *czamlet* in Polish (Tamur, 2003, p. 237).

Figure 1. Riding Coat, around 1760. Materials; Silk and goat's hair. Metropolitan Museum of Art, Inventory No: 1976.147.1

The Oxford English Dictionary's (2017) definition of the word *camlet* may be summarized as "a beautiful, precious oriental fabric," but it also includes various additional comments about the word, such as, "a fabric thought to be made of silk and camel hair, a fabric made of a mixture of wool and silk, a fabric made of cotton and flax with long wool fibres, mostly used in women's clothes." In addition, it is noted that whether the fabric was made of camel's hair is doubtful, and that the word was used for fabrics produced from the fibres of the Angora goat in the 16th and 17th centuries.

In The Grolier Webster International Dictionary (1976, p. 143), the word camlet is described as "a waterproof, durable, special fabric made of goat's fleece, used primarily for cloaks/raincoats in the past." While it is noted that the word has entered English and French as *camelot*, the etymological origins of the word point to *khaml/khamlat* in Arabic. This word in turn derives from *seil al kemel*, which denotes Angora goat in Arabic, according to a source dated to 1874 as quoted by the Oxford English Dictionary (2017). The forms of use of the word over time include *chamlyt*, *chamelet(t)*, *chamlett*, *cham(e)lot*, *chambelot*, *chamblet(t)*, *chamlet*, *camblet*, *chamolet*, *camelott*, *camlott*, *camelot*, and *camlet*. Another claim for the origin of Camlet is that it referred to the River Camlet, where the fabric was made in England (Blum, Ettesvold & Druesedow, 1975, pp. 43-44).

Camlet samples may be found in the New York Metropolitan Museum collection in the United States (Metropolitan Museum of Art, 2017).[2]

Blum, Ettesvold and Druesedow, in a 1975 article, refer to a garment that was recently included in the museum collection. This garment is a riding coat called a *camlet* (pp. 43-44). The Metropolitan describes this item (Inv. No: 1976.147.17) as a British culture riding coat (Figure 1), made of dark brown *camlet*, and states that this is a type of quality fabric that is made of a variety of materials, such as wool, silk, and goat's, or camel's hair. It is also noted that this tightly woven fabric is almost impermeable and therefore compatible with the British climate (p. 44). It is known that the water-resistant feature of mohair was utilized by the Ottomans, too.

Among the products the Ottoman Empire exported to Italy in the 16th century; silk, *sof*, carpets and leather were the most prominent commodities. This valuable fabric was known as *camlet* in English, *camelot* in French, and *ziambelotti* or *zambelotti*

2 There are two English-produced items called *camlet* at the Metropolitan Museum Collection. These are *two panels of printed camlet* dated to the end of the 17th century (Inv. No: 1982.178.1 and 2010.500.5). However, there is no information on whether these were made of mohair.

in Italian sources.[3] Despite the general decline in wool production of the Eastern Mediterranean in the early modern period, *sof* was one of the products regularly exported from the Levant to Europe in the 16th century. At the beginning of the century, *zambelotti d'Angori* (Ankara *sofs*) were among the items dispatched from Ottoman ports to Venice (Kafadar, 2009, p. 100).

Although it is not an equivalent of *sof*, another type of fabric made of Turkish mohair deserves to be mentioned here. This was *Greinen*, produced in Leiden in the Netherlands, in the 3rd or 4th quarter of the 17th century (Wilson, 1960, p.215).

An international rivalry in garment production flourished in the 17th century, and the production of woollen fabrics was of great importance in this competition. The production of *worsted* and fabrics woven with impure yarn were on the decline. *Greinen* or *camlet*, on the other hand, was an exception. The development of these fabrics brought on by the Dutch contrasted with the situation of the English with whom they were competing in the production of woollen fabrics. Starting in 1630, Leiden manufacturers began producing a new kind of *camlet*. Known as the *Leiden Turks*. Camel's or goat's hair were used in this fabric, and later mixed with wool and silk. This fabric sold very well in North and South Europe, particularly in France, and especially in men's wear (Wilson, 1960, p. 217). The Dutch had the advantage of procuring raw materials in face of the worsening general situation of woollen fabrics. The *greinen* produced in Leiden in the 17th century owed its success to the mohair purchased from the Turks at that time.

Demand for Angora goat products began to change by the 18th century. While the identity of the buyers of mohair fabrics in the Ottoman market remains unknown, the domestic trade does not appear to have been too active, either. In addition, the Dutch and the French started to demand mohair yarn rather than mohair textiles. Therefore, it seems likely that focus shifted from weaving mohair fabrics to the production of mohair yarn, an intermediate product. Because this yarn was used in French button industry, and more importantly in textiles in Leiden and Amiens. Likewise, considerable amounts of mohair were used in the manufacture of Dutch woollen fabrics so popular in the 1600s and the 1700s, and in fact, sometimes mohair accounted for 50 percent of the yarns used. This external demand is reflected by the substantial export figures well into the early 19th century (Faroqhi, 2017, p.280).

Greinen samples are found today at the Museum De Lakenhal in Leiden[4]. The fabrics manufactured from mohair yarn most probably obtained from the Ottomans during this period were known as *Turks laken* (cloth) or *Camelots of Turks*. There is a swatch card for these fabrics

---

3 I have learned through my correspondence of 7 August 2017 with Daniela Degl'innocenti, a curator of the Museo del Tessuto (textile museum) in Italy, that there is evidence in Italian archives that *Ciambellotti* (*Zambellotti* in the Venetian dialect) were manufactured; although it was known to have been exported in the 16th century, detecting samples of *sof* in museums was difficult. On the other hand, it is stated that *ciambellotto* in the sources of historical textiles is very limited.

4 Examples from Museum De Lakenhal could not be included in the exhibition because the museum is temporarily closed due to restoration and expansion. Digital print of the fabric Swatch card is included in the exhibition.

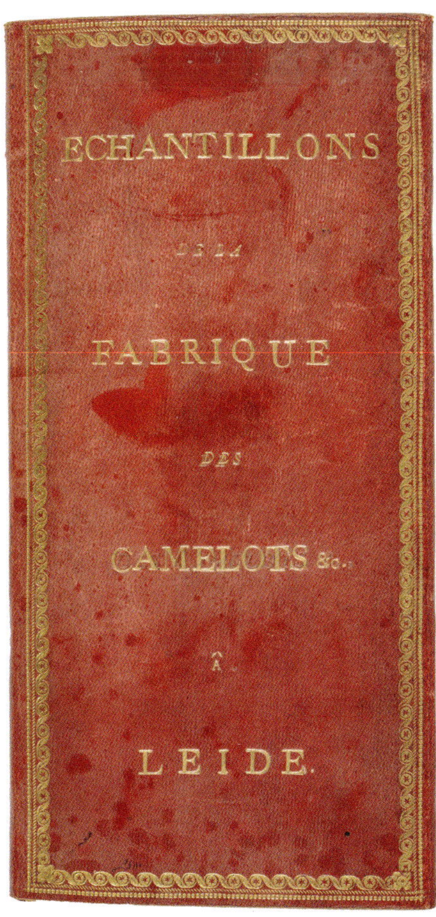

Figure 2 and 3. *Portefeulille met stalen van 'Camelot' of Turks Laken, uit Lieden*
Wallet with samples of *Camelot*, or Turkish cloth, from Leiden (Fabric Swatch card).
Materials: Ink, cardboard, lacquered paper, leather, and paper.
Closed dimensions: 25 x 11.8 x 2.5 cm (250 x 118 x 25 mm).
Open dimensions: 25 x 24.5 x 1 cm (250 x 245 x 10 mm).
Museum De Lakenhal, Inventory No: 1671

in the Lakenhal Museum Collection (Figures 2, 3).

It is also worth dwelling on the English word *mohair*. The word *mohair* was used in English to denote the fleece of the Angora goat, and the yarn or fabric made of this (Merriam Webster Dictionary, 2018). The same dictionary notes that the word was derived from the Italian *mocaiarro*, derived in turn from the Arabic *mukhayyar*, which means *choice*. Leiser (1994) has suggested that *mukhayyar* means "*select*"; and that it appeared as such in Evliya Çelebi's[5] narration of *sof* production in Ankara and in the judicial registries of the period; and that European fabric traders in the Levant may have used (perhaps mistakenly) the Arabic adjective for *select* to describe quality fabrics produced in Ankara, and the Turks may have borrowed it from the Europeans in the course of trade (p. 8).

Sources of the Study

Information on Ankara *sof* can be obtained from various sources. The inseparability of the Ankara *sof* from the Angora goat and mohair and the history of the city of Ankara require that we draw upon diverse fields such as history, folklore, textile engineering, economics, urban history, zoology, zootechnics, and an interdisciplinary approach.

Most of the secondary sources on the Ankara *sof* and mohair weaving benefit from the accounts on the Angora

---

5 Also known as Mehmed Zilli (1611 – 1682), Evliya Çelebi was an Ottoman explorer who travelled through the Empire and neighbouring lands over a period of forty years, recording his commentary in a travelogue called the *Seyahatname* (Travelogue) (T. N.).

goat and *sof* written by travellers of the Ottoman Era, most notably Evliya Çelebi, and foreign travellers. Even the chronology of travellers' accounts from the 15th to the 19th century alone attests to the value of *sof*, its laborious production processes, and most importantly, that it had been significant in accounts on Ankara. Travellers' chronicles impart a wealth of information on the characteristics of the Angora goat and mohair, *sof* weaving and production, and the *sof* trade in the Ottoman Era (Leiser, 1994).

The export of the Angora goat had been forbidden, and the goats were thought to yield low-quality mohair in different climates. Even there had been illegal attempts to cultivate them in various regions, these attempts had failed. In the 19th century, it started to be cultivated across the world, in regions such as South Africa, the United States and Australia. During this period, the Angora goat would also become the subject of many books written in these regions. Among these are Samuel Wilson's (1873) *The Angora Goat: With an Account of Its Introduction into Victoria and a Report on the Flock* is a study of the arrival of Angora goats in Australia and their breeding, along with *The Angora Goat: Its Origin, Culture and Products* by the American author *John Hayes* (1882), which provides information on Angora goat breeders in America. *The Angora Goat*, written by Samuel Cron Cronwright-Schreiner (1898) in South Africa, also contributed to the scientific studies on the Angora goat. American George Fayette Thompson's (1903) *Manual of Angora Goat Raising* imparted essential information about the transportation of the Angora goat to the United States, its breeding, and the development of the mohair industry in America.

Studies on the history of the production of *sof* cover predominantly the 16th and 17th centuries (Ergenç 1975, 1995, Faroqhi 1985, Ongan 1954-1955). Among the main sources used in the literature on *sof* are the accounts of travellers, religious court archives and provincial yearbooks. The studies Ergenç based on documents not only reveal that *sof* was a very important product preferred by the elite, but also provides information on *sof* production, the *sof* trade, and the taxation of *sof* production, especially in the 16th century.

Halit Ongan's Ankara Court Record No. 1 (1958) and Court Record No. 2 (1974) are key sources that list *sof*-related documents. *Ankara Sof Making and Sundry Documentation* (1954-1955), Ongan's study of historical documents on *sof*, reveals the weaving dimensions and dyeing of *sof*, and the strict inspections and control of these in the 16th and 17th centuries.

Studies carried out on the Angora goats during the Republican era also constitute significant sources that contain information about the mohair, the raw material of *sof*, and the goat that is its source. These publications were shaped by such topics as the physical characteristics of the Angora goat, its origins, breeding, characteristics of mohair and its place in the economy (İhsan Abidin [Akıncı], 1924, 1932; Üstar, 1940; Batu ve Okaner, 1946; Batu, 1951; Açıl 1961; Örkiz, 1980; Akman ve Düzgüneş, 1988 ve Akman, 1994).

Some of the sources also are publications that focus exclusively on *sof* and *sof* weaving. The common feature of these publications is that they underline the importance of *sof* and mohair fabric in Ankara and its surroundings during the Ottoman period (Dinçer, 1948 Nisan, 1948 Temmuz, 1948, Ongan,

1954-1955; Ekdoğan, 1955; Ateş, 1968; Su, 1982; Aktan, 1983; Faroqhi, 1985; İmer, 1992; İşcen, 1993; Kılıçbay, 1994; Erdoğan and Jirousek, 2005; İvgin, 2012; Türkoğlu, 2010; Akpınarlı and Yanar, 2016; Uygur, 2017).

Such a holistic approach to *sof* may be found in Erman Tamur's (2003) *The Angora goat and Ankara Mohair Weaving: Cross-sections of the Historical Story of an Exhausted Wealth and Collapsing Industry*. The author traces from his own archive the quest of the Angora goat and Ankara mohair weaving from the 16th to the 20th century.

Regarding Accounts of Travelers...

In Turkish publications which directly and indirectly include the travellers (Eyice, 1972; Şakiroğlu, 1993; Tamur, 2003; Webb Yıldırmak, 2011; Sülüner, 2014) such as Benedetto Dei, Michelé Membre, Ghislen de Busbecq, Hans Dernschwam, Simeon of Poland, Evliya Çelebi, Aşık Paşazade, Joseph Pitton de Tournefort, Aubry de la Mortraye, Paul Lucas, Richard Pococke and Charles Texier. The English article published by Gary Leiser (1993-1994) titled *Travellers' Account on Mohair Production in Ankara From The Fifteenth Through The Nineteenth Century* is worth mentioning, because it provides travellers' accounts of the Angora goat, mohair and *sof* in Ankara in a collective. It is meaningful how for many centuries, accounts of Ankara by people who have come to Ankara for various duties, whom we now define as "travellers," consistently referred to the Angora goat's distinctive mohair, its production and *sof*. When mohair is considered the Angora goat's most prominent feature, it is not wrong to say that accounts of the Angora goat are accounts of mohair and mohair products. In other words, it would not be wrong to define Ankara as the hometown of both the Angora goat and textiles, where the most important commercial activity was *sof* production, despite its decline over time. These accounts not only introduce, as of the 15th century, this creature that has influenced all who came across it, but also allow us to see how the Angora goat and the mohair-based economy identified with Ankara and shaped the history of a city.

The most basic information obtained from all the facts is that Ankara is defined as "the place where *sof* is produced." For example, the Italian Benedetto Dei, a member of the French silk merchants guild who lived between 1418 and 1492, described Ankara when he travelled there in 1467, as a town where *ciambellotti* (*sof*) was made, and this information indicates that *sof* was known in Italy in the first half of the 15th century, and enjoyed international recognition possibly even before that (Webb Yıldırmak, 2006, p.15; Leiser, 1994, p. 9). During this period when Ankara was recorded thus, the *Bedesten*, built at the end of the 15th century by Fatih Sultan Mehmed's grand vizier Mahmut Pasha, and today hosts the Museum of Anatolian Civilizations, and the *Kurşunlu Han* right next to it, were important hubs of the *sof* trade (Ergenç, 1995, p. 17). Leiser (1994), notes that the word *bedesten* derived from the Persian *bazzāzistān* ("place of cloth") and that besides being, with the *Kurşunlu Han*, the centre of *sof* trading in the city, it was also important for the international fabric trade as the station on the Silk Road that linked Istanbul and Tabriz, itself also linked to Bursa (p, 9). Accounts of *sof* and of Ankara, which had gained much recognition due to *sof*, continue with the mid-16th century story of Michele

Membré, a Cypriot merchant of Venetian origin. Travelling with his Armenian and Turkish colleagues to Ankara, Membré recorded his passage through Sivrihisar, arrival in Ankara about ten days later, his sojourn at the *Kurşunlu Han*, later diversion towards Çankırı accompanied by the Turkish traders, where he purchased 25 pieces of *sof* and *mukhayyar* and loaded these on a mule (Şakiroğlu, 1993, pp. 57-58).

Membré's itinerary involves loading his *sof* on a ship at the Port of Samsun to sail for Crimea, where he would continue on to Georgia and Tabriz (Leiser, 1993, p.10), which demonstrates not just the fact that Ankara was the centre of *sof* production and trade, but also that the reputation of the products made of the Angora goat's mohair has become far and wide (Şakiroğlu, 1993, pp. 57-58, Alemdar, 1984, pp. 97-105).

Pierre Belon, a 16th century French naturalist and explorer who came to Ankara in 1548, tells us about the matchless fine wool of the Angora goat, and how this would be plucked by hand rather than sheared. He noted that all moiré and plain *chamelot* were produced from this wool and recorded the earliest description of what we know as the Angora goat, stating that it had fine and long, snow-white hair (Leiser, 1994, p. 10).

The Angora goat and *sof* will continue appear in travellers' accounts throughout the 16th century, such as the *Turkish Letters*, the diaries kept by Austrian Ambassador Augier Ghislain de Busbecq, with the contributions of Hans Dernschwam who accompanied him during his Amasya journey, and French traveller Carlier de Pinon, who reported on *sof* trade in İstanbul, all of which provide very important information regarding *sof* production and trade.

The Flemish-born Austrian Envoy de Busbecq, accompanied by Hans Dernschwam, presented the most comprehensive account of the Angora goat and *sof* fabric of the period. He visited Sultan Süleyman I in Amasya in 1555, as the ambassador of Hapsburg Emperor Ferdinand. He also visited Ankara during this journey (Leiser, 1994, p.10). The *Türk Mektupları (Turkish Letters)*, a compilation of letters (2011) Busbecq wrote to his friend, the Hungarian diplomat Nicholas Michault, is invaluable to those who want to read about the Angora goat and *sof*, as well as a wealth of information about the Ottoman Empire during the Kanuni reign[6]. Busbecq wrote on the Angora goat and *sof*:

... we spent our first night under tents, on account of the heat. The place was called Chiausada [probably Çukurhisar]. Here we saw a subterranean house, which was lighted only by an opening in the roof. We saw also the famous goats from whose fleece — or hair, if you like the word better — is woven the watered stuff known as mohair. The hair of these goats is extremely fine and marvellously flossy, hanging down to the very ground; the goatherds do not shear it, but comb it off, and it is almost as beautiful as silk. The goats are frequently washed in running water. Their food is the scanty dry grass peculiar to these plains, and it is to this that the fineness of their coats is chiefly owing; for it is an ascertained fact, that when the goats are removed elsewhere, their wool does not retain its silky character, but changes with the pasturage; indeed, the whole animal degenerates to such an extent that one would scarcely recognise the breed. These fleeces, after being spun into thread by the women of the country, are taken to Angora [Ankara], a city of Galatia, and

6 Suleiman I, (6 November 1494 – 6 September 1566), commonly known as Suleiman the Magnificent in the West and Kanunî Sultan Süleyman in Turkish ("Suleiman the Lawgiver ") (T. N.).

there woven and dyed; further on I will give you a description of the process. (p.55)

Here we also saw how the famous watered stuff, or mohair, which is woven of the hair of the goats I have already described, is dyed; and how, when water has been poured on, it takes those waves from the action of the press, from which it derives its name, and for which it is prized. The stuff which bears the mark of a very large wave, and keeps its pattern, is considered the best; but if, in any part, smaller and uneven waves occur, although the colour and material be precisely the same, it is worth less by several gold pieces on account of the flaw. Elderly men among the Turks, when they are of high rank, are generally distinguished by dresses made of this material. Sultan Suleiman prefers it to any other dress for state occasions, wearing that which is of a green colour; a hue which, according to our notions, is hardly becoming to a man of advanced years; but their religion, and the example of their prophet Mahomet, who wore it constantly, even in his old age, gives it favour in the eyes of the Turks. (Webb Yıldırmak, 2006, p. 16)

Simeon of Poland, Evliya Çelebi, Kâtip Çelebi and Jean Baptiste Tavernier of France are among the names who reported on the Angora goat and *sof* production they encountered during their visits to Ankara in the 17th century. Evliya Çelebi's testimony is particularly salient:

... Angora goats browse holly leaves up on the mountains of Ankara. The mohair goat is white like milk and there is probably no other animal is as white. Woollen yarn is made of their fleece. The yarns turn out coarse if they are shorn, but they are as soft as Prophet Job's silk if they are plucked. The poor goats bleat to high heaven when they are being plucked, but our elders have found a way to cure their screaming: they mix some lime with some rose water[7] *and wash the goats with this concoction. Their hair fall effortlessly and they become naked. And this is the yarn they use for weaving. The business of men and women is to weave woollen fabrics. Woollen weaving is made in this way: They place a big boiler on the fire and put dye into it for the desire coloured. They half-fill the boiler with water and place decks of woolly fabrics into the boiler. They close the boiler's cover and seal it with dough, and then light the fire. Inside the boiler, the extremely hot steam hits the woollen fabrics and such traces are formed by God that Mani and Behzâd would be powerless incapable to draw. This woollen fabric is actually exclusive to Ankara. There is no possibility of being produced anywhere else on earth.* (Webb Yıldırmak, 2006, p 19. See also Evliya Çelebi, Seyahatname, trans., 2005, p. 137)

By the 18th century, the Angora goat *sof* continued to feature in travellers' accounts. Among the contributors in this period are Joseph Pitton de Tournefort, Aubry de La Motraye, Paul Lucas, Richard Pococke, and Domenico Sestini.

French physicist and botanist Tournefort had recorded that the most beautiful goats of the world lived in Ankara, and that these goats dazzled with their curly, 8-9 fingers-long hair, that all the people in the city earned their lives off the Angora goat's mohair, and that unadulterated yarns were used in *sof* production (Tournefort Seyahatnamesi, 2013, p. 230).

Tournefort's *A Voyage into the Levant* (translated into Turkish as *Tournefort Travelogue* in 2013), with its information on the characteristics of the Angora goat, the economic value of the yarn, and *sof* production, has contributed to the awareness of the Angora goat in the West. Another detailed account in the 18th century belongs to English traveller Richard Pococke. Pococke, besides commenting on the charms of the Angora goat; noted that the goats were sheared in May, that the yarn spun of these would be

7 Different transcriptions of Evliya Çelebi's *Travelogue* translate this as *kül* (ashes) rather than *gül* (rose). (See Kurşun, Kahraman and Dağlı, 1998, p.221).

woven into fine fabrics (*camlet*), which were like the England's best woollen fabrics, and that these were preferred by Turks for summer clothes. The fabrics that the English called *mohair, camlet, prunella,* and the flower-patterned fabrics called *plushes* in Holland were all made from the Angora goat's mohair, England, France and Holland (Webb Yıldırmak, 2006, p.21).

Production Stages and Sites of Ankara *Sof*

By the end of the 16th century, "Ankara was one of Anatolia's major commercial centres, with a population of 25,000. The wealth was derived mostly from the mohair industry" (Faroqhi, 2017, p. 166). Ankara was like a European city, with its international milieu of *sof* trading, and the role of the *ahi*[8] in its administration (Kılıçbay, 1994, Kadı, 2012, p. 29).

According to Özer Ergenç (1995), "dyers and calenderers in *sof* production not only handled the *sof* woven in Ankara but also the products of other *sof*-producing regions such as Tosya, Kastamonu, Çankırı, Sivrihisar and Kalecik. In other words, the processing of the basic *sof* into fabrics of various colours and patterns took place exclusively in Ankara (p.100).

Many families in the 16th century used to weave *sof* in looms they had set up in some part of their homes. Documents from the period, such as bills of real estate transactions, show that there were some three to five looms each in many workshops in the Imam Yusuf, Kâfir-village, Hatun, Öksüzce, Ahi Tura, and Haci Murad neighbourhoods and at the Citadel. Tax records of the period, such as a register dated April 21, 1590, show that tax was received for 621 looms. It is estimated that about 1,000 *sof* looms operated in Ankara in the 16th century (Ergenç, 1995, p. 101).

Faroqhi (2016) notes that while at least some of the farmers found supplementary income sources in Anatolia, where population grew in the 16th century, they were mainly engaged in weaving the mohair fabrics known as *sof* and *mukhayyar*, and most of the preparations for weaving these fabrics were performed by part time village artisans (p. 164). For example, the villages of İstanos, Miranos and Erkeksu at Murtazabad, Ankara did no farming and therefore pleaded to be exempted from some of the taxes levied on agricultural operations (Ergenç, 1984, p.54).[9] Simeon of Poland, who saw Ankara in the 17th century, has mentioned in his travelogue that *sof* was woven in Armenian villages (Tamur, 2003, p. 173).

Investigating the *sof* producing villages of Ankara, Tamur (2003) has noted that Stanos and *Erkapısı* in Simeon's account are İstanos and Erkeksu; and the *Bendos* that was mentioned was most probably Miranos, a mohair and *sof* production destination cited by many foreign travellers after Simeon. He claims that another village, *Alucak*, is Lower Ulucak in the Beypazarı district, mentioned in the Karacabey Endowment, but is no longer registered as residential area (p. 17). In the 19th century, Istanos was the central town of the Zir district, which was founded on a rocky region next to

8 The *ahi* (from the Arabic "my brother") were Sufi guilds of young men dedicated to the betterment of the community focused around Anatolia during the Ottoman Era, since as early as the 13th century (T. N.).

9 See also Ongan, 1974, p. 133, Ankara Court Records, 2/1718.

the Ova Brook, and its name was later changed to Yenikent in the 1950s and is now connected to Sincan. Famous for its *sof* weaving, Zir also caught the attention of Evliya Çelebi, who visited Ankara and its vicinity in the 1640s: "Most of the subjects in these towns are Armenians. There are a thousand looms where *suf* and *mukhayyar* are processed and there is a loom. However, being next to the brook, the air is rather hot, but they produce delightful *mukhayyar*, it is much-praised, and the Armenian girls are legendary." (Kurşun, Kahraman, Dağlı, 1998, p. 229 cited by Tamur, 2003, p.175)

Questions on how *sof* was produced and whether this production process changed over time remain as important as ever, because knowledge of the production technique has been lost over the years. However, we can still refer to travellers' accounts on this subject, too. In the 16th century, the detailed descriptions of Busbecq's companion Hans Dernschwam, in his *Istanbul and Anatolian Travel Journal* imparts information on the *sof* production technique of that period:

We saw only how the Greeks made the sof. First they wash the spun and combed yarn. Then they boil it in hot water; and then put it under the press and drain the water completely. They stretch these yarns tightly from one side to the other and lubricate them with an oily substance, prior to weaving the sof and cutting the yarns. Once the yarns are stretched across the loom, they begin to weave the sof. The woven fabric is thoroughly washed with soap under running water. The sof at this stage looks like mohair. These are stacked into copper boilers, which can be sealed tight. Each boiler can hold 70 pieces. Next, the boilers are filled with fresh water and is left in this state for a full day. Hollow reeds (thin reeds) collected from the shores of the lake are placed between each piece, to make sure that all the pieces are thoroughly inundated. This is how water is delivered between each piece of fabric. Then the sofs are stacked in a press in piles of 70 pieces again. The water in the fabrics is completely removed in this way. The reeds are pulled out prior to placing them under the press. In short, this boiling and pressing process completely removes any water left in the fabrics. Next, the fabrics are spread lengthwise on the ground. Then they are folded and finally readied. All of the sofs we encountered at the township were black (pp. 250-251).

Besides mohair's natural colour, the *sof* fabric was also produced in a variety of colours. Halit Ongan (1954-1955) in his *Ankara Sof Making and Sundry Documentation* has stated that raw and uncoloured *sofs* from the loom were washed by "washers," who next passed them on to the finishing, dyeing and pressing processes applied before they can be offered for sale. He notes that these were quite laborious and costly processes; that dye, tragacanth, and size were the main requirements of the *sof* industry; and that manufacturers who cheat or skimp on the dye mixture could be taken to court.[10] The *sofs* come in a variety of colours, and in addition to Ongan's work, in documents scanned on *sof* in the Ottoman Archives of Prime Ministry of Turkey, we encounter a list of

---

10 There is a second opinion that the *sof* fabric was made of mohair yarn dyed before weaving. The stages of production of *sof* in Necmettin Dinçer's article *The Ankara Sof* (1948, April, p. 31-33, 1948, July, p. 40-41) published in two sections in the Ülkü Halkevi Compendium describes as follows: the preparation of mohair, the combing and separation of long and short fibres, dyeing, washing, a second round of combing the mohair yarn, the spinning and twisting, folding the spun yarn into two, three or four, depending on the type of *sof* to be woven, preparation of the warp and weft yarns, sizing before the yarn is brought to the loom, adjustment of the yarns on the loom, weaving, washing of raw *sofs*, passing through a process of sulfurization and, finally, finishing, polishing, kiln-drying and moiré operations.

the colours *sof* came in: such as crimson, scarlet, dark purple, violet, purple, hyacinth, sky blue, pistachio, rose, bright red, light lilac, cornelian, wine, grass green, orange, Egyptian purple, black, and dark rose.

The *Sof* Trade

Anatolia was not only exporting textiles to the Balkans and the North of the Black Sea, but also to Europe in the 15th and 16th centuries. Expensive fabrics such as brocade and *sof* were produced in Turkey as luxury goods; choice of European elites, among whom were the Russian Tsar and aristocrats, Italian and French princes and princesses, and Swedish bishops (İnalcık, 2011, p. 13). With an income of over 50.000 *akçes*[11] in tax revenues obtained from the dye workshops, 16th century Ankara stands out among the big cities with textile dyeing establishments, and this is due to *sof* exports (İnalcık, 2011, p.123).

Sof trading was conducted in a certain order. The weaving, dyeing and selling of the fabric, along with various methods and rules, was subject to supervision. Various complaints about *sof* production can be found in the 16th and 17th century court records, when of *Sof* production was at its most intense. Today, thanks to these documents, we can learn about the professionals operating in *sof* production, the issues they had to deal with, and order of *sof* production:

The sof weavers, under the supervision of the sheikhs, stewards and guild representatives within the trade order, obtained sof yarns according to their needs and wove fabrics in certain sizes that they would exhibit at the Bedesten or sell them through brokers. They also worked in paid jobs for whoever supplied yarn to be woven into fabric (Ergenç, 1995, p. 101).

Among the actors of the *sof* trade, merchants were as important as weavers, washers, dyers, polishers or pressers in *sof* production.

According to Ergenç (1995), the two main groups of the *reâya*[12] were agricultural producers, namely peasants and small artisans; and another group is made up of merchants. "The merchant is a great businessman who deals with international and interregional trade. In other words, while offering the goods he brings from distant places, he takes or sends the goods he collects in the country to sell elsewhere." Merchants, with a reputation in the Ottoman Empire, were endowed with a privileged position in their activities. Because the merchant "played a role in the fulfilment of the task of obtaining much-needed commodities from regions where these are in abundance, preventing the *reâya* from distress and thus helping the Sovereign in his duty to bring wealth and peace to the land. In addition, one of the merchants' most important functions was their ability to serve the state in various ways. For example, they may lend money to the State or high-level officials when needed, because it always has ready money. Apart from these, a merchant is in the position of the Sovereign's emissary in a foreign country." (p. 109).

The *sof* fabrics produced in many stages in Ankara, was the subject of major trade, especially the 16th century. It was exported to many cities, both inside

11 The *akçe* was the chief monetary unit of the Ottoman Empire, a silver coin (T. N.).

12 The *reâya* were the non-Muslim subjects of the Ottoman Empire, prior to the *Tanzimat* (Ottoman reorganization of 1839 – 1876, T. N.).

and outside the Ottoman Empire. *Sof* sent to cities within the Empire, such as İstanbul, Aleppo, Bursa, and Damascus were sold for the most part to European countries such as Venice and Poland (Ergenç, 1995, p. 113).

By the end of the 16th century, France and Venice had become the two most important actors of the Levant[13] trade. Although trade with Venice was often interrupted due to conflicting relations with the Ottoman Empire, it continues to hold a dominant position in the Ottoman Empire's commercial relationship with the West. Among the wide range of products that Venice purchased from the Levant, Anatolian textiles occupied an important place, and western Anatolia cotton and mohair yarn from the Ankara region were important items in the Ottoman-Venice trade (Eldem, 2006, p. 298). One of the most significant changes that occurred at the end of the century was the rising influence of the British and the Dutch against the Mediterranean powers of Venice and France. While the Venetians' influence in the Levant trade certainly declined, the French would continue to exert some power, albeit being weakened by the war and political impotence until the end of the 17th century. However, with France's recovery, its dominant position in the Levant trade would continue for the larger part of the 18th century (Eldem, 2006, p. 299).

An examination of the Ottoman sources in Venetian archives suggests that the intensity of Ottoman subjects' commercial activities in the Venetian market gradually increased after the 1573 period. The section "Death in Venice (1575)" in Cemal Kafadar's (2009) book *Who Has Been in Here While We Were Not* conveys important information related to the Ottoman-Venetian *sof* trade. The *sof* fabric, which was among Ottoman exports to Italy in the 16th century, was one of the products regularly exported from the Levant to Europe in the 16th century despite the general decline in wool production of the Eastern Mediterranean in the early modern period. At the beginning of the century, Bartolomeo di Pasi cited *Zambelotti d'Angori* (Ankara *sof*) as one of the export items sent to Venice from Ottoman ports (Kafadar, 2009, p. 100). Ankona and Venice were the most important cities in Italy where Ottoman merchants made their presence felt and traded their goods.

Muslim and Armenian merchants from sof-producing Central Anatolian cities like Ankara, Ayaş, Beypazarı, Tokat or Tosya dominated trade in Rialto as of the 1570s. Earlier sources also refer to sof, and Muslim and Armenian merchants who visited Italian cities; however, sof appeared in the Archives of the State of Venice as a very important commercial product, and the merchants of Central Anatolia came to be associated with the cities they came from and with sof trading after the Cyprus War. (Kafadar, 2009, p. 98).

Kafadar questioned whether the appearance of Anatolian *sof* merchants in the Venetian market in the 1570s were more likely to be associated with the Ottoman possession of the once-Venetian colony of Cyprus. Kafadar (2009) believes this to be because Cyprus was an alternative *sof* production centre during the 16th century.

Sometime after the introduction of camels to the island, in the 12th or 13th centuries, and long before Ankara became famous for the sof trade, Cyprus had become an important centre for the production of an

13 The term Levant, "rising," implies the rising of the sun in the east. It was used to denote East Mediterranean countries (Webb Yıldırmak, 2011, p. 20-21).

exclusive type of woollen fabric – today's camel hair. Between 1373 and 1464, when the Genoese reigned over Magosa, sof production appeared as if it was the only production activity in that city; Nicosia was also noteworthy for the production of sof. After taking over the island in 1489, Venice established absolute monopoly on the island's sof, and even gave some of it to Mameluke rulers as a tax. It is no surprise that Selim I, after the Egyptian conquest, asked the Cypriots to pay their taxes in gold rather than sof, because there is plenty of sof in his own Empire (pp. 103-104).

The efficacy of Cyprus within the Ottoman *sof* trade with Venice may still be a matter of research. However, the fact is that *sof* fabric has a major place among the products exported to Italy. Kafadar (2009) documents that *sof* was an important item in the Ankara-Venice trade route of caravans that set off from Ankara; and that payments in kind were made rather than cash in the commercial activities dominated by Central Anatolian merchants from Ankara, Ayaş, Beypazarı and Tosya (pp. 105-106).

Kafadar (2009) also portrays the material world of a 16th century trader from Ayaş, from information gathered from a batch of documents in the Venetian Archives (Archivio di Stato di Venezia). According to the estate of *sof* trader Hüseyin Çelebi bin Hacı Hızır bin İlyas from Ayaş, who went to Venice to trade *sof* and was murdered on March 20, 1575 – a list written in Turkish and translated into Italian on April 8, 1575, of the personal belongings, sold by Huseyin Çelebi's uncle in Venice "in the presence of the Muslims", with information regarding burial expenses, debts and receivables (pp. 114-122).

As Muslim-, Jewish- and Christian-Ottoman merchants from Central Anatolia travelled to Venice; Venetian merchants also came to Ankara in the 17th century for the mohair trade, and even became long-time residents of the city. Indications of such long stays may be traced in historical documents. It is known from the archives that local tax offices attempted to treat these resident foreigners as if they were non-Muslim subjects of the Sultan and intended to tax them as such, but the Venetian merchants avoided paying in 1612 thanks to their ambassadors in Istanbul; and how they were allowed to live within the city walls to assure their security, because rebels had confiscated merchandise left outside the walls (Faroqhi, 2017, pp. 168-169).

Besides Venice, Poland was also a country that imported mohair fabrics. Information on merchants who imported textiles from the Middle East may be found in Ottoman court records of and Polish archives from the mid-16th century to the mid-17th century. Ankara tradesmen are known to have travelled to Poland as well, just as they did to Venice. Andrzej Dziubinski (1999, pp. 40-41), in his article titled *Polish-Turkish Trade in the 16th to 18th Centuries* frequently mentions Ankara merchants, emphasizing that special importance was attached to mohair fabrics in the Polish market (Faroqhi, 2017, p. 169).

Faroqhi (2012) assesses the demand for mohair fabrics in Poland as follows:

Demand came mainly from the male members of the nobility and gentry, for while women dressed in the 'normal' clothes

The demand came mainly from the members of the nobility and gentry, for while women dressed in "normal" clothes of Central Europe, these men asserted what was called a 'Sarmatian'[14] *identity, and*

14 The Sarmatians were a large Iranian confederation in classical antiquity (5 BC – 4 AD).

for this purpose used clothes and arms in 'Turkish' style. Ottoman currency was typically used in these transactions, but bills of exchange were also current; the latter were not only in trade fairs on Polish territory but also in İstanbul and Edirne. Thus, over a century the Polish demand for mohair cloth contributed towards the prosperity of craft production in Ankara and in a broader perspective to a closer link between the Ottoman and Polish business worlds (pp. 169-170).

The fact that the English knew about *sof* fabric can be seen in travellers' accounts in the preceding sections. Queen Elizabeth, with concessions she endowed on 12 traders in 1583, helped establish the Levant Company, a monopoly on trade between England and Turkey (Ottoman Empire). The Company carried out its operations through commercial missions (factors) called "factories," in İstanbul, Izmir and Aleppo. By 1624, the Levant Company had two representatives. These two are thought to have been dispatched from Istanbul to Ankara to carry out the highly valued silk and the Angora goat. The number of representatives declined to one the 18th century (Barnett, 1974, pp. 135-136).

Today, besides the historical documents establishing the history of the Levant Company, another element that proves that English merchants were located in Ankara in the 16th century consists of the tombstones found in the Armenian Church cemetery near Ankara. Hans Dernschwam, who visited Ankara in the 16th century, was the first to mention the Church of the Saint Mary that was linked to the Armenian Monastery. William Hamilton, visiting Ankara in the early 19th century, referred to St. Mary's Church as the centre of the Catholic Armenian Episcopal See, whose power extended to Tokat. He was told that all the European merchants who died in Ankara were buried in the graveyard attached to this church near Lake Çubuk, and the English names on tombstones prove the presence of British merchants in Ankara. Unfortunately, today the church is in ruin; but remnants of the graveyard can be found (Barnett, 1974, pp. 136-137).

Tournefort saw the church graveyard in 1700, encountered the tombstones Scottish merchant John Roos who died on June 22, 1668, and Samuel Farrington, son of London merchant Acidwall Farrington, who died in 1660 when he was just 23 years old. Although these tombs have disappeared, R.D. Barnett, who examined the location, saw the tombstones of William Black, known to be an English merchant who died in 1684 and Henrico Davie, who died in 1703, as well as the tombs of Dutch merchant Theodore Lecker who died in 1679, and French merchant Joseph Guieu, who died in 1770 (Barnett, 1974, p, 141).

One of the documents that shows the British knowledge of and preference for Ankara's mohair fabrics, is in the British Library Lansdowne Manuscripts collection (MS 241, f393a). David French (1972), has brought this document to light in his article *A Sixteenth Century English Merchant in Ankara?* This is a letter from William Harborne, appointed British ambassador on November 26, 1582, to Consul James Towerson. Harborne is known to have come to Istanbul on March 29, 1583 to and conduct the business affairs of the Levant Company. Since Towerson is known to have died

---

Sarmatism is an ethno-cultural concept with a shade of politics based on the belief that Poland originated from Sarmatians (T. N.).

in Aleppo in 1586, and the said letter does not carry a date, the probable date of the letter is thought to be the summer of 1583. In the letter, Harborne listed in detail the fabrics that Towerson is expected to purchase in Ankara. Containing Harborne's detailed orders in the letter mentions the characteristics and various colours of the fabrics. It is a very important document revealing Ankara's textile products of in the 16th century. It is also important regarding the British-Levant trade. A digital copy of the letter received with the permission of the British Library was included in the exhibition.

From Exporting Mohair Fabrics to Exporting Yarn ...

One of the factors affecting the mohair industry and *sof* trade in Ankara is the prohibition of exports of mohair yarns during the Ottoman period up until the mid-17th century; but first the flouting of this law, and later its annulment had significant effects on the *sof* industry and trade:

Until the middle of the 17th century, mohair yarns were used exclusively by sof producers in Ankara, and it was strictly forbidden to sell these yarns to other tradesmen and out of Ankara. Both clerical and administrative authorities, together with the Ankara Pressers' and Dyers' Guild supervised the ban, which began to be flouted as early as 1638. By the end of the century, export of mohair yarn was out of the scope of forbidden commodities. In the 1690s, rules were laid down as to how yarn loads taken out of Ankara would be taxed, and tax rates were established. Now, the name of the yarns spun in Ankara came to be called "İzmir-style yarn" or "yarn purchased in Ankara, paid for in İzmir" (Webb Yıldırmak, 2011, p. 169).

However, due to competition with Europe, Ottoman mining and textile industries, fell into decline in the 1600s and this seems to be related to price movements (İnalcık, 2011, p. 216). One of the events that affected the sale of merchandise in Venice, an important market for mohair merchants during this period, was the long war fought for Crete, which took place between 1645 and 1669. The consequent loss of Venice, in turn an important market for Central Anatolian merchants, led to an excess of mohair fabric domestically with the decline in foreign demand (Faroqhi, 2017, p.279).

By the 18th century, a change was observed in the demand for Angora goat products. While purchasers of the mohair fabrics produced in the Ottoman domestic market have not been identified, the domestic market is thought to be quite sluggish, too. Moreover, it seems that the Dutch and the French now demanded mohair yarn rather than fabrics made from mohair. Therefore, production during this period appears to have shifted from mohair textile to mohair yarn, an intermediate product. Because the "said yarn was used in the French button industry, and more importantly in the cloth manufactures of Leiden and Amiens. For in the manufacture of the Dutch "woollens" that were markedly successful in the 1600s and early 1700s, considerable quantities of mohair were used, sometimes amounting to 50 percent of the fibre employed. This foreign demand is reflected in the export figures, which remained appreciable until the early nineteenth century" (Faroqhi, 2017, p.280).

İsmail Hakkı Kadı (2012), in his *Ottoman and Dutch Merchants in the Eighteenth Century*, which deals with the relations of the Dutch merchants with the non-Muslim merchants in the Ottoman Empire

(Armenian and Greek) in the 18th century, expounds on the Dutch mohair trade with the Ottomans. Kadı's comprehensive study comprises two separate sections on *sof* and mohair trade. These are respectively "The Town of Ankara and Its Mohair Industry" (pp. 29-64) and "The Heyday and Interruption of the Dutch Mohair Trade" (pp. 65-97). In 1700, the Dutch textile industry alone accounted for three-quarters of Ankara's total annual mohair yarn export with some 3,000-3,200 bales, and the Dutch efforts to penetrate the mohair yarn trade deeper had led to a rivalry with non-Muslim merchants who were active in the trade of mohair yarn in the Ottoman Empire (pp. 2-4).

In the 18th century, Britain was an important market in terms of mohair trade between the Ottomans and Europe. Gülay Webb Yıldırmak (2011) presents important information on this subject in her work 18th Century Ottoman-English Mohair Trade, which has been based on large number of documents from British archives. As suggested by Yıldırmak (2011, p.243) a total of 5.545343.2 lb (about 2.518 tons) of mohair yarn was exported from Turkey to England in the 18th Century. Noting that mohair yarn was used in England for men's and women's wear, interior decoration, wigs, toupees, in the military, in buttons, buttonholes and gold ribbons, Yıldırmak points out that (pp. 58-162) while the Angora goat's mohair, a much sought-after material in Great Britain for centuries, created demand for mohair fabrics until the 18th century, when demand veered towards yarn, and then to fleece by the end of the century (p.243). Among the reasons for this shift were, "first of all, the mercantilist/capitalist policies implemented by the UK, and secondly, the invention and advancements of textile machinery with the Industrial Revolution, which shifted the country's necessities from finished goods to raw materials" (p. 243).

French merchants are known to have visited Ankara in the 18th century to buy mohair. The idea of opening a consulate in Ankara was also considered; but the French have to compete with the Armenians, who want to monopolize the mohair trade (Inalcık, 2011, p.113).

Despite the changing foreign demand, the Angora goat still maintained its importance for the Ottoman Empire in the 20th century. An example of this may be seen in the special attention paid to the Angora goat in the *Ankara Vilayeti Salnamesi-Provincial Yearbook of Ankara* 1907. Besides the statistical information on the presence of Angora goats in the Ankara province, the last chapter titled "Mohair Goats: Observations on Goats in General" is about the origins, genera, anatomical structures, characteristics of their home range, economic significance, mohair-to-milk and meat yields of Angora goats, and finally, their diseases.[15] Besides a variety of mohair products, *sof* production continued in early 20th century:

> *According to the accounting of the [Hijri] year [one thousand] three hundred and twenty-two, there were 1,482,782 heads of mohair, and considering that each above-average [goat] yielded one and a half kıyye,[16] this amounts to two and a half million kıyye*

---

15 This work is included in the Sadberk Hanım Museum Collection (Inventory Number: Bulletin No. 2880) and is included in the exhibition. Detailed information about the work is included in the catalogue section of this book.

16 *Kıyye* or *okka* was an Ottoman measure of weight, equal to 400 dirhems. Its value varied,

per annum in Ankara. An insignificant portion of this is used within the province, and the celebrated mohair fabrics, known as the Ankara sof, is woven in the town of İstanos, which is the centre of the Zir district. Some exquisite men's and women's hosiery, neckerchiefs, women's headscarves, and mufflers from the province centre, all mohair; embroidered, natural coloured mohair rugs from Kırşehir; mohair gloves, blankets etc. from Sivrihisar and Akdagmadeni, and fleeces are all prepared and dispatched wholesale to the manufacturing centres of London, Liverpool, Manchester, Vienna, Berlin, and the curiosity of the city. (Ankara Vilayeti Salnamesi, p. 296).

Prof İhsan Abidin [Akıncı], who travelled to Anatolia in 1924 to study the Angora goat and mohair, identified the last few mohair looms in the Zir region, now known as Yenikent (Batu, 1951, p. 40), as opposed to the 1,000 looms that still operated in mid-19th century. It is safe to say that as of the 17th century, the shift in foreign demand from fabric to yarn and then to fleece, was influential in the gradual decline and final collapse of *sof* production in Ankara (Webb Yıldırmak, 2011, p. 169). Other possible reasons may be the fact that the Armenian masters of *sof* weaving of the Ottoman times were unable, for a variety of reasons, to transfer the art to successive generations, and producers who would have provided continuity of information turned to different production activities over time.

Organizing the Exhibition

A holistic approach has been followed to create the exhibition, since *sof* fabric is a final product that cannot be considered independently from Angora goat and mohair weaving. In this context, documents related to mohair weaving and trading, and the Angora goat, source of the raw material, were studied. Various materials from the VEKAM Library and Archives, such as photographs, postcards, publications, stamps, etc. related to the Angora goat, mohair weaving, and trade were inspected and included in the exhibit. In addition to the documents obtained from Erman Tamur's personal archive, samples of the mohair and yarn preparation tools belonging to Erman Tamur and the Özbahar family, who bred Angora goats in Ankara's Ayaş district, were also exhibited.[17]

Since the emergence of the exhibition idea, steps have been taken with the hope of displaying the painting *Gezicht op Ankara*, (View of Ankara, Rijksmuseum Amsterdam collection, Inventory No: SK-A-2055), a work of art that is an important document on Ankara mohair weaving. This painting was thought to portray a view of Aleppo for many years. However, Prof Dr Semavi Eyice has asserted in his 1972 work *An Old Ankara Painting* that Ankara was the subject. One of the biggest factors in determining this provenance is the large number of Angora goats, understood to be undergoing a certain process, located at the lower right edge of the painting.

The upper part of the two-part composition depicts Ankara with its periodic structures and sites, while the

but it was standardized in the late empire as 1.2829 kilograms (T. N.).

17 I would like to thank Ms. Güldane Oğuz, Member of the Board of Directors and Deputy General Manager of Tiftikbirlik, and Onur Bal, who has set his heart on the Angora goat, for their help in contacting the Özbahar family. I would like to thank the Özbahar family and Erman Tamur for their support of our exhibition.

lower part portrays various scenes from the bazaar and city life. This painting reveals the importance of mohair trade and *sof* weaving in the history of Ankara, with its figures of women wearing *feraces*[18] made of *sof*, the wool being woven on the loom, the merchants, and a caravan carrying goods from Ankara. Although the artist is unknown, the work is a vivacious depiction of Ankara with its mohair-based industry, its business life, as well as its topographical features as seen by European eyes. The efforts to borrow and exhibit this work, which is an important document for studies on the history of Ankara, have constituted a large part of the preparations for the exhibition. The work will be meeting Ankara and its citizens for the first time through the exhibition (Weaving the History: Mystery of a City Exhibition Catalog, pp. 170-171).

Although there were many publications about it, *sof* fabric was found only in a few museum collections and not kept on display but in storage, unknown and unseen; and this laid the basis for our purpose of exhibiting *sof* fabric samples. For this reason, samples of *sof* fabrics, woven from the Angora goat's mohair, were sought from many museums and private collections both in Turkey and abroad._

Samples of *Sof* and Mohair from Museums and Private Collections

As the idea of an Ankara *sof* exhibition developed, research was based on the assumption that samples of *sof* and/or accessories made of the fabric could be found in the world textile and fashion circles, and as the literature on *sof* indicated, specifically in the regions where the fabric was exported in the Ottoman period. During studies, conducted mainly between March and October 2017, our very search for *sof* turned into an adventure, like the history of *sof* itself.

The first stage of our research involved creating a list of textile museums, and museums known for their rich textile collections, found in the countries where we knew from scientific studies that *sof* trade had reached. A total of 67 museums, 54 of which were from abroad, such as England, Italy, Poland, Holland, France, Russia, United States, Portugal, Germany, Belgium, Egypt and Greece, and 13 domestic museums were asked whether they had their collections works of *sof* and/or Angora goat's mohair. Considering the possibility that fabrics may have been acquired by private collections through auctions, two international auction houses and one foundation was contacted.

At the outset of our correspondence with the museum, the SEM-EDX (Energy-dispersive X-ray spectroscopy) method, which determines chemical structures by performing elemental analysis of historical textiles, was employed in order to ensure that a late 19th- or early 20th- century, cream-coloured, undyed, plain-weave piece of fabric made of goat's hair, number 10568 in the inventory of Sadberk Hanım Museum, was indeed *sof* (Weaving the History: Mystery of a City Exhibition Catalog, p. 273). The Cultural Heritage Preservation and Natural Dyes Laboratory (DATU), which uses this method to analyse, determined that the yarn used in the fabric was mohair, and that its specifics were compatible with those of the Ankara *sof*.

---

18 A dark, modestly cut woman's robe that buttoned all the way to the throat, fashionable in the 19th Century (T. N.).

This first analysis has served as a model in our quest for the *sof* fabric, in museum collections and shed light on our work. During our research on various samples in museum and private collections that are thought to be made of mohair but unclear as to whether they were *sof*; SEM-EDX, dyestuff analyses, were performed at the Cultural Heritage Preservation and Natural Dyes Laboratory (DATU), and DNA analyses at the Ankara University Faculty of Veterinary Medicine, respectively.

An initial step was to study online museum collections. Collections that may be searched online were queried using especially the English word *mohair* and its equivalent in all relevant languages. The words I used in the first section such as camlet, *camelot* and *greinen*, thought to have been produced from Angora goat mohair in the Netherlands, were also used as keywords. Meanwhile letters were sent to all the museums, referring to the history of the Angora goat, the *sof* fabric and its special characteristics, describing our exhibition project, and querying after *sof* and other mohair artefacts they may have in in their collections.

We were unable to obtain a positive response also from museums that do keep textiles produced during the Ottoman Period such as the British Museum (UK), the Victoria & Albert Museum (UK), the Calouste Gulbenkian Museum (Portugal), the Hermitage Museum (Russia), the Textile Museum (Washington D. C., USA), and the Metropolitan Museum of Art (USA). Metropolitan Museum of Art collection includes artefacts identified as "mohair" by the museum; while a majority of this is dated to the 20th and 21st centuries, a more comprehensive study on mohair clothing, accessories and upholstery fabrics can be pursued. Swiss foundation Abegg Stiftung, which has a collection of works from the Ottoman Empire, was also invited. It can be said that the collections of most of these museums, which featured textile samples from the Ottoman period, consisted of silk and velvet samples, rather than woollen fabrics.

The collection can be found in online searchable museums only when the word "mohair"[19] is searched and museums included mohair-containing artefacts in their collections, such as the Fashion Institute of Design and Merchandising (FIDM), Metropolitan Museum of Art, Museum of London, Manchester Art Gallery, Gallery of English Costume, York Castle Museum, Victoria & Albert Museum, and Kirklees Museum. However, the majority of these constitute works dated to the 19th and 20th centuries. Since the outset of the 19th century, when the Angora goat began to be bred in different parts of the world and especially in South Africa, and mohair yarn and raw mohair exports started, it is very likely that the artefacts dated to these centuries were not produced in Ankara. *Sof* or Angora goat mohair was not detected as a result of our correspondence, except

19 In England, mohair yarns have been used in the manufacture of clothing and accessories by mixing with silk or wool. There are debates whether the term "mohair" was perceived as a kind of "silk in the 17th century." We mentioned this issue in our correspondence of 31 May 2017 with Ms. Clare Browne, senior curator of the Textile Department at the Victoria & Albert Museum, who told us that several researchers, including Peter Thornton, claimed that the term "mohair" denoted a type of silk in 17th Century Britain.

for a piece of upholstery dated to the 18th century found in the Victoria & Albert Collection. Difficulties in carrying out SEM and DNA analyses on a historical piece of dyed fabric has prolonged the process and, unfortunately, although the SEM-analysis of the yarn has determined that it was made of mohair, we were unable to succeed in DNA analysis to prove that is sample is from Angora goat's mohair from Turkey within the deadline of the completion of the procedures required to borrow the respective fabric.

Domestic museums were also contacted through official correspondence. Experts of the Topkapı Palace Museum, Ethnography Museum of Ankara and Sadberk Hanım Museum, affiliated to the Turkish Republic Ministry of Culture and Tourism, General Directorate of Cultural Heritage and Museums were consulted regarding artefacts within the scope of the research, registered in their museum inventories. These experts were Museum Expert Lale Görünür of the Sadberk Hanım Museum, Sultan's Garments Section Curator Sibel Alpaslan Arça of the Topkapı Palace Museum, and Museum Researcher Hatice Ildıroyuk of the Ethnography Museum of Ankara.

Besides the Ethnography Museum of Ankara, the Sadberk Hanım Museum and the Topkapı Palace Museum, all of which have lent artefacts to the exhibition, correspondences were conducted also with the Ankara Museum of Foundation Works, the Istanbul Military Museum and Culture Site Command, the Naval Museum Command, the Konya Mevlana Museum and Istanbul Museum of Mausoleums, which were queried regarding the presence of *sof* fabric artefacts registered in museum inventories. The correspondence was conducted in June 2017. No *sof* could be detected in any of these museums. It should be noted here, however, that because *sof* is difficult to detect – the naked eye can easily mistake it for silk because of its moiré and shiny appearance – although no artefact made of *sof* may exist to our present knowledge, in the future research may be conducted on fabrics found particularly in the mausoleums. Studies conducted on *sof* in the Ottoman Archives of the State Archives General Directorate have revealed that, besides manufacturing *ferace*s and *kerrake*s[20] from *sof* (Fonds number: TS, MA.d Document File No: 2438, Shirt No: None, h.1207 m.1793), drapery made of *sof* were used in the mausoleums (Fonds number: A. {DVNSMHM.d ..., Document File No: 26, Shirt No: 506 h.982 m.1574). Garments of *sof* were assumed to have been made for Dervish orders, too.

Research has revealed that *sof* and mohair production experienced a breakthrough with the establishment of the Republic, and the The Mohair Society of Turkey was founded in 1932 to help increase mohair production and on a scientific basis. In newspaper archives, Cumhuriyet daily dated August 23, 1932 reported that white *sof* fabric produced in The Mohair Society of Turkey's farms was presented to Mustafa Kemal Atatürk. In this context, inventories of the Presidential Atatürk Museum Pavilion, Anıtkabir [Atatürk's Mausoleum] Command, İnönü Foundation The Pink House, all of which were assumed would include the fabric in collections of Atatürk's garments and textiles, were queried; however, to no avail.

---

20 In TDK's Turkish Dictionary, *kerrake* is defined as "a soft, light and narrow top".

Documents on the relationship between Bursa and Ankara in the 15th and 16th centuries and Ankara *sof* in Bursa were studied by Fahri Dalsar (1942). He has revealed that Bursa, an important transit city, marketed Ankara *sof*, and Ankara *sof* would pass through Bursa to be exported to Europe. In this context, our search of museums extended to Bursa, too. We wrote in early October 2017 to the Bursa Cumalıkızık Ethnography Museum, and the Esat Ulumay Ottoman Folk Attire and Jewellery Museum, which keeps a collection of Ottoman costumes, and queried the availability of *sof* fabrics in their inventories. No *sof* samples were found in these museums, either.

Key Challenges Faced

The main challenge that researchers face is the low awareness of the fabric. We hope that *Weaving the History: Mystery of a City, Sof Exhibition* will be effective in overcoming this difficulty, and the word *sof* becomes a household name.

Another problem is related to the fabric's general properties. Experts often cite the difficulty of telling *sof* apart from a silky fabric or raw silk, due to its bright, moiré appearance, its delicacy and silkiness. This difficulty raises several important issues. The first of these is the fact that the structure of the yarn used in a fabric can be determined only by laboratory analysis, if its manufacturer had not provided information on the *sof* fabric and/or garment made of *sof* in the inventory, or if this was lacking when the artefact was received by the museum. This is not always possible, unless special needs arise, considering high costs.

However, inspecting museum collections, samples of mohair may be found among products other than fabrics and garments, such as dolls with mohair hairpieces, mohair teddy bears[21], and up holstery. There are no advanced studies on the provenance of the mohair in samples known by the museums to contain mohair and the majority of which have been dated to the 19th century and later, or museums lack the means to carry out such studies. Deeper research in this area may be possible only by exploring the companies known to have bought mohair yarn imported from the Ottoman Empire and used it as raw material in production, and their present existence.

None of the foreign museums we contacted and performed online catalogue searches came up with artefacts that were proven to be made of mohair and bore the inscription "Made in Turkey" at the same time. However, range of use of mohair abroad is considerably extensive and evaluated in this context, the Victoria & Albert Museum in England, the Gallery of Costume Manchester Art Gallery in England and examples in the United States can be explored in more detail to exemplify the usage of mohair in the West.

Artefacts Detected in Museum Collections at Home

Sadberk Hanım Museum Collection

I would like to start with the works at the Sadberk Hanım Museum, which formed our baseline as we sought *sof* artefacts for the exhibition. As mentioned above, the SEM analysis performed in the TCF-

---

21 Celebrated toy manufacturer Steiff, which owes its reputation to its teddy bears, has used mohair in the teddies since the late 19th century and benefits from the mohair exported from Turkey (Source: Steiff - *The Story*).

Array No	Inventory No	Name	Period
1	SHM 2614-K32	*Sof* Skirt	Ottoman, early 20th century
2	SHM 2714-K130	Mohair Shawl	Early 20th century
3	SHM 2722-K138	Mohair Shawl	Early 20th century
4	SHM10568-D127	*Sof (fabric)*	Ottoman, late 19th - early 20th century.
5	SHM11508-K173	*Sof* Skirt	Ottoman, early 20th century
6	SHM 11935-K502	*Sof* Skirt	Ottoman, early 20th century
7	SHM 13392-K655	*Sof* Şalvar	Ottoman, late 19th - early 20th century
8	SHM 13835-K708	*Sof* Skirt	Ottoman, early 20th century
9	SHM14006-K732	*Sof* Ferace (light overcoat)	Ottoman, early 20th century
10	SHM 14172-K830	*Sof* Skirt	Ottoman, early 20th century
11	SHM 15312-K969	*Sof* Cardigan	Ottoman, early 20th century
12	SHM 17523-K.1078	*Sof* Skirt	Ottoman, early 20th century
13	SHM 17630-K1120	Mohair bed cardigan	1905-1908
14	SHM 18008-K1212	Mohair Cardigan	1925-1930
15	SHM 18357-K1313	Mohair Cape	Early 20th century

Table 1. Artefacts from the Sadberk Hanım Museum Included in the Exhibition

DATU Laboratory of the *sof* fabric sample (Inventory No: 10568-D.127) registered to the Sadberk Hanım Museum inventory was the initial step. Subsequently SEM and dyestuff analyses were conducted on a dark blue *ferace* (Inventory No: 14006-K.732), a mustard cardigan (Inventory No: 15312-K969), a bright pink şalvar[22] (Inventory No: 13392-K.655) and an almond-green skirt (Inventory No: 2614-K.32). Examining the samples taken from these artefacts revealed that they fit the characteristics of the Ankara *sof*. In addition to fabric artefacts, various clothing items knitted from mohair yarn were also included in the exhibition. A list of Mohair artefacts included in the exhibition is presented in Table 1.

22 Traditional baggy trousers (T. N.)

Topkapı Palace Museum Collection of the Ministry of Culture and Tourism

Sof was a fabric of choice preferred by the higher segments of the Ottoman society. Documents show that the palace placed orders for *sof* with Ankara. In 1673, 30 bolts of *sof* were commissioned for Sultan Mehmed IV; in 1687, 40 bolts were ordered for Sultan Mehmed IV again, this time in various colours (Ongan, 1954-1955, pp. 39-40, quoted by Tamur, 2003, p. 83). However, Ogier Ghislain de Busbecq mentions that Suleiman the Magnificent also wore green *sof*, and that wearing *sof* was regarded as a sign of distinction (Türk Mektupları, 2011, p. 55) therefore we assumed we would find sultan's garments made of *sof* included in the Topkapı Palace Museum collection.

However, there are no *sof*-based garments within our knowledge in the Topkapı Palace Museum collection. Hülya Tezcan has conducted a study on the *velense* (1992, p. 108) found among the woollen objects in the Topkapı Palace Museum collection. It was known that the *velense*, named after Valencia in Spain, was commonly used as a blanket, and it is known that some good samples from the 16th and early 17th centuries were included in the Topkapı Palace Museum collection. Some *velense* samples in the collection also appear to have been used as prayer rugs. Of the five mohair artefacts exhibited from the Topkapı Palace Museum collection, three of them were *velense*, while two were Angora goat's hide. Analyses of the works included in the exhibition were performed by the Topkapı Palace Museum. Apart from these examples, analyses have revealed that some other pieces that were thought to be *sof* until now, were actually made of silk. A list of the works included in the exhibition from Topkapı Palace Museum is given in Table 2.

Array No	Inventory No	Name	Period
1	13/482	Angora goat's hide	Ottoman, 17th century, belonged to Sultan Murad IV.
2	13/483	Angora goat's hide	Ottoman, 17th century, belonged to Sultan Murad IV.
3	13/148	*Velense* (ground cloth)	Ottoman, 16th century, belonged to Sultan Süleyman I.
4	13/1191	*Velense* (prayer rug)	Ottoman, 17th century.
5	13/1193	*Velense* spread/ blanket	Ottoman, 17th century.

Tablo 2. Artefacts from the Topkapı Palace Museum Included in the Exhibition

Ministry of Culture and Tourism, Ethnography Museum of Ankara

Sof textiles in the Ethnography Museum of Ankara collection were already known. Feriha Akpınarlı and Ayşem Yanar in their article titled *Traditional Ankara Sof Textiles* (2016, pp.170-179) have studied the five pieces found at the Ankara Ethnography Museum and documented with photographs of features such their warp and weft densities, and thicknesses. In addition to the five *sof* fabrics discussed in this article, another piece was found at the Ankara Ethnography Museum. One of the most beautiful features of these artefacts, besides their Ankara provenance, is their diverse and vivid colouring, such as brown, burgundy, white, blue, and purple. Samples of *sof* fabrics included in the exhibition from the museum collection are listed in Table 3.

Inventory No	Name	Date of Arrival	Size
14193	White *Sof*	25.10.1948	73 x 63 cm
14194	Blue *Sof*	25.10.1948	107 x 73,5 cm
14195	Brown *Sof*	25.10.1948	348 x 73 cm
14207	*Sof* (Purple sof fragment)	25.10.1948	103,5 x 67 cm
23600	*Sof* sample (fabric fragment)	08.11.1978	86 x 65 cm
23601	Maroon *sof* sample (fabric fragment)	08.11.1978	282 x 31 cm

Tablo 3. Artefacts from the Ankara Ethnography Museum Included in the Exhibition

The museum had provided information on the Ankara provenance of the samples, and that the samples of the fabric were originated in Ankara, four of the six artefacts (Inv. No: 14193, 14194, 14195 and 14207) were sent to the museum inventory in 1948 by the Ministry of Economy and Development with the request of Ministry of Education. Remining two fabrics were obtained in 1978 as a gift from Saadet Ayyakın (Source: Ethnography Museum of Ankara). However, the fabrics in the museum inventory had not been dated.

While photographing the fabric samples for the catalogue, the inscription "T.T.C." was found on labels and stamps on the fabrics. T.T.C. is an abbreviation that represents the *Türkiye Tiftik Cemiyeti*- The Mohair Society of Turkey (Tamur, 2003, p. 200), which was established in 1930, became active in 1932 when its bylaws were published in the official gazette, and operated

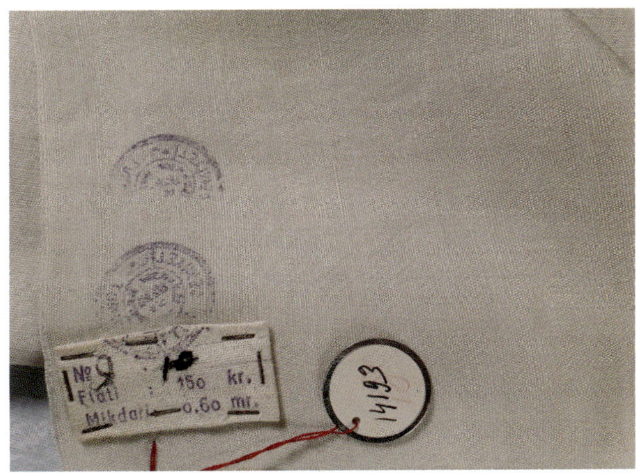

Figure 4. Brown *Sof.*
Photo: Gözde Çerçioğlu Yücel
Ethnography Museum of Ankara,
Inventory No: 14195

Figure 5. White *Sof.*
Photo: Gözde Çerçioğlu Yücel
Ethnography Museum of Ankara,
Inventory No: 14193

until 1951. The T.T.C. built a *sof* textile workshop on a plot in Bentderesi allocated to the Society in 1934 (Gürler, 2006, pp. 41-42). This "*Sof* Weaving House" was created with the hope of stimulating *sof* textile production, and its looms, although seen by the Society as an "encumbrance," continued to weave *sof* because it was "as exclusive to Ankara as mohair" (Gürler, 2006, p.43). Coloured as well as white *sof* was produced at the workshop. For example, a letter sent to provincial muftiates requests that, "robes of muftis, clerics, imams, and orators are sewn from ultramarine *sof*, rather than European fabrics."

Given the premises of the The Mohair Society of Turkey, Sof Weaving House, during studies conducted while preparing the exhibition, from the seals and labels on the fabrics, four of the six pieces of *sof* in the Ethnography Museum of Ankara collection were identified as products of The Mohair Society of Turkey.

Registered at Ethnography Museum of Ankara; There are price tags and/or stamps on the works with the inventory numbers of 14195 (brown *sof* fabric), 14193 (white *sof* fabric) 14207 (purple *sof* fabric), 14194 (blue *sof* fabric).

The label found on the "Brown *Sof*" artefact, inventory number 14195, reads, besides the abbreviation "T.T.C." (*Türkiye Tiftik Cemiyeti*-The Mohair Society of Turkey) the "fiati 155 Kr" price of the fabric, "eni Mr. 75," its width and "mikdari 3.40" its quantity.

Two stamps appear on the artefact "White *Sof*," inventory number 14193 (only the word "Cemiyet" "Society" is legible), and a price tag. The tag bears the numbers 9 and 10 handwritten against the press printed inscription "No.", "Fiati: 150 kr." its price, and "Mikdari: 0.60 mr." quantity can be read.

There is a price tag on the "Sof" (purple-dyed *sof* fabric) artefact with the inventory number 14207, which is also bears the abbreviated T.T.C. title, besides which the label reads, "175", handwritten across the press printed inscription for its price "fiati-Kr.," and "175" across the inscription for its width "eni-Mr.," and "1" for quantity can be read.

A price tag has been stapled to the fabric titled "Blue *Sof*," inventory number 14194, and a seal is visible on the label. The price tag reads a handwritten "6" for "No.," "Fiati: 175 kr.," for its price and "Mikdari: 0.95 mr." for its quantity.

Although the prices are similar, measurements of the fabrics, called "width" and "quantity" differed. Given the data, these *sof* fabrics from the Ethnography Museum of Ankara, are suggested as products of The Mohair Society of Turkey and most likely they were manufactured between 1934 and 1951 whereby the Society had functioned.

Private Studies, Projects, Contemporary Production

As samples of *sof* fabric are few in number and *sof* production did not even exist in our day, our research went on to ask what was currently produced from mohair. The questions of whether it is possible to reproduce the *sof* fabric within the scope of cultural heritage; what the Ankara mohair weaving had left behind; and whether *sof* may be found in private collections determined the framework of our endeavours during the preparation of the exhibition.

One of our priorities was to contact Prof Dr Zahide İmer, who has studied the history of *sof*, its present, and its future. İmer has compared Ankara *sofs* of the past with samples of mohair textiles of Tosya, and observed the latter's weaving techniques and looms. According to İmer (1994), the Ankara *sofs* produced in in the past are different from the ones produced in Tosya. She has noted that in the old Ankara *sof* technique, the mohair was prevented from abrasion and wear by utilizing weaver's reeds (page 87). The Ankara *sof* is known to have been created with the plain weave (taffeta) technique. It owes its fine appearance to the fact that, while the mohair yarn has been hand-spun, the warp and weft is not twisted, but only folded with minimal coiling (pp. 85-86). Pressing and polishing are thought to be the processes that bring about the moiré, and the bright appearance, the most important features of *sof* (pp. 85-86). These soften the fabric, impart it brightness and create a moiré appearance. According to İmer (1994) believes that, instead of the historical, elegant, fine and colourful *sof* fabrics that were used to produce apparel such as *ferace* and *kaftan*, today tougher and thicker fabrics in natural colours may be produced with mohair. İmer (1992) takes up a *ferace* in the Sadberk Hanım Museum collection and two pieces of fabric at the Ankara Ethnography Museum (Inventory Nos. 23600 and 23601). Among the samples İmer collated in her study, a piece of *sof* fabric dated to 1890-1900 is of particular significance. This sample, "Old *Sof*" as she names was produced in Zir, Yenikent. This piece of fabric, measuring 28.1x20.2 cm, has a bright, fine, elegant appearance and is in natural mohair colour. Compared with the fabrics produced in Tosya, the "old *sof*" is found to have a higher frequency of warp and

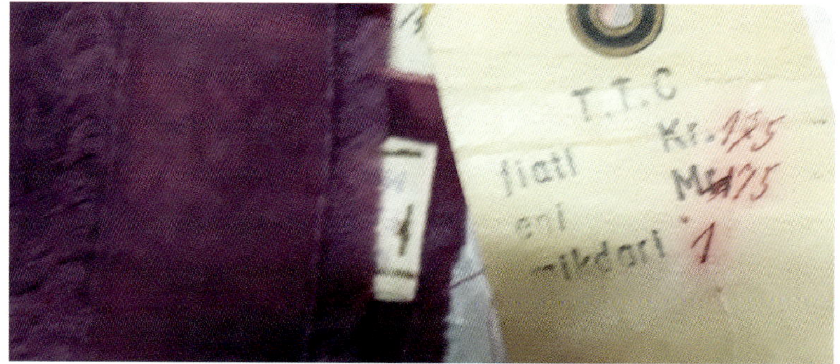

Figure 6. *Sof* (purple *sof* fabric sample).
Photo: Gözde Çerçioğlu Yücel
Source: Ankara Ethnographic Museum, Inventory No: 14207

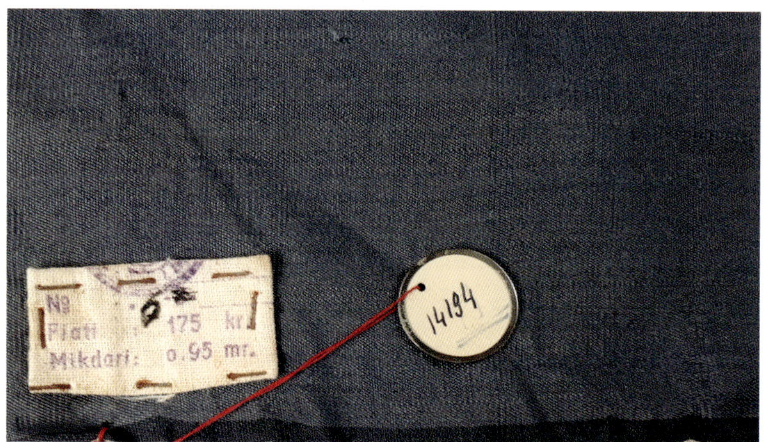

Figure 7. Blue *Sof*.
Photo: Gözde Çerçioğlu Yücel
Source: Ankara Ethnographic Museum, Inventory No: 14194

weft (İmer, 1992, p. 109). In addition, a sample of şalşepik[23] fabric and a sample of *sof* produced in Tosya from İmer's archive were included in the exhibition (Weaving the History: Mystery of a City, *Sof* Exhibition Catalog, p. 278).

Today in Kastamonu's Tosya district, weavers continue to create bath mitts and Tosya sashes on hand looms. However, while the number of weavers working on hand looms is no more than 3-4 people, our observations indicate that maintaining this tradition is also difficult. Both of these products are indigenous. "The weaving is made performed using hand looms with unadulterated yarn. The width of the sashes woven with hand-twisted mohair on hand looms is about 25 to 30 cm. Widely sought-after for lumbar health, these sashes possess their own special pattern because they have been woven on looms with four reeds." (Kastamonu Provincial Culture and Tourism Directorate, 2018). *Waving history: Ayaş*, a documentary produced within the scope of the exhibition and directed by Kerime Senyücel, focuses on the old mohair weavers of the region. We spoke with the now-deceased Nedim Salman's son Mahmut Salman and his wife Melahat Salman, and İsmail Koyuncugil, who used to weave dress textiles for politicians and bureaucrats in the 1950s and continues to earn a living despite his advanced age by creating mitts and sashes, and with Seyfi Bektaş, President of the Tosya Chamber of Mitt and Sash Producers, which has very few members today, on weaving techniques, stages of weaving, and the present and future of mohair weaving.[24]

Projects for reviving and/or bringing mohair weaving back to life were studied. Starting out from published papers (Akpınarlı and Yanar, 2016) we dwelled on the project *Reintroducing Ankara's Historical Sof Fabric into the Cultural and Economic Life of the City*, prepared by the Tiftik and *Sof* Research and Development Association (TİFSOF) and commissioned at Ankara's Kahraman Kazan district in October 2013. We interviewed Bünyamin Zile and Süreyya Zile at the Kahraman Kazan Municipality, and Assoc. Dr Yakup Ömeroğlu with the hope of seeing this project's output (March 2017). The project, under the responsibility of Süreyya Zile; comprised the two phases of weaving and design, involved the selection of 15 disadvantaged trainee women in Kazan. The trainees were given theoretical and practical courses over a six-month period (three days a week) by academicians who were experts in weaving within the scope of the project.

During these interviews, we learned that the fabric was woven from unadulterated mohair yarn within the scope of the project; and products for daily use, such as waistcoats, jackets, skirts, handbags, neckties, etc. were created with the woven fabrics, that difficulties were encountered in attempts to reproducing *sof* out of unadulterated mohair yarn, and that the project was terminated. As Bünyamin Zile, who wrote about the project and project outputs stated in the article published on the website *Ceride-i Mülkiye* [Civil Service Gazette]; difficulties were encountered in the phase of "sizing" of the mohair yarn necessary for weaving,

23 A thin mohair fabric woven around Şırnak.

24 I would like to extend my thanks to the Tosya Municipality, Erman Tamur, Ahmet Dönmez and Ahmet Kaymaz for their assistance in contacting the weavers of Tosya.

and when this process was not performed properly, yarn would be caught between the comb and the reed power in the loom and break. They researched "sizing" techniques, eventually looking into natural materials and experimented with four types of plants. They obtained positive results from one plant, with which they were able to progress through the "sizing" phase and consequently weaving. They have noted, however, that mohair yarn could be woven at a slower pace on the loom, compared to other yarns; but discovered that weaving became much faster when the warp yarns are of cotton, and the weft are mohair. Examples of project output, such as fabrics woven from unadulterated mohair, and the designs of Süreyya Zile produced from the fabric were included in the exhibition (Weaving the History: Mystery of a City, *Sof* Exhibition Catalog, pp. 300-302).

During the research, it was noted that ten years before the project implemented in Kazan, a project titled "Ankara Mohair Goat and *Sof* Fabric" had been initiated by the Ankara *Olgunlaşma* Institute [Advanced Technical Institute for Girls], in 2003. This project was conducted in partnership with the Ministry of National Education, K.T.Ö. General Directorate, Ankara *Olgunlaşma* Institute Department of Research, Weaving Workshop, Ankara Governorship, Çankırı Governorship, Kastamonu Governorship, Şırnak Governorship, Çankırı District Directorate of National Education, Çankırı A.M. and K.M.L. Directorate, Kastamonu Daday H.E.M. Directorate, Kastamonu Tosya H.E.M. Directorate, Altındağ District Governorship Directorate of National Education (Ankara *Olgunlaşma* Institute, 2013). The

Figure 8. *Özbahar* Farm during shooting of the *Weaving the History: Ayaş* documentary, Ayaş, 2018. Photo: Gözde Çerçioğlu Yücel

Figure 9. Angora goats, *Özbahar* Farm, Ayaş, 2018. Photo: Gözde Çerçioğlu Yücel

Figure 10. Goat breeders Bahriye, Bekir and Seda Özbahar at home in Gökçebağ Village, Ayaş, 2018. Photo: Gözde Çerçioğlu Yücel

Figure 11. Tosya bath glove and waistcloth weaver Mahmut Salman is at the loom he inherited from his father Nedim Salman, Tosya, 2018. Photo: Gözde Çerçioğlu Yücel

Figure 12. Weaver Ismail Koyuncugil, at the Tosya Chamber of Bath Glove and Waistcloth Producers, Tosya, 2018. Photo: Gözde Çerçioğlu Yücel

targets of the project were "reviving *sof* weaving, a historic art of the Ankara region, in a bid to keeping cultural values alive," creating collections for the Ankara *Olgunlaşma* Institute with the produced fabrics, promoting *sof* both domestically and abroad, implementing vocational training to housewives from education to employment, supporting national education, and teaching *sof* weaving to a group to be formed in the Altındağ region.

Acting on this information, the Ankara *Olgunlaşma* Institute was contacted, but informed that the outputs of this project were not in the institute's collection. Emine Kıraç, a retired director of the institute, was reached via the institute, and information was obtained. Emine Kıraç had created textiles out of mohair yarns in a bid to evaluate local natural fibres, during the seven years as a village teacher as of 1968. Ms. Kıraç, with a team she formed as general director at the Institute, kick-started the first comprehensive study on the subject with the support of a master in Tosya over the period of 2001-2006. However, they were unable to obtain a satisfactory weave at that time. In the following period, Ms. Kıraç notes that she has worked on mohair weaving in Ankara, Adana, Erzurum, Gaziantep, Cizre and Eruh, with the help of various masters and experts in the sector, and continues to work in all of its phases and following all the scientific developments in this area to resolve problems, especially such as yarn breakage and stiffness of fabrics, with many masters trained in Adana, Gaziantep, Tosya and Çerkezköy. In our interviews, it was noted that the process of applying the *cendere* (press) became a problem because the *cendere* was unknown. The Exhibition features mohair, mohair yarn, and woven fabric dyed with natural and local methods from Emine Kıraç's personal project "Weaving Mohair in Anatolia," and a jacket designed for mohair fabric (Weaving the History: Mystery of a City, *Sof* Exhibition Catalog, pp. 303-305).

In addition, companies that produce with Angora goat mohair were also explored. Altınyıldız Textile and Ready-wear Inc., today owned by Boyner Holding, attracted much attention in the past with its production and export of lavish mohair fabrics. We got in touch with Altınyıldız, who had produced mohair fabrics marketed under the names such as "superior kid mohair" and "silky mohair" in the 1960s and exported these to Europe for dressmaking. The Exhibition includes classifieds advertising the fabrics this company produced, with Tosya, Kastamonu mohair trader Osman Boyner, one of the founders of Altınyıldız in 1952 (Öğüt, 2013), with his mohair tuxedo. (Weaving the History: Mystery of a City, *Sof* Exhibition Catalog, pp. 286-287).

Production of fabric from mohair was observed to decline over time and mohair was no longer preferred by the textile industry as it did before. Therefore, there are very few examples of mohair being converted to final product. That was the reason for inviting the company *Mohair & Angora*, which manufactures male and female shawls, scarves, gloves and socks, using mohair yarn in the homeland of the Angora goat and mohair, to be included in the exhibition (Weaving the History: Mystery of a City, *Sof* Exhibition Catalog, pp. 290-291).

These examples are important for the branding of the Angora goat and guiding its future in textile and knitting industries.

We visited the Anatolian Shepherd Fair, organized by the Ankara Metropolitan Municipality and held at the Atatürk Culture Centre in 18-20 May, where we met with Angora goat breeders and interviewed participating Ayaş district farmers. While their numbers have declined, there are still products such as mohair knitted gloves, shawls, cardigans and vests in Ayaş, Ankara, where goat breeding continues. However, according to the information obtained from the talks, this traditional art is also faces extinction. Particularly the jobs performed by older peasant women: activities that involve laborious steps such as cleaning, washing, spinning the mohair, applying dyes using natural products such as walnut shells, tomatoes, etc., and knitting with the prepared yarns, do not seem likely to be taken up by future generations. We learned at the fair that production continued in the Ayaş, Yağmurdede and Gökler areas. Kerime Senyücel directed the documentary *Weaving the History: Ayaş*, which focused on the production process of Kezban Yıldız, who processes raw mohair (by cleaning, washing, dyeing by natural means, spinning mohair yarn) to create products such as knitted cardigans, vests, shawls, sweaters, at the Özbahar Farm, which is the largest Angora goat breeding farm in Ayaş county (29 January - 2 February 2018). A vest made of mohair yarn dyed with walnut shell, and two natural-coloured mohair shawls produced by Kezban Yıldız are on display at the Exhibition. In addition to these, examples mohair yarns of various hand-spun products from Ayaş, and knitwear such as socks, gloves, two-piece suits, dressing gowns, etc. by the Ayaş Culture House, Hatice Doğruol, Makbule Doğruol, Dicle

Figure 13. Kezban Yıldız knits with the mohair yarn she has personally dyed and spun, Ayaş, Yağmurdede Village, 2018. Photo: Gözde Çerçioğlu Yücel

Vural and Günsel Özyörük were also included in the Exhibition.

The Mystery through the Cracks...

Creating an exhibition on *sof* was an adventure in itself. It was no easy task to find *sof*. We started out with the aim of uncovering a forgotten value, to share it with the public, to demonstrate the existence of such a value Ankara's history, and to raise awareness of the Angora goat, and mohair as a precious material. We only hope that we have achieved these goals.

The story of *sof*, which began with the Angora goat, continued nested within Ankara's history; and, with its production process that involves the whole city, and with the global awareness of it in the world of the past, it has aroused much curiosity. We believe that the relevant institutions and organizations, private companies, textile specialists and individuals we reached during our exhibition preparations, will also trigger initiatives to reproduce *sof* fabric today. Even during the preparations for the exhibition, the *sof* and mohair weaving topics were met with much excitement by the universities, laboratories, the Ankara Development Agency and companies and made way to various initiatives. We now hope that we were able to show through the cracks the mystery of *sof* with this exhibition, which we hope will be a resource for future scientific work. I believe that the significance of the Angora goat must be appreciated while it is still possible to be bred in this country.

References

Açıl, F. (1961). *Ankara keçisi ve tiftiğin memleket bünyesindeki ekonomik önemi.* Ankara: Ankara University, Faculty of Agriculture Publications.

Akman, N. (1994). Ankara keçisi, *Ankara Dergisi, 2*(6), 516.

Akman, N. and Düzgüneş, O. (1988). Türkiye'de tiftik keçisi yetiştiriciliğinin problemleri. *Ziraat Mühendisliği, 209,* 16-19.

Aktan, S. (1983). Ankara sofu. *Turkish Folklore Research Yearbook-1982, 44,* 7-20.

Akpınarlı, F. and Yanar, A. (2016). Geleneksel Ankara sof dokumaları. *Ankara Araştırmaları Dergisi, 4*(2), 170-179.

Alemdar, K. (1984). Seyahatnamelerde Ankara. *Tarih İçinde Ankara Eylül 1981 Seminar Reports,* 97-105.

Ankara *Olgunlaşma* Institute. (2013). *Projects.* Retrieved from http://ankaraolgunlasma.meb.k12.tr/meb_iys_dosyalar/06/01/972455/icerikler/arastrma-projeler_615797.html.

Ankara Vilayeti Salnamesi. (1995). K. Emiroğlu, A. Yüksel, Ö. Türkoğlu and E. Coşkun (Ed.). Ankara: Ankara Institute Foundation Publications.

Ateş, H. (1968). Tiftiğin kullanıldığı yerler ve eski sof kumaş. *İstanbul Ticaret Dergisi, 11*(519), 5.

Barnett, R.D. (1974). European Merchants in Angora. *Anatolian Studies,* C. 24, 136-137.

Batu, S. (1951). Batu, S. (1951). *Türkiye keçi ırkı ve keçi yetiştirme bilgisi.* Ankara: Ankara University Faculty of Veterinary Medicine.

Batu, S. and Okaner, H. (1946). Ankara keçisinin Ankara bölgesindeki yetişme, bakım, beslenme şartları ve beden yapısı üstüne araştırmalar. *Ankara Higher Institute of Agriculture* 2 (5), 444-475.

Blum, S., Ettesvold, P.M. and Druesedow, J.L. (1975). Costume Institute. *Notable Acquisitions (Metropolitan Museum of Art),* 43-44.

Cronwright-Schreiner, S.C. (1898). *The Angora goat.* London: Longsman.

Dinçer, N. (1948, April). Ankara sofu I. *Ülkü Halkevi Dergisi, 2*(16), 31-33.

Dinçer, N. (1948, July). Ankara sofu II. *Ülkü Halkevi Dergisi, 2*(21), 40-41.

Dinçer, N. (1948). Ankara milli tiftik ve sof sanayimiz. *Karınca Dergisi, 6*(135), 22-25.

Dziubinski, A. (1999). Polish-Turkish Trade in the 16th to 18th Centuries. *War and Peace, Ottoman-Polish Relations in the 15th – 19th Centuries,* 38-45.

Ekdoğan, M. (1955, April). Ankara sofçuluğu. *Türk Folklor Araştırmaları Dergisi, 3*(69),1091-1092.

Eldem, E. (2006). Capitulations and Western trade. S. Faroqhi (Ed.), in *The Cambridge History of Turkey* (pp. 281-335). Cambridge: Cambridge University Press. doi:10.1017/CHOL9780521620956.015

Erdoğan, Z. and Jirousek, C. A. (2005). Ankara (Angora) goat hair: the Turkish mohair tradition. *The Fabric of Life: Cultural Transformations in Turkish Society.*

Ergenç, Ö. (1975). 1600-1615 yılları arasında Ankara iktisadi tarihine ait araştırmalar. *Türkiye İktisat Tarihi Semineri 8-10 June 1973,* 145-168.

Ergenç, Ö. (1980). XVII. yüzyıl başlarında Ankara'nın yerleşim durumu üzerine bazı bilgiler. In H. İnalcık, N. Göyünç and H. W. Lowry (Ed.), *Osmanlı Araştırmaları I* (pp. 85-106).

Ergenç, Ö. (1982). Osmanlı klasik dönemindeki "Eşraf ve A'yan" üzerine bazı bilgiler. In H. İnalcık, N. Göyünç and H. W. Lowry (Ed.), *Osmanlı Araştırmaları III* (pp. 85-106).

Ergenç, Ö. (1984). 16. yüzyıl Ankara'sı: ekonomik, sosyal yapısı ve kentsel özellikleri. In E. Yavuz and N. Uğurel (Der.), *Tarih İçinde Ankara (Eylül 1981 Seminer Bildirileri)* (pp. 49-59).

Ergenç, Ö. (1995). *XVI. yüzyılda Ankara ve Konya: Osmanlı klasik döneminde kent tarihçiliğine katkı.* Ankara: Ankara Institute Foundation Publications.

Evliya Çelebi Seyahatnâmesi. (1999). Evliya Çelebi b. Derviş Mehemmed Zıllî, Book II., Topkapı Sarayı Kütüphanesi Bağdat 304 Numaralı Yazmanın Transkripsiyonu-Dizini. Z. Kurşun, S. A. Kahraman and Y. Dağlı (Ed.). İstanbul, Yapı Kredi Yayınları.

Eyice, S. (1972). *Ankara'nın eski bir resmi: tarihi vesika olarak resimler – Ankara'dan bahseden seyyahlar – eski bir Ankara resmi.* Ankara: Türk Taarih Kurumu.

Faroqhi, S. (1985). Onyedinci yüzyıl Ankara'sında sof imalatı ve sof atölyeleri. *İktisat Fakültesi Mecmuası,* (41), 1-4.

Faroqhi, S. (2017). *Osmanlı zanaatkârları.* İstanbul: Alfa Printers Publishing and Distribution.

French, D. (1972). A sixteenth century English merchant in Ankara? *Anatolian Studies,* (22), 241-247.

(2006). Türkiye tiftik cemiyeti tarihçesi. *Lalahan Hayvancılık Araştırma Enstitüsü Dergisi, 46*(2), 39-46.

Hayes, J.L. (1882). *The Angora goat: its origin, culture and products.* New York: Orange Judd.

İhsan Abidin [Akıncı]. (1340/1924). *Ankara keçisinin hâli ve ıslahı.* İstanbul: Vatan Printers.

İhsan Abidin [Akıncı]. (1932). *Tiftik: istihsalden istihlake kadar.* İstanbul: Kader Printers.

İmer, Z. (1992). *Ankara sofunun dünü ve bugünü* (Yüksek Lisans Tezi). Gazi Üniversitesi Sosyal Bilimler Enstitüsü, Ankara.

İmer, Z. (1994, Mart). Ankara sofunun geçmişi ve bugünü. *Ankara Dergisi, 2*(6), 85-86.

İnalcık, H. (2011). *Studies in the history of textiles in Turkey.* İstanbul: Türkiye İş Bankası Yayınları.

İstanbul'dan Anadolu'ya Seyahat Günlüğü. (1992). H. Dernschwam (Author), Y. Önen (Tr.). Ankara: Kültür Bakanlığı.

İşcen, Y. (1993, March). Ankiler - sof ve Ankara. *Anfora Dergisi, 1*(11), 6-7.

İvgin, H. (2012), Ankara'nın somut olmayan bir kültürel mirası: Ankara sofu. *Kültür Evreni Dergisi,* 14, 86-93.

Kafadar, C. (2009). *Kim var imiş biz burada yoğ iken: dört Osmanlı: Yeniçeri, tüccar, derviş ve hatun.* İstanbul: Metis Yayınları.

Kastamonu İl Kültür ve Turizm Müdürlüğü (2018). *Tosya kuşağı.* Retrieved from http://www.kastamonukultur.gov.tr/TR,171377/tosya-kusagi.html.

Kılıçbay, M.A. (1994). Sof şehri Ankara. E. Batur. (Ed.). In *Ankara Ankara* (pp. 65-72). İstanbul: Yapı Kredi Yayınları.

Kurşun, Z, Kahraman, S. ve Dağlı, Y. (1998). *Evliyâ Çelebi seyahatnâmesi II. kitap Topkapı Sarayı kütüphanesi Bağdat 304 numaralı yazmanın transkripsiyonu-dizini.* İstanbul: Yapı Kredi Yayınları.

Leiser, G. (1994). Travellers' accounts of mohair production in Ankara from the fifteenth through the nineteenth century. *The Textile Museum Journal*, 5-34.

Merriam Webster Dictionary, (2018) Retrieved from https://www.merriam-webster.com/.

Metropolitan Museum of Art. (2017). *Collection.* Retrieved from https://www.metmuseum.org/art/collection/search#!?q=camlet&offset=0&pageSize=0&sortBy=Relevance&sortOrder=asc&perPage=50.

Metropolitan Museum of Art. (2018). *Riding Coat.* Retrieved from https://www.metmuseum.org/art/collection/search/81754.

Museum De Lakenhal. (2018). *Portefeuille met stalen van 'Camelot' of Turks laken, uit Leiden* [Fabric Swatch]. Retrieved from http://www.lakenhal.nl/en/collection/1671

Ongan, H. (1954-1955). Ankara sofçuluğu ile ilgili bazı vesikalar. *Ankara Belediyesi Dergisi*, 9/13.

Ongan, H. (1958). *Ankara'nın 1 numaralı şer'iye sicili: 21 Rebiülâhır – 991 – Evahir-i Muharrem – 992 (14 Mayıs 1583 – 12 Şubat 1584).* Ankara: Ankara Üniversitesi Dil ve Tarih Coğrafya Fakültesi.

Ongan, H. (1974). *Ankara'nın 2 numaralı şer'iye sicili: 1 Muharrem 997 –8 Ramazan 998 (20 Kasım 1588 – 11 Temmuz 1590).* Ankara: Türk Tarih Kurumu.

Oxford English Dictionary (2017). Retrieved from http://www.oed.com/

Öğüt, G. (2013, Ekim 8). Boyner ailesinin 150 yıllık aile geleneği. Retrieved from http://www.hurriyet.com.tr/boyner-ailesinin-150-yillik-aile-gelenegi-24845155.

Örkiz, M. (1980). *Ankara keçisi yetiştirme ve tiftik pazarlaması.* Ankara: Gıda Tarım ve Hayvancılık Bakanlığı Lalahan Zooteknik Araştırma Enstitüsü.

Steiff. (2018). *The story.* Retrieved from http://www.steiffusa.com/steiff-the-story/.

Şakiroğlu, M. (1993, Temmuz). Ankara hakkında iki İtalyan gözlemcinin notları. *Ankara Büyükşehir Belediyesi Ankara Dergisi.*

Sülüner, H. S. (2014). Yabancı seyyahların gözlemleriyle Roma ve Bizans dönemi'nde Ankara. *Ankara Araştırmaları Dergisi, 2*(1), 11-21.

Tamur, E. (2003). *Ankara keçisi ve Ankara tiftik dokumacılığı: tükenen bir zenginliğin ve çöken bir sanayinin tarihsel öyküsünden kesitler.* Ankara: Ankara Ticaret Odası.

TDK Güncel Türkçe Sözlük (2018). Retrieved from http://tdk.gov.tr/index.php?option=com_gts&view=gts.

Tezcan, H. (1992). Topkapı Sarayı'ndaki velense ve benzeri dokumalar. *Topkapı Sarayı Müzesi, Yıllık 5*, 223-40.

The English-Language Institute of America, Inc. (1976). The Grolier Webster International Dictionary of the English Language [Grolier Webster İngiliz Dili Uluslararası Sözlüğü]. USA: Grolier.

Thompson, G. F. (1903). *A manual of Angora goat raising.* Chicago: American Sheep Breederco Press.

Tournefort Seyahatnamesi (2013). S. Yerasimos (Ed.), A. Berktay (Çev.). İstanbul: Kitap Yayınevi.

Türk Mektupları (2011). O.G. Busbecq (Author), D. Türkömer (Tr.). İstanbul: Türkiye İş Bankası Yayınları.

Türkoğlu, Ömer. (2010, May-June). Ankara'nın unuttuğumuz değerlerinden sof. *Ankara Eğitim, Kültür ve Sanat Dergisi, 12*(67), 22.

Uygur, A. (2017). Mohair: an endemic fibre from Anatolia. H. Arapgirlioğlu, A. Atık, R. Elliot and E. Turgeon (Ed), in *Researchers on Science and Art in 21st Century Turkey*, (pp. 2857-2868).

Üstar, M. F. (1940). *Tiftik ve tiftikçiliğimiz.* İstanbul: Üniversite Kitabevi.

Webb Yıldırmak, G. (2006). *XVIII. yüzyılda tiftik ipliğinin Osmanlı-İngiliz ticaretindeki yeri / the place of mohair yarn in XVIIIth century Anglo-Ottoman trade* (Unpublished doctoral dissertation). Ankara Üniversitesi Sosyal Bilimler Enstitüsü, Ankara.

Webb Yıldırmak, G. (2011). *XVIII. yüzyılda Osmanlı-İngiliz tiftik ticareti.* Türk Tarih Kurumuu Yayınları.

Wilson, C. (1960). Cloth production and international competition in the seventeenth century. *The Economic History Review, 13*(2), 209-221.

Wilson, S. (1873). *The Angora goat: with an account of its introduction into Victoria and a report on the flock.* Melbourne: Stillwell and Knight.

Zile, B. (2015). Ankara yitiği Kazan'da bulundu. *Ceride-i Mülkiye.* Retrieved from http://cerideimulkiye.com/?p=39853.

Weaving Revolution in Anatolia Historical and Material Value of Wool, from the Neolithic to the Iron Age

ÇİĞDEM MANER
Koç University, Department of Archaeology and History of Art

The history of weaving in Anatolia began in the Neolithic. Cuneiform tablets dated to Sumerian and especially the Old Assyrian Colony Periods reveal that wool and woven fabrics were sold in return for silver, gold and bronze, and show how valuable these were at the time. Although only a small number of fabric fragments were unearthed in excavations, analysis has shown that the earliest textiles were produced from plant fibres, and that the first samples of wool are dated to the Chalcolithic. The use of wool is closely related to the domestication of sheep and goats. That sheep and goats live in suitable environmental characteristics is very important for wool production. The size of the herd determines the amount of wool plucked each year. Technologies were developed for the production of wool and new tools produced for processing wool and producing garments. Information can be obtained on the purpose, usage, development, production and the diversity of fabrics in Anatolia and Mesopotamia, from archaeological remains, depictions, and written sources, after the introduction of writing. Excavations have brought to light various relics related to weaving, such as loom weights, spindle whorls, needles, spools, brushes, awls and pointed tools. While such artefacts are not considered as significant as metals, stamps, ceramics or cuneiform texts, they often give us highly important data about weaving activities. In recent years, many international project partnerships in research and experimental archaeology have been initiated for understanding prehistoric and protohistoric weaving and related developments in Europe and the Asia Minor.

This article aims to discuss the domestication of sheep and goats in the Neolithic period, the production of yarn from wool, weaving, the material value of wool, its place in commerce, and its significance for human life, from the Neolithic to the end of the Iron Age (9000-750 BC / 700 BC), based on archaeological and primary written sources. Gottfried Keller (1874) in his novel, *Kleider machen Leute* [Clothes Make the Man], tells the story of how a tailor's apprentice was mistakenly perceived as a Polish duke because of the garment he was wearing, which shows that clothing can be a symbol of strength, reputation and prosperity. Clothes are very much a part of our lives today, too. How was clothing perceived in prehistoric and protohistorical periods in Anatolia? Was it valued primarily for its functional quality of covering the body? The human transition as of the Late Neolithic, from hunting and gathering to agriculture and animal husbandry, from nomadic to sedentary, brought on many, great innovations in their lives. It is extremely important to study the domestication of the goat and the sheep in the Neolithic in order to understand the beginning of the weaving and clothing.

Domestication Process of the Sheep and Goat

The production of wool is directly connected with the domesticated sheep. Today, the region known as the Fertile Crescent that covers the Levant coastline from the Nile Delta to Northern Mesopotamia, has undergone significant changes in the transition from the Pleistocene to the Holocene (about 10,000 BC). One of the most important of these changes for humans was their transition from the hunter-gatherer culture to sedentary living, and the domestication of plants and animals. The domestication of plants and animals in particular was to influence humanity's livelihood and mode of existence significantly (Peters, Arbuckle and Pöllath, 2012). Archaeological data obtained from the excavations reveal that the neolithization process had begun during 10,000 BC in South-Eastern Anatolia (Özdoğan, 2011, Figure 1); 9,000 BC in Central Anatolia, (Özbaşaran, 2012; Baird, Fairbairn, Martin and Middleton, 2012), 7500 BC in the Lakes Region and 6,500 BC in the Southwest, West and Northwest Anatolia (Özdoğan, 2011). Some of the main factors for the development of the neolithization process in different times are the different geology, climate, soil and topography of Anatolian regions. Transition from hunting to husbandry in the Neolithic period is considered one of the most important changes in the prehistory of the Near East. The domestication of animals was not a linear process, but rather a combination of many factors. During the domestication process, their breeding and feeding were controlled, the life environment was created and new species were born into this. The earliest indirect evidence for breeding efforts seems to be in the form of an accumulation of animal dung found in the Çayönü, Aşıklı Höyük and Çatalhöyük sites (Brochier, 1993; Özbaşaran, 2012; Stiner *et al.*, 2014). The fact that the domestication of livestock began in the northern region of the Fertile Crescent in 9000 BC is considered an indication that Southeast Anatolian societies were actively involved in animal domestication (Peters *et al.*, 2012, p.4).

In the Aceramic Neolithic period of Anatolia, animals known to have existed are the mouflon (*Ovis orientalis*), wild boar (*Sus scrofa*), wild goat (*Capra aegagrus*) and the aurochs (*Bos primigenius*); however, zooarchaeological studies reveal that animal distributions were regional. Archaeological and zooarchaeological data do not reflect whether this regional distribution had any effect on wool production and weaving (Peters *et al.*, 2012). There is no longer any doubt that the mouflon (*Ovis orientalis*) is the domesticated sheep's ancestor (Helmer, 1992, p. 51). The mouflon's coat is made of two types of fibres: smooth and long kemps that covered a layer of short, fine underwool. This short, fine underwool spontaneously moulted once a year in springtime. The first genetic change in the breeding process increased the volume of the underwool; and only this underwool began to appear during the second genetic change that took place in Asia Minor in the Bronze and Iron Ages (Breniquet 2014). Sheep herds are thought to have begun to expand with the use of milk and wool as of the Neolithic period (Becker *et al.*, 2016, p.102). For example, the inhabitants in Arslantepe in the Late Chalcolithic period

Figure 1a. Terracotta brush. Acem Höyük. Museum of Anatolian Civilizations Directorate

Figure 1b. Terracotta spindle whorls found in Ahlatlıbel (2500-2250 BC). Museum of Anatolian Civilizations Directorate

(Layer VIA, 3350-3000 BC) are thought to have specialized in animal husbandry and subsequently underwent significant changes in economy, in which the sheep and the goat played a major role, and the wool production also increased (Bökönsy, 1983; Frangipane *et al.*, 2009 , p. 15). When zooarchaeological data in Anatolia and Mesopotamia are evaluated, 3000 BC is thought to be the major period in the development of the wool-yielding sheep breed, wool production and weaving (Vila and Helmer 2014).

Weaving

Anatolia is an important geography where woven fabrics were produced as of the Neolithic Period, and one of the Neolithic's greatest innovations and inventions was undoubtedly weaving. In Anatolia, very few samples of woven fabric date back to prehistoric and protohistoric times. Therefore, we try to understand weaving activities by examining weaving tools that have been unearthed. We know from fabric remnants that vegetal fibre (such as flax) and wool (from sheep and goats) were used in Anatolia. Among wool's advantages to flax are heat retention, resistance to water, ease in dyeing and in large quantities, handling and less time-consuming plucking and production. Archaeological data offer limited information on the location of the weaving in the settlement, or the kind of places used for the purpose. In general, areas where weaving tools and loom weights are heavily concentrated are considered production places. For example, spindle whorls, awls and pointed tools were unearthed in the monumental structure located at the southwest of the mound in Arslantepe at the Late Chalcolithic period (Layer VII: 3800-3350 BC), and spindle whorls and loom weights were discovered in the houses in the north-east of the mound (Frangipane *et al.*, 2009). These data are accepted as an indication that at Arslantepe during the Late Chalcolithic, weaving was not performed in the palace but at home. Weaving tools such as loom weights, spindle whorls, bone needles and awls were found predominantly in the north and northwestern houses of the palace in Arslantepe (Layer VI A, MÖ 3350-3000). Their proximity to the palace and their presence on the hill suggest that these belonged to high-ranking people, who were also responsible for the weaving (Frangipane *et al.*, 2009, p. 15). Many forms of evidence related to weaving was found, such as looms and dyeing, spinning and combing equipment at the

FIGURE 2A. Terracotta spindle whorls found in Ahlatlıbel (2500-2250 BC). Museum of Anatolian Civilizations Directorate

FIGURE 2B. A decorated terracotta spindle whorl found in Beycesultan Höyük (16th century BC). Beycesultan Höyük Excavation Archive

E1 and H layers of Demircihöyük, dated to the Early Bronze Age, indicating that weaving was important within the settlement (Korfmann 1983, pp. 116, Bachhuber 2016). In Kültepe – Kaneš, plenty of loom weights and spindle whorls in houses in Karum in the Lower City, indicate that women were weaving in the houses (Kulakoğlu and Kangal, 2010). An unusual example dated to the 7th century BC was discovered in Gordion. The building, known as the Royal Storage House, houses fourteen large loom weights, each 60 cm in length and lying side by side, might indicate that this loom was used when the workshop was abandoned, or destroyed (Barber 1991, p. 101-102).

Weaving tools did not appear out of nowhere; their inventions spanned thousands of years. Raw materials used for weaving, variety of fabrics, patterns, symbols of prestige and trade are factors that have played a role in the inventions. Weaving tools are found in the burials, palaces and houses and include spindle whorls, loom weights, awls, pointed tools, needles, spindles, spools, brushes and combs (FIGURES 1A and 1B). Not only the shapes of the spindle whorls and spindle weights, materials and weights inform us about the weaving activities and yarn qualities of those times, weaving tools found in different layers reveal the development, diversity and innovations of weaving activities in that settlement. We shall look at the tools unearthed in the excavations related to weaving in the following section.

Weaving Tools

Spindle whorls and Spindles. Evidence for spinning yarn in Anatolia is provided by spindle whorls and spindles that have been excavated. Spindle whorls are made of clay, bone and stone, found in round, disc, conical, convex and biconvex shapes (FIGURES 2A, 2B). Bone spindle whorls are generally convex or conical in shape, while those made of clay are round, biconical or conical, and those made of stone are disc or convex-shaped. The clay spindle whorl in particular is often ornamented, as a reflection of the user's taste. Examples of spindles are limited, but bone and metal specimens make it possible to get an idea about them (FIGURES 3, 4, 5).

Spindle whorls are generally published together with small finds, but studies and experimental archaeological studies on their application and the thickness of spinned yarn are very few. The Arslantepe excavation team has conducted the most extensive work on this subject. The spindle whorls and weaving remains discovered at

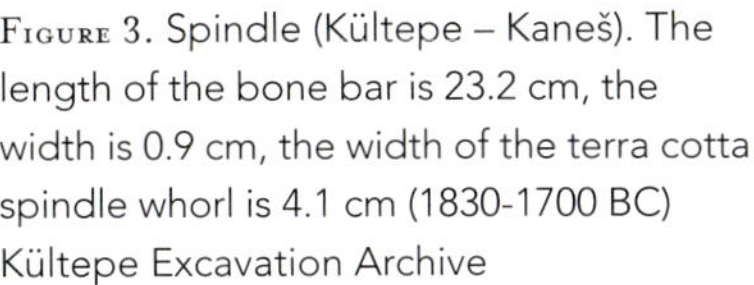

Figure 3. Spindle (Kültepe – Kaneš). The length of the bone bar is 23.2 cm, the width is 0.9 cm, the width of the terra cotta spindle whorl is 4.1 cm (1830-1700 BC) Kültepe Excavation Archive

Figure 4. Bronze spindles found in the Merzifon Göller Cemetery (2500-2250 BC) Museum of Anatolian Civilizations Directorate

Figure 5. Ram's head bone spindle bar, Gordion (8th – 7th century BC) Museum of Anatolian Civilizations Directorate

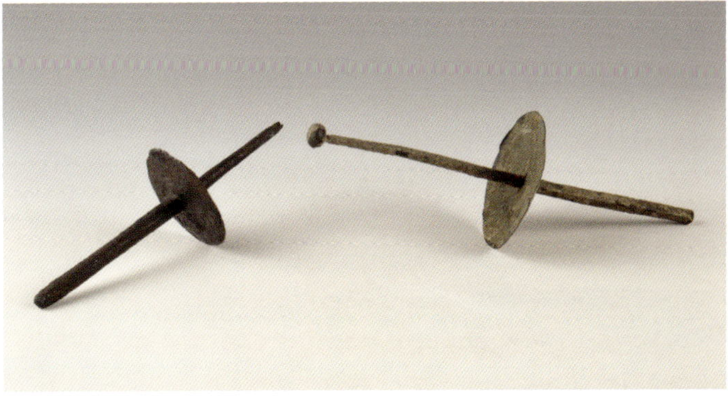

Figure 6. Cylinder seal impression of woman holding a spindle. Kültepe – Kaneš. Source: Teissier, 1994, No. 348

the Arslantepe site in Malatya show that this was an important settlement in terms of the changes, innovations and developments involved in weaving and spinning, from the Chalcolithic to the Middle Bronze Age (4000-1750 BC) (Frangipane *et al.*, 2009; Laurito, Lemorini and Perilli, 2014). Experimental applications in Arslantepe have shown that the weight and diameter of the spindle whorl determines the quality of the yarn and therefore that shape of the spindle whorl depended on parameters such as tradition, and ease of use. Spindle whorls made of bone have a larger diameter than others, and are therefore thought to be used likely for plant fibre, tighter spun yarn (Frangipane *et al.*, 2009, p. 6). Experimental spinning practices have also shown that finer yarns are spun with lighter spindle whorls, while thick yarn is spun with heavier ones. (Anderson, Mårtensson, Nosch and Rahmstorf, 2008). Experimenters have observed that thin yarn broke when spun with a heavy spindle whorl, and that finer spindles failed to spin with thick fibres.

There are a few depictions illustrating women holding a spindle or spinning yarn; extant examples are commemorations in votive scenes or funerary steles. A woman offers a spindle to a goddess sitting in front of her in a votive scene on a cylinder stamp in Kültepe – Kaneš, dated to the Old Assyrian Colony Period (Teissier, 1994, No. 348). A woman holding a spindle was depicted on a Neo Hittite funerary stele dated to 8th century BC, the Iron Age (Bittel, 1976, Figure 313, Bonatz, 2000, Plate 21 C 60). Known as the *Maraş Stele*, it shows a woman holding a spindle

in her left hand, while holding wool in her right. The smaller person depicted across her represents her widower holding a box and stylus (pen), symbolizing that he was a scribe. These depictions reflect the kind of work the deceased person was involved in their life, and yarn is thought to symbolize life and destiny (Baccelli *et al.*, 2014).

Figure 7. Woman, and probably her son depicted spinning wool on the grave stele from the Late Hittite Period, (825-700 BC) found in Maraş. Height: 102 cm, Width: 70 cm. Adana Archaeology Museum Directorate

Figure 8. Crescent-shaped loom weights discovered *in situ* in the Late Bronze Age layer at Beycesultan Höyük excavation (16th century BC). Beycesultan Höyük Excavation Archive.

Figure 9. Crescent-shaped loom weights discovered in Kültepe (1830-1700 BC). Kültepe Excavation Archive

Looms and loom weights. Loom weights found in the excavations help us understand the looms used in the prehistoric or protohistoric ages (Figure 8). Loom weights came in different shapes and weights; and were made of clay, terra-cotta or stone (Figure 9).

The weights and thicknesses of the loom weights are two important parameters determining weaving types (Mårtenson, Nosch and Andersson, 2009). Various weaving experiments have shown that heavier and thicker loom weights were necessary for coarser textile of thicker threads, whereas tight weaving required heavier but thinner loom weights. If loose weaving with fine threads is required, lighter and thicker loom weights must be used, and tight weaving with thick threads requires thin and light loom weights. No depictions of looms belonging to these times in Anatolia have been found yet, but there are depictions on an Archaic *lekythos* (oil bottle) found in Khnumhotep's Tomb in Beni Hasan, in Egypt (1897-1878 BC) (Figure 10).

Researchers believe that the warp-weighted loom, in which warp yarns hang freely, were widely used in Anatolia in the Bronze Age (Frangipane *et al.*, 2009, p. 8, Image 5). Weavers used various loom weights to obtain textiles of varying qualities, thickness, and thinness. As adequate importance was not attached to

Figure 10. Weaving scene depicted on lekythos dated to Archaic period (550-530 BC).
Fletcher Fund, Metropolitan Museum of Art.

Figure 11. Drawing of a weaving scene depicted on the papyrus found in the grave of Khnumhotep (12th Dynasty, reign of Senusret II, 1897-1878 BC) at Beni Hasan, by Norman de Garis Davies (1865-1941).
Rogers Fund, Metropolitan Museum of Art.

loom weights and spindles, they are not often covered in publications, and little experimental work has been conducted to understand the type of weave for which they were used. Important work has been carried out in Arslantepe in this regard. An experimental study was carried out to determine the type of loom and possible fabric and yarn thicknesses based on the number of loom weights found in a room (room no. A933) in a house belonging to an elite person at layer VIA in Arslantepe, dated to the Late Chalcolithic Period (Frangipane *et al.*, 2009, p. 15). Eighteen terracotta loom weights were found in the room. Seventeen of these were conical-shaped, weighing 624-828 g. and 77-95 mm thick. It was possible to weave a 75 cm wide fabric with eighteen loom weights, using nine in the front and nine in the back. It was estimated that to weave a fabric of 2 m. length, 1836 m. of yarn was required and about 37 hours to produce it (Frangipane *et al.*, 2009, p.15). A loom weight found in the same room was lighter (585 g) and thinner (55 mm), and determined that thinner fabrics were woven with such a loom weight. Because a lesser number of loom weights were found at the Arslantepe VI C-D layers (2500-2000 BC), researchers have concluded that a different type of loom must have superseded warp weighted vertical looms in this era (Frangipane *et al.*, 2009, p. 22).

Crescent-shaped loom weights began to be used in the Bronze Age in Anatolia (Figure 8, 9). An experimental study in Lejre Experimental Centre in Denmark and Kültepe-Kaneš have revealed that these crescent-shaped loom weights were used in the production of herringbone-patterned textile (Lassen, 2013, 2015). That this fabric was very special is revealed by the way it was used. Herringbone patterns are seen on garments worn by gods and kings, and on their chairs, or over bull altars, as depicted in Kültepe – Kaneš cylinder stamps (Lassen, 2013, p. 85, Figure 5.17) (Figure 8).

The varieties in loom weights also represent communication between cultures and regions. Crescent-shaped and cylindrical loom weights made of unbaked clay found in Çine-Tepecik in the Late Bronze Age layers indicate that the settlement was associated with both the Hittite cultural region and Western Anatolia (Yılmaz, 2016).

Yarn and Textile Remains Found in Anatolia

Dry soil or permafrost is required to preserve the integrity of fabrics. For example, wooden objects and textiles in ancient Egyptian tombs have been preserved, because they were kept in a dry and airless environment (Figure 12). The textiles that were found in Anatolia were only partially preserved and many were found in burials. In addition to this, information about the types of weaving, yarn thicknesses and application methods may be found in the traces textile leave on clay. (Figure 13). Clay *bullae* (*cretulae*) were attached to seal palace gates, jars, and fabrics to identify trade goods as of the Chalcolithic Period. When the gate was opened, the bulla, which was attached to the door-jamb and wall, was broken, either stored or discarded. It is possible to determine the material and fabric that a bulla adhered to from the marks on its back

Pieces of textile found in Anatolia reveal that weaving was practiced as of the Neolithic, and raw materials, tools, weaving methods and thread-thicknesses changed over time. Analyses show that fabrics were woven out of vegetable fibres, such as flax, and sheep and goat's wool.

Among the Anatolian textile samples examined, the oldest sample was found in Çayönü, in the Cell-Plan Houses Phase (6650-6350 BC). This textile was preserved on a sickle made of antlers (Özdoğan, 1999, p. 55). Textiles were found at Çatal Höyük burials, dating to the Late Neolithic Period (ca. 5950-5880 BC). The first textile pieces made

Figure 12. Linen found in Thebes in Upper Egypt, Sheikh Abd al-Qurna, in the tomb of Hatnefer and Ramose (18th Dynasty, 1492-1473 BC). It is 515 cm in length, 161 cm in width, and weighs 141 grams. There are 46 warps and 30 weft threads per square centimetre.
Rogers Fund, Metropolitan Museum of Art

Figure 13. Texture print on the back of bulla no. KT 90 / K499 found in Kültepe. Source: Özgüç and Tunca, 2001, Plate 107.

of both wool and flax were discovered in the 1960s, in scorched graves in layer VI (Burnham, 1965, Ryder 1965, Mellaart, 2003, p 170, Büken, 2003, Breniquet 2014, p. 56). The textiles were used to wrap the dead, and some were rolled into a ball to insert into the skull after the brain was removed (Burnham, 1965). In 2013, abundant quantities of woven material were discovered in the northwestern tomb of building No 52. A fragment of fabric was found on the shoulder of a terracotta figurine at the Ulucak Mound layer-Vb, dating to the end of 7,000 BC (Çilingiroğlu, 2009, pp. 15-17, Figure 7). These remains may indicate that the figurine was wrapped in textile or might have been the remains of a garment.

160 clay bullae were found in the VIA plate of the Late Chalcolithic Period

Figure 14. Textile fragments found on metal bowl in the royal tomb. Arslantepe Layer VI B1.
Archive of the Archaeological Expedition in Eastern Anatolia (MAIAO), Sapienza University of Rome

Figure 15. Microscope photograph showing the fibres of the raw material (goat's wool) of the fabric found on the metal bowl (y3). Arslantepe, royal tomb, Layer VI B1. (Sample no. 086/2002) Archive of the Italian Archaeological Expedition in Eastern Anatolia (MAIAO), Sapienza University of Rome

Arslantepe, 80 of which presented traces of textile impression. The imprints showed a plain tabby weave and that the yarn was s-twisted, with 8-12 threads per centimetre (Frangipane *et al.*, 2009, p.15). The fragments of textile found at the king's burial chamber at layer VI B impart information on both funerary traditions and weaving practice. The deceased and some grave gifts were found placed on a board in the tomb. Textiles were found on the metal objects and under the pots, close to the shoulder and near left shinbone. Analyses have shown that these were made of vegetal fibres and wool. The piece of woven material No. 086/2002 found inside a metal bowl is of particular interest, because microscopic examinations have shown that it was made of goat's wool (Figures 14, 15) (Frangipane *et al.*, 2009, pp. 19-20, 21). The fabric unearthed in the tomb was one of the oldest animal woven textile ever found in the Old Near East, and it had an extraordinarily fine texture.

Textile samples belonging to the Early Bronze Age were found on metal artefacts and in proximity to the dead found in pithoi and cist graves found in the extramural cemetery (outside the settlement) at Resuloğlu (Tütüncüler, 2006). Analyses underline the fact that textile were woven with flax fibres and were of varying quality, and that different textiles were woven for a variety of intended uses by the people of that era. Textile fragments dated to the Early Bronze Age were found at the Kuruçay 6 A and the 6th construction layers (3620-3350 BC) adhered to bones in a pithos grave on (Duru, 1996, p. 24, Plate 51/1). In Alişar, a fragment of plain tabby weave was discovered in a Chalcolithic grave (e X14) dated to 3000 BC (Fogelberg and Kendall, 1937, pp. 334-335). Microscopic analyses of the fragment were able to detect dark browns and yellows, suggesting that this was the fabric used to wrap the body (Fogelberg and Kendall, 1937, pp. 334-335, Figure 60). Traces of textile woven with plant fibre were detected on an ulnar bone at Samsun, Tepeköy (Kökten, N. Özgüç and Özgüç, 1945, p. 386, Alkım, 1968, pp. 8); and on a dagger, spearhead, piercer, axe, and a tong-shaped instrument in a group of findings at the floor of a building that had been exposed to fire in the "D" opening at İkiztepe (Bilgi 1994, p. 237; Bilgi 2001, p. 4-5, 11-12, Fig. 124). Scraps were also found at Alaca Höyük, at the M.A. and M.C. burial sites famous for their sun disks and deer sculptures (Koşay 1938, pp. 79, 83). The fabric

piece found in the M. A. tomb probably belonged to the deceased's garment; because there are three pieces of oo-shaped, golden clasps used to hold together such a dress. Textile vestiges were observed on a gold-plated copper dagger found in the M.C. tomb. Pieces of textile were also discovered wrapped around a pin in Gaziantep-Gedikli Karahöyük (U. B. Alkım and Alkım 1966, p.17). Nine samples of thread, textile and shoe remains were found in both the Early and Middle Bronze Age layers at the Seyitömer Mound (Bilgen and Tütüncüler Bircan, 2017). Three of these from the Early Bronze Age and one sample from the Middle Bronze Age were analysed. Two of the pieces of textile found on the floor of a burnt chamber from the Early Bronze Age were discovered inside pottery. There were also 5 terracotta brushes, 17 spindle whorls and 17 loom weights unearthed in a room, attesting that the place was a weaving workshop inside a house. Electron microscopy has shown that the textiles were woven from wool (Başer, 2002, p.70, Bilgen and Tütüncüler Bircan, 2017, p. 26, Image 5). The textile was woven in a plain tabby weave, with s-twisted yarn, and it is thought that it was stretched across the mouth of a crock to close it (Bilgen and Tütüncüler Bircan, 2017, p.27). The other piece was fine and loosely woven, like cheesecloth, and used to plug the mouth of a jug (Figures 16, 17) (Bilgen ve Tütüncüler Bircan, 2017, p. 27, Image a-b). The third sample was found with carbonized grains in a bowl, and electron microscope scanning has shown that the raw material is flax (Bilgen ve Tütüncüler Bircan 2017, p. 27, Image a-b).

Fabric fragments dated to the second millennium BC were found in Acem Höyük and Ortaköy. The first piece of textile belonging to the Old Assyrian Colony Period was found at Acem Höyük, at the burnt-down chamber NA-OA / 46, at construction layer III of the Sarıkaya Palace. Among the objects unearthed were ivory objects, textile traces, a gameboard, obsidian and quartz vases and gold ornaments (Özgüç, 1968, pp. 15, 21-22). A peculiarity of the textile-traces are the gilded ceramic beads found inside them (Figure 18). It is thought that this unique piece was from an expensive, imported textile. Some textiles, two pieces of yarn and piece of a shoe was found at the C-phase of layer IV dated to the Middle Bronze Age in

Figure 16. Early Bronze Age spouted pitcher.
Seyitömer Höyük Excavation Archive

Figure 17. Thin and loose woven, muslin-like fabric, twisted to form a stopper to fit into the spout of an Early Bronze Age pitcher (fig. 16).
Seyitömer Höyük Excavation Archive

Figure 18. Textile fragment decorated with gilded fayance beads discovered at Acem Höyük Layer III. (Approx. 18th century BC)
Museum of Anatolian Civilizations Directorate

Seyitömer (Bilgen ve Tütüncüler Bircan, 2017, p. 29, Image 9 a-c). Analyses have determined that the textile was made from wool and three dye spectra were found. The dye used was most probably dyer>s madder (*Rubia tinctorum L.*), also known as "Turkish red." The fabric appears to be a thin belt, woven in a three-line pattern with a macramé or çarpana technique, and it is thought that the piece belongs to a grave cloth or shroud (Bilgen ve Tütüncüler Bircan, 2017, p. 31).

Yarn fragments are very rare. Fragments of yarn spun from wool fibres were found in Seyitömer, in the C and B houses of layer IV (Bilgen ve Tütüncüler Bircan, 2017, s. 31, Image 10 a-c). Behind some of the bullae discovered in the Kültepe – Kaneš layers are fabric traces that provide information on fabrics and their usage (Özgüç and Tunca 2001, Figure 107). The textiles found in Kaman Kalehöyük are dated to the Old Assyrian Colony Period in the Middle Bronze Age (room 150, layer III C). Among them is a small, patterned fragment, made with the *soumak* technique, which constitutes the oldest patterned textile sample discovered in Anatolia so far (Fairbairn, 2004). These textile fragments are thought to be from sacks and garments. The textile remains found in Ortaköy (14th century BC) were probably used to cover the mouths of jars. In the warehouse of Building B, a linen textile fragment was preserved on the shoulders of a jar (A. Süel 1998, p 42, M. Süel 1998, p 571, Figure 19, Gültekin 2005, p.434 Figure 1-13).

These samples generally supply much information on both the raw materials used in weaving and their utilization technique. We find that flax and wool were used in weaving, the earliest textiles were made of vegetable fibre, the oldest goat's wool weaving was found at the Arslantepe VI B layer, and that textiles were used for wrapping the deceased, producing garments, preserving food and for commerce. With the development of writing, it became possible to acquire diverse information about wool and weaving, such as their material values, types of usage and who produced them.

Wool, Weaving and their Material Values in Cuneiform Sources

In Mesopotamia, topics regarding wool, weaving, animal husbandry, wool qualities and plucking began to appear on cuneiform tablets as of 3000 BC. The animals were put to pasture in fields and steppes, and belonged to the ruler, the palace or temple (Sallaberger, 2009, p. 244). The records mention that the weaving in Early Bronze Age Mesopotamia involved both flax and wool, but linen garments were only used for rituals (Sallaberger, 2014). The cuneiform tablets discovered in Kültepe – Kaneš refer to the Assyrian weavers and their wool trade as early as 2000 BC. Wool was a highly valued commodity in Anatolia and Northern Mesopotamia, and was exchanged for silver or bronze (Michel and Veenhof, 2014, p. 216).

Wool was not shorn in Mesopotamia during the Sumerian period. It was instead obtained by plucking or combing in springtime. A ram yielded about 1 kg of fibre, and an ewe produced a little less. The wools were classified according to their quality and washed. Texts from the Early Bronze Age Mesopotamia note that about 100 women worked at the weaving workshop, under the supervision of male guards. Two or three women worked on a loom to produce various fabrics of 2 m. width and 4 m. length. The woven textiles went through various processes. The material would be drenched with sesame and other such aromatic oils and then kneaded. It was washed during the kneading process using various minerals and alkaline. The kneading process hade a felting effect on the surface, which made the fabric more robust (Sallaberger, 2009).

In Mesopotamia, salaries were paid in shares during the Ur III period (2400-2000 BC). The amount varied depending on social status, job, age and sex. The salary was paid with wool and grain (wheat, barley) (Sallaberger, 2009). In general, women were paid less, and children were paid grain and wool according to their age. In the 21st century BC, general measures during Ur III period were as follows (Sallaberger, 2009, p. 245):

- Men (60 litres of grain per month) and one fabric or four *mina*[1] of wool (2 kg) per annum.
- Women (30 litres of grain per month) and three *mina* of wool (1.5 kg) per annum.
- Children (10-20 litres of grain month) and 2 *mina* of wool (1 kg) per annum.

The number of employees paid in kind can be estimated from the city's annual wool disbursements found on the Ur III documents. 34.87 tonnes of wool were paid out according to an account (UET 3 1504). Assuming that each worker had received 4 *mina*, this means that 17,000 people were given wool for clothing (Sallaberger, 2009, p. 246).

Ebla located 80 km south of Aleppo, flourished from the second half of the 3rd Millenium BC until the first half of the 2nd Millenium BC. Tablets found at the Ebla palace archives and dated to the Early Dynastic period contain important information regarding the goods belonging to the palace. Metals, textiles, meat and high-value food belonged to the sovereign. The tablets also include important administrative texts. These record annual expenses and revenues on a monthly basis. Texts on weaving reveal the purpose of their use, and that they were colourful, and that fabric was sent as a gift to rulers of Ebla's neighbouring cities and elders (Sallaberger, 2009, p. 249). These also help calculate the number of high-ranking people in the districts or cities to which goods were sent, since the identities of the recipients were also recorded.

Sumerian merchants sold wool in the 24th and the 21st century, and cuneiform texts reveal that it was a primary barter commodity. It was a significant export commodity in the city of Girsu in the Presargonic Period. The wool was sold in exchange for spices or bartered to purchase silver and copper. The cuneiform texts dated to the Ur III dynasty contain information on accounts of buying and selling, as well as accounts of merchants who acquire commodities from local and foreign markets. At the time, wool was sold only as raw material, not in fabric

---

1 1 mina = approx. 0.5 kg.

from. The administration of the city of Umma exchanged large quantities of wool for gold. In Umma, wool was also sold for bitumen (tar), barley, eggs, women and children. The material value of wool was 30 *shekels*[2] of silver for 5 *talents*[3] wool, (Sallaberger, 2014, p. 99).

Archives show that 2000 people were living in Nabada (Tell Beydar), the second most important Upper Mesopotamian city, in the 24th century BC, and that people used to work collectively in the fields and the workshops. The 18 cuneiform tablets in the archives provide important information about sheep breeding. The tablets recorded whether the animals were inspected by the local government, the number of livestock given to shepherds, the amount of wool sheared in spring, and the number of lost sheep. The sheep belonged to the community, and shepherds were part of that community. These accounts include the name of the shepherd, the type of the animal (sheep or goat), the numbers, and month name. Each herd consisted of 160 to 300 animals, and the high number of rams suggests that these were bred not only for meat, but also for wool. The quantity of the wool plucked and the fact that the plucking process took place during the month of the sun god indicate that plucking was performed during certain periods. The names of the shepherds and the numbers of herds in the texts show that there were about 4,000 sheep in Nabada and a nearly the same number of goats (Sallaberger, 2009, 2014).

The work of wool plucking was performed by women, who were recorded as "working woman" or "woman weaver". For example, a cuneiform tablet from Girsu mentions 816 woman weavers and their supervisor (Waetzoldt, 1972, pp. 14-15). One of the duties of the people between the cities of Girsu and Guana was to classify the plucked wool. The Ur texts speak of ten distinct qualities. The first sorted wool was again sorted into different subclasses, again a process performed by women. Ur III period texts, especially from the Umma archives, provide detailed information on wool production and sheep varieties. There were two varieties of sheep in the herds, these were: a) Local, Sumerian sheep (*udu eme-gi*), and b) Mountain sheep (*udu-kur-ra*), or the fat-tailed sheep. The majority of the sheep were white, while the number of black ones was less than 7%; the black and dark wool was less valuable and was written at the bottom rows of the lists. At that time, wool was not yet dyed. One talent of the Sumerian sheep's wool was 6 shekels, while one had to pay 8 shekels for the same amount of mountain sheep's wool. It is written on a tablet that the herds belonging to the ruler of the city (*ensi*) were kept near the temple. This quite significant information shows that the city's economy, its livestock and agriculture were administered by the temple (Sallaberger, 2009, 2014).

With the introduction of writing to Anatolia, brought by the Assyrian merchants in the early 2nd millennium BC, information began to be recorded regarding wool, weaving and animal husbandry, to be found especially in the Kültepe – Kaneš archives (Kulakoğlu and Kangal 2010). Kültepe is located about 20 km northeast of Kayseri. Cuneiform tablets were found in the houses of the lower city's commercial district *karum* and were dated to the 19th and 18th centuries

2 1 shekel = approx. 7.8 g.

3 1 talent = approx. 30 kg.

BC. Assyrian merchants brought woven goods and tin to Anatolia, and exchanged them for silver and bronze. Until recently, Assyrians were believed to have brought linen fabrics from Assur. The word *kutanum* [type of weave] mentioned in the tablets was misinterpreted to mean flax. However, with the passing of years and more translations of tablets, it was learned that *kutanum* textile was fuzzy, and it was concluded that it must have been made of a woollen fabric. Flaxen fabrics were also woven, and the term *kita'um* was used to describe these (Michel and Veenhof, 2014).

Cuneiform texts from the Sumerian period refer to wool, while those discovered in Kültepe – Kaneš refer to wool and predominantly weaving, i.e. the processed form of wool. Traders would import woollen textiles from Assur to Anatolia in large quantities and it is known that they traded in woollen goods in Anatolia. Commercial texts provide information about the purchasing, handling, transportation, sale and taxation of textiles. Some very rare letters, written by women, contain information on the production of certain textiles (Figure 19) (Michel and Veenhof 2014, p. 210). The price of merchandise was determined by its weight, and every tablet referring to the trade must contain information about weights and prices. The weight units, cited on the hundreds of scales, weights and tablets found in Kültepe – Kaneš, offer significant information about trade in the Middle Bronze Age. Cuneiform tablets impart information about standard weight measures, systems and regional weight systems in Anatolia and Mesopotamia. In Kültepe – Kaneš, two ram-shaped weights were found in layers II and Ib, which weighed 2,530 and 4,898.6 grams (Figure 20) (Kulakoğlu, 2017, p. 348).

The former weight was 5 *minas* and the latter one was 10 *minas* in Assyrian weight system terms. Again, two ram-shaped weights were found in the Chalcolithic strata of Ugarit, Syria, and are thought to represent the wool weight of the period (Matoïan and Vita, 2014; Peyronel, 2014). The ram was a popular motif on jugs and rhytons, and may be associated with the wool trade, too (Figure 21).

Traders categorized fabrics by quality and colour, but also named them by the cities where they were produced. The texts refer to the various qualities of wool. Wool was divided into a number of categories, such as good (*dammuqum*), very good (*dammuqum watrum*), fine, low quality, long (*arkum*), combed (*pusikkum*) (Lassen, 2010). In ancient Assyrian texts, the word soft (*narbum*) was used often to describe wool, but this

Figure 19. Cuneiform clay tablets containing information on shipments of fabrics, tin and donkeys between Kültepe (Kaneš) and Assur (1950-1835 BC). Kt. v / k. 138, 164-138-70
Kültepe Excavation Archive

Figure 20. Ram-shaped stone weight (2530 grams, equivalent to the Assyrian 5 *minas*).
Kültepe Excavation Archive (Kt 1987/k 233)

Figure 21. Ram's head pitcher
Kültepe Excavation Archive

term was not used to describe wool during the Sumerian era. Old Assyrian texts refer to wool dyed red (*samum*),[4] white (*pasium*), dyed (*sinitum*) and dyed red (*makrûm*).

Textile prices were quite specific, and varied from half *mina* to 2/3 *shekel* (Özgüç, 1968, p. 21). Wool was produced in the cities of Kaneš, Luhuzaddiya, Mamma, Hahum, Hurama, Tišmura, Timilkiya, Samuha, Durhumit, Šinahattum and Purušhaddum (Lassen 2014, p. 167, Michel and Veenhof 2014, p. 216). Purušhaddum, located to the west of Kaneš, produced the largest quantities of wool. Sales of 15 tonnes of wool to Kaneš were recorded in tablets (Lassen 2014, p.168). Luhuzaddiya is known as the most frequently mentioned city in the wool trade, cited ten times in some ten thousand texts, which indicates that there was a central wool market there. Although the wool produced in the city of Mamma is mentioned in only one text, it is apparent that its wool was considered the best quality and was therefore expensive: 4 *minas* of wool, which is adequate for producing a fabric, was exchanged for 30 *shekels* of silver (Lassen 2014, p. 167). The city of Tišmura in the Çorum region was probably also a major supplier of wool and was famous for its red wool. When all the texts are taken together, Purušhaddum, Tišmura and Luhuzaddiya stand out as the main production areas, and although the exact locations of the cities are yet unknown, it shows that wool was produced in the north, west and east of Kaneš (Lassen 2014, p. 2).

During the Old Assyrian Colony Period, trade in Kültepe – Kaneš was conducted by family companies that specialized in certain products and recorded detailed information on their activities on clay tablets. In the light of this information, we can infer that donkeys were used to transport the wool from one place to another, and that a wool was put into the sacks which could take up to 45 kg each (Lassen 2010, 167). However, an archive of a family that deals solely with wool is yet to be found. Wool was sold for bronze and silver, during periods when it was profitable to sell (Lassen 2010, p 172, Table 1). A letter written by Puzur-Adad to Imdī-ilum in 1768 BC bears witness to the fact that the palace did not impose fixed price on wool: "I heard that much wool has arrived in Wahsusana city. I will sell the wool for a high or low price and send you the silver" (Lassen 2010, p.173). A few texts impart information about the material value of wool. A woman named Lamassutum is especially active in wool and textile trade. Text Kt 91/k 388.42 in Kültepe – Kaneš indicate that she owned wool for weaving, that she loaned 30 *minas* of wool as credit, and that the textiles were probably woven at her home. Text Kt 87/k 118 cites she purchased with Hapilu 19 *shekels* worth of wool, which would suffice to weave a dozen pieces (Lassen, 2010, pp. 165).

4 *Samum* is thought to be a natural reddish brown.

There were wool merchants from Ebla who traded wool in Anatolia, besides the Assyrian traders, and texts note that they traded wool professionally. Local Anatolian traders, too, are also known to have been involved in the wool trade (Lassen, 2010). Hittite sources are not as detailed as the Kültepe – Kaneš material; in fact, they contain little information about wool's material value. However, laws and official and diplomatic correspondence, treaties, festival-texts, royal victory statements, and cult activities provide information on prized textiles, garments and weavers (Baccelli, Bellucci and Vigo, 2014). Only a few Hittite texts also offer information about spinning wool, cleaning of contaminated wool and weaving on the loom.

Hittite laws refer to the training of male and female weavers. If a person apprentices his son or daughter to the weaver, he has to pay 6 *shekels* (Baccelli *et al.*, 2014, p. 107). This law shows that weaving was an important and valuable occupation. Certain cult inventory texts refer to the fact that weavers were not free citizens, and they could be purchased for 10 *shekels* (Baccelli *et al.*, 2014, p.107). In Hittite texts, coloured wool is often mentioned in the context of rituals. In the Puliša ritual, in the rite to halt the epidemic that had started in the military camp during war, lengths of red, yellow and black woollen yarn were placed in the king's mouth, which the priest would proceed to pull out, so that the pestilence returned to the enemy (Haas, 1994, p. 212). Red and white yarn would be knotted to join the king and the queen (Melchert, 2001, p. 407).

Garments

Garments protect our bodies, but also indicate gender, age, rank or profession. The acceptance of apparel as an element of prestige stems from the material and social value that cultures and civilizations assign to it. In the Gilgamesh epic, Gilgamesh's companion Enkidu, in passing from savagery to urban life, is first dressed, and then learned how to eat and drink (Maden, Trans. 2015).

Cuneiform texts imply that textiles were sold in pieces, rather than ready-made garments. Inventory lists from the Hittite period contain information on clothing varieties. In addition, the iconography of statues, reliefs and figurines from various periods provide information about clothes.

In Mesopotamia, simple woollen wrap-around clothes were worn in the 24th century BC. One of the elements that determined the prestige value of the dress and the rank of the wearer in the 2nd and 1st centuries BC was the garment's hemstitch (*sissiktum* in Akkadian). This border ornament was printed in place of the cylinder stamp, on clay tablets containing legal texts and used for identification (Sallaberger, 2009). In the Neo Hittite king sculptures, the hemstitch on the king's apparel comes to the forefront, and symbolizes his power and rank (Figure 22).

Hittite texts speak in detail on women and men's apparel. In the Tunnawi ritual, the main parts of a Hittite woman's clothing are enumerated: "A pulled-up dress, an embroidered tunic, a mantle, an inner dress, a girdled tunic suit, and a set of silver chest ornaments; these belong to women" (Darga, 1984, p. 86). Among men's clothes are an embroidered dress, tunic, blue socks, shawl or scarf (Figure 23). Garments were also decorated with various colourful and precious stones (Darga, 1984, p. 87). The value of textiles is also apparent from the fact that Hittite kings

Figure 22. Statue of King Mutallu in Arslantepe, Malatya (725-700 BC). Height: 3.18 m.
Museum of Anatolian Civilizations Directorate

Figure 23. Tunics are numbered among menswear in Hittite cuneiform texts. Rams and sheep were depicted as votive animals during the Hittite period.
Alaca Höyük Orthostat, Votive Offering Scene.
Museum of Anatolian Civilizations Directorate

gave fabrics and garments as gifts to the rulers of other countries. Inventory texts found in the archives of the capital Hattuša mention textiles and clothes (Košak 1982, pp. 106-139). Fabrics woven from wool and flax are sometimes referred to with place names, such as Amurus flax or Alašiya (Cyprus) flax (Vigo, 2010, p.291). The inventory lists include names of wool importers, woollen textiles, garments (tunic, tail-tunic, shawl, shirt, robe, dress, leggings, belt, and headscarf), and itemise their quantities, qualities and colours (white, blue, black, green, yellow, red, and purple). Some of these lists hint suggest that certain women's dresses were decorated with gold ornaments (Košak, 1982, p.113). Text numbered CTH 243.6 = Kbo 18: 181 refers to garments of various types, such as Hurri shirts (tunics), Hurri dinner shirt, festival clothes, headscarf, *maršum* headscarf, *sepahi* shirt and *tappaspa* garments (Košak, 1982, pp. 121-123).

While the Kültepe – Kaneš tablets generally relate to weaving, Hittite tablets inform us more specifically on garment types. While the exact reason for this remains unknown, it may be surmised that attire was deemed more important than fabrics.

Understanding and Reviving Anatolian Weaving

The weaving activities that began in Anatolia in the Neolithic Age may be understood thanks to textile fragments, loom weights, spindle whorls, various tools and cuneiform texts discovered in the excavations. Samples found show that textiles were used for wrapping the dead, producing garments and sacks, trading, or covering storage containers. Cuneiform tablets contain much important information, from plucking sheep or goat fibres, to sorting wool by quality, and the production, trade, and material value of woollen and linen fabrics. Wool was deemed as valuable as metals and sold for silver or bronze.

Experimental archaeological studies can detect the type of yarn spun and fabrics woven with the loom weights and spindle whorls found in the excavations (Figure 24). However, very few such experiments have been carried out in Anatolian excavations, and those that have been done do not fully represent the diversity of the wool and textiles sold for silver and bronze during those ages. Weaving has played an important role in every period of Anatolian civilizations. Even today, some places are still famous for their textiles, and one of them is Ankara, with its *sof* weaving. Anatolia, having been the forerunner in wool and textile production in the Near East throughout prehistory and protohistory, has maintained its position until to the present.

Figure 24. Experimental archaeology in Kültepe: weaving with crescent-shaped loom weights.
Kültepe Excavation Archive

Acknowledgments

I would like to thank the Adana Archaeological Museum Directorate, the Anatolian Civilizations Museum Directorate, Prof. Eşref Abay, Prof. Nejat Bilgen, Prof. Marcella Frangipane, Prof. Fikri Kulakoğlu, Prof. Marie Nosch, and Prof. Aliye Öztan for allowing me to use their visuals in this article.

References

Alkım, U. B. (1968). İslâhiye Bölgesi Araştırmaları Gedikli ve Kırışkal Höyük Kazıları. *Türk Arkeoloji Dergisi, XVI/II*, 5-13.

Alkım, U. B. ve Alkım, H. (1966). Gedikli (Karahöyük) Kazısı Birinci Ön-Rapor. *Belleten, XXX/117*, 1-57.

Andersson, E., Mårtensson, L., Nosch, M. L. and Rahmstorf, L. (2008). New Research on Bronze Age Textile Production. *Bulletin of the Institute of Classical Studies 51*, 71-174.

Baccelli, G., Bellucci, B. and Vigo, M. (2014). Elements for a Comparative Study of Textile Production and Use in Hittite Anatolia and in Neighbouring Areas. In M. Harlow & C. Michel & M. L. Nosch (Ed.), *Prehistoric, Ancient Near Eastern and Aegean Textiles and Dress* (pp. 97-142). Oxford: Oxbow Books.

Bachhuber, C. (2016). The Industry and Display of Textiles in Early Bronze Age Western Anatolia. In E. Pernicka, S. Ünlüsoy, S. ve W. E. Blum (Ed.), *Early Bronze Age Troy: Chronology, Cultural Development and Interregional Contacts* (pp. 339-364). Bonn: Habelt Verlag.

Baird, D., Fairbairn, A., Martin, L. and Middleton, C. (2012). The Boncuklu Project: The origins of sedentism, cultivation and herding in Central Anatolia. In M. Özdoğan, N. Başgelen ve P. Kuniholm (Ed.), *The Neolithic in Turkey, Central Turkey and Mediterranean C. 3* (pp. 219-244). İstanbul: Archaeology and Art Publications.

Barber, E. J. (1991). *Prehistoric Textiles: The Development of the Cloth in the Neolithic and Bronze Ages with Special Reference to the Aegean*. Princeton: Princeton University Press.

Başer, İ. (2002). *Elyaf Bilgisi*. İstanbul: Marmara Üniversitesi Yayınları.

Becker, C., Benecke, N., Grabundzija, N., Küchelmann, H. C., Pollock, S., Schier, W., Schoch, C., Schrakamp, I., Schütt, B. and Schumacher, M. (2016). The Textile Revolution. Research into the Origin and Spread of Wool Production between the Near East and Central Europe. In G. Graßhoff ve M. Meyer (Ed.), *Topoi Journal for Ancient Studies, Özel Cilt 6 (pp.*102-151).

Bilgen, A. N. and Tütüncüler Bircan, Ö. (2017). Seyitömer Höyük Buluntularından İp/Urgan ve Dokuma Kumaş ile Deri Ayakkabı Numuneleri. *Arkeoloji ve Sanat 155*, 23-24.

Bilgi, Ö. (1994). İkiztepe Kazılarının 1992 Dönemi Sonuçları, *KST 15.1*, 235-244.

Bilgi, Ö. (2001). *Protohistorik Çağ'da Orta Karadeniz Bölgesi Madencileri Hind-Avrupalıların Anavatanı Sorununa Yeni bir Yaklaşım / Protohistoric Age Metalurgists of the Central Black Sea Region a New Perspective on the Question of the Indo-Europeans' Original Homeland.* İstanbul: TASK Vakfı.

Bittel, K. (1976). *Les Hittites*. Paris: Gallimard.

Bonatz, D. (2000). *Das syro-hethitische Grabdenkmal*. Mainz: P. von Zabern Verlag.

Bökönsy, I. (1983). Late Chalcolithic and Early Bronze I Animal Remains from

Arslantepe (Malatya), Turkey A: Preliminary Report. *Origini 2, 25*, 81-598.

Breniquet, C. (2014). The Archaeology of Wool in Early Mesopotamia: Sources, Methods, Perspectives. In C. Breniquet & C. Michel (Eds.), *Wool Economy in the Ancient Near East and the Aegean. From the Beginnings of Sheep Husbandry to Institutional Textile Industry* (pp. 52-78). Oxford & Philadelphia: Oxbow Books.

Brochier, J. E. (1993). Çayönü Tepesi. Domestication, rythmes et environnement au PPNB. *Paléorient 19*, 39-49.

Burnham, H. B. (1965). Çatal Hüyük: The Textiles and Twinned Fabrics. *Anatolian Studies 15*, 169-174.

Büken, R. (2003). Çatalhöyük Tekstilleri ve Teknik Analizleri. *TAD 3*, 79-86.

Çilingiroğlu, Ç. 2009. Of Stamps, Loom Weights and Spindle Whorls. Contextual Evidence on the Function(s) of Neolithic Stamps from Ulucak, İzmir, Turkey. *Journal of Mediterranean archaeology 22, 1*, 3-27.

Darga, M. (1984). *Eski Anadolu'da Kadın*. İstanbul: İstanbul Üniversitesi Edebiyat Fakültesi Yayınları.

Duru, R. (1996). *Kuruçay Höyük II: 1978-1988 Kazılarının Sonuçları Geç Kalkolitik ve İlk Tunç Çağı Yerleşmeleri*. Ankara: Türk Tarih Kurumu Yayınları.

Fairbairn, A. (2004). Archaeobotany at Kaman-Kalehöyük 2003. *Kaman-Kalehöyük Anatolian Archaeological Studies 13*, 107-120.

Fogelberg, J. M. and Kendall, A. I. (1937). Chalcolithic Textile Fragments. In H. H. von der Osten, J. A. Wilson ve T. G. Allen (Ed.), *The Alishar Höyük 1930-1932 III* (pp. 334-335). Chicago, Illinois: University of Chicago Press.

Frangipane, M., Strand, E. A., Laurito, R., Möller- Wiering, S., Nosch, M. L., Rast-Eicher, A. ve Lassen, A. W. (2009). Arslantepe, Malatya (Turkey): Textiles, tools and imprints of fabrics from the 4th to the 2nd Millennium BCE. *Paléorient, 35*(1), 5-29.

Gılgamış Destanı. (2005). (S. Maden, Çev.). İstanbul: İş Bankası Kültür Yayınları.

Gültekin, A. E. (2005). Çorum-Ortaköy Şapinuva Arkeolojik Alanından Ele Geçen Tekstil Örneği Analizi. In A. Süel (Yay. Haz.). *V. Uluslararası Hititoloji Kongresi Bildirileri, 02-08 Eylül 2002* (pp. 431-443). Ankara: Çorum Valiliği.

Haas, V. (1994). *Geschichte der hethitischen Religion*. Leiden, New York, Köln: Brill.

Helmer, D. 1992. *La domestication des animaux par les hommes préhistoriques*. Paris-Milan-Barcelone-Bonn: Masson.

Keller, G. 2002. *Kleider machen Leute*. Ditzingen: Reclam.

Korfmann, M. (1983). *Demircihüyük: Die Ergebnisse der Ausgrabungen 1975–1978.* Band I: Architektur, Stratigraphie und Befunde. Mainz: Philipp von Zabern.

Koşay, H. Z. (1938). *Türk Tarih Kurumu Tarafından Yapılan Alaca Höyük Hafriyatı, 1936'daki Çalışmalara ve Keşiflere ait İlk Raporlar*. Ankara: Türk Tarih Kurumu Yayınları.

Košak, S. (1982). *Hittite Inventory Texts (CTH 241-250). Texte der Hethiter Heft 10.* Heidelberg: Carl Winter.

Kökten, K., Özgüç, N. and Özgüç, T. (1945). 1940 ve 1941 Yılında Türk Tarih Kurumu

Adına Yapılan Samsun Bölgesi Kazıları Hakkında İlk Kısa Rapor. *Belleten, C.IX, S. 35*, 361-400.

Kulakoğlu, F. (2017) Balance Stone Weights and Scale-Pans from Kültepe-Kanesh: On One of the Basic Elements of the Old Assyrian Trading System. In Ç. Maner, M. Horowitz ve A. Gilbert (Ed.), *Overturning Certainties in Near Eastern Archaeology, A Festschrift in Honor of K. Aslıhan Yener* (pp. 335-394). Leiden; Boston: Brill.

Kulakoğlu, F. and Kangal, S. 2010. *Anadolu'nun Önsözü. Külepe Kaniş-Karumu*. Kayseri: Kayseri Büyükşehir Belediyesi Kültür Yayınları.

Lassen, A. W. (2010). The Trade In Wool In Old Assyrian Anatolia. *Ex Oriente Lux*, 42, 159-179.

Lassen, A. W. (2013). Technology and Palace Economy in Middle Bronze Age Anatolia: The Case of the Crescent Shaped Loom Weight. In M. L. Nosch, H. Koefoed ve E. A. Strand (Ed.), *Textile Production and Consumption in the Ancient Near East Archaeology, Epigraphy, Iconography* (pp.78-92). Oxford & Philadelphia: Oxbow Books.

Lassen, A. W. (2014). Wool in Anatolia in the Old Assyrian Period. In C. Breniquet ve C. Michel (Ed.), *Wool Economy in the Ancient Near East and the Aegean. From the Beginnings of Sheep Husbandry to Institutional Textile Industry* in (pp. 255-263). Oxford & Philadelphia: Oxbow Books.

Lassen, A. W. (2015). Weaving with Crescent Shaped Loom Weights. An Investigation of a Special Kind of Loom Weight. In E. A. Strand ve M. L. Nosch (Ed.), *Tools, Textiles and Contexts Investigating Textile Production in the Aegean and Eastern Mediterranean Bronze Age* (pp. 127-138). Oxford & Philadelphia: Oxbow Books.

Laurito, R., Lemorini, C. and Perilli, A. (2014). Making Textiles at Arslantepe, Turkey, in the 4th and 3rd Millenia BC. Archaeological Data and Experimental Archaeology. In C. Breniquet ve C. Michel (Ed.), *Wool Economy in the Ancient Near East and the Aegean. From the Beginnings of Sheep Husbandry to Institutional Textile Industry* (pp. 151-168). Oxford & Philadelphia: Oxbow Books.

Mårtenson, L., Nosch, M. L. and Andersson, E. (2009). Shape of Things: Understanding a Loom Weight. *Oxford Journal of Archaeology 28, 4*, 373-398.

Matoïan, V. and Vita, J. P. (2014). Wool Production and Economy at Ugarit. In C. Breniquet ve C. Michel (Ed.), *Wool Economy in the Ancient Near East and the Aegean. From the Beginnings of Sheep Husbandry to Institutional Textile Industry* (pp. 310-330). Oxford & Philadelphia: Oxbow Books.

Melchert, H. C. (2001). A Hittite fertility rite? In G. Wilhelm (Ed.). *Akten des IV. Internationalen Kongresses für Hethitologie*, 4-8. Oktober 1999 (pp. 404-409). Wiesbaden: Harrassowitz Verlag.

Mellaart, J. (2003). *Çatalhöyük Anadolu'da bir Neolitik Kent* (G. B. Yazıcıoğlu, çev.). İstanbul: Yapı Kredi Yayınları.

Michel, C. and Veenhof, K. R. (2014). The Textiles Traded by the Assyrians in Anatolia. In C. Breniquet ve C. Michel (Ed.), *Wool Economy in the Ancient Near East and the Aegean. From the Beginnings of Sheep Husbandry to Institutional Textile Industry* (pp. 210-261). Oxford & Philadelphia: Oxbow Books.

Özbaşaran, M. (2012). Aşıklı. In M. Özdoğan, N. Başgelen ve P. Kuniholm (Ed.), *The Neolithic in Turkey, Central Turkey and Mediterranean C. 3* (pp. 135-158). İstanbul: Archaeology and Art Publications.

Özdoğan, A. (1999). Çayönü. In M. Özdoğan ve N. Başgelen (Ed.), *Neolithic in Turkey: The Cradle of Civilization New Discoveries* (pp. 35-63). İstanbul: Arkeoloji Sanat Yayınları.

Özdoğan, M. (2011). Archaeological evidence on the westward expansion of farming communities from eastern Anatolia to the Aegean and the Balkans. *Current Anthropology 52*, 415-430.

Özgüç, N. (1968). Acemhöyük Kazıları. *Anadolu X*, 1-28.

Özgüç, N. and Tunca, 0. (2001) Kültepe-Kanis. Sealed and inscribed clay bullae. TTKY V/48. Ankara: Türk Tarih Kurumu Basımevi.

Peyronel L. (2014). From Weighing Wool to Weaving Tools. Textile Manufacture at Ebla during the Early Syrian Period in the Light of Archaeological Evidence. In C. Breniquet and C. Michel (Ed.), *Wool Economy in the Ancient Near East and the Aegean. From the Beginnings of Sheep Husbandry to Institutional Textile Industry* (pp. 124-138). Oxford & Philadelphia: Oxbow Books.

Peters, J., Arbuckle, B. S. and Pöllath, N. (2012). Subsistence and Beyond: Animals in Neolithic Anatolia. In M. Özdoğan, N. Başgelen ve P. Kuniholm (Ed.), *The Neolithic In Turkey, C. 6* (pp. 1-65). İstanbul: Archaeology and Art Publications.

Ryder, M. 1965. Report of Textiles from Çatal Höyük. *Anatolian Studies 15*, 175-176.

Sallaberger, L. (2009). Von der Wollration zum Ehrenkleid. Textilien als Prestigegüter am Hof von Ebla. In B. Hildebrandt ve C. Veit (Ed.), *Der Wert der Dinge – Güter im Prestigediskurs, Formen von Prestige in Kulturen des Altertums* (pp. 241-278). München: Herbert Utz Verlag.

Sallaberger, W. (2014). The Value of Wool in Early Bronze Age Mesopotamia. On the Control of Sheep and the Handling of Wool in the Presargonic to the Ur III Periods (c. 2400-2000 BC). In C. Breniquet ve C. Michel (Ed.), *Wool Economy in the Ancient Near East and the Aegean. From the Beginnings of Sheep Husbandry to Institutional Textile Industry* (pp. 94-114). Oxford & Philadelphia: Oxbow Books.

Stiner, M. C., Buitenhuis, H., Duru, G., Kuhn, S. L., Mentzer, S. M., Munro, N. D., … Özbaşaran, M. (2014). A forager-herder trade-off, from broad-spectrum hunting to sheep management at Aşıklı Höyük, Turkey, *PNAS Early Edition*, 1-6.

Süel, A. (1998). Ortaköy-Şapinuwa: Bir Hitit Merkezi. *TÜBA-AR 1*, 37-61.

Süel, M. (1998). Ortaköy-Şapinuwa Hitit Şehri. In S. Alp and A. Süel (Yay. Haz.). *III. Uluslararası Hititoloji Kongresi Bildirileri*,

16-22 Eylül 1996 (pp. 559-572). Ankara: Uluslararası Hititoloji Kongresi.

Tessier, B. (1994). *Sealing and Seals on Texts from Kültepe Karum Level 2 PIHANS 70.* İstanbul: The Netherlands Institute of Near East.

Tütüncüler Bircan Ö. (2006). Çorum- Resuloğlu Eski Tunç Çağı Mezarlığı'nda Kumaş Kullanımına İlişkin Yeni Bulgular. *Anadolu / Anatolia 30*, 137-148.

Vila, E., & Helmer, D. (2014). The Expansion of Sheep Herding and the Development of Wool Production in the Ancient Near East: An Archaeozoological and Iconographical Approach. In C. Breniquet & C. Michel (Eds.), *Wool Economy in the Ancient Near East and the Aegean. From the Beginnings of Sheep Husbandry to Institutional Textile Industry* (pp. 22-40). Oxford & Philadelphia: Oxbow Books.

Vigo, M. (2010). Linen in Hittite Inventory Texts. In C. Michel ve M. L. Nosch (Ed.), *Textile Terminologies in the Ancient Near East and Mediterranean from the Third to the First Millenia BC* (pp. 290-322). Oxford & Philadelphia: Oxbow Books.

Waetzoldt, H. (1972). *Untersuchungen zur neusumerischen Textilindustrie.* Roma: Instituto per l'Oriente.

Yılmaz, D. (2016). Geç Tunç Çağı'nda Batı Anadolu'da Tekstil Üretimi: Çine-Tepecik höyüğü tezgâh ağırlıkları. *TÜBA-AR 19*, 93-111.

A Precious Creature That Adorns the Anatolian Highlands: the Angora Goat

BENGİ ÇINAR KUL
Ankara University Veterinary Faculty Department of Genetics, Ankara

Goats, which have taken to the stage as early as humankind's first endeavours to domesticate animals 10,000 years ago, have been of great importance in economic, social, cultural and even religious matters for humanity since time immemorial. Also known as the "poor man's cow," the goat remains a significant livestock particularly for small family businesses in many developing countries, such as Turkey, thanks to its disposability in terms of meat, dairy, hair and skin (MacHugh and Bradley, 2001). Countries such as France and Spain have also developed industries based on goat's milk. Archaeologists and zoologists, and more recently geneticists have conducted researches to find out where and when, and who began to domesticate goats (Zeder, 2008; Amills *et al.*, 2017).

Today, it is reported that there are about 600 goat breeds with different morphological characteristics and yield values in the world (Taberlet *et al.*, 2016). The main breeds raising in Turkey are the *Ankara* (Angora), *Kıl* (Hair), *Honamlı*, *Kilis*, *Norduz*, *Abaza*, *Gürcü* (Georgian) and *Malta* (Maltese) breeds. These breeds continue to have a steadily decreasing presence generally in small family-type enterprises (Özcan and Yalçın, 1985, Porter, 1996, Meat and Milk Board, 2018).

History and Breeding of the of Angora goat

Horn structure, inhabiting areas and genetic makeup are frequently used to investigate the origins of domestic goat breeds (*Capra hircus*). While according to some studies, the domestic goat originated from three wild goat species; namely *C. aegagrus* (bezoar), *C. falconeri* and *C. prisca* (Batu, 1951), other authors have maintained that *C. ibex* and *C. caucasica* also may have contributed genetically (Akçapınar, 1994, Yarkın, 1965).

Short tandem repeats on genomic DNA, Y-chromosomes showing paternal inheritance and mitochondrial DNA genes showing maternal inheritance are frequently used in studies to investigate the origins of breeds. Molecular genetic studies on the history and origin of Angora goats show that Angora goats have not differentiated from other breeds that have existed in this country for thousands of years; in terms of both Y-chromosomes (Çınar Kul and Ertuğrul, 2015) and mitochondrial DNA haplogroups (Çınar Kul and Ertuğrul, 2011); but that they differentiate in terms of the genomic DNA as fundamental causes for such different morphological structures (Ağaoglu and Ertuğrul, 2012). Moreover, the Angora

Figure 1. Angora goat kids, front and side view.
Photograph was taken by Bengi Çınar Kul, from Tahtacıörencik Village, Güdül district of Ankara province.

goats have been shown to originate from the bezoar, like other goat breeds extant in Anatolia (Çınar Kul and Ertuğrul, 2011). Notwithstanding the fact that the name of the Angora goat originates from Ankara, the history and roots of this race are indeterminate. Broadly-accepted opinions on this matter may be grouped under three headings: The first is that this goat was domesticated and bred in Anatolia; the second is that this race, brought to Anatolia in ancient times has changed over time; and the last is that it was brought by the Turkmen and cross-bred with native breeds (Yalçın, 1986; Tamur, 2003, Çınar Kul and Ertuğrul, 2011).

It is believed that the Angora goat, also known as the Mohair or Angora goat, was first bred in Ankara in BC 3000 or 4000 (Yalçın, 1986; Akçapınar, 1994). The Ankara *sof*, made from the mohair obtained from the Angora goat that was bred exclusively in Turkey until early 19th century, attracted of many travellers and scientists. In the 1600s, while Ottoman explorer Evliya Çelebi wrote, "no other creature like it exists on earth," French botanist Pitton de Tournefort described these goats, which he had seen in Ankara in 1701, as "the most beautiful goats in the world are bred in the Ankara region" (Tamur, 2003). Prof Dr Selahattin Batu, a veterinary practitioner who worked extensively in the field of animal husbandry, emphasized its uniqueness, saying, "This precious creature that adorns the Anatolian Highlands is a wonder of the steppes."

Attempts were made as of the 17th century to breed the Angora goat in other countries, in the form of small herds transported to the UK, Holland, Italy and France; however these endeavours failed due to inappropriate upkeep, feeding and incompatible climatic conditions (Menteş Gürler, 2006). However, breeding was successful and mohair began to be obtained as of early 19th century. Today the Angora goat is bred in countries other than Turkey, principally in the United States and the Republic of South Africa, and in smaller quantities in Argentina, Russia, Australia, India, France, Kenya and New Zealand (Tamur, 2003; Menteş Gürler, 2006). These countries, which began breeding with small populations of goats, have brought production in terms of mohair obtained per animal, total production of crude mohair and fibre quality to levels that surpass those of Turkey. In addition, these countries have attained a dominant position in foreign trade of mohair and products (Arıkan and Aral, 2013).

Figure 2. Nannies and Billies of a herd of Angora goats, side and front view. Photograph was taken by Bengi Çınar Kul, from Tahtacıörencik Village, Güdül district of Ankara province.

Physical Characteristics. The Angora goat is a small and delicate animal. The head is more elegant, smaller and trimmer than other goat breeds. The forehead is wide and usually with forelock and the face descends gracefully towards the muzzle and ends with thin lips (Figure 1). Both genders usually have horns and beards (Figure 2). Unlike hair goats, when viewed from the side, the rump (back legs) exhibits a structure where the body resembles a square shape, although with a slightly greater height. Erol *et al.* (2017), studying farm-bred goats in the Ayaş and Beypazarı area, have found live weight, body length, and withers and rump heights of 32.40 ± 0.92 kg, 56.56 ± 0.56 cm, 52.62 ± 0.61 cm, and 54.96 ± 0.51 cm respectively in 2-year-old females, and 48.46 ± 1.52 kg, 63.88 ± 0.52 cm, 60.15 ± 0.59 cm and 61.80 ± 0.69 cm, respectively in 2-year-old males. The average yield of mohair per animal was calculated as 2.18 ± 0.016 kg in goats bred in Ayaş, and 1.81 ± 0.014 kg in goats bred in Beypazarı.

The whole body of the Angora goats, including the head, forehead, ears, jaw and underbelly and legs, is covered with silky, curly, bright and white mohair hanging in tresses. Goats in Konya and its vicinity are usually cream- and yellow-coloured, while those of the Siirt region are pearly grey, brown and black (Akçapınar, 1994; Porter, 1996; General Directorate of Agricultural Research and Policies – TAGEM, Domestic Animal Genetic Resources in Turkey, 2009). This is a robust and disease-resistant breed, well adapted to the various climate and land conditions of Anatolia, able to be raised with minimum upkeep and sustenance. It can be kept in pasture throughout the year and fed at very low cost in stubble fields and fallow fields (TAGEM, Domestic Animal Genetic Resources in Turkey, 2009).

Angora goat in terms of mohair output and the current situation. Although primary purpose of goat husbandry is to obtain both hair and yield characteristics such as meat and milk, Angora goats are bred chiefly for the mohair. Through the many years of improvement policies of Ankara breeders, secondary hair follicles have attained a much higher rate than primary hair follicles (9.0-9.3: 1). This phenotype is practically unique among mammals (Dreyer and Marincowitz, 1967). Hair follicles, which derive from the foetal epidermis, are divided into the two groups of primary and secondary follicles. In general, primary hair follicles produce protective hair, while secondary hair follicles produce dermal hair. Mohair and cashmere are secondary follicles in goats. In mammals, including goats, hair follicle development occurs cyclically. This seasonal cycle is mainly driven by melatonin (Fischer *et al.*, 2008). There are three phases in the cycle: the active (anagen) phase, the regressing (catagen) phase and the resting (telogen) phase. Of these, the pre-active (proanagen) and the pre-regressing (procatagen) phases can be determined within the cycle. The hair begins to grow during the anagen phase, and stops in the telogen stage and curls begin to form in mohair, cashmere and fleece wool at this phase (Wang *et al.*, 2014).

White mohair, obtained exclusively from the Angora goat and considered "true" mohair; (Arıkan and Aral, 2013) is a product preferred by the textile industry due to its high moisture retention, heat resistance, elasticity, high insulation, smooth and sleek surface, dirt-resistance, high quality fibre and ease of dying (Arıkan ve Aral, 2013). The unique characteristics of this unique mohair produced in Ankara and vicinity are attributed to environmental characteristics such as habitat and geographical structure as well as climate features such as humidity and temperature. The *sof* fabric is woven out of this wool. The Ankara *sof*, once considered one of the world's finest fabrics, is no longer produced, but mohair weaving, and production of pouches and belts continues in Kastamonu's Tosya district (Tamur, 2003).

The amount of raw mohair obtained per animal per one year is regarded as mohair yield. Although goats are shorn twice a year in some countries, Angora goats in Ankara are usually shorn in during spring, generally in April. The fineness, elasticity and resilience of the fibres are taken into consideration in grading the yield. Best quality is obtained from goats of 1 to 2 years of age, while goats of 3 to 5 yield the highest quantity. Quantity and quality of the fibres both decline as of 5 years of age, as fibres thicken and lose elasticity and resilience (Tiftikbirlik, 2017). Mohair output obtained from Angora goats in Turkey figures between 1.6 to 2.5 kg per head, whereas these values are in the range of 3.11 - 4.83 kg / head in the United States. Shares of countries in total global output are as follows: South Africa leads with 53.49%, followed by the US and Turkey with 11.63% and 4.07% respectively, while other countries contribute a total of share of 27.31% (Arıkan and Aral, 2013).

Although the world leader some 50 years ago with nearly 6 million mohair goats, Turkey has lost this advantage in the international market, in line with both the decline in numbers and in production (Arıkan and Aral, 2013). Total goat assets in Turkey between 1994 and 2017 and the Angora goat's place in the total are shown in Figure 3. According to this, the Angora goat population of 797,000 in 1994 had dropped to 215,000 heads in 2017. In parallel with this serious decline, the number of mohair goats that have been shorn has decreased by approximately 58% (TURKSTAT, 2018). Arıkan and Aral (2013) have reported that the most important causes of this decline have been mohair's loss of prominence to become a side-product. Producers endeavour to compensate for their loss of profits from declining mohair sales by selling dairy and meat; and because yields of these are low in Angora goats, this in turn adversely affects the number of animals and consequently the mohair production.

The Angora goat and mohair production, despite growing significance in the world, have become ever-increasingly forgotten values in Turkey. The main reasons for this are:

- In spite of being the producer of the world's finest mohair, Turkish production cannot compete anymore with other countries in terms of both cost and quantity.

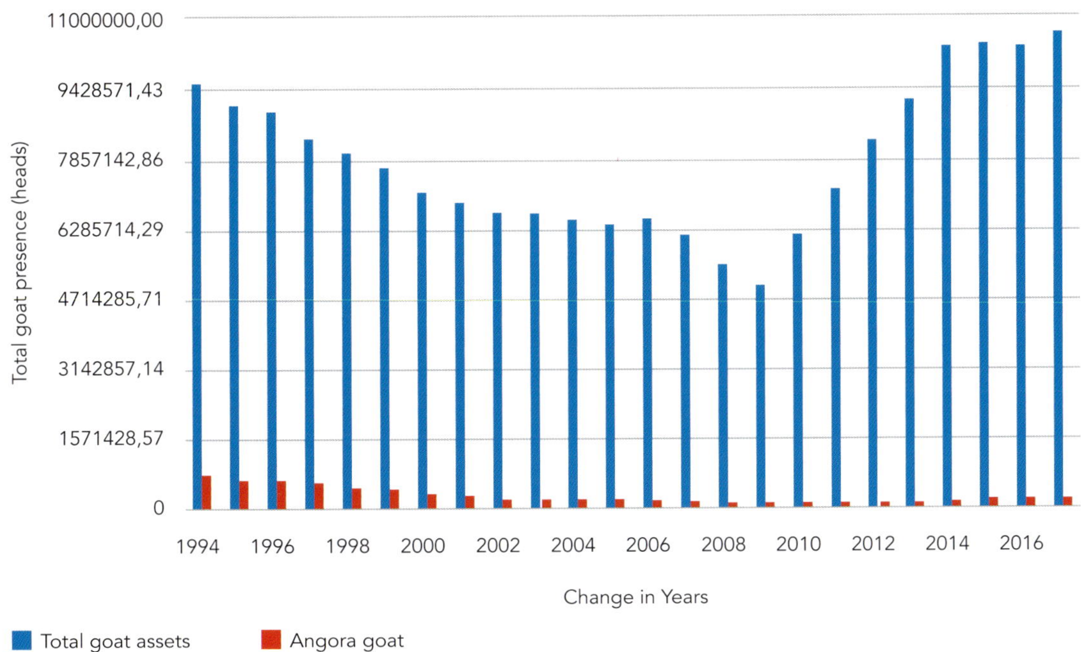

FIGURE 3. The location of Angora goat in total goat presence. The presence of Angora goat, 797,000 heads in 1994, falls to 215,000 heads in 2017.
TURKSTAT Livestock Statistics Database, taken from 2018.

- Turkish farmers have lost their motivation to produce the world's best quality mohair due to the depreciation of the product,
- The Angora goat is not a combined breed, i.e. values of other yields such as milk and meat are low.
- Monopolization in mohair purchasing.
- Migrations to urban areas have caused the number of mohair producers to decline.
- Changing agriculture policies have brought restrictions on goats' habitats by creating obstacles to pasture and woodland utilization.

A number of measures can be proposed so that Angora goats, whose presence is gradually diminishing despite being called "the most beautiful creature on Earth," may continue to adorn the Anatolian highlands for centuries to come. These are:

- Taking urgent measures to encourage local farming,
- Detecting their genetic characterization as gene sources a country's immensely valuable asset,
- Using molecular genetic-based improvement studies in current herds to prevent the bottleneck due to the inbreeding depression.

References

Ağaoğlu, Ö.K., Ertuğrul, O. (2012). Assessment of genetic diversity, genetic relationship and bottleneck using microsatellites in some native Turkish goat breeds. *Small Ruminant Research*, 105(1), 53-60.

Akçapınar, H. (1994). *Lecture notes on goat breeding*. Ankara University School of Veterinary Medicine, Department of Animal Husbandry.

Amills, M., Capote, J., Tosser Klopp, G. (2017). Goat domestication and breeding: a jigsaw of historical, biological and molecular data with missing pieces. *Animal Genetics*, 48, 631–644.

Arıkan, M., Aral, Y. (2013). Ankara keçisi yetiştiriciliği ve tiftik üretiminde mevcut durum, sorunlar ve çözüm önerileri. *Erciyes Üniversitesi Veteriner Fakültesi Dergisi*, 10(3), 185-192.

Batu, S. (1951). *Türkiye yerli keçi ırkları ve keçi yetiştirme bilgisi*. Ankara: Ankara Üniversitesi Yayınevi.

Çınar Kul, B., Bilgen, N., Lenstra, J.A., Korkmaz Ağaoğlu, O., Akyüz, B., Ertuğrul, O. (2015). Y-chromosomal variation of local goat breeds of Turkey close to the domestication centre. *Journal of Animal Breeding and Genetics*, 132(6), 449-453.

Çınar Kul, B., Ertuğrul, O. (2011). mtDNA diversity and phylogeography of some Turkish native goat breeds. *Ankara Üniversitesi Veteriner Fakültesi Dergisi*, 58(2), 129-134.

Dreyer, J.H., Marincowitz, G. (1967). Some observations on the skin histology and fibre characteristics of the Angora goat (capra hircus angoraensis). *South African Journal of Agricultural Science*, 10, 477-500.

Erol, H., Özdemir, P., Odabaş, E., Şenyüz, H.H., Ünal, N., Behrem, S. (2017). Enstitü ve yetiştirici elinde korunan Ankara keçilerinde çeşitli verim özelliklerinin araştırılması. *Lalahan Hayvancılık Araştırma Enstitüsü Dergisi*, 57(1) 1-12.

Meat and Milk Board. (2018) Domestic goat breeds. Retrieved from https://www.esk.gov.tr/tr/11001/Keci-Irklari

Fisher. T.W., Slominski, A., Tobin, D.J., Paus, R. (2008) Melatonin and the hair follicle. *Journal of Pineal Research*, 44(1), 1-15.

Machugh, D.E., Bradley, D.G. (2001). Livestock genetic origins: Goats buck the trend. *Proceedings of the National Academy of Sciences*, 98(10), 5382-5384.

Menteş Gürler, A. (2006) Türkiye tiftik cemiyetinin tarihçesi. *Lalahan Hayvancılık Araştırma Enstitüsü Dergisi*, 46(2), 39-46.

Özcan, H., Yalçın, C. (1985). *Özel zootekni*. İstanbul: İstanbul Üniversitesi Veteriner Fakültesi Zootekni Anabilim Dalı Yayınları.

Porter, V. (1996). *Goats of the world*. Ipswich, UK: Farming Press.

Taberlet, P., Valentini, A., Rezaei, H.R., Naderi, S., Pompanon F., Negrini, R., Ajmone-Marsan, P. (2008). Are cattle, sheep, and goats endangered species? *Molecular Ecology*, 17(1), 275–84.

General Directorate of Agricultural Research and Policies. (2009). *Domestic animal genetic resources in Turkey Catalog*.

Tamur, E., (2003). Ankara keçisi ve Ankara tiftik dokumacılığı: tükenen bir zenginliğin ve çöken bir sanayinin tarihsel öyküsünden kesitler. Ankara: Ankara Ticaret Odası Yayınları.

Tiftikbirlik. (2017). Output of the Angora goat. Retrieved from http://www.tiftikbirlik.com.tr

Turkish Statistical Institute. (2018). Livestock statistics database.

Wang, X., Xu, H.R., Li, T., Qu, L., Zhao, Z.D., Zhang Z,Y. (2014) Expression analysis of KAP9.2 and Hoxc13 genes during different cashmere growth stages by qRT-PCR method. *Molecular Biology Reports*, 41(9), 5665-5668.

Yalçın, B.C. (1986) Sheep and goats in turkey. Food and Agriculture Organization, *Animal Production and Health Paper*, 60.

Yarkın, İ. (1965). *Keçi-deve-domuz yetiştirmesi*. Ankara Üniversitesi Ziraat Fakültesi Yayınları, (243).

Zeder, M.A. (2008). Domestication and early agriculture in the Mediterranean Basin: origins, diffusion, and impact. *Proceedings of the National Academy of Sciences*, 105(33), 11597-11604.

Zeder, M.A. (Ed.). (2006). *Documenting domestication: new genetic and archaeological paradigms*. USA: University of California Press.

An Overview of Angora Goat Breeding and the Ankara Mohair Industry

ERMAN TAMUR
Researcher, Writer

Introduction

Dispatched by King Louis XIV, botanist and French Royal Academy of Sciences member Joseph Pitton de Tournefort travelled to the Aegean islands and certain regions of Anatolia and the Caucasus in the spring of 1700, on a quest to collect new plant species for the palace garden. The travelogue Tournefort produced thereafter became an important source of information not just for the science of botany, but also for his observations and accounts on almost every aspect of local life. In the fall of 1701, when he spent ten days in Ankara and five in the Ayaş-Beypazarı region, Tournefort was fascinated by the goats of Ankara, which he saw everywhere: "They breed the finest goats in the world in the Champaign of Angora. They are of a dazzling white; and their hair, which is fine as silk, naturally curled in locks of eight or nine inches long, is worked up into the finest stuffs, especially camlet" (Tournefort, 1712, pp. 300-301).

Prof İhsan Abidin [Akıncı] (1932), whom we may consider a pioneer of scientific research on Angora goats and mohair in Turkey, speaks of the Angora goats bred in Haymana as follows: "I have encountered the best and purest mohair here, after Ayaş and Beypazarı. They produce mohair that is silky soft, silvery bright, long and bunchy." (P.62).

Prof Selahattin Batu, the author of numerous works on animal husbandry and lead researcher on the Angora goat, is also known as a man of letters. Indeed, while describing Ankara's goats, he cannot help waxing poetic: "This precious creature that embellishes the Anatolian highlands is a beauty of the steppe. As the Arab horse is in the desert, so is the Angora goat in the Anatolian Plateau." (Açıl, 1961, p. 35)

It is possible to find many examples giving utterance to the fascinating beauty of the Angora goat; but in fact, what makes it most important is not its beauty, but its contributions to the economic life in Ankara and its environs for centuries. The Angora goat is a good source of meat, milk, leather and manure; but these are not the primary reasons for farming this most delicate goat breed, but utilizing its full body of long hair that hang to the ground. These hairs, called 'mohair,' have a special place among all vegetable and animal weaving fibres with its functional properties such as strength, water resistance and low thermal conductivity, as well as visual characteristics such as finesse, radiance and whiteness.

Starting from the 16th century or a little earlier, Ankara developed a unique and strong weaving industry based on mohair, the product of its hinterland. Ankara's

mohair fabrics found buyers both domestically and abroad, and the so-called *Engürü Sof*, woven with unadulterated mohair yarn was sold in many European cities for several centuries. This provided the people of Ankara with extensive business opportunities and high revenues. In this context, the Angora goat is one of the original values that comes to mind regarding Ankara and constitutes its historical identity (Figure 1).

Unfortunately, this period was followed by a string of increasingly unfavourable events. Foreign demand for mohair fabrics gradually decreased until Ankara had to settle for selling just mohair yarns rather than fabric. This in turn was followed by a phase in which external demand for mohair yarns was also terminated, which meant that Ankara could no more export finished or semi-finished mohair products other than raw mohair, which, in other words, meant the end of the mohair industry. While Ankara, up to this stage, had the monopoly on raw mohair, at the very least, it lost its position when the Angora goat was shipped to South Africa and the USA. These countries began to breed the mohair goat and thus, Ankara lost that position.

The Origins of the Angora Goat and its Past Existence in Anatolia

The predominant idea until a hundred years ago was that the Angora goat had descended from the wild goat (*Capra aegagrus*), still extant at Anatolian mountains, via the domestic *Capra hircus*, bred since the earliest settlements, was. This was proved to be wrong when in early 20th century zoological data that determine the kinship of goat breeds were evaluated according to scientific criteria; and that the relatives of the Angora goat were found to be breeds from various parts of Asia, such as the Cashmere goat, Bukharan markhor, Tibetan goat and Chinese goat (Figure 2 and 3). Meanwhile in 1913, a fossil of an extinct goat-like species, which had the characteristics of being a common ancestor of these species, was found in eastern Galicia. Studies revealed that this animal, named *Capra prisca*, apparently a steppe animal rather than a mountain dweller, was a common ancestor of relatives of the Angora goat and its relatives in Asia (Batu, 1940).

Figure 1. Southeastern view of Ankara at the end of the 1920s. Ankara and the Angora goats that made its name world-famous, in the same square.
Erman Tamur Archive

Figure 2. The Angora goat and some wild goat species. Above left: Alpine ibex (*Capra ibex*). Above right: Wild goat (*Capra aegagrus*). Bottom left: Markhor (*Capra falconeri*). Bottom right: Angora goat (*Capra hircus ancryrensis*).
Erman Tamur Archive

Figure 3. Various goats. Above centre: Alpine ibex (*Capra ibex*). Above right: Domestic goat *(Capra hircus)*. Bottom left: Cashmere goat, a relative of the Angora goat. Bottom right: Angora goat *(Capra hircus ancryrensis)*.
Erman Tamur Archive

According to historical data, the earliest information attesting to the existence of the Angora goat in Anatolia is from the 15th century. In other words, we have no evidence that societies living in Anatolia before the Turks ever farmed Angora goats. On the other hand, we know that the relatives of the Angora goat had been bred in various parts of Asia for thousands of years. When these data are interpreted in conjunction, it is concluded that the Angora goat derived from a goat breed brought by Turkic tribes from the Iranian Plateaus to Central Anatolia during the 11th - 12th centuries, where it adapted to the climatic conditions and acquired distinct racial characteristics. However, it is thought that the trial-and-error cultivation techniques developed for centuries by Anatolian farmers were also influential in this change.

The Birth, Growth and Decline of the Ankara Mohair Industry

The earliest information compiled on the industrial and commercial activities developing in Ankara city from the mohair obtained from Angora goats farmed in the Ankara and a few neighbouring provinces date back to the 16th century. However, given the intensity of production and trade during this period, it is understood that the beginning goes back to earlier times. Indeed, Mahmud Pasha Bedesten, the major distribution centre of mohair fabrics in Ankara, (today's Museum of Anatolian Civilizations) and Kurşunlu Han, nearby the Bedesten, another centre of mohair fabrics trade, (the museum's administrative department) were both built in the 15th century.

It goes without saying that maintaining a high level of consistent production depends on how satisfactory the benefit created is to the producers, and the stability of customer demand. In Ankara's mohair industry, the export sales were the prevailing drive from the outset, so changes in the European customers' demands were decisive in the type and level of production. Accordingly, we can study the Ankara mohair industry in four distinct periods based on the level of processing.

During the first period, the raw material (mohair) was processed completely

Figure 4. The appearance at the end of the 1920s of a part of the old Avancıklar neighbourhood (today's Yalçınkaya, Başkır and Çeşme neighbourhoods) where intensive weaving activity was carried out in the 16th century.
Erman Tamur Archive

and sold as a fully processed product (fabric). The sale of raw mohair and mohair yarn was prohibited during this stage. This period covering roughly the 16th century and the first half of the 17th century may be described as the "golden age" of mohair-based production and trade in Ankara. At the time, mohair fabrics, called *sof*, *muhayyer* and *şali*, were sold in Ottoman cities such as İstanbul, Aleppo, Bursa and Damascus, but most of them were marketed in European countries like Venice and Poland (Ergenç, 1995, p. 113). The process from mohair to fabric involves the stages of spinning and preparing, weaving, dyeing, washing, mangling and burnishing, all of which require specialized knowledge, skill and experience. The groups of professionals who carried out these procedures endeavoured to work meticulously, in accordance with *ahi*[1] ethics and discipline, and under the guidance of their *sheikh*[2], *kethüda*[3] and *yiğitbaşı*[4]. Ankara's mohair fabrics, especially *sof* gained a reputation far outside the borders of the Ottoman Realm, thanks to their sturdiness, high thermal insulation and low permeability, as well as their eye-catching colours. These colours, which constituted a wide spectrum, were not referred to with simple names like white, black, green, blue, red and brown; but rather adjectives that indicate fine nuances, such as *kâfurî* (camphor), *gülgûnî* (rose), *angûdî* (ruddy), *şarâbî* (wine), *çimenî* (grass), *fıstıkî* (pistachio), *leylâkî* (lilac), and *menevşî* (violet). This shows that the producers endeavoured to offer a variety of products to respond to a wide range of preferences (Tamur, 2003, p. 95).

During this period, the weaving process was carried out by wageworkers who were employed to work in workshops with 3 to 5 looms; but more often by adult family members of both sexes, in rooms set aside as workplaces. A record dated to 1590 notes that taxes had been levied on 621 looms. It can be estimated from this that about 1,000 such looms operated in Ankara, including the sof-making villages in the vicinity (Ergenç, 1995, pp. 100-101). In Ankara, weaving was carried out mainly in the antique Avancıklar district, located at the east of the city, which included today's Yalçınkaya, Başkır and Çeşme neighbourhoods (Figure 4). Washing and painting processes, which constitute another important step of fabric production, and which require a lot of water, were set up at the "Debbağin" (Tabakçılar) neighbourhood, along the Bent Creek. In this period, when fabric production surpassed 100,000 bolts in some years, Venetian and Polish traders were in the forefront of exporting.

The second period of the Ankara mohair industry began with the decline in

1 The *Ahi* Brotherhood was a fraternity and guild, based on a 14th century chiefdom of the same name (Translator's Note).

2 An honorific title in Muslim countries (T. N.).

3 An Ottoman Turkish title meaning "steward, deputy, lieutenant" (T. N.).

4 A *kethüda*'s assistant (T. N.).

Figure 5. The famous *View of Ankara* from Rijksmuseum, Amsterdam. 1700-1799, oil on canvas, 117 x 198 cm. Inventory Number: SK-A-2055, Rijksmuseum, Amsterdam.

fabric production and the emergence of yarn production and trade. The reason for this change was the development of mohair looms in the UK, one of Turkey's major foreign buyers, and its consequent change of demand from fabric to yarn. The mohair yarn imported from Ankara was used in England to weave not only textiles but also to manufacture embroidered buttons, buttonholes and gold ribbons during this period. This period, in which mohair-based production in Ankara shifted from finished fabric to predominantly semi-finished yarn, lasted from nearly the middle of the 17th until the early 19th century. We can describe this as the "silver age" of the mohair production and trade, as Ankara continued to generate high levels of income from this activity in this second period, too. A comprehensive study published in 2011 can give us an idea of the amount of mohair yarn sent to the UK during this period: between 1710 and 1799, this was more than 2,500,000 kg. (Webb Yıldırmak, 2011, p. 243). This means an average of 30,000 kg of yarn per year. If we assume that an average of 1.5-2 kg of mohair can be obtained per goat annually in Anatolia, as is the case today, this amount would account for some 15,000 to 20,000 goats sheared. Considering the demand from the foreign buyers outside the UK and the demand from the Ottoman domestic market, it becomes apparent that the production of mohair yarn has reached large quantities at that time and is a major source of income for Ankara.

Dutch and French tradesmen as well as the British were among the foreign merchants living in Ankara and conducting the export trade during this period. In fact, the famous *Ankara View* painting in the Amsterdam Rijksmuseum, which was probably created on order from a Dutch company in the early 1700s, presents in its lower section the various scenes of Angora goat breeding and the mohair industry and trade (Figure 5).

Figure 6. Sorting mohair to be packed in sacks and exported, in an Ankara business centre, early 1900s.
Erman Tamur Archive

The third period of change in the mohair industry of Ankara began when textile production had completely ended, the production of yarn had declined largely, and unprocessed mohair began to be marketed. This change came through an external development again, when the English replaced the traditional methods of processing mohair using simple *iğ* and *kirmen*[5] with machinery during the early 19th century. This transformed the demand for mohair yarn to raw mohair. The earliest raw mohair exports began in 1820, and this trade has continued to our time, albeit with fluctuations in volume (Figure 6).

The Angora goat began to be reared outside Anatolia as of the mid-19th century. At first, the English shipped a number of goats to South Africa in 1838, where they began to farm it. Eleven years later, the Angora goats gifted by Sultan Abdülmecid to the American agricultural expert Dr Davis in 1849, formed the core of the Angora goat farming in the United States. During this fourth and final period of mohair production and trade, Ankara and Turkey lost its position as the sole producer of mohair in the world, and had to contend with two big rivals such as the Union of South Africa and the United States.

Shipping the Angora Goat Out of Turkey

Cramming the goats on trains
Into ships' holds – not even a kiss goodbye
Stowing away the looms all broken
Trampling on the steppe's most beautiful rose.
Ankara June 14, 1992, Zerrin Taşpınar

5 Different types of traditional spindles (T. N.).

Transporting the Angora Goat to South Africa

The British, important clients of Ankara's mohair products, who developed mohair looms and yarn spinning tools in the process and shifted demand first from fabric to yarn, then from yarn to raw mohair, began by early 19th century to research the practicability of farming within their own dominions (Tamur, 2003, p. 152; Webb Yıldırmak, 2011, p. 243).

The story of the British success in raising Angora goats outside Turkey is an interesting one. According to available information, the first initiative in this regard was Sir Titus Salt's endeavour to ship a quantity of Angora goats to the UK in 1837. Considering the fact that it was not possible for an animal like the Angora goat that requires a very specialized habitat would survive and proliferate in England, it is not difficult to imagine that the animals perished after a while.

The second attempt after Salt's, however, was successful. In 1838, former British naval officer Colonel John Henderson led a herd of twelve bucks and one ewe to South Africa (Kinghorn, 1976, pp. 3, Uys, 1988, p. 3). Uys noted that Col. Henderson's route was through India.

In subsequent shipments, the goats were boarded on vessels in Istanbul, İzmir or a Black Sea harbour, transported from eastern Mediterranean to the west, and then through the Gibraltar into the Atlantic, and proceeded south along the western coast of African continent down to Cape Town or Port Elizabeth. In my opinion, Uys was mistaken in his belief that Col. Henderson's route was through India, unlike subsequent shipments. I think this mistake may have been caused by the similarity of Col. Henderson's goats to the Indian Cashmere goats, previously known in the region. In fact, some have claimed that the first Angora goats that were taken to the USA were Cashmere goats.

There was an interesting incident during Col. Henderson's long and difficult journey with his goats. It turned out that the single female goat in the herd was pregnant, and needed special care. This goat gave birth to yet another male brood before the ship docked, so that a kid was added to the twelve bucks. However, Col. Henderson's pleasant surprise did not last; shortly after he realized something that distressed him immensely: the bucks for which he had paid a lot of money and brought to South Africa through many difficulties had been sterilized prior to being sold to him, and they could not be employed as studs. The only consolation Col. Henderson had was the newly born kid. Indeed, when this kid grew into adulthood, it coupled with its mother, producing another male kid. Thus, the number of Angora goats to be mated and replicated was raised to three. These three goats are considered to constitute the original source of the full-blooded Angora goat stock in South Africa (Kinghorn, 1976, pp. 3-4, Uys, 1988, p. 3). It is known that Col. Henderson's goats were later possessed by Caledonian farmers, H. Vos and W. Hopley. These three Angora goats, on the one hand, mated among themselves, increasing the number of full-blooded Angora goats, while hybrid goats were also obtained by crossbreeding with local Boer goats of the Caledon region. However, although these crossbreeds had Angora goat blood, they did not produce good quality mohair, nor were they suitable for slaughtering. These were further hybridized with domestic goats to achieve goats appropriate for meat.

In those years, Major Bird, another retired British officer also encountered a similar incident. Bird had also brought six Angora goats from Turkey, five of which proved to be neutered, as was the case in Col. Henderson's party (Uys, 1988, p. 3).

In the early 1850s, South African traders led by Adolph Mosenthal and his company decided to import more Angora goats from Turkey to develop mohair production at the Cape Colony. Mosenthal personally made the purchases in Turkey, and imported various numbers of Angora goats to South Africa in the years 1851, 1852, 1857 and 1858. Each of these purchases and journeys were a separate adventure. In March 1856, Mosenthal had just embarked with his goats on a vessel at a Black Sea port when the news of a cholera outbreak reached him, and he had to return to port to wait until August. When they finally sailed and reached the Mediterranean, many of the ports were quarantined and they lost a lot of time. By the time the ship anchored in Southampton, England, the goats had become exhausted and weak. They were taken to Victoria Park through London, where they were rested and fed for a long time so that they could stand the heavy conditions of their next journey. The number of goats who arrived in Cape Town was thirty. Although there is some information about who owned fourteen of these, the fate of the other sixteen is unknown. The number of goats that perished since the beginning of the journey is also undocumented (Uys, 1988, p. 8-9).

The seven bucks and a ewe goat that Mosenthal brought in this time was auctioned off at the city churchyard in Graaf-Reinet, where these animals became the first full-blooded Angora goats in this part of the colony. The local press reported that the farmers who wanted to buy the goats were hesitant because they were disappointed that the goats were so small; but that Mosenthal persuaded them, saying that full-blooded Angora goats were supposed to be delicate (Uys, 1988, p. 9). This interesting auction at Graaf Reinet was also extensively featured in *The Illustrated London News* of September 12, 1857. The journal's South African correspondent reported that each one of the seven bucks and the ewe were purchased by separate farmers, and ewe fetched £60 while the bucks went for £60 to £117 each (Figure 7).

As the view gained a lot of traction that certain regions of South Africa was more suitable for breeding goats instead of sheep, a number of entrepreneurs, including Sir Titus who shipped Angora goats to England in 1837 and learned from experience that it cannot be bred there, imported Angora goats into South Africa through the years 1857 – 1860. These businesspersons were undoubtedly aware of the risks of what they did; but they believed that their venture was worth these risks. In fact, South Africa began to bear the fruits of Angora goat breeding: In 1857, the first mohair exports were dispatched to England. Angora goats were also shipped to Argentina in 1865.

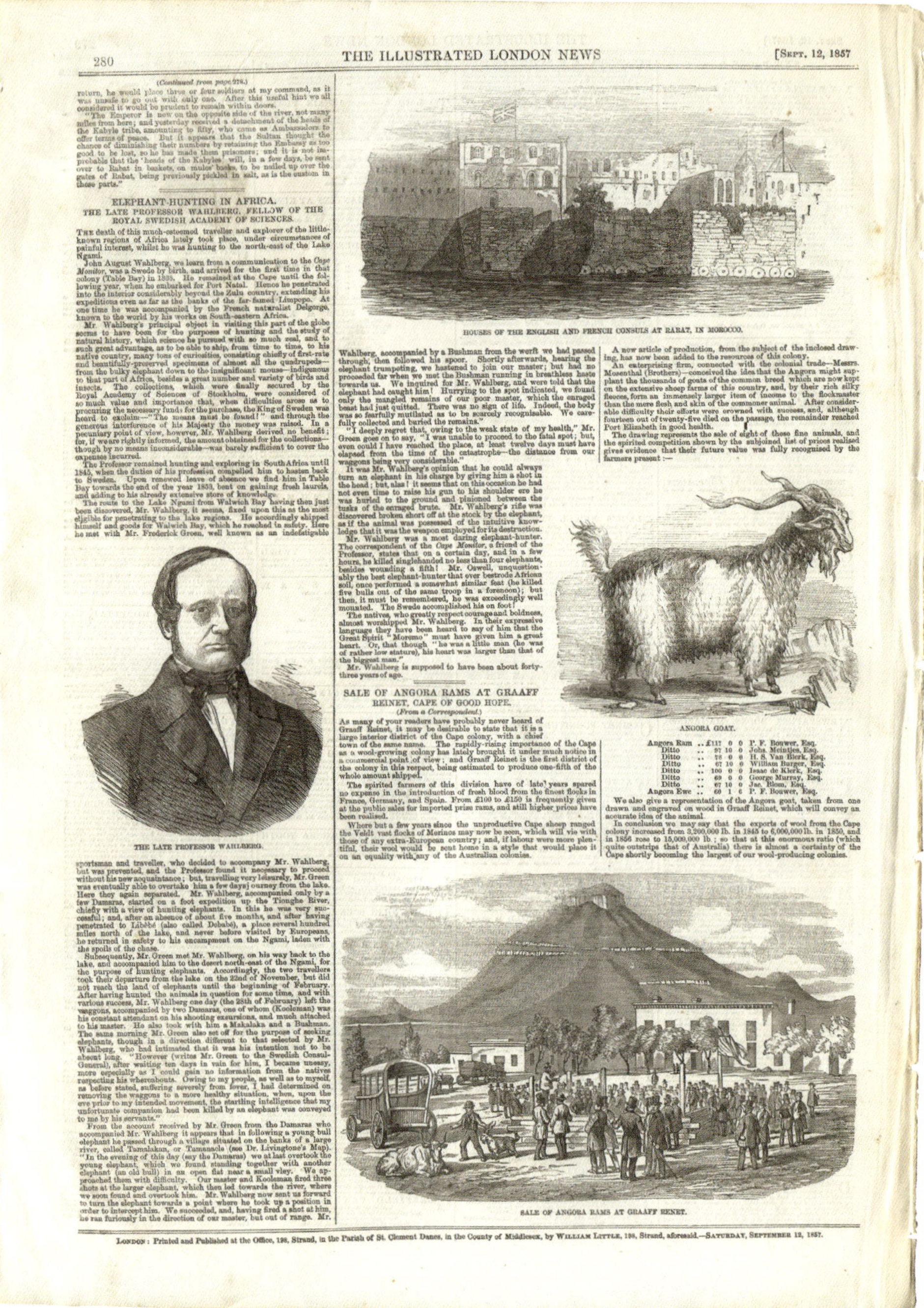

280 THE ILLUSTRATED LONDON NEWS [Sept. 12, 1857

ELEPHANT-HUNTING IN AFRICA.

THE LATE PROFESSOR WAHLBERG, FELLOW OF THE ROYAL SWEDISH ACADEMY OF SCIENCES.

HOUSES OF THE ENGLISH AND FRENCH CONSULS AT RABAT, IN MOROCCO.

THE LATE PROFESSOR WAHLBERG.

sportsman and traveller, who decided to accompany Mr. Wahlberg, but was prevented, and the Professor found it necessary to proceed without his new acquaintance; but, travelling very leisurely, Mr. Green was eventually able to overtake him a few days journey from the lake. Here they again separated. Mr. Wahlberg, accompanied only by a few Damaras, started on a foot expedition up the Tioughe River, chiefly with a view of hunting elephants. In this he was very successful; and, after an absence of about five months, and after having penetrated to Libèbé (also called Debabé), a place several hundred miles north of the lake, and never before visited by Europeans, he returned in safety to his encampment on the Ngami, laden with the spoils of the chase.

Subsequently, Mr. Green met Mr. Wahlberg, on his way back to the lake, and accompanied him to the desert north-east of the Ngami, for the purpose of hunting elephants. Accordingly, the two travellers took their departure from the lake on the 22nd of November, but did not reach the land of elephants until the beginning of February. After having hunted the animals in question for some time, and with various success, Mr. Wahlberg one day (the 28th of February) left the waggons, accompanied by two Damaras, one of whom (Kooleman) was his constant attendant on his shooting excursions, and much attached to his master. He also took with him a Makalaka and a Bushman. The same morning Mr. Green also set off for the purpose of seeking elephants, though in a direction different to that selected by Mr. Wahlberg, who had intimated that it was his intention not to be absent long. "However (writes Mr. Green to the Swedish Consul-General), after waiting ten days in vain for him, I became uneasy, more especially as I could gain no information from the natives respecting his whereabouts. Owing to my people, as well as to myself, as before stated, suffering severely from fever, I had determined on removing the waggons to a more healthy situation, when, upon the eve prior to my intended movement, the startling intelligence that my unfortunate companion had been killed by an elephant was conveyed to me by his servants."

From the account received by Mr. Green from the Damaras who accompanied Mr. Wahlberg it appears that in following a young bull elephant he passed through a village situated on the banks of a large river, called Tamalakan, or Tamanacle (see Dr. Livingtone's Map). "In the evening of this day (say the Damaras) we at last overtook the young elephant, which we found standing together with another elephant (an old bull) in an open flat near a small vley. We approached them with difficulty. Our master and Kooleman fired three shots at the larger elephant, which then led towards the river, where we soon found and overtook him. Mr. Wahlberg now sent us forward to turn the elephant towards a point where he took up a position in order to intercept him. We succeeded, and, having fired a shot at him, he ran furiously in the direction of our master, but out of range. Mr.

The natives, who greatly respect courage and boldness, almost worshipped Mr. Wahlberg. In their expressive language they have been heard to say of him that the Great Spirit "Moremo" must have given him a great heart. Or, that though "he was a little man (he was of rather low stature), his heart was larger than that of the biggest man."

Mr. Wahlberg is supposed to have been about forty-three years of age.

SALE OF ANGORA RAMS AT GRAAFF REINET, CAPE OF GOOD HOPE.

(*From a Correspondent.*)

As many of your readers have probably never heard of Graaff Reinet, it may be desirable to state that it is a large interior district of the Cape colony, with a chief town of the same name. The rapidly-rising importance of the Cape as a wool-growing colony has lately brought it under much notice in a commercial point of view; and Graaff Reinet is the first district of the colony in this respect, being estimated to produce one-fifth of the whole amount shipped.

The spirited farmers of this division have of late years spared no expense in the introduction of fresh blood from the finest flocks in France, Germany, and Spain. From £100 to £150 is frequently given at the public sales for imported prize rams, and still higher prices have been realised.

Where but a few years since the unproductive Cape sheep ranged the Veldt vast flocks of Merinos may now be seen, which will vie with those of any extra-European country; and, if labour were more plentiful, their wool would be sent home in a style that would place it on an equality with any of the Australian colonies.

ANGORA GOAT.

Angora Ram	..	£117	0	0	P. F. Bouwer, Esq.
Ditto	..	97	10	0	Johs. Meintjes, Esq.
Ditto	..	78	0	0	H. S. Van Blerk, Esq.
Ditto	..	67	10	0	William Burger, Esq.
Ditto	..	100	0	0	Isaac de Klerk, Esq.
Ditto	..	69	0	0	George Murray, Esq.
Ditto	..	67	10	0	Jac. Blom, Esq.
Angora Ewe	..	60	1	6	P. F. Bouwer, Esq.

We also give a representation of the Angora goat, taken from one drawn and engraved on wood in Graaff Reinet, which will convey an accurate idea of the animal.

In conclusion we may say that the exports of wool from the Cape colony increased from 3,200,000 lb. in 1845 to 6,000,000 lb. in 1850, and in 1856 rose to 15,000,000 lb.; so that at this enormous ratio (which quite outstrips that of Australia) there is almost a certainty of the Cape shortly becoming the largest of our wool-producing colonies.

SALE OF ANGORA RAMS AT GRAAFF REINET.

LONDON: Printed and Published at the Office, 198, Strand, in the Parish of St. Clement Danes, in the County of Middlesex, by WILLIAM LITTLE, 198, Strand, aforesaid.—SATURDAY, SEPTEMBER 12, 1857.

Figure 7. A copy of *The Illustrated London* News, dated September 12, 1857, reporting on the sale of eight Angora goats in an auction in Graaf Reinet, South Africa.
Erman Tamur Archive

The years 1866 to 1881 saw numerous shipments of Angora goats brought from Turkey to South Africa, and rapid development of husbandry in that country. Major losses were also experienced during transport, due to shipping conditions and means of the era: Of the 400 Angora goats boarded in İzmir in 1866, only 100 were able to reach South Africa. In 1867, about 400 Angora goats were loaded into the ship *Grace Darling* in Istanbul Port to be taken to South Africa, and half the

Figure 8. G. Gatheral (right), British consul in Ankara, and farmer J. B. Evans (left) in Graaff-Reinet, with two of the goats they bought in Anatolia.
Source: Uys, 1988, p.17

Figure 9. Three of the Angora goats brought to South Africa as one of the last purchases from Turkey by Mosenthal Adolph & Co. in 1895. On the carriage: Mr and Mrs W. Mosenthal; Mr. H. Goldschmidt standing behind; the three typically Anatolian villager with caps are Dikraan, Abram and Apik, who serviced the goats during the journey.
Source: Uys, 1988, p. 29.

animals were killed in the storm that hit her shortly after the vessel sailed out. The ship returned to Istanbul to replace the perished livestock and this time picked up 376 Angora goats. By the time she arrived in Port Elizabeth, the number of goats were still somewhat reduced. In 1869, an Ottoman subject named Gulbenkian was employed as an expert to help a South African team purchase 720 Angora goats at the Ankara and Kastamonu regions. An auction held in Port Elizabeth for the sale of these goats, attended by farmers from all over the country, lasted three days. In the same year, another ship bringing in a herd of 5 bucks and 183 ewes was caught in a storm in the Mediterranean, and 22 tons of hay and 26 goats perished. Of the 162 goats on the ship *Good Hope* dispatched to Cape Town, 39 died during this 49-day journey (Uys, 1988).

Meanwhile Gavin Gatheral, Britain's vice-consul in Ankara during the years 1871-1877, was closely involved with transporting the Angora goat to South Africa. Mr Gatheral personally escorted J. B. Evans, a prominent Graaff-Reinet farmer who came to Turkey to purchase Angora goats, and helped him select 30 animals. These goats were first transported to Istanbul, on the back of mules over snowy roads. 17 bucks and 3 ewes survived from this herd of 30 goats and made to Port Elizabeth, travelling from London on the ship *Elizabeth Martin*. In their photographs, Evans and Gatheral seem to have attempted to dress themselves in the local fashion in order to adapt to the environs where they went to buy the goats (Figure 8). These operations to carry Angora goats from Turkey to South Africa continued until the mid-1890s (Figure 9).

The history of the cultivation of the Angora goats in South Africa is the history of the many struggles waged with great courage and determination. The mohair traders of that country proved their mettle not only in the process of shipping Angora goats to South Africa until they reached sufficient numbers, but also in contending with epidemics, fluctuations in the mohair market, and global crises affecting all economic activity throughout the 20th century.

Currently Republic of South Africa is the undisputed leader of world mohair production. This country alone accounts for more than 60% of world mohair production (Akgür and Korkmaz, 2003, p. 16).

The Shipping of the Angora Goat to America

The introduction of the Angora goat to the USA and the establishment of the mohair industry in that country has been described in two separate publications by George Fayette Thompson, an expert of the United States Department of Agriculture Bureau of Animal Husbandry. The first of these is the farmer's bulletin published by the United States Department of Agriculture in 1901 under the title *The Angora Goat* and revised in 1908 as. In this document, Mr Thompson (1908, p.4) described the introduction of the Angora goats to America as follows:

"During the administration of President Polk, the Sultan of Turkey requested of him to recommend some one who would experiment in cotton culture in Turkey. Accordingly, Dr. James B. Davis, of Columbia, S. C., was recommended and received the appointment. The work which he did was so highly gratifying to the Sultan that upon the return of Doctor Davis in 1849 he reciprocated the courtesy of the President by presenting the doctor with nine Angora goats.

The Davis importation of Angoras was frequently exhibited at fairs, and everywhere attracted much attention and received favourable comments.

In 1853 the Davis goats were purchased by Col. Richard Peters, of Atlanta, Ga., with the exception of one owned by Col. Wade Hampton, of South Carolina, one by Mr. Davenport, of Virginia, and one by Mr. Osborn, of New York. Later Colonel Peters imported others, but they did not prove satisfactory. He is generally looked upon as the real founder of the Angora goat industry in the United States."

Thompson's *A Manual of Angora Goat Raising: With a Chapter on Milch Goats* published in 1903; is more extensive compared to the earlier book. It gives an account of how Dr Davis purchased the goats he brought back from Turkey, in a manner similar to the farmer's bulletin of 1901. However, some sections in this book, related by Davis's daughter, Mrs Harriet E. Davis White, were different from the earlier account. According to this, the goats were not gifted to Dr Davis by the Sultan; the former brought them to the cotton farm where he worked from Iran. Apparently, ten of these goats were purebred Cashmeres, and the other two were Tibetan goats. One of the Tibetan goats died, and the surviving female Tibetan goat and Cashmeres were shipped to America by Davis (Thompson, 1908, p. 37). Thompson also claimed that Davis believed that the gift goats were Cashmere goats, whereas eight of them were Angora goats and only one was a true Cashmere.

Another source cites James B. Davis, as a South Carolina farmer who was very much interested in what domestic animals were suitable for the Southern American climate and experimented by bringing various animals from different places to that end. According to this account, the goats Dr Davis brought from Turkey were not presented to him. Davis purchased them himself, and obtained permission from both the Ottoman and US authorities to ship them to his hometown alongside other animals he bought (Barnett, 1987, p.351). It may be worth mentioning that a monthly salary of $15,000 was paid for his services at the model farm in Turkey (İhsan Abidin, 1932, p. 78).

Figure 10. Postcards showing goat breeding in various states in the US. Angora goats appear in Texas (above), Arizona (centre) and New Mexico (bottom).
Erman Tamur Archive

Ultimately, all sources agree that the nucleus of Angora goat husbandry in the United States consisted of the goats that Dr Davis imported from Turkey. Without a doubt, all of Davis's goats were of the Ankara variety. The confusion on this issue may be because Cashmere goats were known in the US in those years, at least due to the famous Cashmere shawls, while Angora goats were probably unheard of.

Colonel Peters, whom Thompson considered pioneer of Angora goat breeding in America, after obtaining Davis's pure stock of six Angora goats, went after the remaining animals purchased by others and bought them all one by one. Col. Peters quickly propagated his goats, not neglecting to keep a quality core group, and Dr Davis distributed the goats' semen to various parts of the country. Meanwhile, new purchases were made in Turkey of 5-6 or 8-10 small herds of goats, and these too were distributed across various regions of the United States. However, just when the number of Angora goats had rapidly risen in many of the states, the eruption of civil war caused great damage to these developments, and the herds in the eastern and southern regions perished. Nevertheless, the situation recovered after a while, and the goats that Col. Peters had previously dispatched to California once again spread to Texas, New Mexico, Arizona and Oregon (Figure 10). In time, Texas became the most successful state in Angora goat breeding. So much so that 97% of the mohair produced in this country is obtained from the Angora goats who were bred in the semi-arid and barren Edwards Plateau of Texas (Barnett, 1987, p. 347).

If small purchases are left aside, after Dr Davis, Winthrop W. Chenery is considered the first person to import Angora goats to the US. In 1861, Chenery shipped 39 goats in the first and 41 on a second shipment to Boston from the Port of Istanbul. During the journeys, two goats from the first and one goat from the second shipment perished. This herd, kept in Chenery's farm, began to develop with 16 kids born in the spring. Unfortunately, caregivers who were unaware that newly shorn Angora goats needed to be protected from the cold, left the animals out in the cold at night, upon which 24 got sick and died. In 1866 and 1867, Chenery brought two more herds of 20 goats each, of which 30 survived the journey to the USA (Thompson, 1908, p. 37-38).

American agricultural magazine *The Country Gentleman* reported on December 12, 1867 that two experts appointed by the American Institute of Agriculture to collate information on Angora goat husbandry, who had been dispatched to Turkey, now brought back a herd of 160 goats to the US. One of the largest brought to the United States, this herd was also claimed to be of high quality goats. There is also an interesting story of an Ottoman subject called Eutichides, who in 1870 or 1871 boarded 175 or 200 Angora goats on a ship bound for the United States, however, the herd were infested with Asian scab. Most of the animals died and he had to sell the remainder at very low prices before he could return home to İzmir.

The four goats that the company C. P. Bailey & Sons shipped to the USA from Turkey in 1901 became the last goats imported from the country after a ban was placed on Angora goat exports as of 1881. Thus, the conveyance of Angora goats to the United States that began in 1849 with the nine animals Sultan Abdülmecid gifted to Davis ended with Bailey's four

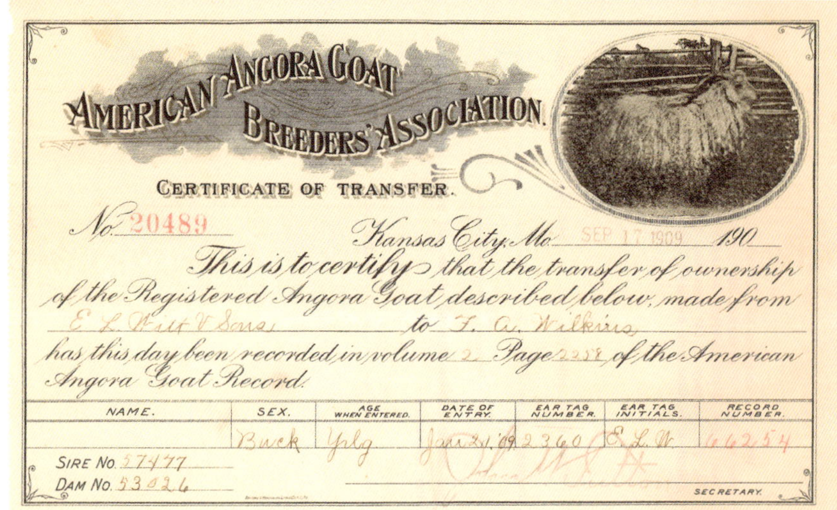

AMERICAN ANGORA GOAT BREEDERS' ASSOCIATION.

CERTIFICATE OF TRANSFER.

No. 20489 Kansas City, Mo. SEP 17 1909 190

This is to certify that the transfer of ownership of the Registered Angora Goat described below, made from E. L. Witt & Sons to F. A. Wilkins has this day been recorded in volume 2 Page 2258 of the American Angora Goat Record.

NAME.	SEX.	AGE WHEN ENTERED.	DATE OF ENTRY.	EAR TAG NUMBER.	EAR TAG INITIALS.	RECORD NUMBER.
	Buck	Yrlg.	Jan 21 '09	2360	E. L. W.	66254

SIRE No. 57477

DAM No. 53026

SECRETARY.

Figure 11. American Angora Goat Breeders' Association; certificate of transfer for Angora goats.
Erman Tamur Archive

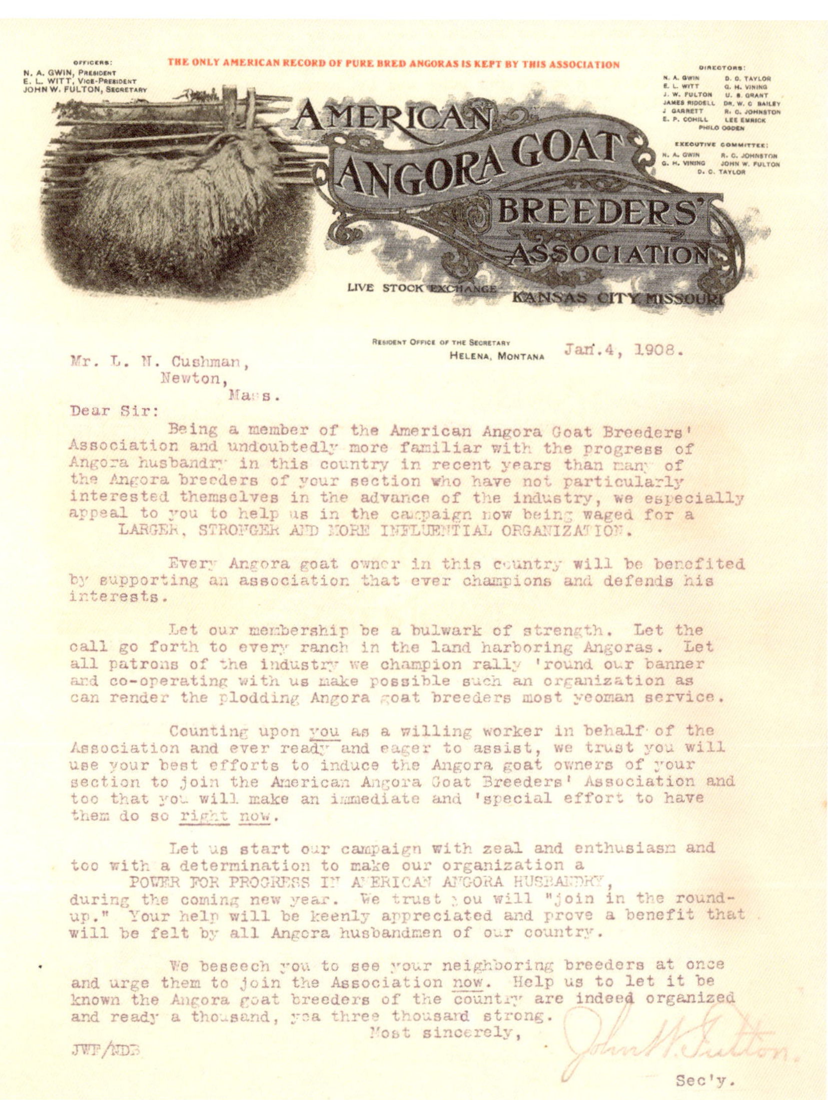

OFFICERS:
N. A. GWIN, President
E. L. WITT, Vice-President
JOHN W. FULTON, Secretary

THE ONLY AMERICAN RECORD OF PURE BRED ANGORAS IS KEPT BY THIS ASSOCIATION

DIRECTORS:
N. A. GWIN, D. C. TAYLOR, E. L. WITT, G. H. VINING, J. W. FULTON, U. S. GRANT, JAMES RIDDELL, DR. W. C. BAILEY, J. GARRETT, R. C. JOHNSTON, E. P. COHILL, LEE EMRICK, PHILO OGDEN

EXECUTIVE COMMITTEE:
N. A. GWIN, R. C. JOHNSTON, G. H. VINING, JOHN W. FULTON, D. C. TAYLOR

AMERICAN ANGORA GOAT BREEDERS' ASSOCIATION

LIVE STOCK EXCHANGE KANSAS CITY, MISSOURI

Resident Office of the Secretary
Helena, Montana

Jan. 4, 1908.

Mr. L. N. Cushman,
Newton,
Mass.

Dear Sir:

Being a member of the American Angora Goat Breeders' Association and undoubtedly more familiar with the progress of Angora husbandry in this country in recent years than many of the Angora breeders of your section who have not particularly interested themselves in the advance of the industry, we especially appeal to you to help us in the campaign now being waged for a
LARGER, STRONGER AND MORE INFLUENTIAL ORGANIZATION.

Every Angora goat owner in this country will be benefited by supporting an association that ever champions and defends his interests.

Let our membership be a bulwark of strength. Let the call go forth to every ranch in the land harboring Angoras. Let all patrons of the industry we champion rally 'round our banner and co-operating with us make possible such an organization as can render the plodding Angora goat breeders most yeoman service.

Counting upon you as a willing worker in behalf of the Association and ever ready and eager to assist, we trust you will use your best efforts to induce the Angora goat owners of your section to join the American Angora Goat Breeders' Association and too that you will make an immediate and 'special effort to have them do so right now.

Let us start our campaign with zeal and enthusiasm and too with a determination to make our organization a
POWER FOR PROGRESS IN AMERICAN ANGORA HUSBANDRY,
during the coming new year. We trust you will "join in the round-up." Your help will be keenly appreciated and prove a benefit that will be felt by all Angora husbandmen of our country.

We beseech you to see your neighboring breeders at once and urge them to join the Association now. Help us to let it be known the Angora goat breeders of the country are indeed organized and ready a thousand, yea three thousand strong.

Most sincerely,
John W. Fulton
Sec'y.

JWF/NDB

Figure 12. A letter dated January 4, 1908, written by the American Angora Breeders' Association to Boston breeder Mr Cushman.
Erman Tamur Archive

REGISTERED ANGORA KIDS. BUCK AND FOUR DOES.
A Good Foundation Flock, $40.00 Northern Angora Goat & Live Stock Co. HELENA, MONTANA.

SPLENDID REGISTERED ANIMALS OF THIS AGE
$10.00 *and* $15.00 EACH
YOUNG BUCK KIDS
Send for our 1907 Price List of Bucks.
Northern Angora Goat & Live Stock Co.
HELENA, MONTANA.

TRIO OF REGISTERED ANGORAS
TWO REGISTERED ANGORA DOES, (*Bred to our Famous Imported Bucks*) AND A REGISTERED BUCK OF DIFFERENT BREEDING
$50.00
Order Now to Secure Early Selection
Northern Angora Goat & Live Stock Co.
HELENA, MONTANA.

Figure 13. Montana-based Northern Angora Goat & Live Stock Company's ads for Angora goats of various qualities. Erman Tamur Archive

goats. Several herds of Angora goats were brought into the US during this 50-year span from South Africa as well. By 1900, the number of Angora goats in the US is estimated to have reached 500,000.

Angora goat cultivation in the United States has developed in an organized and coordinated manner since its beginnings. Government agencies, private associations, farmers large and small have regularly communicated their knowledge and experience with each other. Genealogies of the goats were charted in order to maintain racial purity for mohair quality, and transfer certificates attesting to the quality of the livestock as ratified by the American Angora Goat Breeders' Association (Figure 11). Newcomers to goat breeding were enlightened by unions, and companies categorised their offerings by sex and age (Figures 12, 13).

Endeavours to Revive the Ankara Mohair Industry and Last Word

Towards the end of the 19th century, the Ottoman administration took some measures that indicated an awareness of the importance of Angora goat breeding and the mohair weaving industry associated with it. Abdülhamid II banned the exportation of Angora goats with an edict issued in 1881. Considering the fact that Angora goats had been shipped to South Africa in 1838 and to the United States in 1849, and that goats were dispatched recurrently to both countries for the subsequent 30-40 years, it is clear that this decision was much too late. Moreover, it is also known that this ban was not fully implemented, and Angora goats were transported to the United States and especially to South Africa repeatedly, even after that date.

In the last years of the Ottoman administration, a second attempt was made to encourage the cultivation of Angora goats; once again, during the reign of Abdülhamid II, with the establishing of a Model Pen in Kalaba, Ankara, and a Shepherds' school (Figure 14). The facilities were opened on November 20, 1898. The purpose in opening the Shepherds' School was to teach farmers the fine points of grazing goats, feeding methods, ways of protecting animals from diseases, and techniques for building pens (An Overview of Turkish History of Agriculture, p. 194).

Figure 14. Shepherds' School established in Kalaba, Ankara in 1898. Erman Tamur Archive

We do not have any information about whether the school actually functioned and what benefits, if any, were provided. The final act regarding the cultivation of Angora goats in the last years of the Ottoman rule (or perhaps it would be better to say "Committee of Union and Progress Administration") was a law that was passed by the Ottoman Chamber of Deputies on April 11, 1918. It was titled "Law proscribing the exportation and reproduction abroad of mohair goat brood stock." This law was an attempt to bring into force the Sultan's edict of 1881 that prohibited Angora goat exports, and to remove any loopholes exploited to surmount the ban, and to instate an economic incentive by exempting mohair goat breeders from pasture tax in Article 4 of the Act (Tamur, 2003, p. 192).

In the first years of the Republic, when exploitation of domestic resources were discussed as a prerequisite to development, improving Angora goat farming and reviving the Ankara mohair textile industry came to the forefront. To this end, the Turkish Mohair Association (TTC) was established in 1930. The first action of the society, headed by Yozgat deputy Süleyman Sırrı Bey (İçöz) was to establish a breeding facility (Model Pen) with goats selected from the best herds in Central Anatolia, especially the Ankara vicinity, just as the Ottoman administration had previously done. The aim was to help breeders raise healthy and highly productive livestock by providing high quality brood stock bred at the facilities established at Lalahan (Figure 15).

Another activity of the Association was to reorganize a part of its headquarters near the old Çakırlar Bridge at the Bent Stream, in Ankara, as a mohair textile workshop under the name "*Sof* Textile House" (Figure 16). Looms for weaving *sof* were installed here with a view to reproduce mohair fabrics of old. This initiative was not necessarily valuable economic activity in itself, but a model for the industry.

Only 50 years ago, the Angora goat population in Turkey was in the millions and mohair's share in agricultural exports could not be underestimated. However, in recent years, the total number of Angora goats in the country has declined to a few hundred thousand. The number of Angora goats in Ankara province has fallen from hundreds of thousands to tens of thousands. Although there have been some small positive fluctuations from time to time, the change is generally a negative one.

Angora goat breeding has been state-subsidized for many years, with an additional payment per kilogram of mohair produced. In fact, the constantly dwindling numbers of breeders are able continue their activities today only thanks to that. However, it is also clear that such subsidies have not and will not contribute to the transformation of Angora goat breeding into an added-value economic activity. What needs to be done is to process the mohair with modern techniques and produce high quality Ankara fabrics that will become an international brand, as it used to be. If this is successful, the value of mohair will appreciate, and herds of Angora goats will continue to decorate the Anatolian highlands. This would also be a most appropriate way to honour worthy people who have strived so much for this cause (Figure 17).

Figure 15. Some of the goats in the model herd bred by the Turkish Mohair Association in Lalahan.
Erman Tamur Archive

Figure 16. Headquarters of the Turkish Mohair Association and the *sof* textile house.
Erman Tamur Archive

Figure 17. Turkish Mohair Association president and Yozgat deputy Süleyman Sırrı İçöz by the Lalahan model pen, with a kid on his lap.
Erman Tamur Archive

References

Açıl, F. (1961). *Ankara keçisi ve tiftiğin memleket bünyesindeki ekonomik önemi.* Ankara: Ankara University Faculty of Agriculture Publications.

Akgür, M. and Korkmaz, Ö. (2003). *Türkiye'de tiftik üretimi ve Güney Afrika örneği.* İstanbul: İstanbul Chamber of Commerce Publications.

Barnett, D. E. (1987). Angora goats in Texas: agricultural innovation on Edwards Plateau, 1858-1900. *Southwestern historical quarterly, C. XC. S. 4.*

Batu, S. (1940). *Ankara keçisinin tarihi ve menşei hakkında bir tetkik.* Ankara: T.R. Higher Institute of Agriculture.

Cahen, C. (1979). *Osmanlılar'dan önce Anadolu'da Türkler.* İstanbul: E Publications.

Ergenç, Ö. (1995). *Osmanlı klasik dönemi kent tarihçiliğine katkı, XVI. yüzyılda Ankara ve Konya.* Ankara: Ankara Institute Foundation.

Eyice, S. (1972). *Ankara'nın eski bir resmi.* Ankara. Turkish Historical Society

İhsan Abidin [Akıncı]. (1340/1924). *Ankara keçisinin hâli ve ıslahı ve tetkik raporu.* İstanbul: Vatan Printing.

İhsan Abidin [Akıncı]. (1932). *Tiftik istihsalden istihlake kadar.* İstanbul: Export Office.

Keçi Yetiştirmek ve Bakmak Usulü. (1927). İstanbul: Ministry of Agriculture Publications.

Kinghorn, P. M. (1976). *Angora goat husbandry.* Jansenville: S.A. Mohair Growers.

Okaner, H. (1945). *Türk tiftiğinin en mühim mihaniki vasıfları.* Ankara: T.R. Ministry of Agriculture, Ankara Higher Institute of Agriculture.

Refik, A. (1329 R). *Tiftik keçisi terbiye ve teksiri.* Kastamonu: Farmers' Library.

[Rijksmuseum] View of Ankara [Painting]. (1700-1799). (Inventory No: SK-A-2055), Rijksmuseum, Amsterdam.

Tamur, E. (2003). *Ankara keçisi ve Ankara tiftik dokumacılığı.* Ankara: Ankara Chamber of Commerce Publications.

Tamur, E. (2010). Ankara keçisi ve Ankara tiftik ürünleri. In *Ankara Keçisi Üçlemesi, Sanat, Tarih, Gelenek* (pp. 38-55).

Thompson, G. F. (1908). *The Angora goat.* Washington: U.S. Department of Agriculture.

Tournefort, J.P. (1741). *A Voyage into the Levant*, Vol. III. London: D. Midwinter.

Türk ziraat tarihine bir bakış. (1938). *Birinci Köy ve Ziraat Kalkınma Kongresi.* İstanbul: Devlet Printing house.

Üstar, M. F. (1940). *Tiftik ve tiftikçiliğimiz.* İstanbul: University Bookshop.

Uys, D. S. (1988). *Cinderella to princess, the story of mohair in South Africa 1838 to 1988.* Port Elizabeth: Mohair Board.

Webb Yıldırmak, G. (2011). *XVIII. yüzyılda Osmanlı-İngiliz tiftik ticareti.* Ankara: Turkish Historical Society Publications.

L'acclimatation de la chèvre angora en France et en Afrique du Sud

FRÉDÉRIC HITZEL
CNRS-EHESS-PSL, Paris

De nos jours, lorsque l'on se promène dans les allées tortueuses du Grand bazar d'Istanbul, on découvre une grande variété de foulards, écharpes et châles destinés à une clientèle locale mais également, et surtout, à une clientèle venue des pays du Golfe. En interrogeant les marchands sur la qualité et sur l'origine de ces magnifiques laines soyeuses, on est frappé par l'extrême diversité des noms : pashmina, cachemire, *shatoosh* « la laine du roi » (*Sha-tus*, formé à partir des mots persans : *sha*, signifiant « roi », *tus*, la laine), ainsi que sur l'origine des laines. Celles-ci peuvent en effet provenir de la toison de différents animaux (lapin, lamas, alpaga, chameau, guanaco, yack, etc.), la plus courante étant la fibre naturelle provenant du mouton, la célèbre laine mérinos, et, bien entendu, les poils de la chèvre Angora. Dans ce dernier cas, on préfère la désigner sous l'appellation mohair. Enfin, il n'est pas rare que des noms géographiques servent de label pour indiquer la provenance de ces précieux lainages. On parle ainsi de « laine Shetland » pour désigner une race de moutons élevée sur les îles Shetland, au nord de l'Écosse, ou de la « laine cachemire » pour désigner les chèvres du Cachemire, en Inde.

Cette complexité des désignations se retrouve dans l'histoire de la chèvre d'Angora. Ainsi, pendant longtemps, la France qui recevait des châles tissés en Orient, fut incertaine sur leur lieu de tissage : Tibet, Indes, Tartarie, Turquie ? Il en était de même sur l'espèce animale qui présentait ce duvet fin, léger, doux et chaud. On a supposé que ces poils provenaient d'une espèce rare de chameaux ou de moutons (L'Esprit des journaux, 1780, p.198).

Pour retracer l'histoire de l'introduction de la chèvre angora en Europe, en France et en Afrique du Sud, il faut s'intéresser non seulement à l'histoire naturelle et à la géographie, mais également au commerce et à l'industrie. Elle permet de comprendre comment des hommes, par leurs audaces et leurs témérités ont su braver les distances, parfois les dangers, pour quérir cette matière rare, puis ont cherché à introduire l'animal. C'est à cette quête que nous invitons le lecteur.

Il convient tout d'abord de rappeler que la chèvre angora, telle qu'elle fut élevée au centre de l'Anatolie, est probablement originaire de régions orientales plus lointaines. Sa présence est attestée au Tibet il y a trois mille ans et en Asie Mineure à partir de l'antiquité. Le géographe grec Strabon signalait déjà au premier siècle de notre ère qu'aux « *environs de la rivière Halys (Kızıl Irmak), on nourrit des moutons dont la laine est fort épaisse et fort douce ; et de plus il y a des chèvres qui ne se trouvent pas ailleurs.* » (Pitton de Tournefort, 1718, p.185).

Il paraît certain qu'à partir du XIe siècle, il existait de nombreux troupeaux sur le plateau anatolien, notamment autour de la forteresse byzantine d'Ancyre qui, plus tard, prendra le nom d'Angora. Il s'y développa les premiers ateliers de mohair, mot dont l'origine arabe, *Mukhayyar*, signifie « celle qui est choisie ; la plus belle ».

Dès le XVe siècle, Jacques Cœur (mort à Chio en 1456), qui fut le premier français à établir et entretenir des relations commerciales suivies avec les pays du Levant, fit venir en France un troupeau de « caprins à poil long, ondulé, doux et propre à la teinture ». Ceux-ci furent installés dans une ferme surnommée la « Chevrottière », aux environs de Saint-Pourçain-sur-Sioule, en Auvergne, une commune située à 350 kilomètres au sud de Paris. Le pelage de ces premières chèvres venues d'Orient servit essentiellement au tissage de précieux linges liturgiques et habits sacerdotaux des moines du prieuré du Montet. Hélas les troupeaux ne survécurent pas aux famines et aux guerres de religion qui frappèrent la région à partir de 1568.

Aux XVIe-XVIIe siècles, de nombreux témoignages attestent de la transformation du mohair brut en France, mais également en Hollande et en Angleterre. Les fils de mohair étaient importés d'Angora, région qui va s'affirmer comme la plaque centrale de ce commerce (Kılıçbay, 1994, p. 64-70 ; Kadı, 2012, p. 29-97).

En 1555, Ogier Ghislain de Busbecq (1522-1592), diplomate flamand envoyé auprès de la cour de Soliman le Magnifique, avait remarqué que :

C'est dans ces plaines [d'Angora] que sont les chèvres, dont le poil sert à faire les camelots [grosses étoffes faites de poils de chèvres], il est extrêmement long, très fin & reluisant ; les bergers ne le tondent point, ils peignent seulement leurs chèvres, & on file ce qui tombe de leur toison ; souvent on les lave, elles ne paissent que du chiendent, qui est la seule herbe qui croît dans ces campagnes sèches et stériles. Il est certain que cette espèce de pâture contribue beaucoup à la finesse de leur poil (...). Les femmes qui filent ce poil, le portent vendre à Ancyre. (Lettres du baron Busbec, 1748, p.143).

Deux siècles plus tard, le botaniste Joseph Pitton de Tournefort (1656-1708), qui visita Ankara en 1701, notait également que l'on :

Nourrit les plus belles chèvres du monde dans la campagne d'Angora. Elles éblouissent par leur blancheur & leur poil, qui est aussi fin que la soie, frisé naturellement par tresses de huit ou neuf pouces de long, est la matière de plusieurs belles étoffes, et surtout du camelot ; mais on ne permet guères de transporter cette toison sans la filer, parce que les gens du pays y gagnent leur vie. (Pitton de Tournefort, 1718, p.185)

Un grand tableau conservé au Rijksmuseum d'Amsterdam (Figure 1) nous montre cette activité exercée hors de la ville (Eyice, 1972 ; Tamur, 2008, p. 385-409). En arrière plan figure la citadelle d'Angora ; en bas à droite on assiste à la tonte des moutons ; au centre, plusieurs échoppes où l'on découvre les différentes étapes de la fabrication de la laine : pesage, lavage, filage, tissage, transaction, et des caravanes de chameaux transportant les énormes balles de laine.

Au cours des siècles, plusieurs tentatives d'introduction de la chèvre angora à l'extérieur de la Turquie eurent lieues dans des endroits aussi divers que l'île de Chypre (1598), la Suède (1740), le Palatinat rhénan en Allemagne (1771), Venise (1788) et en France, au château de Rambouillet, où l'on compte un cheptel important, mais qui disparaitra lors de la Révolution française. Ces premières essais, plus ou moins réussis, n'eurent pas de conséquences sur le commerce. C'est seulement au début du XIXe siècle que la chèvre angora allait connaître un extraordinaire regain d'intérêt.

Figure 1. Gezicht op Ankara, Vue de Ancyre (Ankara), 1700-1799
Huile sur toile, 117 x 198 cm, Rijksmuseum, Amsterdam, inv. SK.A. 2055.

Les premières chèvres angoras en France et en Algérie

C'est au lendemain de la guerre franco-turque de 1798-1801, causée par l'expédition des troupes françaises en Egypte, que l'on assiste en France à l'introduction des premiers châles. Le succès est tel que dans les années 1810, les premiers modèles que l'on vit porter par des dames à Paris, étaient de véritables trophées (Lévi-Strauss, 1987, 1988, 1998a, 1998b, 2012). La beauté de ces tissus, leur finesse, ainsi que l'élégance et la richesse de leur drapé, les faisaient rechercher avec empressement. Cette nouvelle mode fut à l'origine d'un nouvel essor des manufactures de tissage.

Ce fut le manufacturier, négociant et homme politique Guillaume Louis Ternaux (1763-1833) qui, le premier, développa les premiers cachemires européens, notamment les célèbres « châles de Ternaux » qui feront sa notoriété et sa fortune, et qui chercha à introduire en France les premières chèvres angoras. Sachant qu'à cette époque l'Empire ottoman interdisait toute exportation du précieux caprin, et pour concurrencer les Anglais qui importait des châles indiens, il chercha d'autres lieux où se procurer le précieux duvet.

Un jour, il apprit d'un voyageur qui se rendait en Tartarie, à la grande foire de Makarief (Kazan), lieu de rendez-vous de tous les commerçants de l'Asie, qu'un Arménien pouvait lui procurer une certaine quantité d'un duvet fort rare s'il se présentait à la prochaine foire. L'année suivante, l'Arménien tint parole et apporta soixante livres (environ 27 kilogrammes) d'un très fin duvet, qui furent aussitôt envoyées à Paris, cachées dans un coussin. Cette précaution était nécessaire car à cette époque l'exportation du duvet était strictement défendue par la cour de Russie. Dans le même temps, le lieutenant de vaisseau Charles Baudin se rendit à Calcutta et rapporta en 1815, quelques petits ballots de duvet provenant de chèvres Tibétaines. Les récits de ces divers voyageurs s'accor-

Figure 2. Achat des chèvres du Tibet par Amédée Jaubert,
Gravure à l'eau forte et au burin d'après 16 x 11 cm
Source : Pierre Martinet.

daient à établir que si la race des chèvres à duvet était très répandue en Turquie, en Perse, et en Inde, on pouvait se procurer quelques spécimens dans les régions de la Volga et dans ce vaste territoire que l'on désignait alors sous le nom de Tartarie. Bien que vagues, ces quelques indications suffisaient pour faire présumer qu'on pouvait, sans entreprendre un difficile et périlleux voyage vers le Tibet, se procurer des chèvres à duvet et tenter de les acclimater en France.

La mission fut confiée par Guillaume Louis Ternaux à Pierre Amédée Jaubert (1779-1847), professeur de turc à l'Ecole spéciale des Langues Orientales (Tessier, 1819 ; Polonceau, 1824). Le savant diplomate, qui connaissait parfaitement l'Orient, ses langues et ses usages pour y avoir effectué plusieurs missions diplomatiques pour Napoléon, accepta la mission que lui confia le roi de France Louis XVIII : acheter des chèvres de race tibétaine à duvet de cachemire et les ramener en France.

P. Amédée Jaubert quitta Paris au mois d'avril 1818, se rendit par bateau à Odessa, Taganrog et Astrakhan, au pied du Caucase. Au cours de son voyage, il apprit que des populations Kirghizes installées sur les bords de l'Oural possédaient une race de chèvres d'une blancheur éclatante, et qui portaient, tous les ans, au mois de juin, une toison d'une finesse remarquable. Les échantillons qu'on lui donna le convainquirent et il acheta auprès de Kirghiz Kara Ağaç et de Kazakhs, 1289 bêtes (Figure 2). Il prit aussitôt le chemin du retour en passant par la Volga et la Crimée. Mais en raison du climat rigoureux de l'hiver, plusieurs bêtes périrent au cours du trajet. En arrivant sur les bords de la mer Noire, au port de Kefe (Théodosie) le 24 décembre, il avait déjà perdu 288 chèvres. Le troupeau fut aussitôt partagé en deux convois : l'un, de 566 bêtes, fut expédié sur un bateau russe et arriva à Marseille vers la mi-avril 1819 ; l'autre atteignit le port de Toulon quelques jours plus tard.

Au total, sur les 1289 chèvres achetées, seulement 400 survécurent. Après une mesure de quarantaine, une partie des chèvres fut placée dans une bergerie royale, aux environs de Perpignan ; d'autres dans les départements du Var et des Bouches du Rhône où elles s'acclimatèrent rapidement à leur nouvel environnement.

Dans les années qui suivirent, on fit des croisements entre les chèvres rapportées par Amédée Jaubert, dites « chèvres à duvet du Cachemire » ou de race tibétaine, avec des chèvres Angora rapportées de Turquie via l'Italie. Cette nouvelle espèce, auquel on donna le curieux nom de *cacho-angora*, ne semble cependant pas avoir eu le succès escompté et fut progressivement abandonnée.

C'est seulement une vingtaine d'année plus tard, sous le règne de Napoléon III (empereur des Français de 1852 à 1870), que le projet d'implanter des chèvres angoras en France est relancé. Cette fois, l'initiative en revient à la Société zoologique d'acclimatation (qui prendra le nom de Société impériale zoologique d'acclimatation), créée à Paris le 10 février 1854. Le but de cette société savante, qui devint une association française de protection de la nature, était de veiller à la protection des espèces animales et végétales sauvages ainsi que des milieux naturels, et au perfectionnement et à la multiplication des races nouvellement introduites ou domestiques (*Bulletin*, 1854, p. XV). Dès les premières années de sa création, la Société acheta ou se fit offrir de nombreux animaux (lamas, kangourous, yacks, perruches, canards de Chine, cygnes noirs de Nouvelle-Hollande, etc.).

Parmi ses prestigieux membres et donateurs figurait le chef religieux et militaire algérien, l'émir Abd el-Kader (1808-1883), qui s'était illustré quelques années auparavant dans sa lutte contre la colonisation française de l'Algérie. Après sa reddition en 1847, Abd el-Kader, sa famille et ses fidèles, avaient été emprisonnés en France, au château de Pau (1848) et au château d'Amboise (1848-1852), puis il avait obtenu de l'empereur Napoléon III d'être exilé à Bursa. Pendant ses deux années de résidence à Bursa (1853-1855), il consacra son temps à l'écriture et au développement d'une ferme agricole. En apprenant que la Société impériale d'acclimatation recherchait les moyens d'acclimater un certain nombre de chèvres d'Angora, il s'empressa d'acheter, à ses frais, et d'envoyer à Paris, un troupeau composé de 11 chèvres et 4 boucs (*Journal des débats*, 1855). Ceux-ci furent installés dans deux départements français (le Haut-Rhin et l'Isère).

D'autre part, la Société impériale d'acclimatation acheta par l'intermédiaire du baron Rousseau, consul de France à Bursa, 72 chèvres d'Angora. Sur ce nombre, 25 chèvres et 10 boucs furent envoyés en Algérie (*Journal des débats* 1854 ; *Journal de Constantinople*, 26 mars 1855). Installé dans un premier temps chez un fermier du Sahel, à Chéraga, dans la banlieue ouest d'Alger, ce cheptel fut par la suite déplacé dans la bergerie de Ben-Chicao, au sud de l'Atlas. Les chèvres d'Angora semblent s'être parfaitement acclimatées au climat chaud et sec de l'Algérie. Cependant, leur installation ne manqua pas d'inquiéter les autorités françaises. Se nourrissant presque exclusivement de broussailles et de végétation arbustive, le gouverneur militaire d'Alger craignit que l'introduction de cette nouvelle espèce n'entraîna une trop grande déforestation. En conséquence, il fut décidé que l'élevage de la chèvre angora serait abandonné (Durand, 1884, p. 113-125). C'est ainsi qu'en France, comme en Algérie, à la veille de la Première Guerre mondiale, il ne restait quasiment aucun vestige des beaux résultats encouragés par la Société zoologique d'Acclimatation. En revanche, l'élevage de la chèvre angora en Afrique du Sud allait connaître d'excellents résultats, le mohair du Cap ne tardant pas à inonder les marchés européens.

L'Afrique du Sud : nouvel eldorado pour la chèvre angora

Si l'initiative de la Société zoologique d'acclimatation d'introduire des chèvres d'Angora en Algérie en 1855 connut un échec, elle ne manqua pas de susciter l'intérêt des colons du Cap. Plusieurs d'entre eux eurent l'idée d'essayer à leur tour d'implanter la chèvre angora en Afrique du sud. Ils furent encouragés dans leurs démarches par le consul en France des Républiques d'Afrique Australe, le chevalier Julius de Mosenthal (1819-1880), membre de la Société impériale d'acclimatation. Il semblerait que ce soit son frère, Adolph Mosenthal (1812-1882), qui, en 1856, avec l'aide de l'ambassadeur anglais à Istanbul, Lord Stratford de Redcliffe, introduisit le premier troupeau de 30 chèvres angoras au Cap (Schreiner, 1898 ; McCall Theal, 2010, p. 12-13 ; Saron & Hotz (ed), 1955, p. 349-352).

Ce premier essai d'acclimatation dans les régions d'Algoa Bay et de Port Natal ayant donné d'excellents résultats, en 1869, une entreprise londonienne, Blaine Brothers, décida de poursuivre l'essai sur une plus grande échelle. 600 boucs et 200 chèvres de la plus belle espèce furent achetés à Ankara et placés sous la garde d'un berger Maltais. L'embarquement s'effectua dans le port d'Inebolu sur la mer Noire, à bord du steamer anglais *Mary*, appartenant à la société Morton & Company de Galata. Le 19 août 1869, le navire transitait par Istanbul, gagnait le détroit de Gibraltar et atteignait le port d'Algoa Bay le 6 octobre (*Levant Herald*, 1869).

L'élevage des chèvres angoras connut une rapide extension, notamment à Aberdeen, Cradock, Graaf-Reinet, Jansenville, Murraysburg, Somerset-East et Willowmore et, dès l'Exposition de Londres, en 1886, les fermiers et industriels du Cap étaient en mesure de présenter pour la première fois une importante production d'articles en laine de mohairs (*Bulletin*, 1890, p. 344). Ces précieuses laines ne tardèrent pas à inonder le marché européen, alimentant notamment le marché de Bradford et les fabriques de Roubaix et d'Amiens qui utilisaient le mohair pour réaliser des tissus d'ameublement connus sous l'appellation « velours d'Utrecht ». Le mohair était également employé dans la confection de tapis, de vêtements de prix, de perruques, et de nombreux jouets (cheveux des poupées et les oursons en peluche, les célèbres Teddy's Bear).

La chèvre angora connut également un formidable développement de l'autre côté de l'Atlantique. En 1848, pour remercier le Dr James Davis qui, envoyé par le gouvernement des Etats-Unis d'Amérique, avait résidé trois ans à Istanbul (1846-1848) pour introduire et développer la culture du coton en Turquie, le sultan Abdülmecid offrit 9 chèvres d'Angora spécialement sélectionnées pour la qualité de leur laine (Cronwright Schreiner, 1898, p. 56). Installé en Caroline du sud, ce modeste cheptel allait rapidement se développer, principalement dans le Texas et le sud des Etats-Unis.

Tandis que l'élevage de la chèvre angora prospérait en Afrique du Sud et en Amérique, la production du mohair à Ankara allait totalement s'effondrer dans les années 1870. Le plateau anatolien fut en effet, coup sur coup, durement frappé par la sécheresse et les invasions de sauterelles qui détruisirent les récoltes et entraînèrent de terribles famines en 1874 et 1875 ; ensuite vint la guerre russo-turque de 1877-1878, puis une épizootie qui décima les troupeaux. En l'espace de quelques années, le nombre de bête diminua de manière drastique. Alors qu'en 1872, on dénombrait 997,247 chèvres dans le vilayet d'Angora, on n'en comptait plus que 724,959 en 1881, soit une diminution de 270,000 chèvres en l'espace de sept ans (*La Turquie*, 8 nov. 1881). La situation nécessitait des mesures urgentes.

Au début de l'année 1881, les éleveurs de chèvres qui produisaient le *tiftik*, adressèrent une requête au sultan Abdul-Hamid II lui demandant d'interdire l'exportation des chèvres et de baisser les taxes (*La Turquie*, 3-4 avril 1881). La première

Figure 3. La chèvre d'Angora, 1755
Dessin
Crayon, encre et lavis, 19,8 x 15,4 cm
Source : Jacques de Sève, 1755a

Figure 4. Le bouc d'Angora, 1755
Dessin
Crayon, encre et lavis, 20 x 15,4 cm
Source : Jacques de Sève, 1755b

requête fut aussitôt appliquée tandis que, par ordonnance impériale, en septembre de la même année, la taxe perçue sur chaque tête de chèvre était diminuée de 6 à 4 piastres (*La Turquie*, 11-12 sept. 1881, 27 Juin 1883). Ces premières mesures semblent avoir eu un effet immédiat. Au cours de l'été 1883, le gouverneur général d'Angora annonçait une augmentation spectaculaire du cheptel qui atteignit 950,518 têtes (*La Turquie*, 3 juil. 1883), soit un chiffre assez proche de celui de 1872.

En 1885, le gouvernement ottoman renforça les mesures pour préserver les chèvres d'Angora. Une circulaire adressée aux vilayets où ces chèvres étaient élevées défendait désormais de manière rigoureuse leur transport par voie de mer, d'un point à l'autre de l'empire. Il était précisé que :

Le transport par voie de terre est permis mais à la condition que le propriétaire du troupeau fournisse une forte caution et qu'il produise ensuite un ilmi haber *de l'autorité douanière de la localité où ces chèvres seront transportées. Cet* ilmi haber *constatera que les chèvres n'ont pas été exportées à l'étranger.*

Faute de ce certificat, le propriétaire perdra la somme déposée à titre de caution et sera en outre poursuivi par voie judiciaire (*La Turquie*, 7 fév. 1885).

Une surveillance sévère et active était désormais exigée des gouverneurs de province. On leur demandait de livrer aux tribunaux tous ceux qui seraient pris en flagrant délit, pour qu'ils soient punis sévèrement. Après la famine, les désastres causés par les sauterelles et les épizooties, une ère de prospérité s'ouvrait temporairement pour Angora. Elle allait cependant être de courte durée en raison des nombreux conflits qui n'allaient pas tarder à secouer l'Anatolie au début du XXe siècle.

La chèvre d'Angora, se distingue des chèvres classiques par leurs oreilles pendantes, leurs cornes en spirale et surtout par leur poil blanc très long, très fourni, très fin qui s'enroulent en longs tire-bouchons (Figure 3, 4). C'est principalement pour ce poil, qui se file comme la laine, et dont on fait des étoffes chaudes et légères, que cette race de chèvre est mondialement connue.

Depuis le XVIe siècle, l'Europe reconnaît les grandes qualités de cette laine et essaie d'acclimater cet animal sur son territoire. Les premières tentatives d'élevage de chèvres angora en France s'étant toutes soldées par un échec (surtout en raison des épidémies et des famines), longtemps la légende s'est établie que cette chèvre ne pouvait être élevées ailleurs que sur le plateau anatolien. Mais au XIXe siècle, sous la pression des industriels du textile, et grâce aux nouveaux moyens de transport, plus sûrs et plus rapides, la chèvre angora suscitait un nouvel intérêt. Il ne faudra que quelques années pour que celle-ci s'adapte et se développe sur le continent sud Africain et en Amérique.

Aujourd'hui, le mohair est une production que l'on trouve sur tous les continents. Les principaux producteurs restent l'Afrique du Sud (66 %), les Etats-Unis (11 %), la Turquie et l'Iran, qui se disputent la troisième place, en attendant l'arrivée d'un nouveau concurrent de poids : la Chine.

Sources

Bulletin Consulaire Français: Recueil des rapports commerciaux. (1890). XIX (1e yarıyıl).

Bulletin de la Société zoologique d'acclimatation. (1854). n 1. XV.

Durand, M. (1884). "La chèvre en Algérie". *Bulletin mensuel de la Société nationale d'acclimatation de France.* 31, 113-125.

Eyice, S. (1972). *Ankara'nın eski bir resmi: tarihî vesika olarak resimler Ankara'dan bahseden seyyahlar eski bir Ankara resmi.* Ankara: TTK.

Gezicht op Ankara. (1700-1799). (SK-A-2055). Rijksmuseum, Amsterdam.

Journal de Constantinople. (26 mars 1855).

Journal des débats politiques et littéraires. (26 décembre 1854).

Journal des débats politiques et littéraires. (20 mai 1855).

Journal des débats politiques et littéraires. (10 janvier 1855).

Journal des débats politiques et littéraires. (6 mars 1855).

Kadı, İ. H. (2012). *Ottoman and Dutch merchants in the eighteenth century.* Leiden: Brill.

Kılıçbay, M. A. (1994). Sof şehri Ankara. In E. Batur (ed.), *Ankara* (pp. 64-70). İstanbul.

L'Esprit des journaux, Français et étrangers, dédié à Son A. R., le duc Charles de Lorraine & de Bar. (1780). VI (IX) juin, 198.

La Turquie. (8 novembre 1881). 15 (258).

La Turquie. (3-4 avril 1881). 15 (77).

La Turquie. (11-12 septembre 1881). 15(210).

La Turquie. (27 juin 1883). 17.

La Turquie. (3 juillet 1883). 17(150).

La Turquie. (7 février 1885). 19(30).

Lettres du baron Busbec. (1748). (M. L'abbé de Foy, çev.). Paris: C.-J.-B. Bauche.

Levant Herald. (20 août 1869).

Levant Herald. (22 novembre 1869).

Lévi-Strauss, M. (1987). *The romance of the cashmere shawl.* Mapin Publishing.

Lévi-Strauss, M. (1988). *Cashmere shawl.* Abrams Inc.

Lévi-Strauss, M. (1998a). *Cachemires parisiens, 1810-1880.* Paris: Musée Galliéra.

Lévi-Strauss, M. (1998b). *Cachemires: L'art et l'histoire des châles en France au XIXe siècle.* Paris: Adam Biro.

Lévi-Strauss, M. (2012). *Cachemires: La création française, 1800-1880.* Paris: La Martinière.

Martinet, Pierre. (coll. Particulière). [Achat des chèvres du Tibet par Amédée Jaubert]. Paris.

Pitton de Tournefort, J. (1718). *Relation d'un voyage du Levant, fait par ordre du roi.* Paris: Imprimerie Royale.

Polonceau, A. R. (1824). *Notice sur les chèvres asiatiques à duvet de Cachemire.* Paris-Versailles.

Polonceau, M. (1826). "Rapport sur des essais de croisement de chèvres asiatiques à duvet de Cachemire, avec des boucs Angora". In *Mémoires d'agriculture, d'économie rurale et domestique* (p. 182-187). Paris: Chez Madame Huzard.

Saron, G. ve Hotz, L. (ed). (1955). *The Jews in South Africa, a History.* Cape Town: Cumberledge & Oxford University Press.

Schreiner, S. C. C. (1898). *The Angora goat and a paper on the Ostrich.* Londra: Longmans.

Sève, Jacques de. (1755a). Ankara keçisi. Ankara Fotoğraf, Kartpostal ve Gravür Koleksiyonu (Env. No: 1850), Koç University VEKAM Archive, Ankara.

Sève, J. (1755b). Ankara tekesi. Ankara Fotoğraf, Kartpostal ve Gravür Koleksiyonu (Env. No: 1851), Koç University VEKAM Archive, Ankara.

Tamur, E. (2008). *Amsterdam'da bir Ankara resmi.* Kebikeç İnsan Bilimleri için Kaynak Araştırmaları Dergisi, 25, 385-409.

Tessier, A. H. (1819). *Mémoires sur l'importation en France des chèvres à duvet de cachemire.* Paris: Imprimerie de Mme Huzard.

Theal, G. M. (2010). *History of South Africa since September 1795.* Cambridge: University Press.

“Sheep go to Heaven, (Angora) Goats go to Hell” A Spatiotemporal Analysis of the Angora Goat Economy in Ankara Province (1889-1905)[1]

SEMİH ÇELİK
Koç University, Department of History

In this article, I will endeavour to present new perspectives on the meaning of rural-urban relations from the late 1880s to the first years of the 1900s in the Ankara province through changes in the density of the Angora goat population. The period covered here is coined as the Ottoman industrial revolution (Clark, 1974), the empire's incorporation into the global capitalist economy (Kasaba, 1988), an age of agricultural crisis and restructuring (Quataert, 1975), or the decline/degeneration period of the Ottoman Empire (Lewis, 1958), as defined by Ottoman historians within the context of the empire's cultural and economic dependence on the West; widely conceptualized by the decline literature . The narrative in the literature, regardless of the various parameters examined, shares a common belief in an rapid urbanization where the rural-urban divide has deepened. It has been largely believed that the installation of the railway as of 1890s has accelerated this process. To put it in terms of economic historical terms, it is an accepted fact that this period has formed the basis for the transition from an organic economy an industrial economy (Wrigley, 2016). In this context, the prevalent view is that agricultural production and livestock professions (the primary sector), which are the decisive elements of the agricultural economy, are losing ground in favour of the more "urban", industrial and service sectors.

The historiography developed against this background has begun recently to digress from structural analyses and human actors and take up the history of other actors in nature, especially animals. It would not be wrong to say that we have passed a historiographical turning point

1 An earlier version of this article was presented at the International Congress of the Ottoman Social and Economic History (ICOSEH) conference in Sofia, Bulgaria, on 24-28 July 2017. I am grateful to all attendees of the conference, and Johannes Petrus Gerrits and Uygar Karaca of Koç University for their substantial assistance in implementing ArcGIS. I would also like to thank Assoc. Prof Dr Erdem Kabadayı from Koç University and Sinan Kaya from May 29 University, who read commented on the draft. The compilation of the data used in this study and H-GIS analyses were carried out within the scope of the ERC-Starting Grant, project 679097 UrbanOccupationsOETR conducted by Assoc. Dr M. Erdem Kabadayı of the Department of History of Koç University, where the author has also served as post-doctoral researcher.

for Ottoman historians from the growing interest in animals and human-animal-nature relations. In this context, literature is yet to develop, apart from a study examining animal human relations in the Ottoman Empire compiled by Suraiya Faroqhi (2010), and Alan Mikhail's (2013) monograph which examines the role of animals in the public sphere and the evolution of this role in Ottoman Egypt. It should be said that these kinds of studies, examples of which we shall see more in the future, also represent a partial critique of the history reading outlined above.

This article, besides being a contribution to animal historiography, aims to propose a new method of studying the history of an animal species with its highly specific characteristics, and more generally the effects of agricultural reforms or industrial revolutions on a well-defined economic activity. To that end, the article aims to examine whether there has been a vital change in the Angora goat economy during the observed 17 years between 1889 and 1905. It aims at realizing the said examination by means of Historical Geographical Information Systems (H-GIS) tools, which help us grasp the change over time in the selected qualities of the specific place (animal density in this example).

I shall explain what I mean by the concept of "economy of the Angora goat" before delving into the essence of the argument. Economic historians have been interested so far in the market/exchange value of the Angora goat as a commercial commodity. Thus, a limited analysis is brought about on the different perspectives of Angora goat breeding, involving the decline of the economic value of the Angora goat and its by-products with the collapse of the *sof* industry.

However, I use the concept of "the economy of the Angora goat" in this chapter to express the relationship between the goat breeders, their households, the goats and the natural environment in the broader sense. As Koray Çalışkan (2007) claimed, the commodification of a product in agrarian societies requires close and intimate relations not only between producers and market actors, but farmers, breeders, veterinarians, traders, workers, women, insects and even bushes. Therefore, the "economisation" of a commodity requires the repositioning in a complex way of information, actors, time and space. Following Çalışkan's conceptualization, I put forth here that the Angora goat economy was a vibrant one that reacted not only to the inter-imperial market dynamics in the last quarter of the 19th century, but also to local, economic and climatic changes such as famines or the establishment of the railway system in Ankara. More particularly, it is possible to say that the economy of Angora goat continued to dominate the reorganization of the space in Ankara in the first decade of the 20th century.

The Angora Goat Economy

For centuries, the Angora goat has come to be highly valued thanks to its unique fur, mohair. To say that Ankara's economic activities depended on the existence of this animal will not be wrong in this context. Mohair and the *sof* industry made Ankara a significant junction for merchants of various backgrounds in the empire. With changes in global production relations, especially in the 16th and 17th centuries, and the development of production technology in the 18th century, the market value and profitability of the

Ankara *sof* decreased considerably. The Ankara *sof* industry had reached its final days by the middle of the 19th century. During the second half of the century, Ankara had become just a source of mohair fibre and raw mohair, and finally an exporter of Angora goats for more developed industries. In the same period, the Angora goat was successfully cross-fertilized in the USA and Cape Town (Planhol, 1975-1977; Faroqhi, 1994; Tamur, 2003; Kadi, 2012; Tan, 2014). Despite the decline in the market value resulting from all these, the Angora goat population increased in the last decade of the century (Graph 1). The fact that the Angora goat needed specific climate conditions to survive, coupled with its delicate nature further placed the sustainability of its economy on the edge. This situation makes efforts to re-evaluate the economy of the Angora goat at the end of the 19th century even more meaningful.

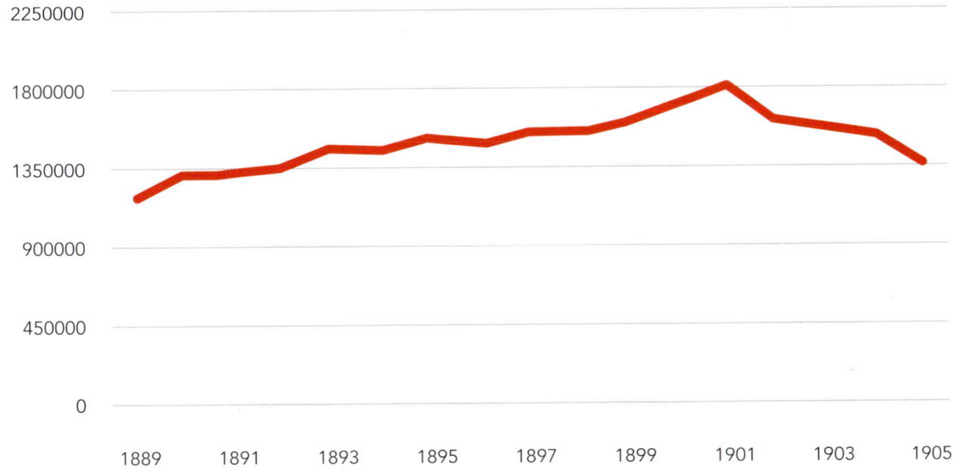

Graph 1. Changes in the Angora Goat Population in the Ankara Province (1889-1905).
This was obtained by compiling the data in (1325/1907) of the Ankara Province Official Yearbook, a royalty-free source.

Historians have portrayed the decline of *sof* production in Ankara not only as the end of an industry, but also as the total expiration of the Angora goat economy in the region (Tamur, 2003, Tan, 2014). However, although the *sof* and shawl industry seemed to have disappeared, it has been able to sustain its economic existence in a broad sense. Undoubtedly, goat breeders played a significant role in this sustainability. So much so that the breeders have opposed countless times the exportation of the Angora goats in the late 19th century. We know that the reactions of 1865, 1878 and 1897 to that end have failed. According to İhsan Abidin (1924), Angora goat breeders tried to make their voices heard by state authorities, but they could not prevent exports (p. 17). Breeders who suffered from this situation secretly gelded the bucks earmarked for export at different times (Şahin, 2013).[2] These and similar reactions show that the economic value of the Angora goat remained important to the breeders, although its market value has declined.

Although the demands of goat breeders were often ignored, Ottoman administrators, especially those in the provinces, ascribed more importance to the Angora goat than its market value. Administrators endeavoured to revive *sof* production in the face of intense competition from Europe in the 1860s. Around the middle of 1868, the Ankara Trade Council decided to establish a mechanized *sof* and shawl production facility (BOA, 1311/1895). The issue of mechanization of *sof* production continued to be discussed even in the 1880s and 1890s. A model farm and shepherds' school established in the outskirts of Ankara in 1890 aimed to educate Angora goat breeders on scientific husbandry (Keskin, 2010).

2 The success of the cross-fertilization efforts in Cape Town is said to be due to a single female goat bearing a male foetus, even though all male goats had been secretly sterilized.

The decline of the *sof* economy and struggles to revive the Angora goat economy continued with efforts to breed the goat outside the limits of the Ankara province. The fact that the geographical location of the Angora goat was limited to the Ankara province was held to be a "delusion" ("bunun başka yerde yetiştirilmesinin imkânsızlığı efkâr-ı batıl [olması]"), for which attempts were made to disprove in the 1870s with efforts to breed the Angora goat in the *Hüdavendigar* province (BOA, 1290/1873). Meanwhile exportation of the Angora goat outside the province, especially to port cities such as Istanbul and İzmir, was banned,. The animals to be exported to said cities had to be selected from castrated bucks ("wethers") older than five-year-olds or "rejects" (BOA, 1323/1905).

Despite its decrease in the market value, the economic value of the Angora goat increased in other aspects. İhsan Abidin states that the centuries-long tradition of not milking Angora goats was abolished by the end of the century. Although the amount of milk they produce is relatively small in comparison to other goat species, Angora goat breeders tried to increase the surplus value in this way. On the other hand, the Angora goat has functioned traditionally as a wet nurse for babies, due to its milk's affinity to human milk. This illustrates that the Angora goat's use value was important beyond its exchange value. We also know that young Angora goats that have not yet been pastured are considered a family member and even children's "playmates." Moreover, the relatively poorer breeders who did not have pens to shelter their herds in winter, kept their goats in their homes (Cronwright Schreiner, 1898, pp. 69, 128). Early republican era literature often portrayed scenes where Angora goats were natural and intimate family members (Oyal, 2013).

This intimacy was further enhanced by the exceptional care required due to the "delicate" nature of Angora goats. Ankara's 1907 yearbook mentioned specialized shepherds selected to tend to Angora goats were difficult to come by. Shepherd dogs also had to be specially trained (Tamur, 2003). Angora goats were also thought to be harmful to the environment due to their appetite for young shoots of trees. As early as 1848, Tabib Hayrullah (1264/1848) stated that the Angora goat was a species harmful to forests and that it was "fairly impetuous and perfidious and disposed to wandering". Almost eighty years after that, İhsan Abidin (1924) stated that the Angora goats were fierce enemies of foresters, to the extent that foresters endeavoured to curb the reproduction of this species (p. 11). Besides the damage to the forest economy, the goat economy was mutually exclusive with sheep economy (Cronwright Schreiner, 1898, p). A quick glance at 1845 *temettuat* registers will show that sheep population was very low in towns and villages where the Angora goats dominated.[3] The same is true from the opposite angle as well. Despite its delicate, fragile and demanding qualities, the value of the Angora goat for breeders and other actors at a time when the *sof* industry was collapsing reflects on the numbers of Angora goats in the last quarter of the century.

---

3 This author has conducted a general research examining the Angora goat economy and sheep economy in the same region within the framework of the Koç University, ERC-Starting Grant, 679097 UrbanOccupationsOETR project, yet unpublished.

Counting the Angora Goats in Ankara

Since its establishment, the Ottoman State has closely followed the dimensions of agricultural production and animal husbandry within the borders of the empire. Behind this was the motivation of collecting taxes and procurement of the capital's provisions. Especially sheep were the animals of great significance for Istanbul's meat consumption. From the 1780s until the mid-19th century, the meat of the city and the army was provided by a system called the "sheep tithe." The system was based on the obligation of sheep breeders in Rumelia to sell one tenth of their produce to the palace at the going rate. One result of this system consists of the livestock registers/censuses in the Ottoman archives (Uzun, 1997). The state and its representatives, on the other hand, were receiving taxes in kind (sometimes also in cash) at varying rates of sheep and goats during the early-modern period (Emecen, 1988).

The system changed as of the middle of the nineteenth century and replaced with a system that would provide the capital's meat requirement directly from the market. The tithe system was rescinded in favour of a goat tax in cash that covered the whole empire. Thus, taxable animals and by-products were counted on an annual basis to calculate tax amounts (Emecen, 1988).

Beyond tax issues, property problems in the second half of the century forced Ottoman rulers to set legal norms for ensuring animal ownership. For this purpose, in 1867, "the decree for the prohibition of theft of buffaloes and water buffaloes and asses and horses" was published. This decree was intended for the identification and supervision of individual animals by means of proprietary permits (Barakat, 2015, p 111). Other regulations designated marketplaces where livestock and goats were to be sold. Later, in 1904, a new tax regime forced Ottoman rulers to classify livestock and goat under the heading of "domesticated animals." All these developments show that animal censuses under scrutiny here and elsewhere are not static by nature. The classification of these censuses and their rationale and forms reflect the changes in the ideas of Ottoman rulers regarding animals and their ever-changing nature and functions. The change in the concepts that define and classify animals from livestock to domesticated animals was due to the change in value that Ottoman rulers attributed to the different species within different political-economic frameworks. Besides, the results obtained in the censuses were highly problematic. Breeders often tended to declare smaller numbers of animals, relocating some of their livestock to stockyards in other regions during the census or bribing the census officer. Moreover, in the process of converting the micro-data of the census to macro-data, plenty of errors were made in the calculations, with the resulting figures not quite related to reality (Bolton, 2007; İhsan Abidin, 1924).

For the analysis in this section, I used the domesticated animal records for the past 17 years in the 1907 Ankara yearbook (BOA, 1323/1907). For deficiencies or inconsistencies, I applied data that existed in the annals of those years.

In addition to the inconsistency problems, the data I have cited here for the H-GIS study also present the abovementioned problems. However, the following graphs I created to test the representation and reliability of the data show that the data correctly reflect the patterns of

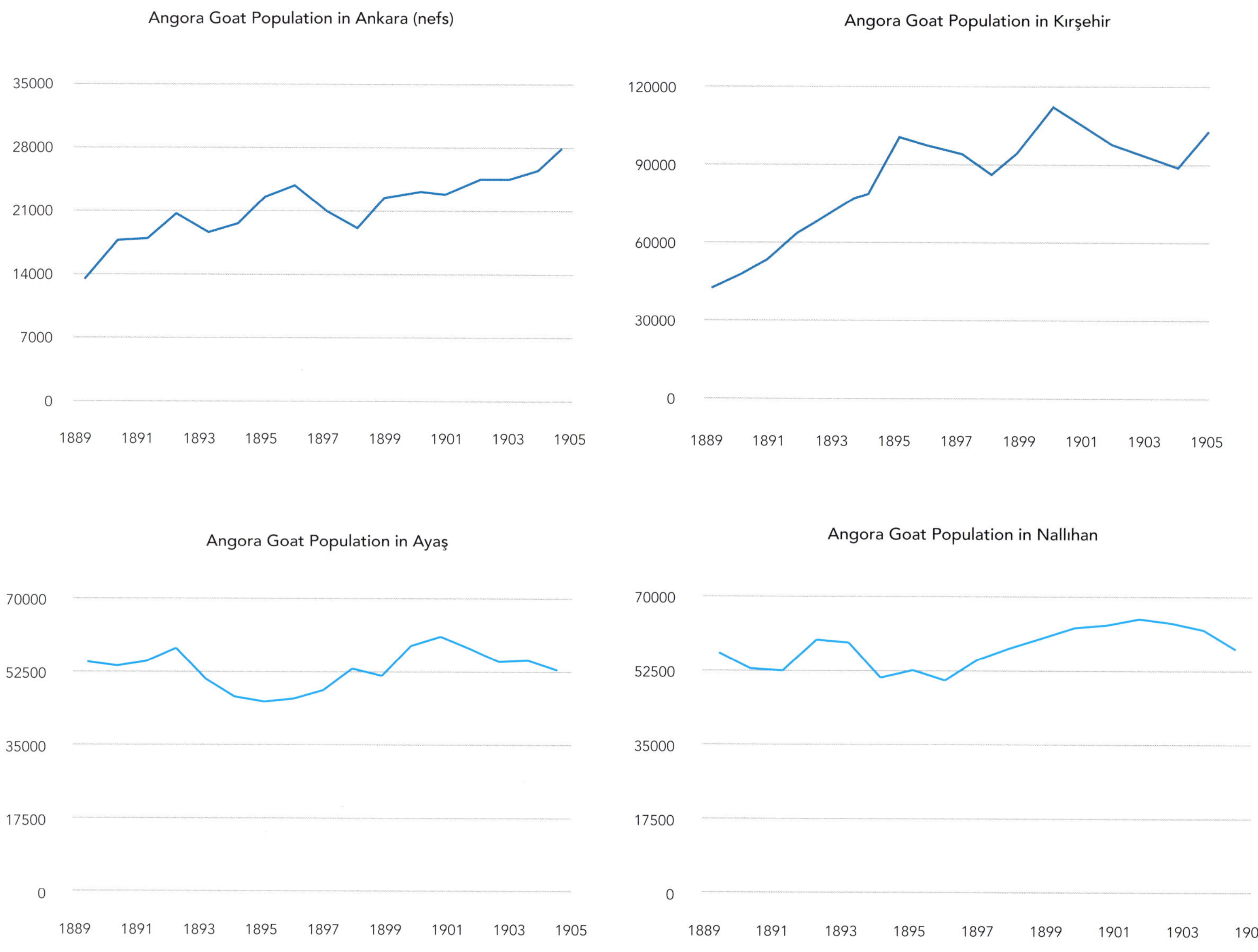

change of similarly structured spatial units, even though this data does not reflect actual figures (Graphic Set 1).

Although this article aims to go beyond them, it may be possible to reach meaningful conclusions about the economy of the Angora goat in the Ankara province by merely looking at the numbers. We can see in the table above that the relatively urban administrative centres such as Ankara and Kırşehir had increased Angora goat populations. Meanwhile predominantly rural areas such as Ayaş, Nallıhan and Beypazarı, where the larger section of the populace subsists on farming and animal husbandry, and historically the Angora goat is intensively bred, the number of goats remained fixed within a certain range. This becomes more visible post-1894, when the railway arrived in Ankara. Looking at the graphs, establishing a positive correlation between the increase in the population of Angora goats in the administrative centres and the decrease

Graphic Set 1. Change in Angora goat population in some Ankara districts (1889-1905). This was obtained by compiling the data in (1325/1907) of the Ankara Province Official Yearbook, a royalty-free source.

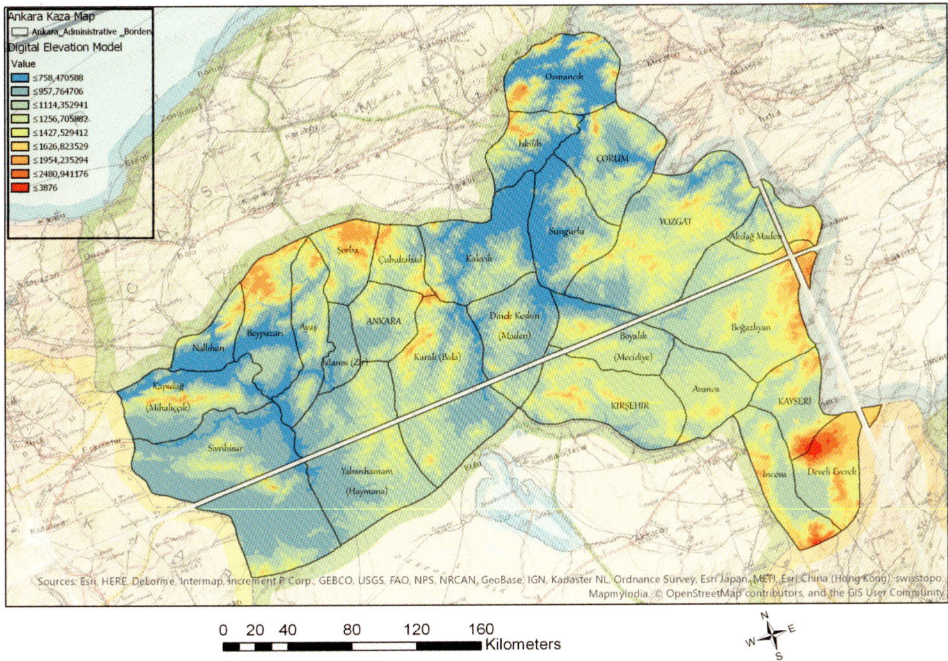

Map 1. The Ankara province's 1899 district boundaries and Angora goat habitats, based on the Digital Elevation Model (DEM). Geographical reference and analyses were carried out using ArcGIS PRO software, with reference to R. Huber, Empire Ottoman: Division Administration, 1899, dressée d'après le Salname 1899 map.

in provincial districts during 1892-1896 becomes possible. It may be speculated that this decrease in the regions where the agricultural production and livestock determined the economy is caused by the "migration" of the Angora goat to the administrative centres. The fact that the change in the goat population in some provincial districts not reflected in the graphs accounts for 50% of the population demonstrates, besides its significance of such activity, the vivacity and fluidity of the Angora goat economy. Looking merely at the numbers, although it allows all these interpretations, may lead at least partially to misleading results.

Estimating Angora Goat Density via Historical Geographic Information Systems (H-GIS) Tools

In addition to its characteristics as a species, the fact that the Angora goat's home range is limited by the climatic and geographical conditions compels us to go beyond census values in order to understand the Angora goat economy. During the period covered here, the Angora goat ideally bred at an altitude of about 800-1,200 metres. This necessitated that pens were built within this range, too (Ihsan Abidin, 1924, p 26, Cronwright Schreiner, 1898, pp. 66). While looking only at the numbers makes it possible to say that the Angora goat economy was sustainable at the end of the 19th century, adding altitude to our analysis will allow us a deeper look into the different aspects of this economy's change of direction. The following Angora goat density maps (Map Set 1) do not show merely the areas of goat numbers concentrated in a limited geographical area. Beyond that, and more importantly, they show the significance of systems and actors that would be otherwise marginally visible. The fact that the Angora goat is concentrated more in districts less favourable for breeding in comparison to those with areas that are more suitable demonstrates the insistence of breeders and other actors in maintaining this economy despite the lack of physical space in these districts. When the change in density of Angora goat numbers in the same district is compared with the change in the goat population, the existence of an organic economy that determined social and economic relations in spite of industrialization and urbanization is revealed.

The first step towards estimating the density of the Angora goat in the Ankara province was to find a map where we could geographically reference the administrative borders of the Ottoman state. The most suitable example for this was the map drawn by R. Huber in 1899. The map was appropriate for both the temporal and procedural purposes of this section, because Huber also had based his map on the 1899 annals. Once the Huber map is geographically referenced in real space, the next step was to input the administra-

DEM Angora Goat Density 1890

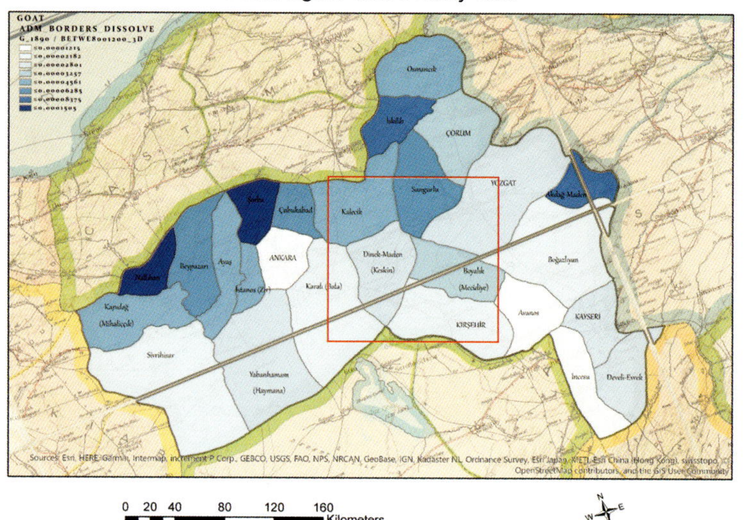

DEM Angora Goat Density 1893

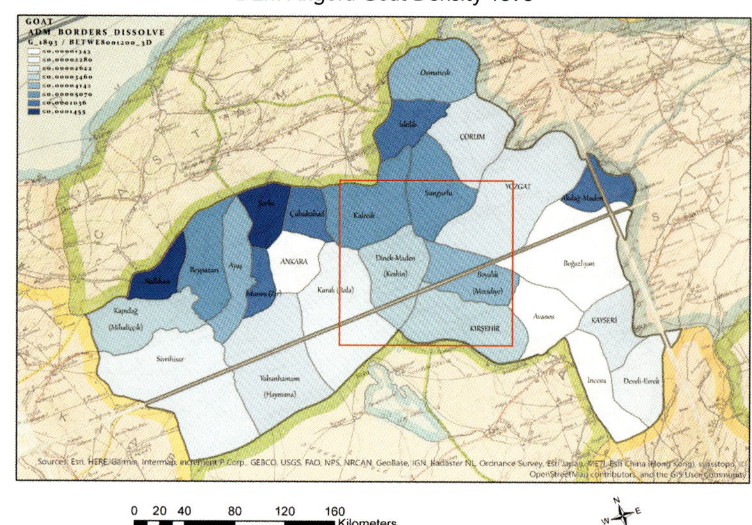

DEM Angora Goat Density 1895

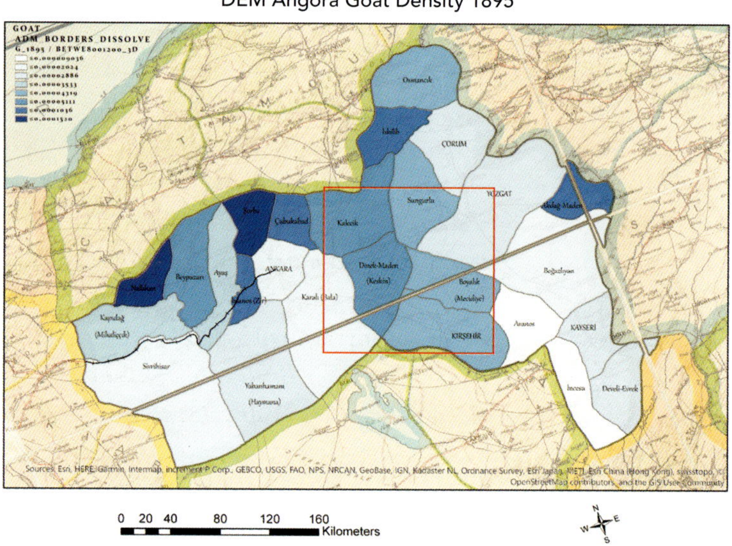

DEM Angora Goat Density 1898

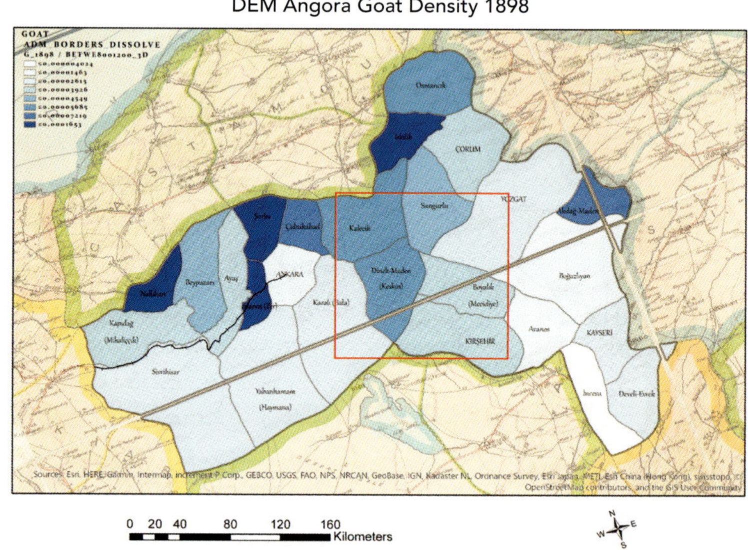

DEM Angora Goat Density 1901

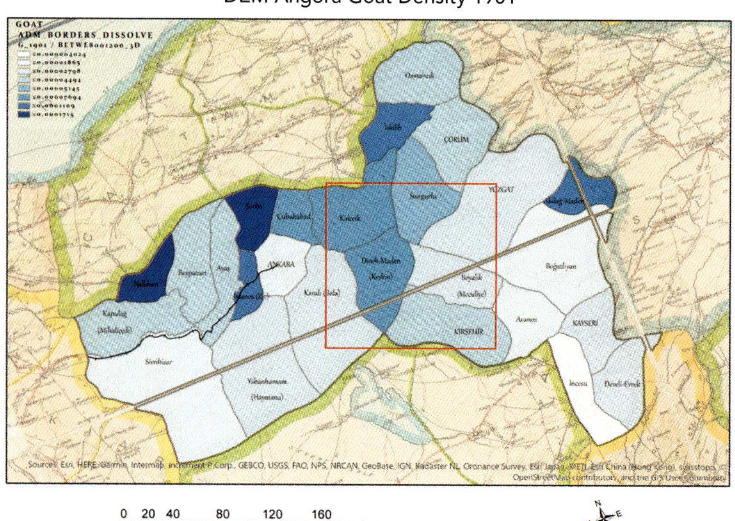

DEM Angora Goat Density 1904

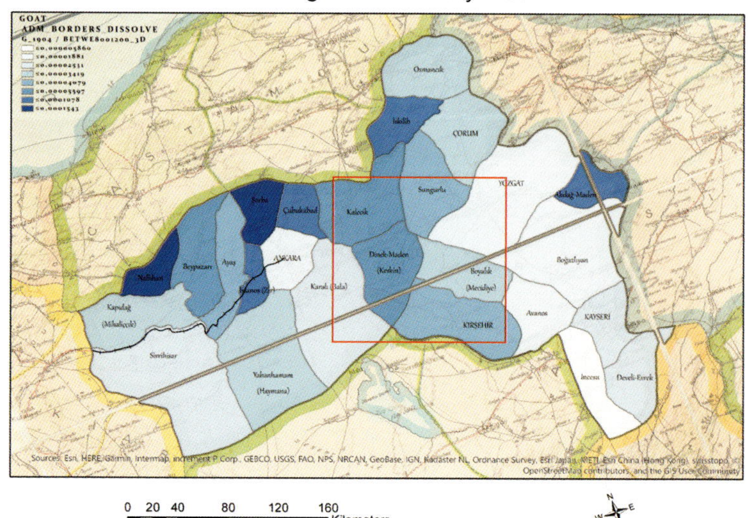

Map Set 1. Digital Elevation Model (DEM)-based Angora goat density maps in the Ankara province districts (1890-1893-1895-1898-1901-1904). Geographical reference and analyses were carried out using ArcGIS PRO software, with reference to R. Huber, Empire Ottoman: Division Administration, 1899, dressée d'après le Salname 1899 map.

tive boundaries into the ArcGIS software in the form of polygons to construct the two-dimensional geography of the Ankara province. Then the whole of these two-dimensional polygons was superimposed on the Digital Elevation Map (DEM) that contains the elevation data on modern Turkey's spatial references, and three-dimensional geographical areas of each district were calculated. The rivers and lakes were masked because these were outside the Angora goats' habitat. Thus, the ideal geographical area where the Angora goat can be bred in the Ankara province was mapped (Map 1).

Map 1 shows us the home ranges of Angora goats and neighbouring areas. Green areas represent elevations of 800-1,200 metres, the ideal home range of the Angora goat. We have assumed that the Angora goat did not breed in other areas in theory. Looking at this map, we see that the Angora goat habitat is particularly concentrated in the Sivrihisar, Yabanhamam and Bala districts, in the southern and southwestern regions.

The above maps (Map Set 1) allow us to carry our analysis to 3D space by superimposing the Angora goat census data on the Digital Elevation Model. Density maps suggest that the Angora goat economy moved towards the more limited (marked red) districts when compared to the Angora goat habitats in Map 1. Beyond this, we may also arrive from these maps at the following conclusions:

- In particular, with the advent of the railway in Ankara in 1894, it can be said that the economy of the Angora goat began to concentrate in the middle and southwestern districts in the province. Although our maps do not reflect the change of density of the goat in the Ankara district centre, it can be seen in the increase in the number of animals in the centre and in the goat density in the neighbouring districts. In this context, particularly the Kalecik, Mecidiye, Kırşehir and Denek-Maden districts stand out.
- These districts have "jammed" high numbers of goat populations in relatively smaller areas of land suitable for grazing and breeding Angora goats. Looking at the density maps, we can say that the development of the railway did not deepen the rural-urban divide, but rather facilitated an increase in the number of goats in towns with administrative centres by bringing pastures, goat pens, shearing tools and Angora goat breeders that make up the Angora goat economy closer to these areas.
- Maps of Angora goat populaces indicate that the climatic imperatives for sheltering, feeding and shearing of the stock play an important role also in determining the locations of human settlements. One can expect that human settlements in regions where the Angora goat economy is concentrated to appear in the same elevation range. Further research into human geography and their comparison with the geography of Ankara will tell us more on this (Yıldırım, 2006).
- It can be said on a macro-economic scale that the successful cross-fertilization of the Angora goat in the USA and South Africa, marginally influenced the Angora goat economy in Ankara over a 17-year period. Although in the US there were some 900,000 Angora goats in the 1900s, Ankara maintained the role of the main mohair supplier worldwide. Similarly, the British trade did not change much in volume although the British Empire found an inexpensive source for mohair by officially adding South Africa

to its colonies in 1902 (in the 1880s there were close to 1 million Angora goats in Cape Town). This reality of the Angora goat economy, that is, the sustainability of the economy becomes clearer from the following letter written by George Gatheral to S.C. Cronwright Schreiner (1898) in April 1897:

The mohair clip of Asia Minor has been for generations a kind of investment, and the entire stock of the staple is never thoroughly cleared out. We have a familiar proverb among the native dealers that Asia Minor is like an old flour sack, no matter how much you beat or shake it, you will always shake some dust out. (pp. 162-163)

It is possible to say that while the period examined is not long enough to allow us to make analyses on a macro-scale, we can safely say that the Angora goat economy maintained its vitality at a time when we could expect global demand for mohair and *sof* to decline.

• Just as many tools used to represent historical reality, H-GIS applications obscure more than they expose. There are also some issues here regarding analysis.

Although Ankara's goat economy was able to survive climatic anomalies (the agricultural crisis in the 1890s), the conjectural decline in global demand, and technological developments, what was the prevailing economy in the Ankara region for centuries was now being replaced by an economy based on cereal production and exports. With the establishment of the railway in 1894, grain exports exceeded mohair for the first time in history (Kaynar, 2016).[4] Of course, it is not possible to see this detail in Angora goat density maps at this point.

Similarly, climatic changes and changes in vegetation entail a deeper analysis. İhsan Abidin (1924), although not too clearly, suggests a positive correlation between the decline of the *sof* industry and Angora goat economy, and the deforestation of Central Anatolia (p. 26). Although we can see that the Angora goat survived during the 17 years observed in this analysis, more long-term studies should also take into consideration the changes in climate and vegetation cover.

• While this section has attempted a reassessment of the economics of the Angora goat within the historical framework, the method of applying it to resources can serve as a model for future studies. As Geoff Cunfer and colleagues (2006) have claimed, using the Historical Geographical Information Systems tools to position animals in time and space can give us the opportunity to conduct Long-Term Socio-Ecological Research (LTSER). From this perspective, other more extensive studies on different aspects of climate and geography, using different sources such as current animal censuses on the Angora goat, will enable historians, economists, climate scientists, zootechnics specialists and other experts in the field to join forces to analyse the past and the future of this unique species.

---

4 One of the reasons for this was the promotion of agricultural production to refugees from the Balkans and the Caucasus, who were placed in fertile areas along the railway line in the late 19th century.

References

Barakat, N. (2015). Marginal actors? The role of Bedouin in the Ottoman administration of animals as property in the district of salt, 1870-1912. *Journal of Economic and Social History of the Orient, 58*(1-2), 105-134.

Bolton, M. (2007). Counting llamas and accounting for people: livestock, land and citizens in southern Bolivia. *The Sociological Review, 55*(1), 5-21.

Clark, C. E. (1974). The Ottoman industrial revolution. *International Journal of Middle East Studies, 5*(1), 65-76.

Cronwright Schreiner, S. C. (1898). *The Angora goat and a paper on the Ostrich.* New York, NY: Longmans, Green, And Co.

Cunfer, G. *et al.* (2006). From LTER to LTSER: Conceptualizing the socioeconomic dimension of long-term socioecological research. *Ecology and Society, 11*(2), 13.

Çalışkan, K. (2007). "Markets and fields: An ethnography of cotton production and exchange in a Turkish village." *New Perspectives on Turkey, 37*(3), 115-145.

Emecen, F. (1988). Ağnam Resmi. In *TDV İslam Ansiklopedisi* (pp. 478-479). Vol. 1, İstanbul: Türkiye Diyanet Foundation.

Faroqhi, S. (1994) Mohair manufacture and mohair workshops in seventeenth-century Ankara. *İstanbul Üniversitesi İktisat Fakültesi Mecmuası. 41* (1-4), 211-236.

Faroqhi, S. (2010). Introduction. In S. Faroqhi (Prep. by) *Animals and people in the Ottoman Empire* (pp. 11-55). İstanbul: Eren.

Huber, R. (1899). *Empire Ottoman: Division Administration, 1899, dressée d'après le Salname 1899.* F. Loeffler.

Ihsan Abidin [Akıncı]. (1340/1924). *Ankara keçisinin hâli ve ıslahı.* İstanbul: Vatan Matbaası.

Kadı, İ. H. (2012). *Ottoman and Dutch merchants in the eighteenth century: competition and cooperation in Ankara, Izmir, and Amsterdam.* Leiden: Brill.

Kasaba, R. (1988). *The Ottoman Empire and the world economy.* New York, NY: SUNY Press.

Kaynar, İ. S. (2016). *Engürü'den Ankara'ya: 1892-1962 arasında Ankara'nın iktisadi değişimi.* (Unpublished PhD Thesis). Marmara University, İstanbul.

Keskin, Ö. (2010). Osmanlı İmparatorluğu'nda modern ziarat eğitiminin yaygınlaşması: Ankara numune tarlası ve çoban mektebi. *Osmanlı Tarihi Araştırma ve Uygulama Merkezi Dergisi OTAM, 28* (28), 87-106.

Lewis, B. (1958). Some reflections on the decline of the Ottoman Empire. *Studia Islamica, 9*, 111–127.

Mikhail, A. (2013). *The animal in Ottoman Egypt.* Oxford: Oxford University Press.

Oyal, Ö. F. (2013). *Keçi, zanlı, kurban, cefakâr.* İstanbul: Yapı Kredi Yayınları.

Planhol, X. (1975-1977). Rayonnement urbaine et selection animale: une solution nouvelle du probleme de chevre d'Angora. *Bulletin de la Section de Geographie, Etudes de Geographie Historique 82*, 179-196.

Şahin, G. (2013). Türkiye'de Ankara keçisi (Capra hircus ancryrensis) yetiştiriciliğinin dünü bugünü ve yarını. *CBÜ Sosyal Bilimler Dergisi, 11* (2), 338-352.

Quataert, D. (1975). The Agricultural Bank and agricultural reform in Ottoman Turkey, 1888-1908. *International Journal of Middle East Studies, 6*(2), 210-227.

Tabib Hayrullah. (1264/1848). *Fenn-i ziraatten beyt-i dehkani.* İstanbul.

Tamur, E. (2003). *Ankara keçisi ve Ankara tiftik dokumacılığı: Tükenen bir zenginliğin ve çöken bir sanayinin tarihsel öyküsünden kesitler.* Ankara: Ankara Ticaret Odası Yayınları.

Tan, S. (2014). XIX. Yüzyılda Anadolu'dan Güney Afrika'ya tiftik keçisinin yasal ve kaçak sevkiyatı. *Osmanlı Tarih Araştırma ve Uygulama Merkezi Dergisi OTAM*, 35 (35), 137-152.

T. C. Başbakanlık Osmanlı Arşivi (BOA). (1290/1874). HR.I.3 419/25.

T. C. Başbakanlık Osmanlı Arşivi (BOA). (1311/1895). SD. 1536/21.

T. C. Başbakanlık Osmanlı Arşivi (BOA). (1323/1905). DH.MKT.882 /42.

Uzun, A. (1997). İstanbul'un *et ihtiyacının sağlanması: ondalık ağnam uygulaması (1738-1858).* (Ph. D. thesis). Istanbul University, Istanbul.

Yıldırım, B. E. (2006). *Ankara Sancağı'nın tarihi coğrafya bakımından yerleşme ve nüfusu (1871-1907).* (Unpublished Master's Thesis). Ankara University, Ankara.

Wrigley, E. A. (2016). *The path to sustained growth: England's transition from an organic economy to an industrial revolution.* Cambridge: Cambridge University Press.

View of Ankara: The Story of A Painting

FEYZA AKDER
Koç University Faculty of Humanities, Department of Archaeology and Art History

The 18th century saw a proliferation of various perceptions that embraced cultural differences, rather than othering different cultures. One of these was *Turquerie*, which involved the use of various aspects of Ottoman culture in visual, literary and architectural works. At the same time, eastern countries sought various solutions to meet the demands of the political and commercial relations that emerged from Europe's view of different cultures, and their adaptation to and interaction with them. The trade race that England, France, Holland and Denmark ran to the far corners of the world influenced these developments, and many people travelled east. These travellers' letters, their memoirs and travelogues, such as French botanist Joseph Pitton de Tournefort's travel writings, were met with much interest and considered reliable sources (Avcıoğlu and Flood, 2010, pp. 8, 9, 11). The "Turkish" imagery, depicted by Europeans such as the French painter Jean Baptiste Vanmour who came to Istanbul with the French diplomatic mission and spent his entire life there, was known in that context.[1] Cornelis Calkoen, Dutch Ambassador to Istanbul from 1727 to 1744, was among the people who created such collections. The *Rijksmuseum View of Ankara* (Figure 1), together with Vanmour's paintings, has reached our day as part of the Calkoen collection called the *Vanmour Series*.[2]

The Western artists who came to the Ottoman Empire in the 18th century were embassy officials and their families. These artists favoured subjects such as the silhouette of the historical peninsula, harbours, the shores of the Bosporus and its villages, the city's great mosques and archaeological remains, the bazaars, the fountains, the mosque courts, coffee houses and the resorts. However, Anatolia, and by extension Ankara, perceived as Eastern Turkish rather than Arabic, were rarely taken up by Western artists (Germaner and İnankur, 2008, pp. 22, 36, 202).

---

1 Jean Baptiste Vanmour (1671-1737) was born in Valenciennes. There is not much information about his art education prior to coming to Istanbul. He arrived in the city under the patronage of the French Ambassador and died there in 1737. Vanmour's most significant achievement is a series of paintings preserved as the legacy of [Dutch envoy] Cornelis Calkoen in the Rijksmuseum, which portray daily lives of Turks. However, Vanmour also produced an album which depicted the attire of not only the Turks, but also those of people of various creeds living in other regions such as Greece, Hungary and Wallachia. The artist probably worked in a large workshop, with apprentices selected from the Greek community for their experience in icon painting. Most researchers believe that Vanmour met Cornelis Calkoen, who is known to have purchased 64 of his paintings (Bull, 2003, pp. 25-29).

2 The painting registered as *Gezicht op Ankara / View of Ankara* in the Rijksmuseum Collection is referred to as the *Rijksmuseum View of Ankara* in this article.

Travels to Istanbul and the Arabian East resulted in many literary, musical, architectural and artistic works. However, fewer works appear to have emerged from voyages to Ankara. The most noteworthy of these are travelogues. In fact, the only oil painting of Ankara painted in that century is the *View of Ankara* at the Rijksmuesum today. We do not know who the painter was or when the painting was made. We will be arguing, contrary to previous studies on this painting, that the painting possesses a dominant cartographic language, and that this is related to the European city atlases. Similarly, it will be shown that the artist used classifications that everyone can understand in an attempt to provide detailed and accurate information about 18th century Ankara.

There are many other questions that we seek to answer. For example, the artist's identity would have told us how he or she interpreted and reflected the scenes he or she saw. We may be able to get a better understanding of the reality of 18th century Ankara, and thereby judge the accuracy of the information provided by the painting. In addition, as far as we know, this is the only oil painting of Ankara dated to the 18th century. Most Ottoman landscapes covered Istanbul. Who would have had gone and painted a picture of Ankara? At the time, Ankara was a rather strange choice as a subject. This makes the work even more interesting in terms of art history.

The painting's 20th-century adventure began when it was included into the Rijksmuseum collection in 1902. Then, it was recorded in the museum registry as *A View of Aleppo*. Sixty-eight years later, art historian Semavi Eyice saw a reproduction of the painting in the book *De "Turkse" schilderijen van J.B. Vanmour en zijnschool, De Verzameling van Cornelis Calkoen, ambassadeur bij de Hoge Porte,* written by Remmet Van Luttervelt and detected some inconsistencies: "The city of Aleppo has a diverse ambience, but this cannot be found in the *View of Ankara*. The second point that differs the view from Aleppo is the Angora goats located at the lower right corner, as Angora goats cannot survive in Aleppo's climate." In addition, the fact that the architectural structures depicted in the painting matched Ankara buildings established that this, indeed, was a *View of Ankara* (Eyice, 1972, p. 99).

The painting is a document of Ankara's architecture, city plan and social and commercial life. Most significantly, it deals with the mohair trade that almost single-handedly made Ankara and its region a wealthy area between the 16th- and 18th centuries. Eyice's discovery attracted the attention of urban history researchers and the painting took its place in many studies as a valuable source for its visual information, as no other document exists that visualizes 18th century Ankara and its inhabitants in such detail.

The *Rijksmuseum View of Ankara* deals with the general view of the city and the mohair market at the bottom part of the painting. The city has been depicted against a dark sky, with adjacent houses behind the fortifications, and white minarets interspersed between them. It is difficult to know what season has been portrayed. We can infer that it may be springtime, because the Angora goats appear to be ready for shearing. The city's layout is not some distant silhouette. Rather, the city's chief architectural structures have been clearly depicted. For example, the windows of the *Mahmut Paşa Bedesten*,[3] the sole ten-dome

3 Bedesten is a covered bazaar.

Figure 1. Anonymous, *Rijksmuseum View of Ankara*, 117x198 cm, oil on canvas, 1700-1799, Inventory no: SK-A-2055, Rijksmuseum, Amsterdam.

structure at the top left, or the *filgözü*[4] of the baths are visible. The midsection of the painting shows three companies of travellers on the roads emerging out of the city, and two streams of water flowing by. At the bottom is a marketplace scene, depicted at the foreground. The market expands from the merging of the streets extending from both sides of the single mosque at the bottom of the painting. There are nearly 150 people in the market. Outside, at the bottom right corner of the painting, are the goat shepherds and the herd of Angora goats. Very few colours appear to have been used in the picture, mostly tones of brown, black, red and white. The light is shimmering over the city, as if the sun was rising from the lower right corner. The walls of the houses facing this side are illuminated, and the rest remain dark. The light around the city leads towards the horizon, revealing the roughness of the land. The sky is quite dark. Transitions between light and shaded areas are sharp, resulting in a crisp image. In the market scene on the lower left of the painting, the one-storey shops are the darkest areas, but the vendors inside the shops are well-lit, as if stripped of their shadows. The short shadows of the figures found in the pavilion extend slightly to the upper left. There are more women than there are men at the very lively marketplace.

Contemplating the painting's composition and comparing it to other paintings and engravings printed in books of the same period is a useful window on the painting. It is very difficult to associate the composition of the *Rijksmuseum View of Ankara* with 18th-century European landscape paintings. From the 17th century onward, a new understanding of space had emerged in European landscape painting. This involved the reconstruction of space based on observation. This understanding had

4 *Filgözü*-elephant's eyes are small, star-shaped windows across the dome of a Turkish bath's sıcaklık section (room with hot bath) that enable the seepage of sunlight at all hours of the day.

brought about innovations such as the *camera obscura*[5] and depictions of sky (Clark, 1952, pp. 16-20).

However, the construction of the space and the use of light in the *Rijksmuseum View of Ankara*, probably painted in the 18th century, are different from 18th-century European paintings. Firstly, the market on the lower left corner of the picture is a set-scene created by the painter, as if highlighting a section of the city. In this way, the continuity of the landscape is cut off. Secondly, the sharpness is virtually the same at every point, whereas the human eye does not perceive nature in this way. The contours of receding or distant objects become obscured, their colours lose their vibrancy, and after a while, the human eye is unable to perceive details. However, in the *Rijksmuseum View of Ankara*, the colours and shapes of the trees beneath *Hıdırlık* Hill, just behind the ramparts, are distinctive. Therefore, references to distance and proximity are unclear. Thirdly, the city walls were painted much higher than they were, so that the entire city and the marketplace could be seen. The minarets of the mosques were also depicted very high, to attract attention, and the floors of the shops in the marketplace are shown from different aspects. All of these considerations lead us to question the picture's perspective. Indeed, the very idea of perspective involves the question of how three-dimensional objects may be placed on two dimensions.

5 Camera obscura: from Latin, meaning "dark room": camera "(vaulted) chamber or room," and obscura "darkened, dark"), an optical phenomenon that occurs when an image of a scene at the other side of a screen (or for instance a wall) is projected through a small hole in that screen as a reversed and inverted image on a surface opposite the opening.

Most books on art history speak of perspective as a development, a skill, a problem that artists have progressed through by combining their experiences over the centuries. If the perspective in a painting does not conform to the rules of linear perspective that were becoming more and more important in European painting towards the end of the Renaissance, this would indicate a lack of training, or incompetence. Because the art of painting has evolved for the better with this understanding of perspective. Erwin Panofsky, however, considers perspective not as an evolutionary development but as a symbolic form. Panofksy (1991) explains that perspective, which he describes as a matter of opinion can be established in more than one way, and that these differences are not a measure of competence, but choice:

But if perspective is not a factor of value, it is surely a factor of style. Indeed, it may even be characterized (to extend Ernst Cassirer's felicitous term to the history of art) as one of those "symbolic forms" in which "spiritual meaning is attached to a concrete, material sign and intrinsically given to this sign." This is why it is essential to ask of artistic periods and regions not only whether they have perspective, but also which perspective they have (p. 40).

Panofsky argued that perspective is a form of thinking and problem solving to reproduce the landscape on canvas, wall or paper, as a result of collected experiences of art history. Perspective has changed with the changes in cognizance of space and the idea of landscape with the philosophy of the First Age, Scholastic thought and the Enlightenment. In a nutshell, the lifestyles of societies have changed individuals' lives, their perception of the world, and the perspectives they used. Therefore, we may be able to get a little closer to the reality of the painting by examining the *Rijksmuseum View of Ankara* not by our aesthetic judgments, but by paying attention to the features that the painting seems to communicate.

The perspective of the *Rijksmuseum View of Ankara* has not been fixed to a focal point on the horizon. That is, linear perspective, considered "correct" since the Renaissance, was not applied. If it had been, the painting's integrity would have felt different, but this much detail could not have been covered. According to Panofsky (1991), "perspective is by nature a double-edged sword" (p. 67): in other words, it is not possible to draw the way that human beings perceive and at the same time show all the details as they are in the *Rijksmuseum View of Ankara*. One must choose between the two. Nevertheless, having already chosen an unconventional subject, what could be the painter's purpose in painting it in an even less conventional way? Could it really be that the painter was unable to use linear perspective because he or she was not trained in it, or even more dramatically, simply incapable in spite of his training? Perhaps what we are encounter today is a bit of heart-breaking whimsy. However, progress from this interpretation onwards is problematic. Worse still, such a claim also blights the credibility of the information visualized in the painting. For this reason, we may rely on the painter's artistic abilities and assume that the painter preferred to show all the details for a reason. It is also worth noting that the precarious intercultural interactions of the 18th century encouraged a different aesthetic and approach. Therefore, it is possible that the painter was working to order.

When we study the composition and the choice of perspective employed in *Rijksmuseum View of Ankara* against the European city view drawings that had been developing since the 16th century we may be able to make some assumptions as to why and how it was painted. City atlases were made to depict European cities in the 16th century. Such atlases featured city views, information about the city, etc. These drawings were usually bird's-eye views, emphasizing city boundaries. Features of the surrounding land (woodland, agricultural and mountainous areas etc.) were added, city gates were indicated, roads to and from the city were shown with human figures walking on them, and important buildings like the local parish, etc. were drawn more distinctly than others.

City drawings took the form of an atlas with Abraham Ortelius, a Dutch cartographer and geographer. Ortelius drew the first atlas, the 53-page *Theatrum Orbis Terrarum,* in Antwerp in 1570.[6] The purpose of the Atlas was to publish maps of the world's cities. The Atlas consisted of bird's-eye plans and views of the cities. Georg Braun, a geographer and topographer from Cologne, who helped Ortelius with the *Theatrum Orbis Terrarum,* later contributed by developing local features such as costumes, production, etc. (Rees, 1980, p. 64). The language of cartography, which includes city views, continued to evolve over successive centuries. Information on costumes, work force and local folk traditions were visualized in Dutch maps of the 16th century. In the 17th century, shortly after Europe began

---

6 While Ortelius drew the maps of the Atlas, Frans Hogenberg created the engravings. Hogenberg, influenced by Ortelius, decided to make an atlas on major cities in Cologne and started working with Georg Braun. Recruiting Simon van den Neuvel, the group published a city atlas titled *Civitates Orbis Terrarum* in 1572 (Keuning, 1963, p. 41).

to conduct systematic and metrological cartographic field studies, landscape-sketching techniques became very useful for scientists, engineers and natural scientists. These methods continued to be used in 18th century England in ordnance cartography education (Rees, 1980, p. 63)

We may take the engraving *Tivoli* (Figure 2), dated 1578 as an example of Abraham Ortelius' city-views. While the general view is at the upper section of the engraving, information about the city is presented in the cartouche at the lower left corner, and a detail that is not visible in the general view has been enlarged and shown in the plate at the lower right corner. There are people walking on the roads to the city. Prominent structures of the city have been accentuated out of the cluster of buildings. These features are also found in the 18th century *Rijksmuseum View of Ankara*. A second relevant example is the *View of Ankara* drawn by Claude Aubriet in Ankara, in 1702 (Figure 3).

The earliest depiction of Ankara with a date (as far as we know) and artist's name in the 18th century, was created when Claude Aubriet, a painter who specialized in botanical drawings, and famous French botanist Joseph Pitton de Tournefort arrived in Anatolia in 1700-1702. This engraving must have been created in 1702. It was published in 1717 in Tournefort's travelogue (Tournefort, 1717, pp. 442, 452, 464). Aubriet's *View of Ankara* uses the cartographic language mentioned earlier.

Tournefort was an eminent scientist, celebrated for his book *Eléments de Botanique*, an account of his studies of the European and Mediterranean coasts, published in 1694. While working on *Eléments de Botanique*, Aubriet was the principle artist of the book. At the time, Aubriet was working on his drawings at the Royal Collection of France. Six years after the publication of the book, Tournefort proposed to Aubriet that he join him for an expedition trip to the East. Alongside the two was also a German botanist and physician named Andreas von Gundelsheimer. In addition to teaching at the Tournefort's Academy, which was the main objective of the Anatolian journey, he had been adding new species to the plant collection of the *Jardin du Roi* (Royal Garden). Tournefort's team set out on a journey to the East to explore the Aegean Islands, Istanbul, Anatolian cities and Georgia to study natural history, antique and contemporary geography, and trade

2

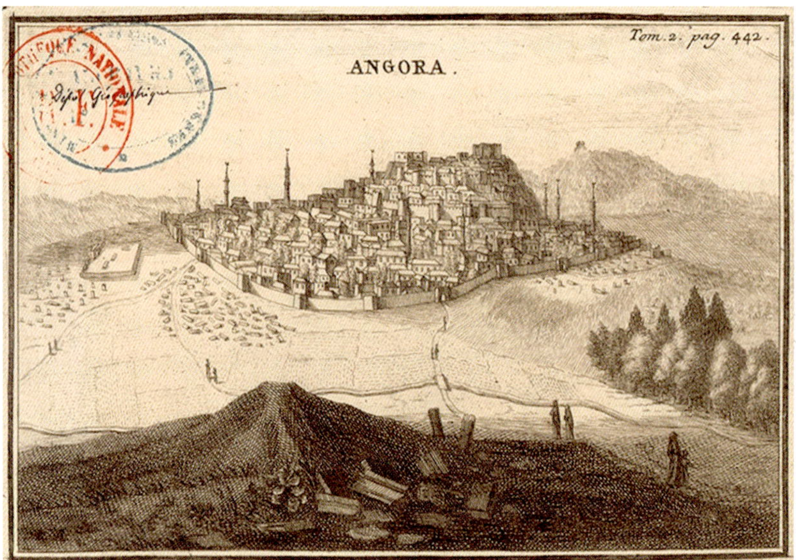

3

Figure 2. Abraham Ortelius (draughtsman), Joris Hoefnagel (engraver), Georg Braun (writer), Frans Hogenberg (writer), *Tiburtum vulgo Tivoli*, 1578, 36.5 x 48.5 cm, engraving, Bibliothèque nationale de France, département Cartes et plans, CPL GE DD-2987 (5455).

Figure 3. Claude Aubreit, *Ankara (Angora)*, 1717 (printed), 13x18 cm, Engraving, 10x15 cm, Bibliothèque nationale de France, département Cartes et plans, GE DD-2987 (6558).

4

5

Figure 4. Anonymous, *View of Ankara* – detail, 1700-1799, 117x198 cm, oil on canvas, Inventory no. SK-A-2055, Rijksmuseum, Amsterdam.

Figure 5. Claude Aubreit *Ankara (Angora)*-detail, 1717 (edition), 13x18 cm, Engraving, 10x15 cm, Bibliothèque nationale de France, département Cartes et plans, GE DD-2987 (6558).

and religion, between 1700 and 1702 (Speake, 2013, p. 1188). Tournefort's travelogue, published upon his return journey, was received with great acclaim, and came to be used as a reference source for architectural studies conducted in Europe within the scope of *Turquerie* (Avcıoğlu, 2012, pp. 48, 202).

As a scientist, Tournefort needed a professional draughtsman because accurate and systematic drawings were required to document plants or minerals. Many Turkish sources cite or imply that Tournefort was the creator of the *View of Ankara* and the *Angora goat* (Figure 28), but this is incorrect. *Bibliotèque nationale de France* records also confirm that that was Aubriet.[7]

Aubriet came to Ankara with this expedition team on 22 October 1702, and then left the city to travel to Bursa on 2 November 1702 (Tournefort, 1717, pp. 442, 452, 464). He worked most probably with the botanist while drawing. Throughout the journey, Aubriet painted the plants, landscapes, antique remains and local attire wherever they went. Aubriet returned to France earlier, when he became ill during the last year of the journey, but not before he had made botanical drawings with robust contours and clear forms, which some art historians believe represent a style derived from the medieval illustration tradition (Blunt and Stearn, 1994, pp. 113-115).

Aubriet's *Ankara* is a general view of the city. Virtually all of the engravings Aubriet created for Tournefort's travelogue show the city in the middle of the paper, drawn from a bird's-eye- view. The roads leading to the city, the city gates, and the walls are distinct. There are people moving on the roads to the city. Prominent architectural structures have been accentuated out of the cluster of buildings. All of these elements have been used in the same way in the *Rijksmuseum View of Ankara*.

Aubriet's engraving and the *Rijksmuseum View of Ankara* greatly resemble each other when studied in detail, because they use the same language: the ramparts that demarcate the city's borders, the gates used for entrance to and exit from the city, the roads leading to the city, and the prominent architectural structures within the city all have been highlighted separately. Both Ankara views are symmetrical along an axis drawn through the *Hıdırlık* Hill. In the *Rijksmuseum View of Ankara*, *Hıdırlık* is the hill that appears next to the ramparts at the upper left of the painting, while in Aubriet's *View of Ankara*, it is the crosshatched hill on the upper right part of the engraving.

In that case, the Rijksmuseum painter may have used the perspective and composition in this way to create, perhaps to order, a picture similar to the cityscapes

7 Accessed from http://gallica.bnf.fr/ark:/12148/btv1b23005662?rk=128756;0

Figure 6. Anonymous, *Hochepied Reception Ceremony and View of İzmir*, oil on canvas, 155.5 x 243.5 cm, Invertory no. SK-A-4085, Rijksmuseum, Amsterdam.

appearing as of the 16th century. It is hard to imagine that the *Rijksmuseum View of Ankara* oil painting was the first such view of Ankara. It would not be surprising to find one or more preliminary studies, both as an 18th century painting, and for such a detailed and large canvas in general. The *Rijksmuseum View of Ankara* may have been transferred on to the canvas after it was first conceived on paper. Unfortunately, we have not come across a painting (except for Aubriet's drawing), neither in Ankara nor in the archives that could have been the sources of the drawing erroneously called Aleppo.

The *Hochepied Reception Ceremony and View of Izmir* (Figure 6) also features similarities in composition and subject with the *Rijksmuseum View of Ankara* (Figure 1). In addition, just like the *Rijksmuseum View of Ankara, the Hochepied Reception Ceremony and View of Izmir* was a part of the *Vanmour Series* painting collection, which was transported to the Netherlands upon the death of Calkoen, and passed on to Rijksmuseum in 1902. Remmet van Luttervelt has written about this in detail[8]. It is also unknown who painted the *View of Izmir*, or when. This painting also depicts Izmir from a birds-eye-view. The entrance and exit points of the city and its borders have been delineated, and prominent buildings in the city are highlighted against the others. We know more about this picture is than we do the *Rijksmuseum View of Ankara*, because the welcome ceremony in the lower right corner of the picture is a well-documented event. Baron Daniël Jan de Hochepied, the Dutch envoy to Izmir, arrived in the

8 On the other hand Eveline Sint-Nicolaas (personal communication, July 31, 2018) states that "View of Ankara and View of İzmir were part of the collection of the Directorate of Levantine Trade, as was the Calkoen collection, but their provenance must have been different".

city in 1696 (Luttervelt, 1958, p. 35). Luttervelt assumes that a person from the "painting school" of the city of Izmir was the painter. In fact, the way Izmir was drawn is the same as an engraving made by Du Mont in 1699, and the painter had merely added the lower reception hall to the engraving. The types and clothes there also represent the 18th century (Luttervelt, 1958, p.36). In fact, we may even state that the cultural encounters we have been describing since the beginning of this paper are present on the canvas: the stylization of the clouds, the cartographic view of the city and the composition of the pavilion on the lower right corner of the table bear traces of different cultures.

The first noticeable difference in style between the Izmir painting and the Ankara painting is in the sky. The shape of the clouds in the Izmir painting is conspicuously reminiscent of the cloud stylizations used in [Turkish] miniature art. The clouds have been shaped in the form of spirals with extending, pointed tips. The colours used in this painting are also limited.

Luttervelt studied the Izmir and Ankara cityscapes while examining the Rijksmuseum collection of Cornelis Calkoen, Dutch Ambassador to Istanbul from 1727 to 1743. Calkoen bought a large number of the paintings of Jean-Baptiste Vanmour, who lived in Istanbul in the same years as himself, and who had been painting the lives, the attire, and court ceremonies of the Turks. After Calkoen's death, the collection of paintings first went to Levantsche Handel, then to the Ethnography Museum in Leiden, and finally to the Rijksmuseum in 1902 (Luttervelt, 1958, pp. 1-7). Luttervelt deals with the Ankara view very briefly. His focus is on the Vanmour paintings in Calkoen's *Vanmour Series* collection. The author notes that the reason for sending the *Rijksmuseum View of Ankara* to the Netherlands was unclear: perhaps it was painted during the Near East journeys of the envoy (Luttervelt, 1958, p. 39). The painting was recorded in the collection as the *View of Aleppo*, which Luttervelt accepted as such. According to Luttervelt, the painting was illustrative and primitive, and anecdotal. That is, the painting attempted to present a particular event simply by specifying its main characteristics. The use of light and shadow, perspective and colour was different from 18th century European art, and a series of interrelated small-scale scenes were seen in the picture. The painter had chosen a birds-eye point of view, so he or she could easily show the buildings and the market scene in front of the picture. This is a feature of Byzantine art. Therefore, the painter might have been an Izmir Greek who knew Byzantine art[9]

---

9 Byzantine art is the name given usually to artworks created in Eastern Roman (Byzantine) Empire and in countries that inherit this empire's culture. Although the empire was overthrown with the conquest of Istanbul in 1453, many Orthodox countries in Eastern Europe and Muslim countries on the Mediterranean coast continued for many centuries to create artefacts bearing Byzantine influences. Among these, icon paintings and church architecture first come to mind. This style is characterized by the artistic expression of the theological ideas of the church. For example, the sizes of the people in the works are determined by the rank they have been ascribed in the Bible. The various symbols are again resolved by references to the Bible. After the collapse of the Eastern Roman Empire, the Byzantine influence was felt in European art until the 13th and 14th centuries, especially in the Sienese School of painting and Gothic style. Luttervelt means by his statement that the artist who created the painting may have had a close understanding of Byzantine art was

intimately and in fact, worked in that style (Luttervelt, 1958, p. 39). Luttervelt covers the *View of Izmir* more broadly, but arrives at the same conclusion as he does with the *View of Ankara* regarding the cultural sources of the painting.

But the tradition Luttervelt called the Byzantine influence, which the Greek community in the Muslim countries carried forward after the collapse of the Byzantine Empire in Eastern Rome, can be detected in Sienese, Venetian and northern European illustrations as of the 13th century. Indeed, Aubriet's understanding of drawing were assessed this way. Greek Orthodox drawings and medieval illustrative techniques share their roots in the Byzantine influence. These are the traces of a cultural interaction, which appeared in Ankara in the 18th century, but had occurred long before.

Erman Tamur is another researcher who, after Luttervelt and Eyice, examined how the painting may have been painted. Tamur, in his article titled *A Painting of Ankara in Amsterdam*, offers a somewhat different and elaborate account as to where and how the painting may have been painted. *Levantsche Handel* was a Dutch company that traded with the Ottoman Empire in the 18th century. For many years, the *Rijksmuseum View of Ankara* was in the Levantsche Handel headquarters at the Dam Square in Amsterdam (Tamur, 2003, p. 29). According to Tamur, the fact that the company owned a painting related to the mohair trade indicates its regional mohair connection. Additionally, there must be a relationship with Vanmour as the painting is part of the *Vanmour Series*. However, the painting is different from Vanmour's compositions. So, according to Tamur, in the 18th century, one (or more) of Vanmour's apprentices, who worked in a workshop in Istanbul, were dispatched to Ankara upon the request of Levantsche Handel and created sketches for the painting; while a different artist, in Istanbul or in Holland, composed the *View of Ankara* using these sketches (Tamur, 2008, pp. 25-26). Eyice (1972), however, believes that the painter was a Dutch subject with modest ability: he or she studied Ankara from the distance and drafted some sketches. They also created some drawings that very closely represented the city and its trade and industry life, and then went back to their country, where he or she brought these together on a canvas (page 115). All three researchers of the *Rijksmuseum View of Ankara* are sceptical about the painter's skills (Luttervelt, 1958, pp. 42-43, Eyice, 1972, p. 104, Tamur, 2003, p. 26).

The three researchers endeavoured to detect the provenance of the work: who painted it, and who ordered it, to what purpose. According to Luttervelt, the painter was probably a Greek from Izmir's Orthodox Christian community. Tamur and Luttervelt have noted that this member of the Orthodox community may have worked at Vanmour's workshop in Istanbul. Eyice believes that the painter must be Dutch. The *Rijksmuseum View of Ankara* is more likely to have been created by someone familiar with this tradition originating from Europe, given the relation of the painting with the cartography. Because the composition of the work, the style of expression and general tendencies indicate the cartographic tradition. The influence of the Byzantine

---

that he must have been a member of the Greek Orthodox community living in the dynastic Muslim Ottoman Empire, and he must have been closely acquainted with church architecture and iconography.

painting traditions on the Orthodox community and Vanmour's painting of Istanbul are the possibilities offered by the general conditions of the 18th century. However, the cartographic tradition refers to a more precise point, as it has originated from the composition of the painting. Vanmour may have portrayed Istanbul and may have worked with his apprentices from the Greek Orthodox community in that city (Bull, 2003, pp. 25-29). This is based on the presumption that an apprentice painter had learned to paint with Vanmour but was unable to apply linear perspective successfully. The landscapes Aubriet created during the same period as the painting indicate that this presumption is not the only option. Aubriet had stayed in Ankara for only two weeks and working with Tournefort, created a drawing very similar in composition to the *Rijksmuseum View of Ankara*. Thus, the *Rijksmuseum View of Ankara* offers us the possibility that the painting was created by a painter who implemented cartographic city views and recognized the European tradition.

Could the painter have based his composition on a drawing like Aubriet's, and added the market scene in the lower left corner of the table? Luttervelt has suggested this possibility when discussing the *Hochepied Reception Ceremony and View of Izmir*. In which case, we need to consider two painters. One of the two painters completed the painting in this way who was an apprentice at Vanmour's studio and who painted the *View of Ankara* appropriately for cartography and was a member of the Greek Orthodox community. The other painter who composed the painting, and was influenced by this European practice. All of these arguments suggest that the artist who created the composition of the painting was either European, or had been trained in Europe.

If we focus on the *Rijksmuseum View of Ankara* once again, once we have studied the composition, perspective and light of the general view, we can examine the market scene at the lower left corner of the painting where many consequent events seem to be happening: shearing, dyeing, weaving, trading, bartering, praying and fighting. So, did these activities we really happen all together in 18th century Ankara? This question is necessary in order to understand the painting's relation to reality. It is important how the artist painted the scene. One way would be to go to Ankara, examine a street where there were shops and *sof* trade, draft some small sketches and later mentally combine them. However, the way the artist has brought together scenes from different quarters of Ankara like a succession of movie frames, in order to create a composition that differs from the actual image of the city, but highlights the flow of the mohair trade, conforms to the Greek Orthodox and Byzantine influences extending to northern Europe that Luttervelt indicates.

Towards the end of the 16th century, weaving activities were scattered among different parts of the city, between today's *Denizciler Caddesi*, *Bentderesi* and *Cebeci* districts (Tamur, 2003, p. 111). Also, in the 16th century, the most crowded neighbourhoods were close to the business districts, and some occupational groups, including *sof*-makers occupied the same neighbourhood (Ergenç, 1995, p. 56). In the first half of the 19th century, yarns suitable for weaving *sof* were marketed at the *Atpazarı*, and the *İplik Pazarı* (Yarn Market), west of *Kurşunlu Han*. The number of looms and workshops located in Ankara during this period is unknown, but documents show that certain foundations demolished derelict shops and converted them into *sof* workshops (Özdemir, 1998, pp. 39, 239). *Mahmut Paşa Bedesteni* was the centre of the *sof* trade during 16th –18th centuries. *Sof* looms were often located in rooms at the lower floors that had been converted into workshops. Dye houses, on the other hand, were located on the banks of the *Bentderesi*, because their processes required a lot of water (Tamur, 2003, pp. 110, 113, 118).

Considering the fact that the populace involved in the *sof* business cohabited in the same neighbourhoods, and specific commodities were traded at specific marketplaces, there must have been a dense population working close to each other. However, the fact that the dye houses should be adjacent to the marketplace is unexpected in light of this information, since dye houses are located near rivers which were in a completely different neighbourhood. At this point, we may surmise that the images on the market scene are composed of actual places and actions in different parts of Ankara combined in one place in the painting. We can imagine a production process that is lined up on the same linear plane in the painting, but we have to assume that the actual scenes that took place were somewhat different. The spaces have been arranged in the sequence of the *sof* production process, unlike their actual locations in Ankara.

So far, we have compared the *Rijksmuseum View Ankara* with similar works of the 18th century. We assumed that a visual, cultural element proceeds with reference to prior visual work, and that a large part of art history has developed in this way. However, verbal portrayals were regarded as sources of paintings and even architectural structures in the 18th century. For example, the architectural depictions in Tournefort's travelogue are regarded as ample bases for architectural examples. We find that at the end of the 18th century, it was usual for architects to refer to travelogues in order to assert the authenticity of their designs. Tournefort's travelogue was one of these (Avcıoğlu, 2014, p. 200). Could the artist who painted the *Rijksmuseum View of Ankara* have benefitted from such a source?

Tournefort's travelogue does not mention Ankara's mosques, the *Bedesten* and the single-storey shops in the marketplace. He found the Temple of Augustus to be the most interesting building in Ankara. The only thing in Tournefort's travelogue that could be a source for the *Rijksmuseum View of Ankara* is Aubriet's drawing. The text is not sufficiently explanatory. In the 18th century, British anthropologist Richard Pococke's travelogue contains more verbal representations of Ankara from among other travellers who recorded information about the city, such as French antique trader Paul Lucas, Tournefort himself, and French traveller Aubry de la Motraye. Drawings of Ankara are only available in Tournefort's and Lucas's travelogues.

Pococke (1745) begins his portrayal of Ankara by mentioning a herd of Angora goats near the city. He refers to the *Sakarya* River, the *Tabakhane* Creek, and the *Çubuk* Stream that flows next to the ramparts. There are many rivulets near the city; people who live in the upper neighbourhoods of the city carry home water in leather bags on horseback, while those by the riverside walk to the fountain (pp. 86-87). Indeed, two rivers with bridges across them, on the right and left sides of the painting, are connected with the roads leading to the city. The roads are easily recognized with their lighter colours. There is also a large fountain at the entrance to the city.

Pococke (1745) recounts houses of civil architecture in the city. "Though many of the houses of the city are very good within, yet the buildings on the outside make a very mean appearance, being all of unburnt brick; the streets are narrow, and the city irregularly laid out" (p. 87). When we try to imagine the streets between the buildings inside the walls in the painting, we do feel that they may well be narrow and the construction erratic. However, the exterior walls of the buildings in the painting are clean; the colours of the mosques and minarets are almost white. The painter must have shaped the types of buildings so that their functions may be distinguished. The houses are built to a rectangular plan, with two or three storeys, a shingled, triangular roof and plenty of windows. Eyice (1972) stated that the Ankara houses in the painting are not realistic and may have been imagined (page 101). We believe

Figure 7. Claude Aubreit, *Ankara (Angora)*-detail, 1717 (edition), 13x18 cm, Engraving, 10x15 cm, Bibliothèque nationale de France, département Cartes et plans, GE DD-2987 (6558).

Figure 8. Anonymous, *View of Ankara*-detail, 1700-1799, 117x118 cm, oil on canvas, Inventory no. SK-A-2055, Rijksmuseum, Amsterdam.

Figure 9. Anonymous, *Hochepied Reception Ceremony and View of Izmir*-detail, oil on canvas, 155.5x 243.5cm, Invertory no. SK-A-4085, Rijksmuseum, Amsterdam.

7

8

9

that the artist's purpose was not to reveal local architectural features of the buildings. When details of the buildings in the works we cited above (Figures 7-8-9) are examined, we find that, although they were created by different artists in different times, and in images painted for cities in different regions, they were made in a similar manner. There is no marked difference between details of houses in Aubriet's *View of Ankara*, the *Rijksmuseum View of Ankara*, and the *Hochepied Reception Ceremony and the View of Izmir*. We may say that this is the visualization of the function and social class of the architectural work, in a way that Europeans can understand. Buildings have become virtually symbols in the legends of the maps. The visual meaning of these houses is that they are civilian architecture, and they belong to townsmen.

There is a similar classification of religious architecture in the painting. Religious architecture may be discerned at first sight from among the crowded city, thanks to the white minarets with the single- or double-*şerefe*[10]. Pococke (1745) provides information on the classification of religious structures in the city:

(...) the principal mosque called Hadjee-Biram [Hacı Bayram], near which is the temple of Augustus (...) it is an oblong square building of white marble (...) and there is a corniche round at the top, both inside and out (...) open like a portico, there is a grand door, the frame of which is very richly carved (...) they have about twelve large mosques with minorets (sic.), and several small ones, near a hundred in all. (pp. 87-88).

Pococke's text tells us that there were large mosques with minarets and small mosques without and their numbers, and the floor plan of the most beautiful mosque in the city. Pococke cites something like twelve mosques with minarets, while we can count fifteen in the painting. Some are portrayed with domes, while others have triangular roofs. Pococke did not specify the number of the domed mosques, and in fact failed to mention the locations and features of any mosques other than *Hacı Bayram*. However, the architectural plans of the domed mosques located in the landscape at the upper part of the painting in the *Rijksmuseum View of Ankara*, and the market scene at the bottom are the same as the *Hacı Bayram* Mosque described in the text. Eyice encounters some difficulties trying to determine the mosques in the painting, because some of

10 *Şerefe* is the balcony of a minaret from which the *muezzin* makes his prayer call (T. N.).

the structures shown as domed mosques actually have triangular roofs.[11]

The main topics Eyice and Tamur put forward in their writings about the painting involve the identities of the architectural structures and their realism. The first and foremost reason why Eyice dwelled on the issue was, of course, to illustrate that the city was not Aleppo, but Ankara. Tamur tried to expand the scope. Although Tamur associated 35 buildings in the painting with Ankara, the structures that Eyice definitively identified were the ramparts, the *İzmir* Gate, the *Erzurum* Gate, *Hacı Bayram* Mosque, the Julianus Monument, *Zincirli* Mosque, *Hıdırlık* Shrine, the *Namazgâh* Gate, *Mahmut Paşa Bedesteni*, and *Akkale*. Eyice was very meticulous in scientifically identifying the buildings in accordance with Von Vincke's 1859 map of Ankara and their recognized architectural features. While Eyice and Tamur named the structures in the picture, they reported varying opinions (Eyice, 1972, 101, Tamur, 2008, pp. 393, 394).

This issue can be examined by comparing the *Rijksmuseum View of Ankara* with the photographs of Ankara taken over time. The photograph of *Hacı Bayram* Mosque taken in 1928 and the structure of the

10

Figure 10. *Hacı Bayram Mosque*, 1928, black and white postcard, original, 14x9 cm, VEKAM Library and Archives, Collection of Ankara Photographs, Postcards and Engravings, Inventory no. 0940.

11

Figure 11. Anonymous, *Hacı Bayram Mosque and Augustus Temple – View of Ankara*-detail, 1700-1799, 117x198 cm, oil on canvas, Inventory no. SK-A-2055, Rijksmuseum, Amsterdam.

12

13

14

Figure 12. Anonymous, *Zincirli Mosque- View of Ankara*- detail (According to Erman Tamur's definition), 1700-1799, 117x118 cm, oil on canvas, Inventory no. SK-A-2055, Rijksmuseum, Amsterdam..

Figure 13. *Zincirli Mosque*, 1954, black and white photograph, copy, 18x24 cm, VEKAM Library and Archives, Collection of Ankara Photographs, Postcards and Engravings, Inventory no. 0551.

Figure 14. Anonymous, *Zincirli Mosque – View of Ankara*-detail (According to Semavi Eyice's definition), 1700-1799, 117x118 cm, oil on canvas, Inventory no. SK-A-2055, Rijksmuseum, Amsterdam.

11 Eyice was unable to pinpoint the locations of the Mukaddem Mosque, and the Ahi Elvan, Ahi Şerafettin (Aslanhane), Cenabi Ahmet Paşa mosques, the Geneği Masjid and the Karacabey Baths near the Bedesten on the painting. There are domed buildings in the painting where there should be certain timber or tiled roofs. Moreover, some buildings are far from where they should be. However, Tamur was bolder in detecting structures (Eyice, 1972, pp. 102-103, Tamur, 2008, pp. 393, 394). Eyice and Tamur believed that the building on leftmost side of the painting was the İğneli Belkis Mosque; however, this is not a domed but a tile-covered structure, as shown on the postcard (Eyice, 1972, p. 111, Tamur, 2008, pp. 393-394).

Figure 15. *Aslanhane Mosque and Shrine*, 1953, black and white photographic copy, 18x24 cm, VEKAM Library and Archives, Collection of Ankara Photographs, Postcards and Engravings, Inventory no. 0580.

Figure 16. Anonymous, *Aslanhane Mosque (Ahi Şerafeddin) (?) and Shrine – View of Ankara*-detail, 1700-1799, 117x118 cm, oil on canvas, Inventory no. SK-A-2055, Rijksmuseum, Amsterdam.

15

16

Figure 17. *Cenabi Ahmet Paşa Mosque and Complex*, VEKAM Library and Archives, Collection of Ankara Photographs, Postcards and Engravings, Inventory no. TKVOO81.

Figure 18. Anonymous, *Ahmet Paşa Mosque (bottom left of the painting) (?) – View of Ankara*-detail, 1700-1799, 117x118 cm, oil on canvas, Inventory no. SK-A-2055, Rijksmuseum, Amsterdam.

Figure 19. Anonymous, *Cenabi Ahmet Paşa Mosque* (upper half of the picture, within the cityscape) (?) – *View of Ankara*-detail, 1700-1799, 117x118 cm, oil on canvas, Inventory no. SK-A-2055, Rijksmuseum, Amsterdam.

17

18

19

Figure 20. *Vilayet Plaza (İğneli Belkıs Mosque)*, 1900, black and white original postcard, 9x13 cm, VEKAM Library and Archives, Collection of Ankara Photographs, Postcards and Engravings, Inventory no. 1235.

Figure 21. Anonymous, *İğneli Belkıs Mosque – View of Ankara*-detail, 1700-1799, 117x118 cm, oil on canvas, Inventory no. SK-A-2055, Rijksmuseum, Amsterdam.

20

21

Figure 22. *The Road from Anafartalar to Hacıbayram Mosque (Kurşunlu Mosque)*, 1928, black and white original postcard, 13x9 cm, VEKAM Library and Archives, Collection of Ankara Photographs, Postcards and Engravings, Inventory no. 0941.

Figure 23. Anonymous, *Kurşunlu Mosque – View of Ankara (?)*, 1700-1799, 117x118 cm, oil on canvas, Inventory no. SK-A-2055, Rijksmuseum, Amsterdam.

Figure 24. *Kurşunlu Mosque*, VEKAM Library and Archives, Collection of Ankara Photographs, Postcards and Engravings, Inventory no. TKV0200

22

23

24

mosque in the painting are similar. The photograph of *Zincirli* Mosque from 1954 resembles the triangular roof in the painting that Eyice noted. The *Aslanhane* Tomb is easily distinguishable in both the photograph and the painting with its hexagonal prismatic roof. In the photo, however, the structure with a triangular roof is depicted with a dome. The same incompatibility is also applicable to the *İğneli Belkis* Mosque. *Cenabi Ahmet Paşa* Mosque and Complex has been depicted twice. One is in the upper half of the painting, within the landscape, while the second appears in cross-section within the marketplace scene at the bottom left. The number of the domes were depicted correctly in the painting, and the arched entrance is shown in detail at the bottom left of the painting. The photo of the *Kurşunlu* Mosque taken in 1928 shows its minaret, and the structure can be seen in the VEKAM archive photograph. The form in the painting is reminiscent of the other. The rectangular entrance floor below the domes of the mosque were painted to show simultaneously the right, left and front façades. While this formatting provides information about the structure, it makes it difficult to pair it with photographs (Figures 10-23).

Specific features of various groups were revealed by the observations in travelogues. Determining and compiling features necessitate a classification. The tendency to classify is a characteristic of the Turquerie trend of the 18th century. One of the sources for Turkish mosques and Turkish manners (*manieré*) is the 18th century travelogue (Avcıoğlu, 2014, p. 14). We may ask the following question: has Pococke, and more importantly the painter, endeavoured to determine the general properties of the mosques by making a classification? The text does not quite answer this question, and although Pococke imparts ample material for a specific classification, he does not mention the difference between the roofs and the domes. However, the painter has observed these features, or has learned them from a source. In either case, there are certain typologies for Turkish mosques and minarets in the 18th century. For example, the minarets are the same in all of the Anatolian cities Aubriet depicts.

The last of the architectural elements that Pococke referred to, and which appears in the picture is the *Mahmut Paşa Bedesten*. Aubriet also included the *Bedesten* in the overall image of the city, but in the *Rijksmuseum View of Ankara*, the shops in the market place conform to Pococke's description. In addition, these shops are not mentioned at all in other travelogues. Pococke (1745) described the shops in the *Mahmut Paşa Bedesten* as follows: "But

25

26

Figure 25-26. Anonymous, *Shops, View of Ankara*-detail, 1700-1799, 117x118 cm, oil on canvas, Inventory no. SK-A-2055, Rijksmuseum, Amsterdam.

27

28

Figure 27. Anonymous, *Angora goats, View of Ankara*-detail, 1700-1799, 117x118 cm, oil on canvas, Inventory no. SK-A-2055, Rijksmuseum, Amsterdam.

Figure 28. Claude Aubriet (draughtsman / date of drawing: 1702). "Chevre d'Angora," p. 185, Joseph Pitton de Tournefort (1718). *Illustrations de Relation d'un voyage du Levant*, Bibliothèque nationale de France. (For visuals see: ark:/12148/btv1b23005662).

they are sold in single-storey shops, with small domes, very beautiful stones, and a treasure house." (p. 87).

In addition, these shops are not mentioned in other travel destinations. Pococke (1745) portrays the shops inside the *Mahmut Paşa Bedesten* as follows: "They have however, a handsome stone building covered with cupolas, which is a bezestan (sic.) for rich goods; there are buildings only of one floor with shops in them (...)" (p. 87).

Like other travellers, Pococke writes most extensively about the goats in Ankara. He provides information on raising and shearing the goats, and selling and exporting mohair and *sof*. In fact, the Angora goat is a subject treated affectionately by the travellers who wrote about Ankara. The common view was that the Ankara breed were the most beautiful goats in the world.

A view of a goatherd and herdsmen shearing the animals appears on the lower right corner of the *Rijksmuseum View of Ankara*. The goats were painted according to their distinguishing physical properties, so much so that Eyice, as mentioned at the beginning of this article, realized that the city in the painting was Ankara. Claude Aubriet is the sole person we know definitely came to Ankara in the 18th century and created drawings of the city. Aubriet has actually placed the goat in a fictional Ankara landscape, but revealed its physical properties. Moreover, Aubriet was, in fact, renowned for his scientific drawings. Goats in the *Rijksmuseum View of Ankara* are depicted as a herd in the distance. Nevertheless, their hair, their horns, and their clustering within the herd were represented.

If we query once again whether Pococke's travelogue is one of the painting's sources, we must note that while it is the only travelogue in the 18th century that alluded to specific points that appear in the painting, there are details in the painting that are never mentioned in the text. The overall appearance of the city seen in the painting constitutes a specific and coherent classification, and this is more detailed than what Pococke and other travellers revealed. The answer is that Pococke does not contain enough information to be the source of the painting, but it can inspire us to ask another question. If there is a classification in the architectural elements in the picture, has it been implemented in other elements, for example in the market scene?

There are over 150 people in the market scene: vendors, shoppers, shopkeepers, yarn spinners, dyers, weavers, porters, fighters, hookah smokers, people

29

30

praying, chatting, talking with their children, working with their children, etc. The first thing that comes to mind when speaking of the "Turkish type" of the 18th century were the types who appeared in Jean-Baptiste Vanmour's costume albums, rather than the actual people who lived in Ankara. The images Vanmour produced in Istanbul were perceived as Turkish daily life and Turkish types, and Vanmour's costume albums were influential in the establishment of eastern forms. In fact, Vanmour's pictures were formed inside the authentic source (Avcıoğlu and Flood, 2010, p.17). Vanmour's characters are people who lived or worked in Istanbul's *Topkapı* Palace. His oriental characters are rich, beautiful, happy, flamboyant and confident. Of all the drawings published in the travelogue, Aubriet was the one to discuss the "types" living outside Istanbul. His travelogue includes a Turkish man, Greek and Armenian clerics, and women in Istanbul and the Greek islands. Muslim women were never depicted.

After Ankara became first the headquarters of the Republic during the Independence War and later became its capital, the number of photographs of the city increased and portraits of its citizens gradually began to reappear, about two

Figure 29. Anonymous, *View of Ankara*– detail, 117x118 cm, oil on canvas, 1700-1799, Inventory no. SK-A-2055, Rijksmuseum, Amsterdam.

Figure 30. "Figure 5: Shearing", (Üstar, 1940, p. 26).

31

Figure 31. Anonymous, *View of Ankara*-detail, 117x118 cm, oil on canvas, 1700-1799, Inventory no. SK-A-2055, Rijksmuseum, Amsterdam.

32

Figure 32. "Figure 19: Portage inside the warehouse – detail", (Üstar, 1940, p. 60).

centuries after the painting was created. These portraits are similar to those in the *Rijksmuseum View of Ankara*.

What is surprising is that, although it was only in 1972 that the *Rijksmuseum View of Ankara* was understood to portray Ankara, the traces of the types in the painting appear to be from the future, rather than the past, from the years 1861, 1905 and 1930s. The link between the photographs

33

34

Figure 33. Anonymous, *View of Ankara* – detail, 117x118 cm, oil on canvas, 1700-1799, Inventory no. SK-A-2055, Rijksmuseum, Amsterdam.

Figure 34. "Istanbul Trade and Produce Exchange Hall", (Üstar, 1940, p. 43).

Figure 35. Anonymous, *View of Ankara* – detail, 117x118 cm, oil on canvas, 1700-1799, Inventory no. SK-A-2055, Rijksmuseum, Amsterdam.

Figure 36. *A Camel Caravan in Ankara,* 1920, black and white postcard, original, 9x13 cm, VEKAM Library and Archives, Collection of Ankara Photographs, Postcards and Engravings, Inventory no. 1551.

35

36

Figure 37. Anonymous, *View of Ankara* – detail, 117x118 cm, oil on canvas, 1700-1799, Inventory no. SK-A-2055, Rijksmuseum, Amsterdam.

Figure 38. *Mohair Workers and Mohair Traders*, 1905, Black and White Postcard, Original, 8.13 cm, VEKAM Library and Archive, Collection of Ankara Photographs, Postcards and Engravings, Inventory no. 0763.

37

38

Figure 39. Anonymous, *View of Ankara* – detail, 117x118 cm, oil on canvas, 1700-1799, Inventory no. SK-A-2055, Rijksmuseum, Amsterdam.

Figure 40. *Armenian Women Spinning Mohair,* 1861, Black and White Postcard, Original, 8x14 cm, VEKAM Library and Archives, Collection of Ankara Photographs, Postcards and Engravings, Inventory no. 2003.

39

40

and the painting is very strong. Actually, when one looks at travelogues and Jean Vanmour's engravings, one can assume that the 18th-century types did not appear in the painting. Indeed, the picture offers a different and more detailed narrative. However, photographs of city dwellers taken in the 20th century prove that the painting had captured the characters of the city, which have remained unchanged over a period of more than two centuries.

An adult and a child, possibly a father and son work together as goats are sheared.

Porters carrying heavy sacks on bent backs perform the hardest jobs of the entire production process.

The stock market that had spontaneously formed in the marketplace was reinstated in Istanbul during the Republican era, in line with modern economic guidelines. Part of the Istanbul stock market belongs to mohair traders and experts. In this way, the price of mohair can be determined.

Transportation with camels has been used for a long time.

Mohair merchants examine the quality of the goods by viewing or perhaps touching a batch.

Women spin the yarn. Unlike the women walking around in *çarşaf*[12], they wear colourful clothes, and these two women, who do not wear the *çarşaf*, are part of the production process. Their clothing is possibly a sign that they are non-Muslim. In addition, all of the female figures on the market screen show that women are active in social life as customers or artisans, too.

The *Rijksmuseum View of Ankara* is the most detailed visualization of Ankara from the 18th century. Not all of the information it offers is entirely accurate nor clear when compared against different sources. This will continue to be a point of discussion until definitive documentation emerges about the identity of its creator or its purpose, because the 18th century has abstruse boundaries drawn by much more insightful and curious eyes than the specific cultural outlooks of specific groups. The most important point that we can determine about the picture is that it possesses the cartographic language seen in European cityscapes.

The similarities between the photographs of Ankara denizens in the 1930s and the painting are astonishing. If the context of the painting had been known by Ottoman or early Republican artists, we might surmise that this painting was the beginning of the visual tradition on this subject. However, this was not known. Looking at the *Rijksmuseum View of Ankara*, we may say that the artist also foresaw scenes from the future.

---

12 Simple, loose, essentially robe-like Turkish women's over-garment.

References

Road from Anafartalar to Hacıbayram Mosque (Kurşunlu Mosque). [Postcard]. (1928). Collection of Ankara Photographs, Postcards and Engravings (Inventory no. 0941), Koç University Vehbi Koç Ankara Studies Research Centre (VEKAM) Library and Archives, Ankara.

A Camel Train in Ankara. [Postcard]. (1920). Collection of Ankara Photographs, Postcards and Engravings (Inventory no. 1551). Koç University Vehbi Koç Ankara Studies Research Centre (VEKAM) Library and Archives, Ankara.

Ankara Chamber of Trade and Industry Guidebook. (1933). Ankara.

Aslanhane Mosque and Shrine [Photograph]. (1953). Collection of Ankara Photographs, Postcards and Engravings (Inventory no. 0580). Koç University Vehbi Koç Ankara Studies Research Centre (VEKAM) Library and Archives, Ankara.

Aubriet, C. (1717). Angora goats [Engraving]. *Illustrations de Relation d'un voyage du Levant* (p. 185). Bibliothèque nationale de France, Paris. Accessed from ark:/12148/btv1b23005662.

Aubriet, C. (1717). *[Ankara] Angora* [Engraving]. Département Cartes et plans (Inventory no. GE DD-2987 [6558]), Bibliothèque nationale de France, Paris. Accessed from http://gallica.bnf.fr/ark:/12148/btv1b23005662?rk=128756;0

Avcıoğlu, N. (2014). *Turquerie ve temsil politikası: 1728-1876*. Renan Akman (Trans.). Istanbul: Koç University Publications.

Avcıoğlu, N. and Flood F. B. (2010). Globalizing cultures: art and mobility in the eighteenth century. *Ars Orientalis*, 39, 7-38

Blunt, W. and Stearn, W.T. (1994). *The art of botanical illustration: an illustrated history.* New York: Dover Publications.

Bull, D. (2003). Ressam ve sanatı. E. Sint Nicolaas, D. Bull, G. Renda ve G. İrepoğlu (Ed). In *Lale Devri'nin bir görgü tanığı Jean Baptiste Vanmour* (p. 25-39). Istanbul: Koçbank Publications.

Cenabi Ahmet Paşa Mosque and Complex. [Photograph]. (t.y.). Collection of Ankara Photographs, Postcards and Engravings (Inventory no. TKVOO81). Koç University Vehbi Koç Ankara Studies Research Centre (VEKAM) Library and Archives, Ankara.

Clark, K. (1952). *Landscape into art.* London: John Murray Publishing.

Portage inside the warehouse [Photograph]. (Undated). *Tiftik ve Tiftikçiliğimiz* (p. 60). Ankara: Üniversite Bookstore.

Ergenç, Ö. (1995). *XVI. yüzyılda Ankara ve Konya.* Ankara: Ankara Foundation Institute.

Eyice, S. (1972). *Ankara'nın eski bir resmi.* Ankara: Turkish Historical Society.

Germaner, S. and İnankur, Z. (2008). *Oryantalistlerin Istanbulu.* Istanbul: Türkiye İş Bank Publications.

Hacı Bayram Mosque [Photograph]. (1928). Collection of Ankara Photographs, Postcards and Engravings (Inventory no. 0940). Koç University Vehbi Koç Ankara Studies Research Centre (VEKAM) Library and Archives, Ankara.

Hochepied Reception Ceremony and View of İzmir [Painting]. (1657-1723). (Inventory no. SK-A-4085), Rijksmuseum, Amsterdam.

Istanbul Trade and Produce Exchange Hall [Photograph].(undated). *Tiftik ve Tiftikçiliğimiz* (p. 43). Ankara: Üniversite Bookstore.

Keuning, J. (1963). The 'civitates' of Braun and Hogenberg. *Imago Mundi*, 17, 41-44.

Kurşunlu Mosque. [Photograph]. (t.y.). Collection of Ankara Photographs, Postcards and Engravings (Inventory no. TKV0200). Koç University Vehbi Koç Ankara Studies Research Centre (VEKAM) Library and Archives, Ankara.

Luttervelt, R. (1958). *De Turkse schilderijen van J. B. Vanmour en zijn school: de verzameling van Cornelis Calkoen, ambssadeur bij de hoge porte.* Istanbul: Nederlands Historisch-Archaeologisch Instituut.

Montagu, J. (1799). *A voyage performed by the late Earl of Sandwich round the Mediterranean in the years 1738 and 1739.* London: Printed for T. Cadell Jun. and W. Davies.

Ortelius, A., Hoefnagel, J., Braun, G. ve Hogenberg, F. (1578). *Tiburtum vulgo Tivoli.* Département Cartes et plans (Inventory no. CPL GE DD-2987 [5455]), Bibliothèque nationale de France, Paris.

Özdemir, R. (1998). *XIX. yüzyılın ilk yarısında Ankara.* Ankara: Ministry of Culture Publications.

Panofsky, E. (1991). *Perspective as symbolic form.* C. S. Wood (Trans.). New York: Zone Books.

Pococke, R. (1745). *A description of the East and some other countries.* C. II, London: W. Bowyer.

Rees, R. (1980). Historical links between cartography and art. *Geographical Review*, *70*(1), 60-78.

[Rijksmuseum] View of Ankara [Painting]. (1700-1799). (Inventory no. A2055), Rijksmuseum, Amsterdam.

Speake, J. (Ed.). (2013). *Literature of travel and exploration: An Encyclopaedia.* Oxford: Routledge Publishing.

Tamur, E. (2003). *Ankara keçisi ve Ankara Tiftik dokumacılığı.* Ankara: Ankara Chamber of Commerce Publication.

Tamur, E. (2008). Amsterdam'da bir Ankara resmi. *Kebikeç*, 25, 385-409.

Sof Looms of Mohair Society. [Photograph]. (undated). Ankara Chamber of Commerce Guidebook (p. 42).

Armenian Women Spinning Mohair. [Postcard]. (1861). Collection of Ankara Photographs, Postcards and Engravings (Inventory no. 2003). Koç University Vehbi Koç Ankara Studies Research Centre (VEKAM) Library and Archives, Ankara.

Mohair Workers and Mohair Merchants. [Postcard]. (1905). Collection of Ankara Photographs, Postcards and Engravings (Inventory no. 0763). Koç University Vehbi Koç Ankara Studies Research Centre (VEKAM) Library and Archives, Ankara.

Tournefort, J. P. (1717). *Relation d'un voyage du Levant.* Paris: De L'Imprimerie Royale.

Üstar, M. F. (1940). *Tiftik ve tiftikçiliğimiz.* Ankara: Üniversite Bookstore.

Vilayet Plaza (İğneli Belkıs Mosque). [Postcard]. (1900). Collection of Ankara Photographs, Postcards and Engravings (Inventory no. 1235). Koç University Vehbi Koç Ankara Studies Research Centre (VEKAM) Library and Archives, Ankara.

Zincirli Mosque [Photograph]. (1954). Collection of Ankara Photographs, Postcards and Engravings (Inventory no. 0551). Koç University Vehbi Koç Ankara Studies Research Centre (VEKAM) Library and Archives, Ankara.

Natural Dye Sources Used In Ankara *Sof* Processing

TCF DATU
Turkish Cultural Foundation | Türk Kültür Vakfı
Cultural Heritage Preservation And Natural Dyes Laboratory

The Cultural Heritage Preservation and Natural Dyes Laboratory (DATU), established by TCF[1] in Istanbul in 2010, maintains the world's most extensive collection of natural dyes. The inventory consists of 680 dye plants, dye insects, seashells, and natural organic lake pigments.

The laboratory has produced 30 natural organic lake pigments, organic dye of vegetal and animal origin. These pigments may be used also as natural, organic ink in traditional Turkish arts such as paper marbling (*ebru*), illumination (*tezhip*) and miniatures. Natural organic pigments have been used in the past in sacred books, paintings, icons, manuscripts, leather and murals. Organic natural lake pigments are used also in restoration work in these fields.

DATU – Cultural Heritage Preservation and Natural Dyes Laboratory also produces printing dyes, which play a vital role in the textiles industry. Dyestuffs of plant and animal origins manufactured by DATU are non-toxic, non-carcinogenic and non-polluting. Fabrics dyed and printed using eco-friendly and human-friendly natural organic dyes can be imparted natural antibacterial, antifungal, anti-UV and antimicrobial properties of plant origin. The laboratories also carry out R&D work, using traditional dyeing prescriptions to research increased durability against light, sweat, friction and water. The laboratory is involved in various projects, such as TUBITAK projects, publishes all its research in international and national journals, and presents it in symposiums and conventions.

The secret of Turkish Red, a pigment and dyeing process which held an important place in the dyeing industry, was lost for over two hundred years. It was rediscovered through research work supported by TCF and undertaken by DATU and patented by the Turkish Cultural Foundation (Turkish Patent Institute patent number TR 2015 00638 B).

---

1 This part is provided by the Turkish Cultural Foundation (TCF), Cultural Heritage Preservation And Natural Dyes Laboratory (DATU). The Turkish Cultural Foundation (TCF) was established in 2000 by Drs. Yalçın and Serpil Ayaslı. The mission of TCF is to support the preservation and promotion of Turkish culture and heritage worldwide. TCF is a U.S. tax-exempt public charitable organization supported by a Trust established by the Ayaslı family and private donations. It has offices in Boston, Washington, D.C. and Istanbul, Turkey. The mission of TCF is to increase knowledge of Turkey's cultural heritage and to highlight Anatolia's contributions to world culture and humanity while building people-to-people cultural exchanges across the world. TCF has been accepted into official relations with UNESCO in 2015.

The material characterization, dyestuff analysis, colour measurement and technical analyses of archaeological and historical objects are conducted at the DATU Laboratory via non-destructive microanalysis methods and the highest technology. Information regarding weave types, warp and weft densities, direction and number of yarn twists etc. is acquired through technical analyses. These measurements and analyses, often conducted free of charge with the support of the Turkish Cultural Foundation, provide significant data for restoration and conservation. Moreover, these analytical methods also hep to correctly date historical and archaeological artefacts. Scientific and technical support is provided for the restoration of works in accordance with the acquired data.

The history of natural dyeing is virtually as old as that of weaving. Archaeological excavations conducted at the Mohenjo-Daro site, in the Indus Valley within today's Pakistani borders, have revealed a small amount of blue pigmentation in cracks in the ground stones. The indigo dyestuff found in this settlement that has been dated to BC 3,500 is the oldest and most important natural dye that has been recorded. Considering that this region belonged to India at the time, it is assumed that the first place where indigo was ever used was probably India. Another excavation conducted later at the same site unearthed two red coloured money pouches made of cotton fibre dated to BC 3,000. These were probably dyed with madder species (*Rubia sp.*). However, these money pouches were not properly preserved and disintegrated after the excavation. Clay tablets found in Nippur, one of Sumer's largest cities, reveal that spinning, weaving and dyeing were developed towards the end of BC 4000, during the same period when indigo was used in India. In addition, vat dyeing and mordant dyeing were mentioned also in other tablets discovered in the Mesopotamia Region. Natural dyeing, now known to date from 5,000 to 6,000 years ago, continued until 1856 when William Henry Perkin synthesised aniline dyes. Use of natural dyes has gradually decreased since that date.

The Ankara *Sof*

The Ankara *sof* is a kind of fabric woven from mohair harvested from the Angora goat, which is prominent among animal fibres in the textile industry for its length, robustness and brightness. From spinning of the mohair fibre into yarn, to weaving the yarn into cloth and finally dyeing the cloth, all phases of *sof* production comprise a distinctive craft widespread in Ankara and neighbouring provinces. The *sof* weavings preferred by the society elite throughout history were traditional weavings peculiar to the province of Ankara and Central Anatolia. In this respect, the Ankara *sof* holds a significant place within the cultural heritage of this geography. The finer-spun mohair was, the more desirable *sof*, the woven fabric would be regarded. Ankara *sof* was appraised for its fine weave, and soft, shiny and silky appearance. These fabrics were also highly durable. *Sof* fabric production was known to involve some long and arduous production stages, listed as the process steps below.

1. Procurement of mohair wool (shearing, collecting, aeration, cleaning, sorting, screening),
2. Combing,
3. Spinning,

4. Dyeing,
a) Mordanting,
b) Dyeing,
c) Washing,
5. Sizing,
6. Placement / adjustment / spooling,
7. Weaving (four-fold, four-treadle, three-fold),[2]
8. Washing/dry finishing,
9. Buffing,
10. Watering.

Natural Dye Sources Used In Ankara *Sof* Processing

1 – Madder (*Rubia tinctorum* L.): Dyer's madder (*Rubia tinctorum* L.) is the best-known red dye, used since ancient times. The roots of these plants are used for dyeing. Best for the purpose are 3-year-old roots. Dyer's madder contains various dyestuff groups, but alizarin and purpurin are the best-known dyes. Dyer's madder is known in Anatolia under many different names: dye root, dyer's root, dye *pürç*, dye çil, red root, red dye, scarlet root, dye ivy, egg dye and tongue bleeder, etc. Many different colours may be obtained through the method of dyeing with dyer's madder with various mordant materials. These are red, rose, purple, reddish-brown, orange, reddish-black, and reddish-blue. The red obtained by the application of dyer's madder with multiple mordants and further dyeing has been known historically as *Turkey Red* or *Edirne Red*. Anatolia very likely is the motherland of dyer's madder. In Anatolia, the most common farming ground is the Central Anatolia region. Nevertheless, it seems to have spread naturally to the Caucasus, Iran, Midwest Asia and the Himalayas. Dyer's madder is known to have been used particularly for dyeing Ankara *sof*, the same way it has been used across Anatolia. There is evidence that dyer's madder was traded between the East and the West as far back as the 1st Century. According to one writer from ancient Greece, the earliest trade for dyer's madder took place between India and Anatolia. The Egyptians, the Greeks and the Romans used this plant in dyeing. The Romans first brought the plant to Central Europe and cultivated it there. Farming for dyer's madder began in Europe in the 8th century, albeit in small quantities. Later, Baghdad became the major trading centre for dyer's madder. By the 10th century, Netherlands and Germany had accomplished many advances in the production of dyer's madder. In Europe in the 18th century, dyer's madder had become a highly important economic crop. In the 19th century, France became an important producer of dyer's madder in Europe. French producers managed to compete with manufacturers of synthetic dyes until 1870. In fact, French governments dyed the uniforms of their troops using dyer's madder. Up to this day, dyer's madder has been identified in analyses to be the source of the red colouring in many eastern carpets, Ottoman carpets, *Hereke* carpets and many other fabrics from different periods.

2 – Weld (*Reseda luteola* L.): The weld (*Reseda luteola* L.) is a biennial plant that can grow to a height of up to 1.5 metres. There is no need for fertile soil for the plant to grow. The weld can grow in moist, sandy and pebbly soil. This plant

2 There are three types of *sof*: Thick fabrics are woven with yarn twisted four-fold. The four-treadle weave is the most sought-after, patterned and highest quality *sof*. Three-fold weaving creates plain *sof* (Translator's Note).

has been observed to grow spontaneously at waysides a year after road construction, as well as rocky places of 400-1,500 metres high. All aboveground parts of the plant are used in dyeing. The main colouring dyestuffs of the plant are *luteolin* and *apigenin*. Weld produces a yellow pigment, but khakis and olive greens may be obtained using different mordants. This plant is cultivated intensively in Anatolia, particularly in the Ankara region, north Marmara, the Aegean region, as well as western Black Sea. It is known that weld has been used in textile dyeing as far back as prehistoric times. Weld seeds from the Neolithic era were found in a lake excavation in Switzerland. It was widely cultivated and used in dyeing during Hellenistic and Roman times. Weld is believed to have been used to dye nuns' habits and wedding dresses. Pliny the Elder claims that only women's dresses were dyed with weld. Dyestuff analyses of Coptic textiles from the 3rd to 10th centuries have revealed that weld was extensively farmed in Egypt. These textiles were yellow from weld, and orange made from a mixture of weld with madder; and green, from a mixture of weld and woad(indigo). Yellow colorant analyses have revealed that during the 16th century, one of the most brilliant periods in the history of Turkish carpet making, the Uşak-made carpet type *Lotto* was dyed with weld. Weld was a highly popular dyeing plant during Ottoman times, and has been used frequently in dyeing both wool and silk. It was used in the yellow colours of Ottoman fabrics and as the yellow component with woad (*Isatis tinctoria L.*) used for green. Weld has been cultivated in Europe and America for centuries. Cultivation of the plant in Turkey and in Europe has continued until the end of the 19th century.

3 – Anatolian Buckhorn (*Rhamnus petiolaris* Boiss): *Rhamnus petiolaris* is a buckthorn species known in Anatolia with a variety of names, such as *altin agaci* ("gold tree"), *alacehir*, *boyacı dikeni* ("dyer's thorn") and *akdiken* ("white thorn"). There are 22 species of *Rhamnus sp.*. Small yellow-green flowers bloom during May to June. Green seeds (drupes) formed from these flowers turn brown or black after a long while. The drupe, 6 to 7 mm in diameter, is yellow inside a brown shell. *Rhamnus petiolaris*, the "gold tree," is endemic in Central Anatolia. This plant is cultivated in Central Anatolia, Turkey, particularly in the Ankara, Kayseri, Çorum, Gaziantep, Sinop, Afyon, Uşak, Yozgat, Tokat, Nevşehir, Niğde, Kahramanmaras and Konya vicinities. The drupes of the buckthorn are used in the dyeing process. The main colour obtained from *Rhamnus petiolaris* is a deep, bright yellow. Colours like orange-yellow, khaki and olive green are also obtained using a variety of mordants. Its main dyestuffs are *rhamnetin*, *isorhamnetin*, *quercetin*, *kaempferol* and *emodin*. Dyestuff analyses show that buckthorn was used to obtain yellow pigmentation for many Anatolian carpets woven in the 15th to 17th centuries. It was also exported from Anatolia to many countries around the world for its use in dyeing silk wool and mohair fibres until the early 20th century. Buckthorn was used as the yellow component of yellow and green-yellow Ottoman fabrics in the 16th century. It was also an important dyestuff in the 19th century. *Rhamnus petiolaris* continued to be cultivated in the 20th century, too. Buckthorn was used often for the yellow–coloured parts of the earliest examples of Hereke carpets. This plant is known to have been used also for dyeing Ankara *sof*.

4 – Walnut Shell (*Juglans regia* L.): The outermost green shells and leaves of the common walnut are used in dyeing. It is known as a very important dyestuff fur brown pigmentation. The green walnut shells and leaves of walnut have been used in brown dyeing since ancient times. The most effective dyestuffs contained in walnut shells are *juglone* and tannic acid groups. Ancient Greek and Roman literatures reveal that the walnut tree was cultivated during those eras. Roman Pliny the Elder imparts prescriptions for grey and brown-coloured hair dyes made of walnut shell. The Romans have carried the walnut tree from Greece to Italy and then over the Alps into France, and then to Germany. England and Germany developed their own production, when the walnut tree came to their countries. Quite a few sources cite the use of walnut shells for brown dyeing. Although walnut shell dyestuffs were not used in 15th to 17th century Turkish carpets, it was used in Iranian carpets of the same period. Today, however, walnut shells are used in brown dyeing in both Iran and Turkey. One of the basic dyestuff sources used in the Medieval Europe was the bark, branches and leaves of this tree. In France, walnuts played a significant role in the textile dyeing industry in the 17th century. It was used to dye soldiers' uniforms during the American Civil War of 1861-1865. The uniforms of Turkish soldiers in the Independence War (1919-1922) were dyed with walnut dyestuff. Nowadays, it is still in use, albeit in small amounts, in Anatolian textiles.

5 – Valonia Oak (*Quercus ithaburensis* Decaisne): The Mount Tabor oak is a plant species endemic in Greece and Turkey, and especially in the Aegean region of Anatolia. There are upwards of 20 distinct species of Quercus (oak) in Turkey. Their fruits are generally called "acorn" without any distinction. This is the part of the plant used in dyeing. The main colour is a milky brown, and a scale of grey to black may be obtained using various mordants. The dyestuff that acorns contain are tannic acid groups. The most effective ones are the ellagic acid and gallic acid dyestuffs. Acorn has been used as human and animal food since the Stone Age (50,000 BC and earlier). It has been used frequently in the past, in leather dyeing and tanning. It has been used often with iron mordant to obtain the black dye used in Turkish carpets and kilims. It was also combined with iron for black ink used in historical manuscripts. However, this plant's iron complex develops a strong acidic effect over time, which causes damage and deep cuts on the applied surface.

6 – Safflower (*Carthamus tinctorius* L.): The safflower plant is cultivated primarily as an oil crop, but has numerous uses in various other fields, such as art, paper, textiles, food and cosmetics. Dried petals of safflower are used to produce yellow and red pigments. Obtaining red colouring is somewhat more demanding than yellow dye. The most effective dyestuff it contains is *carthamin*. It is mostly cultivated in Anatolia in the Ankara region, as well as in the Afyon, Kütahya, Eskişehir, Çankırı, Isparta and Şanlıurfa provinces. It is known in Anatolia as *cartham*, *aspur*, *asfur*, "bastard saffron," parrot feed, and dyer's safflower.

This plant has been widely used in textile dyeing processes in the past for its yellow and red pigments. In the 16th and 17th centuries, between 1557 and 1628, safflower was used in silk carpets belonging to Shah Abbas I of Persia. There are also Anatolian resources that attest to the use of this plant in dyeing. Analyses of historic Ankara *sof* dyestuffs in museums have revealed use of this plant.

7 – **Woad** (*Isatis tinctoria* L.): Nearly 30 species of woad grow naturally in Turkey. It comes into yellow flowers in June-August. Woad has been used for its blue dye in Mesopotamia in ancient times. It was also known in Ancient Greece and the Roman Empire as a source of indigo dyestuff. Analyses of blue Masada textiles of AD 73 and blue Palmyra textiles of AD 273 have revealed woad (indigo). The blue colours of these textiles were most likely obtained from the woad plant. Dyes obtained from woad are used also as pigments in other areas, in addition to textile dyeing, such as murals, art and dyed papers. Woad was widely cultivated in France and Germany in medieval times. Dyer's woad is used in the Ankara *sof* fabrics as the blue component of the green colouring.

8 – **Dyer's Sumac** (*Cotinus coggygria* Scop, syn. *Rhus cotinus*): Dyer's sumac has been known as a dyestuff source since the Romans. It was widely used in Europe during the middle ages; and represents an important niche economically. Roman author Pliny the Elder, who lived between the years AD. 23 - 79 wrote about its use in leather dyeing. It is known that dyer's sumac (*Cotinus coggygria* syn. *Rhus cotinus*) has been used widely in Europe in the 19th century for yellow in dyeing fabrics, especially silk. Uniforms and tents of Turkish soldiers during the First World War were dyed using the leaves and thin branches of this plant. It was also used in 19th century Anatolia to dye yarn yellow. Dyer's sumac was observed to have been used especially in the yellow colours of *Taşpınar* carpets and in Ankara *sof*.

9 – **Kermes** (*Kermes vermilio* Planchon): This dye insect is a parasite of the *Quercus coccifera* (kermes oak), *Quercus ilex* (evergreen oak) and *Quercus robur* (common oak) species of evergreen oaks, found in parts of the Mediterranean coast and up to the Zagros Mountains of Iran.

The word "*kermi*" in Sanskrit means worm. This became *qirmiz* in Arabic, *kermes* in Persian, and *kırmızı* in Turkish, all meaning "red." The English word crimson is derived also from the same root. Kermes dyeing held an important place in the Near East and Southern Europe for many centuries. The use of the kermes for dyeing was known also by the Sumerians around BC 3000. Many Sumerian clay tablets depict weaving and dyeing techniques for woollen fabrics. It was known in ancient Mesopotamia that the kermes insect was the chief source for red pigment. A clay tablet found in archaeological excavations in Babylonian *Nuzi*, modern *Yorghan Tepe*, near Kirkuk in Iraq, tells us that the kermes insect was used in dyeing textile fibre red. Texts in Torah indicate that kermes insects were used in dyeing processes in BC 1400s. Persians used kermes insects to obtain the red colouring of their fabrics and many carpets. In fact, it is a well-known fact that red dye was spread worldwide by the Persians. Romans termed dyes obtained from kermes *scarlatum*. The kermes insect, during this period, was used for dyeing different types of fibres, such as silk, wool, etc. Pigments obtained from these insects were used also in their murals and icons. Kermes were collected at Venice and Marseilles during the middle ages and exported to other European countries. Venetians considered the red pigment obtained from kermes a superior colour. They have overseen kermes production techniques and maintained its quality. Thus, their kermes dyes came to be known all over the world as "Venetian red." After the conquest of Istanbul (1453) by the Ottoman Empire, Fatih Sultan Mehmet banned the use of seashells in dyeing, thus increasing the prominence of kermes dyeing. The Roman Cardinals' ban of 1464, also prohibiting the use of seashells greatly increased the use of the kermes.

10 – Cochineal (*Dactylopius coccus* Costa): The Cochineal is a scale insect native to Central America, and lives as a parasite on a cactus known as *Opuntia cochenillifera*. It was brought to Anatolia with the acceleration of geographical discoveries in the early 16th century. Dye analyses have revealed that the bright red palace fabrics were dyed with the pigments obtained from the cochineal. It was also determined that the insect has been used in mohair, as in the Ankara *sof*, as well as in wool dyeing. Cochineal was one of the most important dyestuff sources used in colouring textiles red in its motherland Mexico around BC 1000. The insect was not known outside Mexico until the early 16th century. However, a species found in the Old World (Asia and Europe), at Mount Ararat and the banks of the River Aras, was known as the "Ararat cochineal". Cochineal was discovered by the Spanish in Mexico in 1512, and they began to use it as a dyestuff in various fields, but mainly textiles in Europe and Asia. The Spanish first shipped the cochineal from Mexico to Spain. Later they traded it with other countries in Europe and Asia. This insect found a very good niche in the market, because it contained more dyestuffs than various similar insects in Europe and Asia (the Ararat cochineal, lac insects, and Polish cochineal) and yielded brighter and more sumptuous colours. Nearly 1100 tons of cochineal are consumed annually in the world. Statistics show that in 2002, 1045.9 tons were produced. Today it is used in food colouring and cosmetics besides dyeing textiles. Peru leads world production of cochineal.

Source: Turkish Cultural Foundation – TCF

11 – Saffron (*Crocus sativus* L.): Saffron consists of the dried stigmata of the crocus species *Crocus sativus* L. (*Iridaceae*). It is a tuber plant, which can grow up to 20 centimetres and blooms with large purple flowers in the autumn. It is cultivated in Safranbolu villages. Saffron is used as a fragrance and a dyestuff.

Anatolia is the saffron plant's motherland, where it has been cultivated in the region since 3000 years. It is used not only as a dye plant but also in the fields of medicine and cosmetics. Homer, Hippocrates, Pliny, and many other ancient authors have mentioned saffron. This plant had been cultivated in ancient times, and then spread through Iran to further east. Arabs carried saffron to Europe via the Moors of Spain. Today saffron is cultivated in Morocco, Spain, Sweden, Iran and Kashmir. Saffron was used to dye textiles in ancient cities such as Sidon and Tyre. Ancient Persians cultivated *Crocus sativus* in Derbena, Isfahan (modern day Iran), and Khorasan (modern day Afghanistan) by the 10th century BC. Saffron was also used as a dye plant in the woven fabrics offered to the gods. Saffron was used for yellow and orange colour in illuminations of 13th century and medieval manuscripts.

Angora Goat and Mohair Supply Chain[1]

A. HALİS AKDER
Middle East Technical University, Department of Economics, Retired Faculty Member

This study is on the importance of the Angora Goat and Mohair in the economy in Turkey and the decline of their significance thereafter. The study will touch upon former periods, but the weight is on the period beginning from the sixties up to now. The Angora Goat and related problems are addressed through various disciplines. The issues will be evaluated here from the economic point of view and problems will be shown along the supply chain.

How Important Was Angora Goat and Mohair during the Republican Era?

The number of Angora Goats reached its highest level in the year 1959. This peak of six million goats was achieved in spite of the problems surrounding farming and trade, not because of any solution or progress toward one. A. Fethi Açıl stated the importance of the Angora Goat in a brief sentence in the introduction of his book "*The Importance of Angora Goat and Mohair in the Country's Economic Structure*", published two years later: "The aim of this study... is to identify the measures to increase the production and develop the exports of this important source of foreign exchange" (Açıl, 1961, p.3). All studies written before and after this book identify the importance of mohair as generator of foreign exchange earnings. Although Turkey was a large producer country, she never became a mohair processing country during the Republican era although the preferences and developments were different concerning the cotton and wool weaving industries. When studies done on Angora Goat are reviewed, they invoke the impression that Sümerbank preferred woolen weaving to mohair (Açıl,1961, s.112; Üstar, 1940 s.108).[2] This may be explained by the absence of a common and easy applicable technology for mohair processing (Anuk, 1969). How far the aim to earn foreign exchange was realized may be followed from the tables of the same study (Table 1).

The first importance indicator calculated by Açıl is the share of mohair exports in total exports. This share has fluctuated between 1938-1960 from 0.48% to 6.01%. It reached close to 5% several times during the 1950s. During the same period the average was 2.6%. Açıl has used the share of mohair exports in total

1 This paper is translated from Turkish to English by the author.

2 Yapağı-Tiftik A.Ş. Genel Müdürlüğü (General Directorate for Wool and Mohair Incorporated Company) was founded in the year 1955 but has been criticized because of its interest in wool procurement and neglect of mohair.

exports of animal products as an indicator, too. This share varied between the years 1938-1959 from 8% to 70%, It was 48.05% in 1959 and the average of these years was 37,3%. These numbers represent high and important magnitudes for that period. The second indicator used by Açıl is also interesting. (Table II); He calculated the share of the top fifteen products in total exports. Thirteen out of the fifteen products were agricultural products and only two of them were minerals.

The total shares of these fifteen products make up almost 81% of total exports. Mohair ranks sixth, after tobacco, cotton, hazelnut, wheat and raisins. This confirms the importance of mohair in exports and is a success indicator. Another success indicator is the achievement of the top rank of global mohair production for several years. Mohair achieved the expected importance and maintained a high export performance until the 1980s.

The importance of Angora Goat may be reiterated in ways that go beyond a pure statistical ranking. Agricultural production has always been a difficult activity in Anatolia because of challenging climate and soil conditions. For the same reasons it is a challenge for Anatolian farmers to produce a product with global competitive power. This valuable product has been produced in this challenging geography until the 1980s and has been exported with a competitive power in large quantities. The achievement of this level of production and exports with minimal input is a great success and is of great importance. Mohair is also today in spite of all its problems among the least import input dependent agricultural products. This success and importance is also not that recent. During the Roman period the saying was "If grain kept Galatia alive, wool brought it wealth". Natural historian Pliny said that Galatia was most famous for wool (Mitchell, 1993, p. 146). Mohair and "sof"[3] were also the source of wealth in Angora and Central Anatolia during the Ottoman era.

Table I. The Share of Mohair Exports in Total Exports
Source: Açıl, 1961, p.5.

Years	Total Exports 1.000 TL	Mohair Exports 1.000 TL	Share in Total Exports
1938	144947	3575	%2,5
1939	127389	7653	%6,01
1940	111446	6582	%5,91
1941	1233081	9765	%0,79
1942	165034	9862	%5,98
1943	257152	14221	%5,53
1944	232530	9764	%4,20
1945	218929	1828	%0,83
1946	432094	2079	%0,48
1947	625244	3912	%0,63
1948	551038	4191	%0,76
1949	693910	5816	%0,84
1950	737547	15975	%2,17
1951	879429	16154	%1,84
1952	1016158	16058	%1,58
1953	1018971	28592	%2,81
1954	937787	21276	%2,27
1955	877370	23687	%2,70
1956	853972	26302	%3,08
1957	966608	39518	%4,09
1958	692358	20015	%2,89
1959	990536	45177	%4,56
1960	900875	44498	%4,94

3 Ottoman mohair-textile

		Export (TL)	Share[4]
Tobacco	1	257.020.000	%25,95
Cotton	2	154.705.000	%15,62
Hazelnut	3	118.552.000	%11,97
Wheat	4	61.028.000	%6,16
Dried Raisins	5	50.945.000	%5,14
Mohair	**6**	**45.127.000**	**%4,56**
Chrome	7	28.195.000	%2,85
Barley	8	22.447.000	%2,27
Lentils	9	15.149.000	%1,53
Animal Prd.	10	12.718.000	%1,28
Wool	11	10.311.000	%1,04
Opium Poppy	12	8.974.000	%0,91
Dried Figs	13	5.650.000	%0,57
Fishery	14	4.557.000	%0,46
Copper	15	2.101.000	%0,21

Table II. The Share of Various Products in Total Exports in the Year 1959
Source: Açıl, 1961, p.7.

Graph I. Number of Angora Goats in Turkey
Source: TurkStat, for earlier periods see Üstar, 1940, p.7; Açıl, 1961, p.23

The number of Angora Goats increased from the beginning of the Republican era up to the 1960s (Graph 1). It has reached the peak in 1959. Over the decade from 1959 to 1969, it decreased by one million to five million. From 1969 to 1971 the number of goats fell further, losing one million over three years before leveling at four million. In 1983 it decreased to a number less than three million, one year later in 1984 to two and in 1992 down to one million. In other words, in thirty-three years the number of goats fell by almost five million. In 2009 the numbers dropped to the minimum number 146,986. The number of Angora Goats has shown a slight improvement according to the latest statistics and increased to 215,645 in 2017.

Supply Chain of Angora Goat

The supply chain of a product demonstrates its structure and the integral links and relationships from inputs to final product movement through the stakeholders such as producer, wholesaler, distributor, processor, retailer and consumer. It covers all successive nodes that are passed through from production to the final consumer. This is the most suitable tool to discuss how stakeholders are affected by various problems. If it would be possible to calculate the added cost or value at each node this could be transformed to a value chain. The "supply chain" approach has been preferred for the continuation of this study.

The value chain map displayed on the next page is to some extent the outline

4 The shares of raisins and barley were misprinted in the original table. They are corrected here. The ranking from large to small has been arranged also for this study.

of this study. Moving from the inputs upwards (vertical analysis) for example as one ton of mohair is carried over, changes hands and is processed, its value will increase. The value will increase by productivity and quality improvements and will multiply by transformations. The upward, vertical analysis opens also the discussion of how the added value is distributed. The value may increase but is the distribution of the increased value fair? The horizontal relationship on the other hand indicates competition. Those at the same level will compete for resources to pass up to a higher level. The whole of the map represents supply: at the very top it shows the final demand of the (foreign) consumer for the mohair products. The input demand in between is derived from this final demand.

First Node of the Supply Chain: Inputs and the Angora Goat Herd

The inputs are rowed horizontally at the bottom of the Angora Goat and Mohair supply chain map. The aim at this level is to feed and maintain an Angora Goat herd by these inputs. The most important inputs are according to their cost levels: the fee of the shepherd, feed and interest payment for credit. The sum of these three items may add to 75-80% of total cost or may even be higher than this level. Other inputs may be sorted as dog maintenance, payment for the pasture, salt, shelter maintenance or rent, insemination fee, donkey, gas, firewood, depreciation of tools, tax, cartridges, veterinary services and medicine, transportation expenses. The availability of the shepherd is the most problematic of all these inputs. Considering inputs as cost, dead and lost animals may also be accounted as input costs.

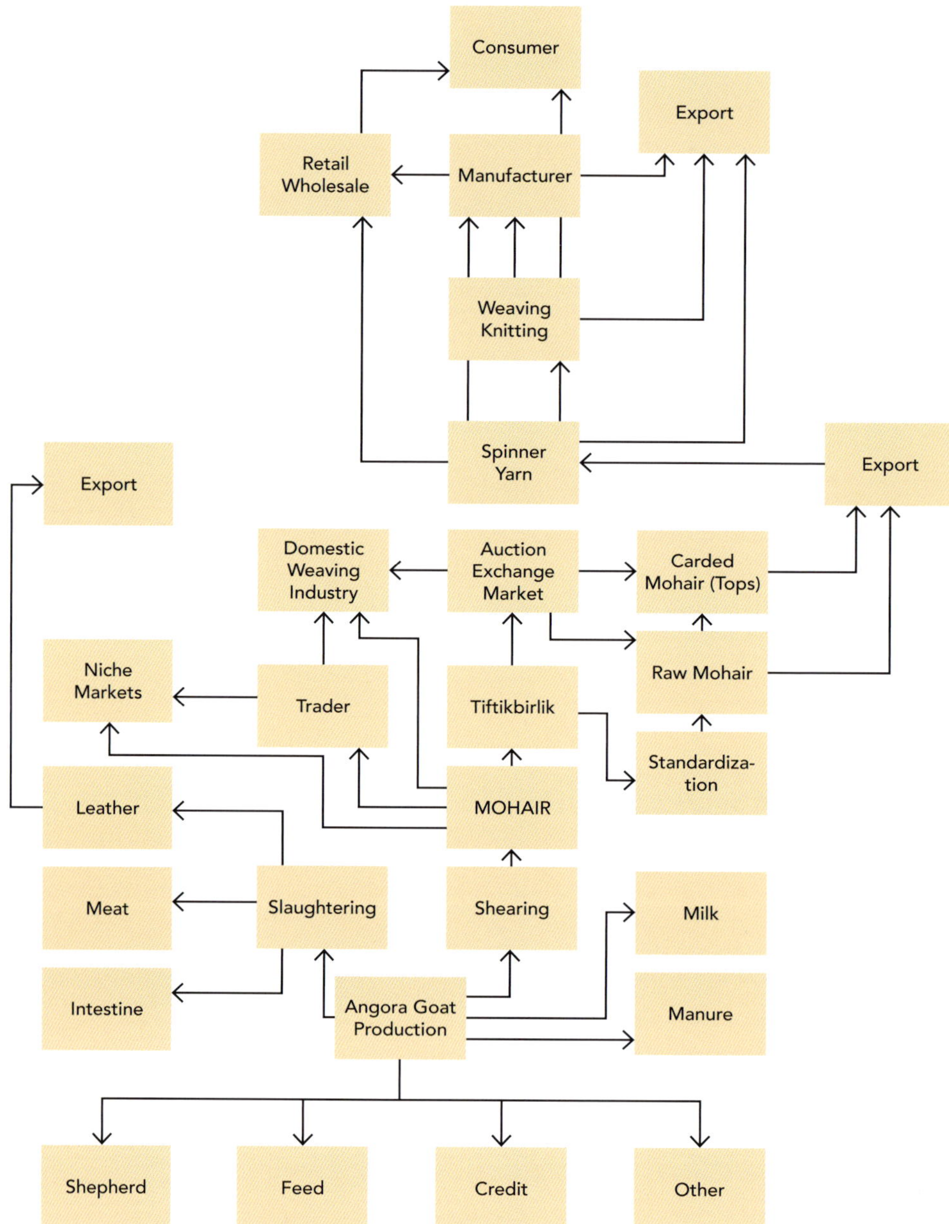

Map I. Angora Goat and Mohair Supply Chain Map olacak.

Angora Goat and Mohair Supply Chain Map:

The main output to be harvested from the herd is the mohair. The meat, milk, leather, intestines even the manure of the goat are byproducts. The herd is composed according to the targeted amount of mohair, depending on the age and gender of the goats. The ideal composition of a large herd is one third doe (female goat), one third kids (baby goat) and one third wether (castrated male goats). The goal is to bring the herd to the composition that will yield the desired amount of mohair and then to keep it at that level.

This will be possible if new-born goats replace those goats that have reached old age and produce a low quality mohair and will be sent to slaughter, those who died because of disease and other reasons, and those that are unproductive. So, the herd may be looked upon as a means of production. The new-born goats that replace the lost ones or ensure an increase are the Angora Goat herd's production. It was not common to replace or increase the size of the herd by trade[5] (Üstar. 1940, p.135). Live Angora Goat exports were also banned by law until 2009.

Mohair Production: Shearing

An Angora goat is sheared in Anatolia during April to obtain mohair. An experienced shepherd or the owner of the herd can do the shearing if the herd is small. But large herds are sheared by a specialized shearer. The shearing starts with the bucks (male goats), goes on to wethers, kids, and does that have had a kid. The logic of this sequence is sorting of the raw material according to its quality before it is brought to the market place but one cannot claim that this sequence is followed strictly all the time. Shearing is done by machine or with a pair of shears. A mature goat is sheared in a maximum of 25-30 minutes. During shearing the rough dirt clinging to the fleece is also removed. The best quality mohair is obtained from kids up to one year but the amount obtained is less than the amount sheared from mature goats. Mohair obtained from young goats is used for weaving dress fabrics, that obtained from older goats is used for the production of rugs and upholstery. Average mohair yield per Angora Goat is between 1.6kg and 2.5 kg but there are also goats that yield up to 5 kg. Shearing is performed in Turkey once a year. It is done twice, in February and August in the USA and South Africa. The yield increases there up to 4-4.5 kg on the average due to double shearing. Single shearing gives Anatolia the reputation for longest mohair fiber produce.

Byproducts

Although mohair is obtained each year from each animal in the herd, byproducts are obtained from a limited number of animals according to the herd's composition. Leather, meat and intestine products are limited by the number of goats that will be sent (because of old age) to slaughter. Leather has competitive power and may be exported. The supply chains of the byproducts are not added to the map here. For example, the supply chain of leather is at least as complicated and stratified as the supply chain of the mohair. Goat leather is used for shoe making, gloves, suede jackets, lady's suits. Recent price increases of the price have raised the value of meat in the domestic market. There is interest for Angora Goat meat in regions where ordinary goat meat is traditionally con-

5 According to Üstar's exposition "It is not possible to explain the reason why there is no market for Angora Goat in our Country... If steps will be taken to establish such a market it will be observed with satisfaction that it will serve to the increase of these precious, invaluable animals." The observation stated by Üstar in 1940's does not mean that there was no trade of Angora Goat at all. He means probably that trade was very small.

sumed. But the meat yield of the Angora Goat is not high. Efforts to increase leather production and mohair production support each other. Efforts to improve the quality of leather by better feeding will also improve the mohair quality. Another byproduct is milk but the numbers of the goats that yield milk are limited to does that have a kid. Besides, the milk of the Angora Goat is not much and milking will affect the healthy growth of the kids adversely. To include ordinary male goats into the herd to increase the milk and meat yield, on the other hand, conflicts with the goal to produce good quality, pure mohair (Daşkıran ve Koluman, 2015, p. 29). The herd grazes during the summer in the steppe, it is therefore not possible to collect the manure and only the amount collected in the winter shelter may be profited from.

The inputs on the supply chain may be labeled up to this point in two different ways. The monetary value of the inputs reveal an important part of the value added and also production cost. The revenue received from the byproducts and mohair is income. The difference between income and cost is profit (Üstar 1940 p.135; Açıl 1961, pp 50-59; Kıral, Özçelik, Fidan, Yılmaz, 1996).[6] The mohair price is the most important variable that determines this equation, it is (derived) reflected back from the supply and demand price of the final good in the export destination where the mohair was sold and was processed into an end product. As mohair producers were making losses or expecting that losses would continue, they have given up raising Angora Goats and may have preferred herding sheep.

Years	Average purchase price (TL/kg)	Direct support payment (TL/kg)	Quantity (ton)	Total Product Payment (TL)
2007	5,00	8,0	193	958.212
2008	5,00	8,9	141	695.952
2009	5,00	10,7	144	677.202
2010	5,00	13,8	126	525.222
2011	5,34	14,6	140	747.119
2012	7,02	17,0	152	1.067.076
2013	6,87	17,0	185	1.270.334
2014	7,09	20,0	213	1.509320
2015	7,88	22,0	218	1.725.386
2016	10,43	22.0	169	1.762.146

Tablo III. Mohair purchase price, Quantity and Value of Mohairunion (2001-2016)
Source: Mohair Report, 2018, p.9.

Domestic Trade of Mohair

Government intervention to the mohair market started after the Angora Goat numbers decreased approximately by one million during the years 1969-1971 (Üstar, 1940).[7] The most important stakeholders in the mohair market are shown in a study published in 1980 as "collector", "trader", "exporter", "Wool-Mohair General Directorate"[8] and "Mohair and Wool Agricultural Sales Cooperative[9]" (Örkiz, 1980). Throughout Republican history large mohair exporting companies in Istanbul needed employees that would collect the product from many

6 For former profit accounting examples.

7 The book written by M. Faik Üstar is an excellent reference source for the mohair market in earlier years.

8 The Wool&Mohair General Directorate (Türkiye Yapağı ve Tiftik A.Ş. Genel Müdürlüğü) was closed down in 1995.

9 The name of this cooperative is shortened to "Mohairunion" (Tiftikbirlik).

small producers. The producer was on the other hand always, even in the years when government procured but paid with a delay, in need of cash. The trader and collector did not only buy the mohair but made advance payments and covered to some extent the finance needs of the producer. Besides it might be good to point to the nuance that there were two types of traders, one of them may be called a commissioner (Üstar, 1940, p.33). This trader does not buy the product from the producer but mediates the sale of the mohair for a commission. The other trader buys the product and markets it thereafter. Sometimes the producer brought the remaining product to the market place himself and maybe some left over mohair was put into his stock. Competition increased after the public organizations entered the market to make support purchases. Marketing channels changed as a result and markets leveled at around support prices. The support prices put some brake on the price decrease; however global prices continued to fall due to the decrease in final good demand. During the 1980s the mohair producer was able to sell their produce to the collector, trader, General Directorate for Wool&Mohair and to the Mohairunion. The collector delivered the mohair to the trader, to Directorate of Wool and Mohair, or to mohair processing rug and textile factories. The trader was using the same channels. Mohair exporters, Mohairunion and Directorate for Wool&Mohair were directing the product to export after the expertise process (Örkiz, 1980).[10] The directorate for Wool&Mohair might have processed some amount (1984-1998) to tops in Afyon, Sincarlı and blended it probably with other fiber (probably wool) and used it in Sümerbank textiles. The share of the traditional stakeholders of mohair, the traders and the collectors has decreased recently almost to disappearance. Mohairunion[11] is now the only and most important stakeholder in mohair trade. The Union procures almost all mohair production in the name of the government for achieving producer price stability and for protection against foreign competitors. This is performed according to the instructions of the Union and on the basis of expertise procedures. The procured mohair is processed in the installations of the Union and is exported or marketed to domestic firms. The Union makes prepayments for shearing, additional help is provided for medicine, concentrated feed and breeding to achieve high quality and high yielding mohair production (Tiftikbirlik, 2018). Purchases after 2000 may be evaluated as not usual support procurements but rather support efforts to protect the Angora Goat from the threat of extinction.

Manufacturing in the Domestic Market

Blended with other fibers, mohair has been used in the domestic weaving industry, rug and blanket production. There are also niche markets where traditional production continues in small amounts. One encounters touristic good production like mohair kese and belly band in Tosya and knitted socks in Ayaş and its surroundings. Carding of mohair for export may be considered as semi

10 See the presentation of this schema in the book written by M. Örkiz.

11 Mohair and Wool Agricultural Sales Cooperative (Tiftik ve Yapağı Tarım Satış Kooperatifi) has been founded in the year 1969.

processing and tops production may be evaluated as domestic manufacturing. Mohairunion claims that mohair production is consumed in recent years totally in the domestic market and if there will be quality and quantity improvement there will be no marketing problem at all (Tiftikbirlik, 2018). The foreign trade statistics support this view.

Raw and Carded Mohair Exports

There were raw mohair exports between the years 2007-2016 only in the years 2010, 2011 and 2014, respectively at the amounts $4,670,339 (107.636 kg), $491,899 (60.274kg) and $21,036 (23.373 kg). Semi processed mohair was exported in the years 2007 and 2008 at respective amounts $351,000 and $72,000. It is no longer possible to learn semi processed mohair trade figures separately after the revision of the foreign trade chapters in 2009. Foreign trade figures of mohair are aggregated with other fibers but it is assumed that the largest share is that of mohair. "Combed or carded" in other words the average value of semi processed animal hair exports between 2009-2016 is $1,262,941. Average import value during the same period is $5,408,983. These numbers indicate that Turkey has transformed to a mohair net importing country (Tiftik Raporu, 2018, pp. 5-7).

Spinning

As can be seen from the supply chain map, Turkey's exports of raw and semi processed mohair continue their journey further in foreign countries. In next stages its value increases the more it is processed. An important characteristic of mohair is its versatility, it can be dyed easily, it is a light and shiny fiber. Raw mohair is washed and prepared like a thick rope ball for spinning and is send to dying and roving. In this form it is called tops. Tops are drawn by spinners into rovings that are then spun into different types, sizes of yarn. Each type is for a different market: dressing textile, upholstery, felt hat; knitting yarn of different sizes, blended with natural (wool) and synthetic fibers (nylon, viscose, acrylic) are sent to knitting and weaving. Home knitting yarn may be sent from this stage directly to the retailer. Tops and yarns may also be exported at this stage and reach foreign processors and consumers.

Knitting and Weaving

Knitted textile or weaving is the last stage in mohair's processing (transformation). Textile or knitted wear may go directly to manufacturing and may also be exported. Especially knitted wear may be produced at this stage or design products (shawls, scarves or pullovers) may also be processed.

Manufacturing

Manufacturing in this context means the use of knitted or woven textile or even yarns for the production of final goods. Luxurious suits for men and women, home textile, furnishing, rugs, upholstery and similar products are produced at this stage. A large amount of mohair goes into furnishing fabrics. Such fabrics are often used for upholstery, particularly in prestige locations including the first class areas of ships, yachts, cars, airplanes. These fabrics are preferred be-

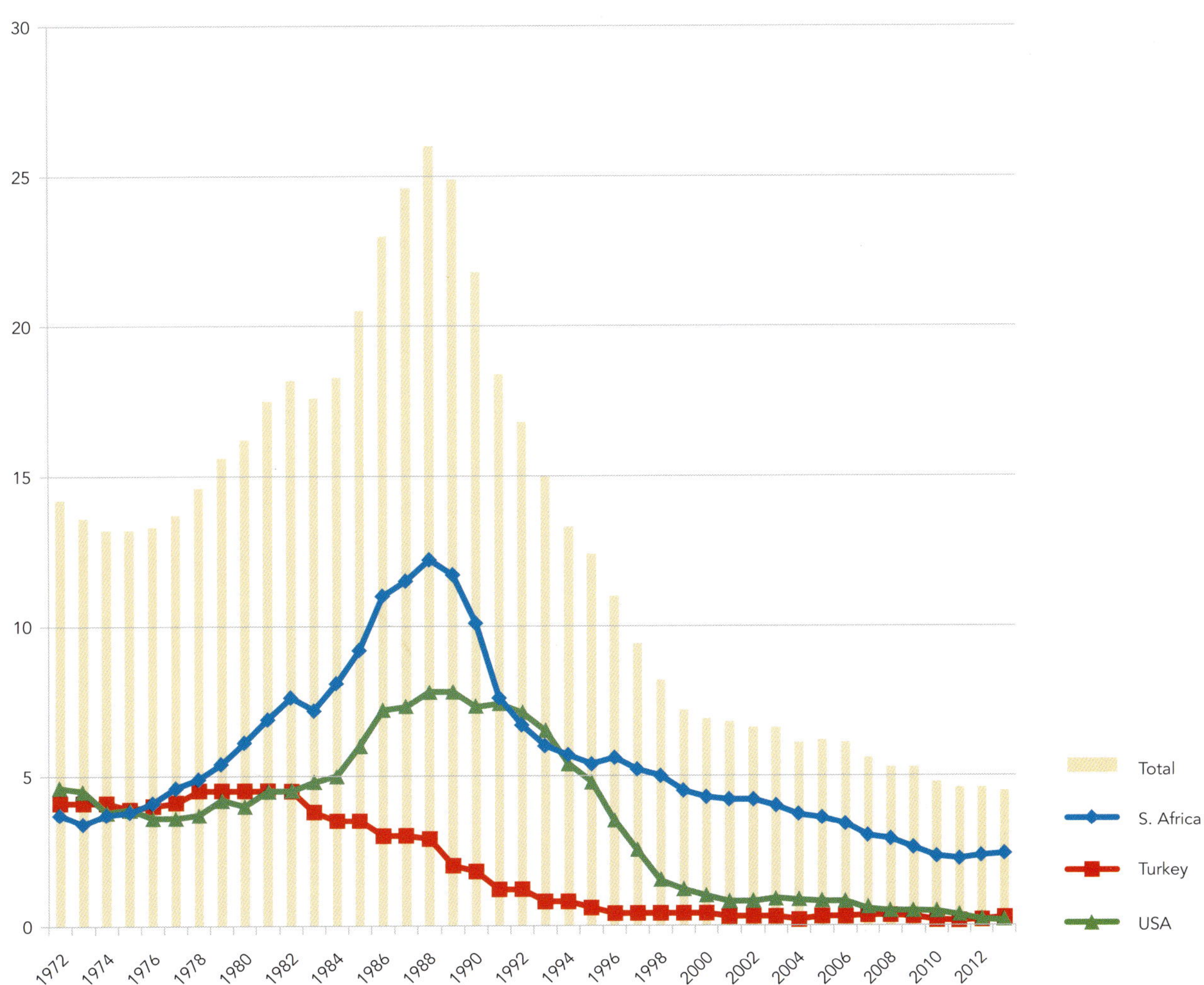

Graph II. (1972-2013) Global Mohair Production (million kg)
Source: Mohair South Africa, 2012, p.19.

cause they are extremely hard wearing d fire resistant. Manufactured products are channeled to the retailers in the domestic or foreign markets.

Wholesale - Retail

Mohair is a luxury product therefore it is important that it is supplied to the producer unlike ordinary goods but as a branded product and this will add value to it. Yet, as observed in the example of South Africa, big enterprises have merged design, manufacturing, wholesale, retail under the same roof. To clarify some issues now it may be useful to preempt the discussion of the problems at the end of the study. First, mohair reveals itself not as a homogeneous product. Mohair is of different quality according to the body part of the goat where it is sheared from. Quality classification implies that different qualities will be used for different product markets. Second, many countries that don't produce mohair in Europe and Asia are processing mohair. Preparation of tops, spinning, weaving, knitting and manufacturing, each of these activities may be performed in different countries.

How and Why Did the Importance and Success End?

Most of the studies that try to explain the decline emphasize the persisting problems. Basic requirements that couldn't reach a satisfactory solution and stated repeatedly are low yield due to insufficient care and feeding, expanding arable farming on the steppe, unsatisfactory management of the goat and woodland relationship, animal health issues, continuing breeding problems, and unsuitable herd composition. These are important problems and each demands determined effort to solve them. These problems may also hinder a new start if prices would rise again. But one should not forget that at its highest levels of mohair production these problems were there and were not resolved.

These problems may have affected the decline of mohair compared to other countries earlier and harder. But the main reason for the decline after 1988 is not the observed production problems in Turkey but demand and price problems arising from the final product processing countries (GRAPH II).

There aren't many countries in the global mohair market. The Angora Goat has been smuggled in the past outside Anatolia, yet it can still be grown in an climatically restricted area similar to that of Central Anatolia. It is produced much less than other natural fibers such as wool and cotton, and even less than cashmere and alpaca. The main producer countries are South Africa, the USA and Turkey. The USA and South Africa are at the same time mohair processing countries. Turkey, on the other hand, is only a raw material, mohair producing country.

Global mohair production in 1988 reached 26 thousand tons and this is the highest known level. At this level Turkey is producing three thousand tons. Argentina, Australia, New Zealand, and Lesotho may also be listed among mohair producing countries. As the decline started after 1988 the production levels of these countries remained at very low levels. Two countries that don't produce mohair but process mohair are the United Kingdom and Italy. Several large and small countries in Europe and Asia may be added to the processor list. As can be observed from Graph II the production of three major countries, USA, South Africa and Turkey is declining together and very fast[12]. None of them is increasing its share at the cost of the other. This implies that the problem is related to the final good market. In other words the decline of mohair production depends on the declining demand for final goods produced from mohair. The demand decrease for mohair final goods is decreasing the raw material (mohair) demand.

Looking at the graph one may notice that these three countries had the same production level during the 1980s. Then, as two of them were increasing their production Turkey's output starts to fall. One may think that the market share lost by Turkey is won by the others. However, the total increase is higher than Turkey's loss. The production starts to fall of all three together after a short while. Output of the USA has decreased almost below that of Turkey. (United States Department of Agriculture 2017, p.14).[13] Although the output is recently less than its 1972 level, by producing half of the global output, South Africa is struggling to hold on, and they were even able to improve their position in 2012. Studies done in Turkey have looked for the cause of this decline in Turkey's production process. It is better to call this "not wrong but misses the point". The apparent cause of this decline is the flow of cheap clothing from developing countries to developed countries due to trade liberalization. Cheap clothing has substituted mohair products.

---

12 The countries that are not shown on the graph are considered in the category "total".

13 The Number of Angora Goats in USA is in 2016, 150,000and in 2017, 152,000.

Mohair has been blended parallel to this development in larger quantities with synthetic fibers or mohair has been replaced with cheap mohair imitations such as acrylic textile or knitting. As demand for mohair products was also not stable anyhow, price fluctuations have affected the situation for the worse.

In South Africa the mohair industry and retail market is divided into three segments. The kid's mohair is used for elite, luxury products; sophisticated men's and women's wear is produced from this fine mohair. This is a fashion market, yet, it is stable but small. Angora and other fine wool products are the competitors. The second segment is the fashion market. Demand in this market depends on the continuously changing fashion. Therefore demand is unstable. The demand lasts a few seasons and prices follow demand. Prices increase or decrease with demand. The retail market is blending mohair with other fibers more and more. The spinners may give up mohair as its price increases and use other fibers and as its price decreases they come back again. The third segment is the non-fashion manufactured product market and this is actually the largest segment. Mohair is used here in very large quantities and is influenced very much because of the fashion price fluctuations (*Agricultural Marketing Extension*, 2018). These changes impact also primary mohair production market and the price fall causes the producers to exit.

Wool, cotton and synthetic fibers are the most important substitutes of mohair; kids mohair's price is twice that of wool. The wool price is about threefold that of cotton and other synthetic fiber (polyester, acrylic, nylon, polypropylene) (Mohair, 2012; FAO, 2009). The main reason for the decline in mohair production is its substitution by cheap synthetics but especially by acrylic. Acrylic is marketed as a mohair look-alike product. Acrylic damages the luxury image of mohair beyond substituting it. The substitution of mohair with synthetic fibers started during the 1960s in the USA but its recent impact has been much stronger compared to periods before 1988.

Recommendations Starting From the Consumer to the Producer Along the Supply Chain

Starting from the end of the supply chain, from the consumers, what might be the concerns and related recommendation for Angora Goat and mohair? The observed problem related to mohair consumers is their reluctance to buy mohair products. Here is the endpoint where problems ball up and this is a demand problem. The most feasible solution is to increase the awareness of the consumer of mohair products. This may be expected from the retail sector with a brand name in respective countries. A contribution to the solution from the other end of the ball, from Turkey, seems to be impossible. In the first instance one might think that there aren't many mohair product consumers in Turkey but there is need for enhanced awareness here, too. To see Angora Goat and mohair only as foreign exchange earning didn't create a persistent awareness. As the numbers of Angora Goats were approaching extinction only a small group showed concern about it. If the importance emphasizes foreign exchange earnings, a great majority may not even notice the decline in the number of Goats and Mohair exports as these are compensated for very fast by increased cotton textile and other product exports.

The retail sector is expected to contribute to "awareness" yet the sector itself demands traceability. It is known that spinners and manufacturers are expressing concern about the lack of qualified technicians. The traceability is here also a concern.

Development of new mohair processing equipment for new products requires innovative contribution and it is an area that goes beyond agriculture. The same problem has limited in the past Turkey's willingness to process mohair domestically, too. The development of new machinery is a solution on the supply side but new product development might become a solution on the demand side. Trade is placed in the most critical position for mohair as it provides the feedback of both sale and production. The most frequently observed problem of trade is finance. Trade is also at a critical position concerning traceability. It is important to trace that hazardous chemicals have not been used. Trade is also the location for quality classification.

Angora Goat husbandry is done in Turkey by farmers who live in mountainous areas and who have little land and income and have little opportunity to produce an alternative product. Those producers are the ones that couldn't solve Angora Goat husbandry problems due to the conditions under which they live. It might be more convenient to apply for rural development programs under these circumstances. It might be also appropriate to keep a financial program ready for those who will start if a new chance evolves.

To preserve the domestic textile industry and foreign trade the quality has to be raised to an acceptable level and the achievement of an approved standardization by importing countries is indispensable. It might be advisable under these circumstances to involve the textile industry to a trial for contract farming. The improvement of the quality by breeding is not a short-run policy but may have very high returns in the long run. The continuous effort of public organizations in this regard is the most promising investment in the future.

Conclusion: Is a Comeback in Mohair Trade Possible?

In 1959 Turkey was producing 10,269 tons of mohair (Açıl, 1961 p.19). Global mohair production in 2013 was 4,500 tons (Graph II). Solutions to problems arising in undiscovered final good markets due to unknown consumer demand may not be expected from efforts that deal with Turkey's supply problems. The USA, Australia, New Zealand, and South Africa are countries that have solved the problems observed in Turkey long ago and are still helpless against existing problems. It is unrealistic to expect a comeback to the old days. This doesn't mean nothing can be done or should be done. An increase in fuel prices may lead to an increase in synthetic fiber prices; an increased awareness of sustainability may cause a return from synthetics to natural fibers; income increases may make luxury consumption more affordable. All these may give a chance for a new start. Yet, it is important to be ready at that time.

References

Açıl, A.F. (1961). *Ankara keçisi ve tiftiğin memleket bünyesindeki ekonomik önemi*. Ankara: Ankara Üniversitesi Ziraat Fakültesi Yayınları.

Agricultural Marketing Extension Training Paper No: 8 Wool and Mohair. Retrieved from http://www.nda.agric.za/docs/GenPub/8WoolMohair.pdf

Anuk, M.N. (1969). Tiftik elyafının işlenmesinde teknolojik güçlüklerin nedenleri. In *Tiftik Semineri*, (pp. 144-194). Ankara: Türkiye Ticaret Odaları ve Ticaret Borsaları Birliği.

Daşkıran, İ., Koluman, N. (2015). Ankara ili tiftik (Ankara) keçisi işletmelerinin güncel analizi ve sürdürülebilir yetiştiriciliğe ilişkin yaklaşımlar. *Ç.Ü.Z.F. Dergisi*, *30* (1): 25-38.

Food and Agriculture Organization of United Nations (FAO). (2009). *Why natural fibers? Five good reasons*. Retrieved from http://www.fao.org/natural-fibres-2009/about/why-natural-fibres/en/

Kıral T., Özçelik, A., Fidan H., Yılmaz D. (1996). *Ankara tarım işletmelerinde tiftik üretiminin ekonomik analizi*. Ankara: T.H.K. Basımevi.

Kooperatifçilik Genel Müdürlüğü. (2018). *Tiftik raporu 2016*. Retrieved from http://koop.gtb.gov.trdata58e5f6ac1a79f54dd851b460/2016%20Tiftik%20Raporu.pdf

Mitchell, S. (1993). *Anatolia, Land, Men and Gods in Asia Minor, Volume I, The Celts and the Impact of Roman Rule*. Oxford: Calderon Press.

Mohair South Africa. (2012). *Mohair review*. Retrieved from http://www.mohair.co.za/application/storage/upload/mohair_review_2012.pdf

Örkiz, M. (1980). *Ankara keçisi yetiştirme ve tiftik pazarlaması*. Ankara: Gıda-Tarım ve Hayvancılık Bakanlığı Lalahan Zootekni Araştırma Enstitüsü Genel Müdürlüğü (GTBKGM). Ankara.

Tiftikbirlik. (2018). Retrieved from http://tiftikbirlik.com.tr/

United States Department of Agriculture. (2018). *Surveys: Sheep and goat inventory*. Erişim adresi: https://www.nass.usda.gov/Surveys/Guide_to_NASS_Surveys/Sheep_and_Goat_Inventory/index.php

Üstar, M.F. (1940). *Tiftik ve tiftikçiliğimiz*. İstanbul: Üniversite Kitabevi.

How Did the Angora Goat Come to Represent the Country's Agriculture? The Angora Goat in Paintings, Stamps and Banknotes

FEYZA AKDER
Koç University Faculty of Humanities, Department of Archaeology and Art History

This paper is concerned with the creation of images of the Angora goat in paintings on canvas, stamps and banknotes between 1923 and 1956, and their relation to each other. An image identifiable with agriculture, such as the Angora goat, came to represent the country's agriculture thanks to the persistent and dedicated efforts of artists, journalists and politicians working together. A wide variety of agricultural products besides the Angora goat did appear in paintings, stamps and banknotes. The aim was to promote the spread of cultural policies related to agriculture as well as new agricultural policies. But it was the Angora goat, a symbol unlike other animals that symbolize importance and power, such as the eagle, the lion or the wolf, that was elected to promote the young Republic on stamps and banknotes through such efforts.

Illustration of agricultural images as the symbol of the Republic dates back to the years of the Independence War[1]. One of the earliest examples we were able to access is a drawing in the *Dersaadet Newspaper* dated 12.8.1920. The next image is an envelope sent by Master Kadri (*Kadri Bey*) from the İzmir Economic Congress to the incumbent Foreign Minister İsmet İnönü on 17.2.1923. These two items, together with one side of the *One Turkish Lira* banknote that entered into circulation on 5.12.1927 are early examples where agricultural images represent the state (Figures 1, 2, 3). The *Dersaadet Newspaper*, illustrated and published in Istanbul by the eminent journalist of Republican history and newspaper owner Sedat Simavi supported the Independence War in Anatolia (Gökman, 1970, p. 26). In Simavi's drawing, an elderly person, a father or grandfather, points out the sunrise to a child as they work an ox plough together. On the envelope with the İzmir Economic Congress letterhead of 1923, a lone young peasant ploughs towards the rising sun. This is a variation of the *Dersaadet* drawing, and highlights the state and agriculture relationship, too. In fact,

1 The Turkish War of Independence, also known as *İstiklâl Harbi* (19 May 1919 – 24 July 1923) was fought between the Turkish National Movement and the proxies of the Allies after parts of the Ottoman Empire were occupied and partitioned following the Ottoman defeat in World War I. It resulted in the establishment of the Republic of Turkey.

the first İzmir Economic Congress held between February 17 and March 4, 1923 did not only determine the principles of production, but also specified that "history is analysed to determine, on a secular basis, the underlying economic, political and judicial structures of the Turkish people, or the new Turkish State" (Hafızoğulları, 1999, p. 296). On the banknote circulated in 1927, the Grand National Assembly building appears behind the farmer and his plough. The banknote image clearly relates the Republic to agriculture. The farmer and plough image is also repeated in paintings on canvas such as the *Karasabanlı Çiftçi* (Farmer with Plough) by Hasan Vecih Bereketoğlu, *Çift Süren Köylü* (Peasant Ploughing) by Nazmi Çekli, and *Çiftçiler* (Ploughmen/Farmers) by Ayetullah Sumer (Yasa Yaman, 1996, p. 31, 32).[2]

There are two Council of Ministers decrees published between 1923 and 1950, regarding the use of agricultural images. The first of these, dated 1931, referred to

2 Hasan Vecih Bereketoğlu's *Karasabanlı Çiftçi* and Ayetullah Sumer's *Çiftçiler* are at the Ziraat Bank Collection; Nazmi Çekli's *Çift Süren Köylü* is in the Central Bank Collection. Another example that can be given is the image of a young girl holding grapes, Turgut Zaim's *Üzüm Toplayan Yörük Kızı* (Yörük Girl Picking Grapes), which was exhibited at the 1939 State Painting and Sculpture Exhibition and purchased by the Ministry of Customs and Monopolies (Prime Ministerial Republican Archives, 1939). A similar photograph of a girl holding a bunch of grapes on the *Hundred Lira* banknote, circulated in August 1942, also appeared on the weekly *Yedi Gün* (Seven Days) magazine covers of May and July of the same year (Yedi Gün, 1940, E3, one hundred Turkish Liras, reverse side, 1st Lot, monetized on 15.08.1942, withdrawn on 25.04.1946). It also appears on the stamps issued for the 1943 İzmir International Fair, in denominations of 13 ½ *kuruş* and 4 ½ *kuruş*.

a process that ended with disappointment. According to the document, when postage stamps were reprinted in Latin letters following the alphabet reform of 19283, agricultural symbols were intended for their use. However, the designs created for this Interior Ministry project were not satisfactory. Eventually it was decided that a design with a portrait of Mustafa Kemal surrounded with the inscription "*Türkiye Cümhuriyeti*" (Republic of Turkey) and "*Posta*" (Mail) would suffice (State Archives of the Prime Ministry of the Republic of Turkey, 1931). This decision indicates that use of agricultural-related images was intended, but these designs were not sufficiently competent or original yet at the level that the bureaucrats demanded.

As use of the image of the young peasant working his plough on banknotes and paintings attests, and the 1931 decree indicates, agriculture is a highly appropriate area to show visually the interaction between the state, art and the press during 1923-1950. In the early years of the Republic, many artists began to take up subjects such as sowing, reaping, harvesting, farmers with ploughs, tractors, farmer families etc. (Yasa Yaman, 1996, p. 32).[4] The state, simultaneously with the artists, used similar or the same images on their stamps and banknotes, as did other periodicals which supported the government.

Six of the 29 images that appear on the reverse sides of the banknotes issued between 1923 and 1950 are agriculture-themed, which meant that one fifth of the banknotes in circulation presented an agrarian scene. Two of these feature Angora goats (Republic of Turkey Banknotes, 2014, pp. 21-98). However, books about the Turkish mohair industry are the only medium where photographs of the Angora goat were widely used in the Republican era. Angora goats are not featured too frequently in newspapers, magazines or paintings. Even then, the Angora goat remained in circulation as a figure on stamps and banknotes until 1952.

Mohair's economic significance is the main reason why the Angora goat figure was preferred over many other images that could symbolize agriculture. The Angora goat helped develop Ankara and its periphery thanks to mohair as a foreign trade product between the 16th and 18th centuries. The focus of trade during this period was the *sof* fabric woven from the Angora goat's mohair. However, the *sof* trade declined in the 19th century for a variety of reasons. By the 20th century, *sof* fabric was no longer produced for the foreign market but mohair was exported as raw material. Between 1926 and 1928, major economic crises upset global markets and adversely affected the mohair trade. In 1931, the situation began to improve somewhat with Soviet Russian purchases of mohair from Turkey (Üstar, 1940, pp. 68, 70). The Mohair Association of Turkey, founded in 1932, conducted valuable studies on Angora goat husbandry during and after the crisis. After this period, mohair continued to

3 The current 29-letter Turkish alphabet was established as a cultural reform in 1928. Hence the Arabic alphabet was given up and Latin letters became the official alphabet. As a result of this reform many printed materials had to be reprinted.

4 A significant study on how the peasant and farmer theme was taken up as a new subject during the 1923-1950 period is an article titled *Peasant/Farmer Theme in Art as a Political/Ideological Discourse of Modernism*. This study describes how the prominence of agriculture in the Republican period affected the art of painting (Yasa Yaman, 1996, pp. 29-37).

Figure 1. Sedat Simavi, "Dersaadet Newspaper First Page Drawing," no. 36, 12.08.1920 (Gökman, 1970, p. 27).

Figure 2. Envelope with İzmir Economic Congress letterhead, dispatched to Foreign Minister İsmet Paşa on 17.02.1923 (Temiz, 1996, p. 26).

Figure 3. One Turkish Lira, reverse side, First Lot, monetized 05.12.1927, demonetized 25.04.1939 (Banknotes of the Republic of Turkey, 2014, p. 21).

be significant as foreign trade until the 1970s, although prices fluctuated. In 1959, the share of mohair exports was higher than the export value of products such as barley, opium, dried fig, livestock, wool, copper and chrome, and almost near that of raisins. In 1961, mohair exports accounted for 4.94% of all exports (Açıl, 1961, p. 114).

Another reason for preferring the Angora goat as a figure in paintings, stamps and banknotes was the fact that this animal was a symbol of Ankara. From the 16th century onwards, the *sof* production and trade in the city drew the attention of all travellers to Ankara. Foreign merchants came to Ankara mostly for the mohair and *sof* trade, which was a substantial business in the 16th century. The *sof* fabric was sold in Istanbul, Aleppo, and Bursa as well as European markets such as Venice, and Poland. The Angora goat was the essential factor that connected the city to the outside world from the 16th century, thanks to *sof* trading (Ergenç, 1984, pp. 53-54, Yıldırmak, 2011, pp. 11, 353). Thus, travellers and merchants have identified Ankara with this animal for three hundred years.

The first major documentary film where the Angora goat was used as a symbol of Ankara was *Ankara, the Heart of Turkey*. The film was made in 1933 by Sergei Yutkevich, a film director and screenwriter who was on the official USSR delegation that came to Ankara for the celebrations of the Tenth Anniversary of the Republic. In the film, a herd of Angora goats and its proud herdsman stand atop a hill overlooking the city on the morning of October 29, 1933 (Yutkevich, 1933, 1'33" – 2'15").[5] The Angora goats directly refer to Ankara and thus to Turkey in the documentary. While the Angora goat as a symbol of Ankara goes back to the Ottoman era, there was also significance in the fact that the mohair trade had just begun because of the trade agreement with Soviet Russia in 1931.

The Angora goat was first seen on canvas in Republican period painting in 1933. This was a work by Turgut Zaim titled *Eastern and Western Peoples Offer Gratitude to Atatürk:* a triptych currently at the MSGSÜ Museum of Painting and Sculpture. The painting portrays a scene where Anatolian people offer their products to Atatürk and thank him. The work was created for the Tenth Year Celebrations (Yasa Yaman, 2006, p. 60). In the east wing of the triptych, an Angora goat gambols forward at the front of the group walking towards Atatürk. A second Angora goat figure stands at Atatürk's right hand side at the central panel.

In reviews of the painting, no comment has been offered regarding Zaim's use of the Angora goat as a figure. However, Zaim's choice of an Angora goat to represent Anatolian products during the Tenth Year Celebrations is highly consistent with the contemporary economic developments described above.

Two years later, Turgut Zaim presented the Angora goats once again, this time more clearly within the composition. They can be seen in the paintings titled *Kavun Satan Yörük Kadın* (Nomadic Woman Selling Melons), *Ürgüplü Yörükler* (Nomads of Ürgüp) and *Yaylada Yörükler* (Nomads in the

5 The documentary *Ankara, the Heart of Turkey*, filmed in 1933 and screened for the first time in 1934, was a Soviet production. Although a documentary film, the film follows a script that promotes the Republic's Tenth Year Celebrations. The film was ordered at the request of Ataturk. It is preserved at the VEKAM Library and may be viewed by everyone by appointment.

Figure 4. Turgut Zaim, *Yaylada Yörükler*, 1935, oil on canvas, 175x134 cm, Ankara Museum of Painting and Sculpture.

Highlands), which appeared in the fifth exhibition of the *d Grubu* in 1935 (Image 5-4, Yasa Yaman, 1992, p. 105).[6] The shepherds in the paintings were depicted in a harmonious and happy atmosphere, with women and children nearby. The goats are portrayed as part of the *Yörük* (nomadic) life, which will prove to be a most significant subject in the artist's repertoire (Tansuğ, 1976, pp. 27-28).[7]

Turgut Zaim was an artist who saw an emotional connection beyond the economic between Angora goats and the people. This bond is often impressively portrayed through the affection and embraces between children and goats. In 1935, Turgut Zaim painted the Angora goats beyond the provincial borders of Ankara, too. The most important reason for this is

---

6 d Grubu is a pioneering artistic circle that was active between 1933 and 1947. Catalogues of the collections do not specify when the paintings were created. However, Zeynep Yasa Yaman has determined the dates of the paintings in her doctoral dissertation. Considering that Turgut Zaim, who was born and raised in Istanbul, set off on his Anatolian adventure in 1930, these paintings must have been created between 1930 and 1935, and most probably in 1935 when they were exhibited (Yasa Yaman, 1992, p. 105).

7 Studies of the nomadic Yörük, resettlement policies of Ottoman and Republican eras, and the different lifestyles of the said tribes, together with Turgut Zaim's paintings, reveal that a variety of interpretations can emerge. For example, while the camels in the background and the landscape indicate the impressions of the nomadic lifestyle at the highlands in Zaim's *Yörükler*, in *Ürgüplü Yörükler* the Yörüks who have crossed over to sedentary living tend to Angora goats, which are not adaptable to breeding in high pastures. It is highly probable that Turgut Zaim may have depicted different groups under the Yörük epithet. However, this article focuses only on the goat figures. See related issue (Kasaba, 2012). See especially for migration on camels (Tuztaş Horzumlu, 2014).

that Zaim had associated the goats with the life cycle of nomadic people, rather than a region. A second reason is that Zaim may have seen Angora goats outside Ankara for the first time.

Born in Istanbul in 1906, until the 1930s Zaim only left the city to visit Paris and Bursa for just a few days. The artist went to Paris to resume his art education, and it was highly unlikely that he would encounter Angora goats there. After he returned home, he lived in Konya and Sivas. He settled in Ankara in 1932 (Tansuğ, 1976, p. 28) and must have seen Angora goats for the first time in the early 1930s, in Konya and Sivas. While Ankara and its surroundings were the natural habitat of the goat, this is a steppe animal and is able to survive in areas that are characterized as steppe (Batu, 1951, p. 63). The density of Angora goats in Konya, Sivas, Bursa, Ürgüp and Istanbul attests to the possibility that the painter might have seen Angora goats for the first time in Konya and Sivas, and then in Ankara. The number of Angora Goats in Ürgüp, which was 35,225 in 1929, rose to 160,322 in 1937 (Üstar, 1940, pp. 7-17).

The reason for Zaim's appreciation of the Angora goat independent of its economic significance is probably the fact that although work had been conducted until 1935 to develop the mohair industry, the adverse effects of the 1929 crisis had not yet been completely erased. In 1935, mohair had not reached yet the economic potential that it would gain in the following years. The fact that mohair was not profitable at the interim indicates that mohair, and therefore, in Zaim's paintings, the goat were important for the peasants for the products made of the wool, such as rugs, socks, garments, etc. In this context, Zaim portrays the peasants, not as the farmers that the Republic wanted to highlight, who appreciated modern agriculture, supported modernization and carried their products to the highest potential, but those who retained their traditional methods of animal husbandry. As a result, the Angora goat figure took its place in Zaim's paintings as a source related to Anatolian folklore.

Zaim's goats, besides representing the agricultural drive high on the Republican agenda, were vital to the paintings' compositions. The emphasis on dark and light colours are visible in similar elements. For example, while black blots may form a woman's bonnet, a black cat, or a foal, white areas are usually made up of goats (Tansuğ, 1976, pp. 11-13).[8]

In 1935, when Zaim exhibited his paintings, the Prime Ministry issued a second decree concerning postage stamp images. This time, in response to an appeal from the Ministry of Public Works, it was decreed that "stamped and illustrated postcards that combined the many beautiful and historical landscapes of our country, and innovations in the field of Public Works and Economics" would be issued (State Archives of the Prime Ministry of the Republic of Turkey, 1935). This decree once again attested to the administration's

8 The artist recounted his experience of painting peasants as follows: "Most of the paintings I made during my training at the Academy were studies of nature. Again, in those years, in order to adapt myself to working without a model, i.e. from memory, I tried to recreate at home the studies I practiced with models outside school. This kind of work was very helpful during my trip later in life. I would make sketches of the peasants and landscapes, and then transferred these to large paintings on canvas. There were times when photographs I took were very useful, too." (Tansuğ, 1976, pp. 11-13).

Figure 5. Anonymous (1936), "The Provincial Department works among the peasants. Photographs showing the work of this Department easily explain its activities." Detail from photograph (Ankara Halkevi, 1936, p. 44).

Figure 6. Şerif Renkgörür, *Ankara Keçileri*, 1938, oil on canvas, Ulus Newspaper insert for Painting Exhibitions.

determination to use agriculture a symbol on stamps, banknotes and postcards. A second matter that the decree emphasized unequivocally was that instruments used in communication, such as stamps, would be regarded as a means of representing the country, not only at home, but abroad, too. In this period, the economy was founded on agriculture, and two thirds of the population was employed in this sector, therefore, agriculture was vital for representing the country both home and abroad.

Another event that would affect Angora goat images was the appointment of ex-military officer and painter Şerif Renkgörür to the *Ankara Halkevi* (Community Centre) in 1935 (Prime Ministerial Republican Archives, 1936)[9]. Two years after this date, he exhibited his painting *Ankara Keçileri* (Angora goats) (Figure 6). During the 1930s, the *Ankara Halkevi* presented documentary films on agriculture issues, produced by the Higher Institute of Agriculture, and working in the Ankara neighbourhood via its Village Branch.[10] The Drama Branch where Şerif Renkgörür was employed travelled with the Village Branch to villages where they staged shows. The aim was to modernize Ankara and its surroundings, and to introduce and educate the farmers of the region on modern farming methods (Image 5, Anonymous, 1933, pp. 112-128).

Renkgörür exhibited *Ankara Keçileri* in 1938. The work was part of the Second United Painters and Sculptors Exhibition opening at the Ankara Halkevi in June. We do not know in which collection this painting has been preserved. However, a black and white photograph was printed in the exhibition insert of the newspaper *Ulus* (Doğan, 2009, p. 109).

In the painting, five Angora goats stand a little apart from their herdsman. The goats are in a hilly area and there is a mountain in the background but it is not possible to tell to which city the landscape belongs. A review of the exhibition published in *Ulus* criticised the painting,

9 The very first Western style painting lessons in an official establishment were scheduled at "*Mühendishane-i Berri-i Humayun*" (Military School of Engineering) in 1793 in Istanbul during the Ottoman era. In this school classes were categorized as military and drawing. Graduates from the drawing classes were intended to work as engineers, cartographers or drawing teachers for the army. A number of these men became eminent artist both in Ottoman and Republican eras. They were called *asker ressam*, literally "military painter". Şerif Renkgörür is one of the less recognized ones.

10 The Ankara Halkevi Village Branch visited the villages and townships of Karaağaç, Kayaş, Kusunlar, Bayındır, Kutludüğün, Balkat, Kara Kusunlar, Yalıncak, Gölbaşı, Çakallar, Üreğil, Mamak, Zir, Solfasol, Lodum, and Yakacık in 1935; and Balkat, Lodomu, Karakusunlar, Möhye, Bitik, Karalar, Zir, Gölbaşı, Pursal, Orhaniye, Küçükyozgat, Hılkavun, Yabattal, Çubuk, Karaoğlan, Çakal, Etimesut, Kayaş, Bayındır and Kutludüğün in 1938 (Ankara Halkevi, 1938, p. 63, Ankara Halkevi, 1936, p. 39).

noting, *"Şerif Renkgörür's landscapes are beautiful, but the Angora goats are too docile. It is probably their hair. They should have been a little pluckier in colour and movement."* (Doğan, 2009, p. 109).

The painting's composition and the formatting of the goat figures was an endeavour to depict them as they were, in their natural form. Nahit Sıtkı Örik, who wrote art criticism and news in other contemporary periodicals such as *Ülkü*, *Varlık* and others, found Renkgörür's Ankara landscapes "sentimental" (Örik, 1938, pp. 81-82). In fact, animals did not constitute a subject of choice for Renkgörür, as can be seen from the exhibition catalogues. From that point of view, Renkgörür's choice of subject was bold.

We have small information on Şerif Renkgörür's life and no source is available to show us how he created his works. However, artists of the period were known to rely on quick sketches and photographs they have taken. There is an undated and anonymous photograph strongly resembling Şerif Renkgörür's painting (Figure 7). Renkgörür may have used this photo when creating the painting. A second possibility involves a particular method of producing stamps. This method requires that when a painting or an engraving is to be transferred on a stamp, a photograph of the artwork needs to be made into a stereotype (Akoba, 1963, p. 63). However, it is very difficult to decide on this issue without access to the original of the photo and the painting.

The second Angora goat image of 1938 appears on a banknote. A herd of goats in front of a farm depicted on the Fifty Turkish Lira banknotes that were issued in April (Figure 8). The banknote certainly fulfils the duty of *"promoting innovations made in the field of public works and economy, at home and abroad,"* mentioned in the 1935 decree. A flat landscape extends towards a mountain in the distance. The environment is barren, save for a few trees.

Figure 7. Angora goat, black & white photograph, 18x24 cm, VEKAM Library and Archives, Collection of Ankara Photographs, Postcards and Engravings, Inventory no. 0083, Ankara.

The herd on the banknote, with a group standing apart from the rest of the herd, and the goat appearing in profile exhibit various characteristics of the species. There is a modern pen at the lower left corner of the banknote and an expanse of land towards the right. Although herds of goat have been around the region for centuries, they appear as an image of modern agriculture and development image of the Republic for the first time on this banknote. The fact that they are featured on a banknote emphasizes this meaning. In many photographs of the new Ankara, which began to take shape with Republican-style modern buildings as of 1923, one sees such a building in a vast plateau against the background of a mountain in the distance. The pens depicted on the banknote are important in this context, and may be considered a repetition of the mentioned photographs. Pens were a matter of importance in Angora goat breeding in the 1930s – the more modern the pen, the higher quality of the mohair. Books on Angora goat breeding

Figure 8. Fifty Turkish Lira banknote (reverse side), E-2 group, in circulation from 1938 until 1952, 8x17.5 cm (Banknotes of the Republic of Turkey, 2014, p. 36).

Figure 9. Fifty Turkish Lira banknote (reverse side), E-3 group, in circulation from 1942 until 1952, 8x17.5 cm (Banknotes of the Republic of Turkey, 2014, p. 53).

Figure 10. Angora Goats, Stamp, VEKAM Library and Archives, Collection of Ankara Documents, Inv. no. A032_38, Ankara.

expound scientific methods of organizing pens (Üstar, 1940, pp. 27-30). Scientific or modern methods are crucial to the productivity of the trade, as is the case with any other agricultural matters. One of the conditions that will provide this are the pens. Therefore, pens must be modern and scientific, essential structures. The location of the goat pen in the photograph has not been documented. However, the most noteworthy modern goat farm at the time was the experimental pen built at Lalahan, Ankara, by the The Mohair Society of Turkey (established in 1932) (Tamur, 2003, p. 195). The banknote would remain in circulation until 1952.

In the 1940s, the group of goats in Şerif Renkgörür's painting gained importance. It was used in 1942 on banknotes, and in 1943, on stamps. This is the most significant example of the Angora goat's image being used one-to-one in paintings, banknotes and stamps. The news that the stamp would be printed was announced by Ali Nusret Pulhan, who was a leading name in Turkish philately, in his column on stamps in the daily *Yedi Gün* (Seven Days) in 1941. A stamp bearing the image of an Angora goat (alongside 19 other stamps in the *Atatürk-İnönü Series*) was to be printed using the *Taydus* method at the Vienna State Press, in sufficient quantity to meet the two-year stamp requirement of the country. Pulhan commended the artistic expression and the idea of ordering them abroad to insure quality, and congratulated the Postal Administration from his column (Pulhan, 1941, p. 4).

The goat figures in the Şerif Renkgörür painting, the 1942-banknote, and the postage stamp of 1943 are identical. Comparing them, however, one notes that the landscapes are dissimilar. The Fifty Lira banknote printed in 1942 differs from the painting, the postage stamp and the photograph (Figures 6, 7, 10) in that there is no mountain in the background. Comparing the stamp, the banknote, the photograph and the painting, one can see that the large white cloud cluster on the upper left corner of the stamp is not present in the others (Figures 7, 8, 9). Like

Figure 11. Cemal Tollu, *İstihsal* (Production), 200x300 cm, oil on canvas, 1954, İş Bank Collection, Istanbul.

Figure 12. "Cemal Tollu with preparatory work on the *İstihsal* painting", (Berk, date unknown, p. 11).

the mountain at the end of a vast expanse, the white clouds gathering had become part of the new Ankara landscape as of the 1930s, especially in the Ankara scenes created by Austrian photographer Othmar Pferschy for his album *Turkey in Pictures*. Were the immense white clouds that frequently appear behind the *Victory Monument* at *Ulus* district in the photographs, added to give a powerful atmosphere to the landscape when placed behind the goats? There is no clear document explaining the composition of the image on the stamp, or how it came about; but data at hand indicates to such a conclusion.

Seven years after the printing of the stamp, and five years after the end of World War II, in 1950, the Democrat Party (DP) came to power and brought about changes to Turkey's culture and arts policies. One of the changes was that when the banknotes issued by the outgoing government were withdrawn from circulation, visual content related to agriculture would no longer be used. In banknotes, tourism replaced agriculture.[11] The year 1952 is a demarcation: the relationship of postage stamp, banknote and paintings in the context of agriculture began to weaken after this date.

A second significant change concerned the state's culture and arts policies. From 1923 onwards, state institutions and community houses had carried out art and cultural events almost entirely on their own. These were mostly group exhibitions involving a large number of artists. The DP government, on the other hand, did not appear to be interested in cultural and artistic activities other than continuing the State Painting and Sculpture Exhibitions. Non-governmental establishments began to be involved in artistic activities. The *Work and Production*-themed art competition organized by the Yapı Kredi Bank in 1954 is a good example of this (Yasa Yaman, 1998, p. 96). Cemal Tollu's painting *İstihsal* (Production) that took part in this contest was an important work in which the Angora goat was depicted once again during the DP administration (Figure 11).[12]

At the centre of the *İstihsal* are Angora goats. Tollu did not offer any direct

11 These changes can be detected easily in the catalogue *Republic of Turkey Banknotes* published by the Central Bank (Banknotes of the Republic of Turkey, 2014, pp. 21-181).

12 This Cemal Tollu painting is registered under the title *Keçili Kompozisyon* (Compostion with Goats) in the İş Bank Collection.

explanation for his choice of the Angora goat. However, in an article he wrote later about the contest, he noted that competition rules required "paintings had to demonstrate the various production activities in Turkey's economic life," and that a bank spokesman, speaking of the competition rules had told them that, "beyond anything else, you must create works that reveal production in Turkey and that this production transpired in Turkey" (Tollu, 1954, p. 1). Given the figures mentioned at the beginning of this article regarding the Angora goat's place in Turkey's agriculture and foreign, Tollu's decision to include these animals in his painting was coherent.

The Yapı Kredi Bank's specifications share common points with the Prime Ministerial decrees of 1931 and 1935, which were discussed in the section above, and the information about the competition that Cemal Tollu received. The 1931 decree recommended the creation of paintings that represented agricultural subjects, while the 1935 decree prescribed beautiful and historical landscapes, public works and economic innovations. All three specifications point to agriculture under the conditions of the country. Private sector Yapı Kredi Bank's creation of a suitable environment for the production of agricultural images is a good example of the above-mentioned changes brought about as of 1950.

The distinct figures in Tollu's *İstihsal* are other symbols used since the declaration of the Republic in various forms, in printed publications, paintings, and government-sponsored photographs, stamps and currency: the Citadel of Ankara, the rising sun, farmlands, peasants, wheat, the Angora goat, peasant playing *bağlama*, etc. The only living creature in the table that is clearly rendered but not one of these symbols is the black cat walking confidently at the lower left corner of the painting.

Tollu uses an almost symmetrical composition in his work *İstihsal*. The Citadel, with the sun rising behind, seems to witness the busy work and lives of the villagers. Three young figures each on the right and left sides of the couple conversing at the centre approach each other with their products. The complex composition consists of groups of interlaced colours and blots. Although the contours of the blots are not indicated with paint, evidence of his work on them may be seen in a photograph that shows the artist with the preliminary sketches in his studio (Figure 12). There is no single random area, or an uncalculated dot in the painting. Tollu would work on the Angora goat theme once again in 1956 with the painting titled *Anadolu Çobanları* (Shepherds of Anatolia), kept at the Mimar Sinan University of Fine Arts Museum of Painting and Sculpture.[13]

The Angora goat was taken up in the first thirty years of the Republic as a symbol in paintings, postage stamps and banknotes. As it became one of the leading images in promoting agricultural and related cultural policies, the Angora goat came to represent not only Ankara, but also the Turkish economy as a whole.

The relationship between Angora goat paintings with postage stamp and banknote images indicate that agricultural policies had influenced art. The paintings

---

13 An oil-painted preliminary study on a red background and a large-scale drawing of this composition is found also at the Mimar Sinan University of Fine Arts Museum, Painting and Sculpture collection. The drawing titled *Çoban ve Tiftik Keçileri* (Shepherd and Angora goats) is dated 1955. For the paintings see: (Çoker, 1967, pp. 10, 12).

of Turgut Zaim and Cemal Tollu point at the Angora goat's niche in rural life from different angles. Şerif Renkgörür's painting has become widespread by its presence on postage stamp and banknote images produced directly by the state. This example shows that some agricultural images originate from a multi-source interaction. Although the Angora goat has been associated with Ankara since the 16th century, the first thirty years of the Republic was a period when the Angora goat, regardless of its docile nature, came to represent the state and the national economy.

References

Açıl, A. F. (1961). *Ankara keçisi ve tiftiğin memleket bünyesindeki ekonomik önemi.* Ankara: Ankara University Press.

Akoba, M. M. (1963). *Türkiye'de pul ve pulculuk.* Istanbul: Ceylan Publications.

Anameriç, H. and Rukancı, F. (2011). *Posta pullarında başkent Ankara seçmeler* (1922-2008). Ankara: Vehbi Koç Ankara Studies Research Centre.

Ankara Halkevi (1933). *Halkevleri 1933.* Ankara: Ankara Halkevi.

Ankara Halkevi (1936). *Ankara halkevi bir yıl içinde 300.000 yurddaşı çatısı altında topladı 1935-1936.* Ankara: Ankara Halkevi.

Ankara Halkevi (1938). *Ankara halkevi bir yıl içinde 475.651 yurddaşı çatısı altında topladı 1937-1938.* Ankara: Ankara Halkevi.

Batu, S. (1951). *Türkiye keçi ırkları ve keçi yetiştirme bilgisi.* Ankara: Ankara University Press.

Berk N. C. (undated). *Tollu.* Istanbul: Academy of Fine Arts Publications - Ahmet Sait Press.

Çoker, A. (1967). *Tollu desenler.* Istanbul: DGSA Publications.

Doğan, Ç. (2009). *Ankara halkevi sergileri.* Unpublished postgraduate thesis. Ankara University Institute of Social Sciences, Ankara.

Elvan, N. and Sönmez, N. (2004). *Resim tarihimizden: "İş ve istihsal 1954 Yapı Kredi resim yarışması."* Istanbul: Yapı Kredi Publications.

Ergenç, Ö. (1984). 16. Yüzyıl Ankara'sı: ekonomik, sosyal yapı ve kentsel özellikleri. Yavuz, E. and Uğurel, N. (Comp.). In *Tarih içinde Ankara: Eylül 1981 seminer bildirileri* (pp. 49-60). Ankara: Middle East Technical University.

Ersel, H. (2014). *Kazım Taşkent Yapı Kredi ve Kültür Sanat.* Istanbul: Yapı Kredi Publications.

Gökman, M. (1970). *Sedat Simavi.* Istanbul: Apa Ofset Press.

Hafızoğulları, Z. (1999). İzmir İktisat Kongresi görüşler ve değerlendirmeler, In *Av. Dr. Faruk Erem armağanı* (pp. 289-311). Ankara: Turkish Bar Association.

Kaçar, D. A. (2015). *Kültür/mekan: Gazi Orman Çiftliği, Ankara.* Ankara: Koç University Vehbi Koç Ankara Studies Research Centre.

Örik N. S. (1938). Ankara'da bir gravür sergisi, *Ülkü, 61*(11), 81-82.

Pulhan, A. N. (1941). Pul köşesi: yeni pullarımız. *Yedigün, 460*(18), 4.

T.C. Başbakanlık Cumhuriyet Arşivi. (1931). *Posta pullarının basılmasına ilişkin kararname.* Date: 25.02.1931, Place: 30-18-1-2 / 18-13–9.

T.C. Başbakanlık Cumhuriyet Arşivi. (1935). *Resimli ve pullu kartpostal ve kartlar çıkarılması.* Date: 26.11.1935, Place: 30-18-1-2.

T.C. Başbakanlık Cumhuriyet Arşivi. (1936). *Ankara halkevi ressamı Şerif Renkgörür'ün sicil dosyası.* Date: 01.04.1936, Place: 490-1-0-0 / 382-1617–2.

T.C. Başbakanlık Cumhuriyet Arşivi. (1939). *Sergievinde açılan resim sergisinde gümrük ve inhisarlar bakanlığı Turgut Zaim'in üzüm toplayan yörük kızı adlı tablosunun gümrük ve inhisarlar bakanlığınca satın alındığı.* Date: 13.07.1939, Place: 173-196-1.

T.C. Resmi Gazete. (1932, Nisan). *Türkiye tiftik cemiyetinin esas nizamnamesi. 10* (2073), 1349-1352.

T.C. Ziraat Bankası Resim Koleksiyonu. (1993). T.R. Ziraat Bank. Ankara: Ajans Türk.

Tamur, E. (2003). *Ankara keçisi ve Ankara tiftik dokumacılığı: Tükenen bir zenginliğin ve çöken bir sanayinin tarihsel öyküsünden kesitler.* Ankara: Ankara Chamber of Commerce Publications.

Tansuğ, S. (1976). *Beş gerçekçi Türk ressamı.* Ankara: Gelişim Publications.

Temiz, Y. (1996). *Pullarda İnönü.* Istanbul: Burak Philately Inc. Cultural Publications.

Tollu, C. (1954, 15 Eylül.). San'at tenkitçileri ve bir netice. *Yeni Sabah.*

Tör, V. N. (2010). *Yıllar böyle geçti.* Istanbul: Yapı Kredi Publications.

Türkiye Cumhuriyeti Banknotları. (2014). Ankara: Republic of Turkey Central Bank Publications.

Üstar, M. F. (1940). *Tiftik ve tiftikçiliğimiz.* Ankara: Universite Books.

Yasa, Y. Z. (1992). *1930-1950 yılları arasında kültür ve sanat ortamına bir bakış: D grubu.* Unpublished postgraduate thesis, Hacettepe University Institute of Social Sciences, Ankara.

Yasa, Y. Z. (1996). Modernizmin siyasal/ ideolojik söylemi olarak resimde köylü/ çiftçi izleği. *Türkiye'de Sanat, 22*, 29-37.

Yasa, Y. Z. (1998). 1950'li yılların sanatsal ortamı ve temsil sorunu. *Toplum ve Bilim, 79*, 94-136.

Yasa, Y. Z. (2006). Ötekinin varlığı: Her resim bir öykü anlatır/ Modern Türk sanatında kadının imgesel dönüşümü. Carol Ann La Motte (Trans.) In *Kadınlar, resimler, öyküler: Modernleşme sürecindeki Türk resminde kadın imgesinin dönüşümü* (pp. 8-85). Istanbul: Pera Museum.

[Cover]. (1940, 7 Mayıs). *Yedigün, 374*(15).

Yıldırmak, W. G. (2011). *XVIII. Yüzyılda Osmanlı-İngiliz tiftik ticareti.* Ankara: Turkish Historical Society.

Yutkevich, S. (Director). (1933). *Türkiye'nin kalbi Ankara.* (56', Black & white, Russian, Turkish). USSR.

Anki

SADIK KARAMUSTAFA
Graphic Designer

For the first time in Turkey, a local government implemented a corporate identity design project for the city it serves, under the guidance of contemporary visual design discipline. The main elements of the project were a charming, shaggy animal, and a museum artefact unearthed in archaeological excavations.

In 1989, Social Democratic People's Party (SHP) candidate Murat Karayalçın was elected mayor of Ankara Metropolitan Municipality. The mohair-goat *Anki*, designed during his tenure, symbolized the City of Ankara, and a newly commissioned reinterpretation of the logo based on the older "Hittite Sun" formed the visual identity of the Ankara Metropolitan Municipality.

When Welfare Party candidate Melih Gökçek was elected mayor of Ankara in the 1994 municipal elections, one of his first actions was to change the logo. A jury of municipal officials and "artists" selected, through a design contest, a new logo, which was approved by the Municipal Council (Ankara Metropolitan Municipality, 1994). The logo change has caused much controversy and met with extensive media coverage.

The purpose of this article is to convey the story of the design processes and logo replacement debates of Ankara's corporate identity projects.

Corporate Identity of Ankara City and Ankara Metropolitan Municipality during Murat Karayalçın's Term (1989-1994)

In 1989, I was offered work in the election campaign for Murat Karayalçın, the candidate for Erdal İnönü's Social Democratic People's Party (SHP), in the Ankara Metropolitan Municipality elections. I was to conduct the campaign's visual communication design work with two of my friends, one of whom was a writer and the other, a filmmaker. I accepted the offer and started to work. Later we were joined also by a photographer friend. We went to Ankara a few times, talked to the authorities about campaign promotion strategy and learned about the projects pledged in the election bulletin. We dwelled on the idea "Ankarayalçın" as a portmanteau of the words Karayalçın and Ankara. We took photos of Karayalçın, to be used in the campaign. Advertising panels, posters, brochures, press releases and other means of communication were designed and produced. At the time, Murat Karayalçın was a decidedly popular executive who was entering politics. Karayalçın's contender was Mehmet Altınsoy of the Motherland Party (ANAP). I do not know how far our publicity work helped, but Karayalçın won the election and became mayor of Greater Ankara.[1]

Corporate Identity Project for Ankara

Before we had the time to rest after this arduous campaign, our team was asked to design the corporate identity and publicity projects of the Ankara Metropolitan Municipality. This involved a long stretch of work. Each one of us three were freelance designers. The municipality wanted to deal with an institution. To that end, we established a promotion and design agency limited to this project. The founders of the agency and the consultants who later became a part of the staff were people who knew Ankara well: most lived in Ankara, were educated in Ankara schools, and some had worked in Ankara for some time. We submitted our program proposal with the agency file. It was approved, and thus we became the design and promotion agency of the Metropolitan Municipality of Ankara. In fact, we were offering a culture and identity project rather than promotion.

At the time, the concept of corporate identity was newly entering the terminology in Turkey. Corporate identity comprises the programming and design of visual identities for companies, banks, public institutions, local governments, foundations, educational institutions, and non-governmental or similar organizations that produce products or services. Corporate identity design begins with determining of the corporate logo[2] and colour scheme. This is followed by designs for correspondence documents, selection of fonts to be used in corporate communications, and design plans for in-house and external routing elements and institutional tools, all within the framework of institutional integrity. Corporate identity design should not be confused with promotional activities. Corporate identity design is a perpetual, long-term task, while activities to promote products and services are period dependent.

Urban identity and corporate identity are similar and divergent concepts both. The common feature of institutions and cities is change. Institutions are organizations with certain functions. Each institution, whether it is one year- or a hundred-years-old, has an unpredictable lifespan – they are born, they grow, and then they die. The existence of institutions established by a person or persons depends on human will. Whereas cities, regardless of their founding myths, are independent of human will. They continue to live, as long as natural disasters or wars that "raze the city to the ground" do not destroy them.

Today we use – because of their differences – the word "logo" for institutions, and "symbol" for cities in the terminology of identity. For instance, Berlin's symbol is the "bear" figure. Copenhagen is symbolized by the "mermaid" figure.

The Project Process

The first step for corporate identity design required being acquainted with

---

1 At the time, Turkish equivalents of the term, "Greater Municipality" was used instead of "metropolitan municipality". The word "metropolitan" came into use during the Karayalçın administration.

2 The term "emblem" or "trademark", which was used until the 1990s, was later replaced by "logo," which is still in use.

the institution. Once our proposal had been approved, our first job was to go to Ankara and begin our research. We had to observe through professional eyes the city we thought we knew.

However, we found ourselves faced with an arduous and complex job, considering our subject matter was not simply an institution, but Turkey's capital city, its second largest city, and that city's municipality. I realized that I had not learned much about Ankara during 1957-1964 when I was a boarder at the TED Ankara College. The seven-year secondary school programme had not offered anything worthwhile outside the "official history" of the city in which we lived and studied. Atatürk's mausoleum "Anıtkabir," districts of Kızılay and Ulus, the May 19 Stadium, a few cinema houses, the "Cyprus is Turkish" rally, the military coup (May 27, 1960) and two coup attempts (February 22 and May 21, both by Talat Aydemir), and that was that... None of the city's cultural values and social and economic history were covered by the curriculum.

Figure 1. Anki logo, 1990
Sadık Karamustafa
Sadık Karamustafa Archive

Ankara's Symbol: The Mohair Goat

We talked much about the economic and social history of the city in meetings held with Mr Murat Karayalçın and his team. These interviews culminated with a decision to work towards separate designs for the city and the municipality. The idea of using the "mohair goat," historically a significant source of income, prevailed as a symbol for Ankara. As for the Ankara Municipality logos, it was decided that the present logotype "Hittite Sun" should be revamped and continued. Historians surmise that Ankara's name is derived from the Galatians, believed to have founded the city in the 3rd century BC (Lequenne, 1991, p. 50). Accordingly, the Galatians had captured a golden anchor as loot in one of their conquests. They named the city "Ancyra" to commemorate their spoils of war. The city was referred to as Angora during Seljuk and Ottoman times, and it became Ankara in the Republican era. Using all three names in the Ankara symbol was decided.

We spoke about the concepts of Ankara and "Ankara the Capital" during those meetings. The symbol of the city would be the mohair goat, in other words, the Ankara goat, which represented historically Ankara's most significant economic force. Ankara and its vicinity held a unique distinction in the production of *Sof* (woollen fabric woven with mohair) from the Ankara goat, thanks to its highly favoured fibre. Besides Mardin and periphery, which were less significant, Central Anatolian flatlands had the monopoly on being home to this delicate creature, since as far back as the 14th to the 19th centuries (Kafadar, 2014, p. 98).

Figure 2. Drawing for Anki figure
Sadık Karamustafa
Sadık Kaaramustafa Archive

As we resumed our work, we needed to address an important question: in addition to Ankara Metropolitan Municipality and Ankara City, there was also the question of its identity as the capital. That Ankara was the nation's capital was a separate factor. Was it necessary to separate these two statuses and design a separate logo / icon for "Ankara the Capital?" No, it was not so. Ankara was the capital of the Republic of Turkey and its administrative headquarters; the capital's logo was naturally the national flag and no other emblem was required.

The Hittite Sun logo and the Mohair goat symbols would be used together or separately, depending on subject matter, in urban communication materials such as banners, information booklets, press advertisements, promotional films, and corporate tools, to impart the following messages:

Youthful Ankara ... Beautiful Ankara
I am an Ankara Resident.
I love Ankara.
Ankara Deserves the Best.
Turkey's Heart is Ankara Forever
Ankara, the Culture Capital
The New Ankara... Young Ankara...
One Ankara... Contemporary Ankara

Anki

We decided at the consultations with the Karayalçın team to name our mohair symbol "*Anki.*" It was to be a youthful, happy and vigorous figure. Anki would be voicing campaign pledges for the upcoming elections.

I went to the Ankara Zoo to see some mohair goats. I have had an aversion to animals being incarcerated and exhibited ever since I was a child: I just do not like zoos. I was saddened by the appearance of the few mohair goats there, their indifferent gazes at visitors, the way they seemed so bored with nothing to do. They were not very conducive to creative inspiration for a designer. I was uncomfortable with this outlook, so I took a few photographs and went away.

The first draft studies I made on my return to Istanbul were not very promising. Inspecting the photos I took, I felt as if I was losing my incentive. My first drawings were rather charmless and faltering. I shut my sketchbook and took a few days off work. When I returned, I set out to draw the Anki of my dreams, rather than the unhappy goats in the photos. Instead of a logo drawn with a ruler and a setsquare, I picked up my pencil and began to produce some freestyle sketches. Presently I began to feel as if I was beginning to catch the spirit I wanted.

The Ankara Metropolitan Municipality Logo

We may describe the "Hittite Sun" object that was excavated from Alacahöyük and is currently on display at the Ankara Museum of Anatolian Civilizations, and employed as a logo by a number of institutions, especially the University of Ankara, in the following form:

A circular frame symbolizing the sun,
Bottom of this frame has been truncated by an arc,
A U-shaped curve below the arc that forms a rectangular area when joined to the arc,
A grid consisting of three horizontal and three vertical lines inside the circle,
Eleven extensions that resemble abstract human figures that radiate from the intersections of the lines that make up the grid with the circle,
Three moving rings on the grill hanging from the top of the circle.

It is believed that the sun disk was placed on spear tips in battle, so that it would produce a sound with the movements of the soldier or horse that carried it. It is assumed that the noise emanating from hundreds of the disks together was used to frighten the enemy. We can assume that this object, in a strange coincidence, had been used historically as a means of communication.

The "Sun Disk," adhering to the original, is currently a part of the Ankara University logo.

The historical Hittite Sun object was redesigned as a municipality logo by painter Oya Katoglu, its originality partially preserved, presumably during Vedat Dalokay's term as mayor in the 1970s. Katoğlu transformed the eleven abstract extensions on the outside the object into concrete figures of women, men, and children in various attire, representing the diverse cultures that coexisted. This was the logo used until Karayalçın's term.

The logo I designed was a work that would provide a contemporary interpretation of the original, not attempting to imitate the original, free from excess, and free from problems in serving as the principal actor of the corporate identity programme. The logo design and "Anki" were approved by the Ankara Municipal Council.

The project lasted about two years. We completed all the design work we had been ordered. Only the productions of the promotional films continued. My writer partner and I parted, leaving the company with our filmmaker partner.

Logo Change

The Ankara Metropolitan Municipality passed on, as I mentioned above, to the Welfare Party after the 1994 local government elections. Ankara's new mayor, Melih Gökçek staged a new competition, based on the claim that Modern Turkey and Ankara's history began with the Battle of Manzikert, and that the Hittite Sun had nothing to do with "our" history. The winner of the competition, a logo comprising a minaret, Atakule, the moon and stars was ratified by the Municipal Council as Ankara's new logo. The logo change caused much controversy in the media. The Governor's Office rescinded the Gökçek Municipality's modification. However, Mr Gökçek refused to abide with the Governor's decision and went on to use the new logo.

The media controversy was plagued with much misinformation. For one thing, an expanded version of another Hittite (or Hatti) piece, created by sculptor Nusret Suman on commission from the Ankara Metropolitan Municipality during Vedat Dalokay's term, was confused with the original artefact. Secondly, the contest was presented as if it was for "Ankara the Capital," whereas in fact a municipal logo was sought.

Political circles, non-governmental organizations and the press joined "the debate." NGOs gathered signatures protesting the new logo. Periodical Tempo magazine reported with the title "Goat Prattle in Ankara." Writers Hadi Uluengin, Serdar Turgut, Doğan Hızlan, and Derya Sazak carried the issue to their newspaper columns.

In the meantime, Anki bore the brunt of it all. More precisely, while everyone was discussing the Hittite sun, the symbol of the city of Ankara disappeared in the hubbub.

What came of the logo I designed that was based on the Hittite Sun? Well, from time to time, I see shipping companies, educational institutions; trade associations, etc. happily use my design in corporate identities, obviously without my consent.

References

Ankara Municipal Council (July 4, 1994) Capital Ankara Emblem Grand Prize Competition Specifications, Decree No. 259.

Kafadar, C. (2014). *Kim var imiş biz burada yoğ iken* (5th edition). İstanbul: Metis Yayınları.

Lequenne, F. (1991). *Galat'lar.* (Trans. S. Albek,). Ankara: Atatürk Kültür, Dil ve Tarih Yüksek Kurumu, Türk Taarih Kurumu Yayınları.

Weaving The History: Mystery of a City, Sof

Rahmi M. Koç Museum Ankara
12 May-16 September 2018

Sof... a moiré, silky, fine and deluxe fabric woven with the yarn spun from mohair goats, once exclusively bred in and around Ankara... Sof, produced exclusively in and around Ankara since the 15th century was a commodity of choice for Ottoman, Venetian, Polish and British tradesmen, as well as Italian and French princes and princesses. It was considered the most important commercial product of Ankara, which was a textile centre of the Ottoman Period. It remained a major theme of foreign visitors' accounts of Ankara for many centuries to come. While once upon a time this cherished fabric was a luxurious commodity sought by European elites, it turned into a forgotten value and an urban mystery by the 19th century, because of the dwindling away of sof weaving and production techniques thereof.

Pursuing sof fabric's centuries-old adventure begins in the city where the Angora goat, which has drawn much attention throughout history with its unique fibres, which has been named after its homeland: Ankara. The most salient and distinctive feature of the Angora goat is the mostly white, silky-soft, locks of mohair wool that cover the entire body, including the head, the forehead, ears, below the muzzle, below the belly and legs. In the West, the yarn obtained from the Angora goat came to be called diamond fibre thanks to its brilliance. Throughout history, the best mohair was obtained from the Angora goat growing in and around Ankara. The sof fabric woven from this mohair has been recognized in the world since the 15th century with mohair's lustre, finesse and softness.

Page 170-171
Gezicht op Ankara (View of Ankara)
1700-1799
Anonymous
117x198x6,5 cm
Oil on canvas
Loan from Rijksmuseum, Amsterdam, Env. No: SK-A-2055

For many years, this painting in the Rijksmuseum, Amsterdam was thought to depict a view of Aleppo. However, Prof. Dr. Semavi Eyice, put forth that the painting represented Ankara (An Old Painting of Ankara, 1972). Eyice's work has revealed the picture to be a very significant document for academics studying the City of Ankara.

One of the primary factors in determining the painting's provenance was the large number of Angora goats, which appear to be undergoing a certain process, located on the lower right edge of the painting. The upper and lower parts of the painting show Ankara in two separate compositions, such that some epochal edifices and sites are depicted at the upper part, while the lower part features various scenes from Ankara's bazaar and city life. Although anonymous, the painter has portrayed Ankara through European eyes, revealing besides its topography, the lively, mohair-based trade and *sof* weaving history with images of women in *sof* feraces (tunics), woollen materials on looms, merchants and a caravan carrying goods from Ankara.

Erman Tamur's (2008) study of the painting have shown that the work was received into the Rijksmuseum inventory during the early 20th century, as part of the so-called Vanmour Series from a company called Levantsche Handel that conducted trade with the Ottoman State in the 18th century. In fact, the painting once hanged in said company's headquarters in Amsterdam before it was included in the museum inventory. In the painting, the trade center Bedesten was portrayed directly and with emphasis. In addition to this, the mohair yarn trade between the Ottoman Empire and Netherlands in the 18th century, points out to the possibility that work and the artist were somehow related to the commercial links with the Netherlands; and strengthens the painting's provenance with this company.

An interactive screen was designed for the exhibition. On the interactive screen, photographs from the late 19th century and onwards are used to match the sites, crafts and tools which can be detected on the View of Ankara painting. The interactive screen comprises Erman Tamur's (2008) article "An Ankara Painting in Amsterdam", Semavi Eyice's (1972) book An Old Painting of Ankara, Feyza Akder's (2018) article "Story of a Painting: Rijksmuseum's View of Ankara", Koray Olşen's photographs taken for the interactive screen, VEKAM Library and Archive's Ankara Photograph and Postcard Collection, Gönül Öney's (1971) book Turkish Period Architecture in Ankara, and M. Faik Üstar's (1940) book Mohair and Our Mohair Industry. This interactive screen can be experienced at the Koç University, VEKAM Library and Archive in the aftermath of the exhibition.

The Angora Goat

Physical Characteristics, Origin and Habitat of the Angora Goat

Purebred Angora goats are defined as small, delicate animals. Their heads are smaller and more elegantly shaped compared to hair goats, the body structure is diminutive and dainty, with a straight back, and withers and sacrum heights virtually at the same level. The body is long, wide and round; legs short and shapely; and eyes are bright and foreheads wide. Both males and females have horns. The ears are long and drooping. They are mostly white, but sometimes also leaden, black, and yellow (Müftüoğlu ve Öznacar, 1972, p. 20).

Origins of the Angora Goat

Factors such as horn structure, areas of propagation and genetic structures are frequently used investigating the origins of domestic goat breeds (Capra hircus). Some studies have alleged that the domestic goat was derived from three the three wild goat species of C. aegagrus (bezoar), C. falconeri and C. prisca, while other works suggest that the C. ibex and C. caucasica also may have contributed genetically during the domestication process.

Molecular genetic studies on the history and origins of the Angora goat have shown that this goat has not differentiated from other races inhabiting the region for thousands of years but has differentiated in terms of the genomic DNA, which is at the root cause of such different morphological structures. Scientific studies have also revealed through that the Angora goat has originated from the bezoar, like other goat races extant in Anatolia.

There is a lot yet to be discovered about the history and origins of the goat that took its name from Ankara. However, there are three widely accepted views: the breed was domesticated in Anatolia; or a breed which brought to Anatolia many ages ago has changed in time; or it was bred by the Turkmen by combining it with various indigenous races. Husbandry of the Angora goat, or the Mohair or Angora goat, dates back 3,000 to 4,000 BC, since its beginnings in Ankara (Çınar Kul, 2018, s. 66).

Habitat of the Angora Goat

In the Ottoman period, despite efforts of Europeans' wish to cultivate the Mohair goat in face of various bans, the Angora goat could not be displaced beyond the climate it inhabited and thrived across only a limited region. The geographical features required for breeding the Angora goat are available in Central Anatolia at 700-1000 metres elevation, warm in the summer, and cold in the winter and relatively low in moisture. In addition, the climate conditions of the plant cover in this region play a role on the quality of the mohair. It used to be believed that not only the Angora goat is unable to survive outside the land it belongs, the mohair, too, degenerates outside of Anatolia. While the Angora goat is particularly fond of aromatic herbs that grow in these climatic characteristics, such as soapwort, veronica, wild rue, cock's-foot, mullein and marjoram, it also likes to browse holly oak, all of which are thought to be effective in the formation of beautiful mohair (İmeryüz, 1965, p. 2).

These goats were bred during the Ottoman period at Kastamonu province of Gerede, Kengırı, Mudurnu and Bolu municipality, at the Eskişehir, Kütahya, Aziziye and Afyonkarahisar municipalities of the Hüdâvendigâr province, in the Akşehir province of Konya province, Karacadağ Highlands and Tuzkarahisar Province and the Ankara provinces of Boğazlıyan, Akdağmadeni and Provinces of the Çorum Sanjak. Since mohair has been Ankara's most important commercial product throughout history, some regions were particularly celebrated for breeding the best goats and producing the best mohair. These were Gerede, Ankara's Zir (now known as Yenikent), Beypazarı and Ayaş provinces, and the Eskişehir and Kütahya regions (Ankara Vilayeti Salnamesi, 1325/1907, p. 294).

From the 15th century onwards, the Angora goat attracted the attention of many travellers and scientists traveling to Ankara and its regions; thus much information about how both the Angora goat, and the *sof* fabric woven from this goat' mohair has been included in accounts of Ankara. Among the names mentioning the Angora goat and *sof* fabric are Benedetto Dei, Michelé Membre, Ogier Ghiselin de Busbecq, Hans Dernschwam, Simeon of Poland, Evliya Çelebi, Aşıkpaşazade, Pitton de Tournefort, Aubry de la Mortraye, Paul Lucas, Richard Pococke and Charles Texier (Leiser, 1994; Webb Yıldırmak, 2006).

Despite the prohibition of exporting the Angora goat and its most precious mohair in the Ottoman times, attempts were made in the form of small herds smuggled to England, Holland, Italy and France as of the 17th century; but these failed due to improper handling, feeding and varying climatic conditions (Akman, 1994). However, Angora goats began to be produced in many parts of the world as of the 19th century; and today grows in many countries, led by South Africa and the United States, Australia, New Zealand, Argentina, Russia, Australia, India, France and Kenya (Çınar Kul, 2018, p. 66).

The number of Angora goats that stood at 1,835,401 in 1922 (Batu, 1951, p. 35) is now 215,645 goats in 2017, 133,590 of which were bred in Ankara according to TURKSTAT data. The Angora goat, famous for its mohair for centuries, has become one of the forgotten values, as revealed by these decreasing numbers. Reassigning these values depends not just on understanding cultivation-related problems and finding their solutions, but on understanding problems related to the global mohair market.

French painter Claude Aubreit, who specialized in botanical drawings, and the famous French botanist Joseph Pitton de Tournefort, travelled to the east between 1700 and 1702 to explore the natural history, antique and modern geography, trade and religion of some Aegean Islands, Istanbul, Anatolian cities and Georgia and arrived in Ankara at some point in their itinerary. This is when Claude Aubriet made the drawing, and it was included in the travelogue published by Tournefort in 1717 for the first time, Relation d'un voyage du Levant. The presence of an inscription in English, A Goat of Angora, indicates that this copy was used for one of the English editions of the book. The first edition of the book in English was published in 1718.

The dates of birth and death of Jacques de Sève are unknown. This artist illustrated many books of science and literature during 1742 – 1788. Most striking were the Dictionnaire Iconologique by Honore Lacombe de Prezel in 1756, Histoire Naturel, générale et particulière, avéc la description du Cabinet du Roi by Georges-Louis Leclerc, Comte de Buffon, Oeuvres de Racine, d'après l'édition de 1760 by Jean- Baptiste Racine. This drawing was made by Jacques de Sève for Figures pour l'histoire des quadrupèdes by M. de Buffon (1755).

Chèvre d'Angora, A Goat of Angora
1702
Claude Aubriet
Engraving
10x15 cm
VEKAM Library and Archive, Inv. No: 2684

La Chèvre d'Angora (The Angora Goat)
1755
Jacques de Sève
Engraving
25x20 cm
VEKAM Library and Archive, Inv. No: 1850

La Bouc d'Angora (The Angora Goat)
1755
Jacques de Sève
Engraving
25x20 cm
VEKAM Library and Archive, Inv. No: 1851

Chèvres d'Angora

Angora Goats
1896
12x16,5 cm
Black & White photograph
VEKAM Library and Archive,
Inv. No: 1709

The inscription Chèvres Angora in French (Angora Goats) appears on this photo.

Angora Goats
1920
9x13 cm
Black & White postcard
VEKAM Library and Archive, Inv. No: 1552

The inscription *Ankara Kazası, tiftik keçileri* (Ankara town, mohair goats) in Ottoman Turkish appears on the back side of the postcard.

Angora Goats and the Goatherd
1926
9x14 cm
Black & White photograph on a postcard
VEKAM Library and Archive, Inv. No: 2466

Angora Goats
Before 1938
Black & White photograph (copy)
18x24 cm
VEKAM Library and Archive, Inv. No: 0083

Angora Goats-Delegation Trip
05.10.1938
9x14 cm
Black & White photograph
VEKAM Library and Archive, Inv. No: 2504

Angora Goat
1953
9x14 cm
Black & White photograph
VEKAM Library and Archive, Inv. No: 0780

Angora Goats
Date Unknown
9x13 cm
Black & White photograph
VEKAM Library and Archive, Inv. No: 1550

Angora Goats and Goatherd
Date Unknown
9x13 cm
Black & White photograph
VEKAM Library and Archive, Inv. No: 0764

The inscription *Ankara Tiftik Keçileri, No: 50* in Turkish (Angora goats, No: 50) appears on the lower left corner of the photograph.

About the Angora Goat...

The Angora goat is a rare animal that has subsisted exclusively in and around Ankara for many centuries. It has drawn much attention with its highly valued, unique mohair. French botanist Pitton de Tournefort (1656-1708) who set out during 1700 to 1702 on a journey East to study the history of the Aegean Islands, İstanbul, Anatolian cities and Georgia, as these locations related to natural history, ancient and contemporary geography, trade and religion between 1700 and 1702, and happened to stop by Ankara during this trip. His book *Relation d'un voyage du Levant*, published in English as *A Voyage Into the Levant*, and in Turkish as *Tournefort's Travelogue*, was composed of letters, notes and sketches drawn during these travels. It comprises the Angora goat's characteristics, including information on its economic value and information on the production of *sof* and has contributed greatly to Western awareness of the Angora goat.

The Angora Goats, exports of which were long-banned, were thought to yield low-quality mohair when farmed in different climates. Although bans were surmounted at times and animals smuggled elsewhere, efforts failed in cultivating it. Finally, in the 19th century, Angora goats began to be bred in other, diverse parts of the world, such as South Africa, the United States, and Australia. Books on Angora goat husbandry are published during this period.

One of these publications is Samuel Wilson's (1832-1895) *The Angora Goat: An Account of Its Introduction into Victoria and a Report on the Flock* (1873). The work includes a review of the Australian author's evaluation of the Angora goat that had been cultivated in the second half of the 19th century, in the Victoria region of Australia, and a report on the herds of Angora goat by Zoological and Acclimatisation Society of Victoria.

The Angora goat: Its Origin, Culture and Products, a book published in 1882 by American writer John Hayes (1812-1887) provides information regarding the provenance of the Angora goats as well showing the guidelines on husbandry. While portraying the observations of the leading American Angora-goat breeders of this period, this book also points to current growing interest in Angora goat husbandry in the USA.

Another climate where the Angora goat was bred in the 19th century was South Africa. *The Angora Goat* penned in 1898 by South African author Samuel Cron Cronwreight-Schreiner (1863-1936) consists of sections on the evolution of the Angora goats from wild goats, the province of Ankara, the localization of purebred Angora cattle, breeding Angora goats in South Africa, Turkey's mohair regions, Angora goat farming in Turkey and Turkey's mohair trade. It has served as a significant resource to myriad scientific studies on this subject.

Written by the American, George Fayette Thompson (1860-1906), a US official who worked for the US Department of Agriculture's Bureau of Animal Husbandry, and considered an important authority in Ankara, having served as an arbitrator in many animal exhibitions, *A Manual of Angora Goat Raising* (1903) contains noteworthy information on transporting to and breeding of the Angora goat in the US, and the development of the mohair industry in the US. It is considered an important source and guide for following the American adventure of the Angora goat, from its importing from Ankara, in relation to the major stateside entrepreneurs.

A Voyage into the Levant
1741
Joseph Pitton de Tournefort
London: Printed for D. Midwinter
21x13,4 cm
VEKAM Library and Archive, Rare Collection,
Call No: VEKAM.RARE/DS47 T68 1741 v. 3

Although the Angora goat had begun to be farmed elsewhere as of the 19th century, it remained important as the source of mohair, one of the city's most vital products for Ankara's economic and social life. During the Ottoman period, the Angora goat continued to be valued high in the Ankara province, although Ankara came to be a province that changed from *sof* fabrics to fibre exports, and then from fibre to mohair in the 19th century, for various reasons in time. One such example is the *Ankara Vilayeti Salnamesi* (Provincial Yearbook of Ankara) published in 1325 Islamic (AD 1907). In addition to statistics of the goat population in the province of Ankara, information on the origins, genus, anatomical features, and characteristics of their habitats, their economic significance, mohair, milk and meat yields, and finally diseases of the Angora Goats are discussed in the section titled Tiftik Keçileri Umûm Keçiler Hakkında Mutâlaât (General Observations on Mohair Goats). This work is a highly important resource for monitoring the numeric existence of the Angora goat and following the regions where it was raised in the Ottoman period.

The Angora Goat
1898
Samuel C. Cronwreight-Schreiner
Londra: Longmans, Green and Co.
23,4x15,6cm
VEKAM Library and Archive, Rare Collection, Call No:
VEKAM.RARE/SF385 .S37 1898

A Manual of Angora Goat Raising
1903
George Fayette Thompson
Chicago: American Sheep Breederco Press
22,3x15,2 cm
VEKAM Library and Archive, Rare Collection, Call No:
VEKAM.RARE/SF385 .T46 1903

The Angora Goat: It's Origin Culture and Products
1882
John Hayes
New York: Orange Judd
23,5x15,4 cm
VEKAM Library and Archive, Rare Collection, Call No:
VEKAM.RARE/SF385 .H39 1882

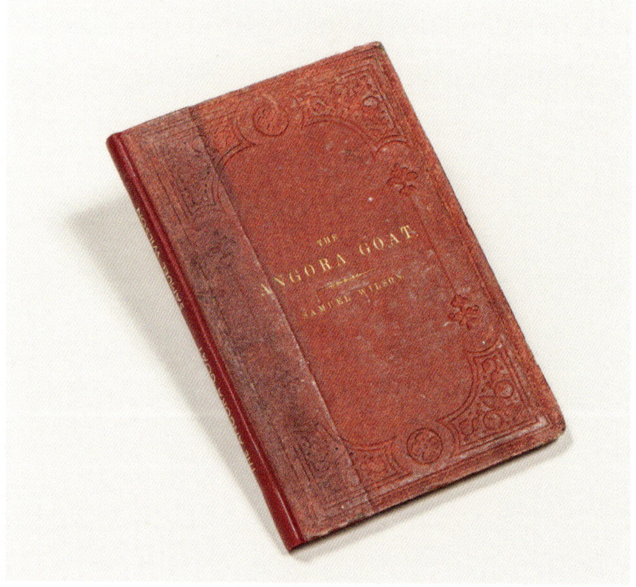

The Angora Goat: With an Account of its Introduction into Victoria and a Report on the Flock
1903
Samuel Wilson
Melbourne: Stillwell and Knight
21,5x14,5 cm
VEKAM Library and Archive, Rare Collection, Call No:
VEKAM.RARE/SF385.W55 1873

Ankara Vilayeti Salnamesi (Provincial Yearbook of Ankara)
1325 (1907) Def'a: 15.
23x16 cm
Sadberk Hanım Museum Library, Hüseyin Kocabaş Collection,
Inv. No: Küt. d. No. 2880

The book is not in its original cover and there is an old map on its last page.

Angora Goat Density Maps

Maps that are exhibited here visualize the per- square kilometre number of Angora goats within the Angora goat habitat and the changes in that number, on a sub-district level for the Ankara district at the turn of the twentieth century (1889-1905). Doing so, they aim to demonstrate the regional and geographical dynamics of a dying economy, which had for centuries shaped social and economic life in and around Ankara. Within the 17 years in question, the number of Angora goats increased, and the Angora goat density shifted from the sub-districts in the north, towards those in the centre.

The number of Angora goats per sub-district per year are gathered from *Ankara Vilayeti Salnamesi* Provincial Yearbook of Ankara 1325/1907. The sub-district borders are drawn using ArcGIS Pro, a Geographical Information Systems (GIS) software, based on the 1899 map, R. Huber *Empire Ottoman: Division Administrative, dressée d'apres le Salname 1899*. Angora goat habitat is set as areas with 800-1200-meter elevation based on a modern Digital Elevation Model (DEM). Data on the mohair production of 1899, 1893, 1899 and 1901 are compiled from the official provincial yearbooks of Ankara from the respective years.

Data collection and GIS analysis for this study have been conducted in the framework of ERC-Starting Grant, 679097 UrbanOccupationsOETR project, carried out at Koç University by Assoc. Prof. M. Erdem Kabadayı.

ANKARA KEÇISI
188

0 25 50

ANKARA KEÇISI
189

Angora Goat Density Maps
Dr. Semih Çelik
2018

RINDA ANKARA KEÇISI YOĞUNLUĞU
A BAZINDA - ADET/KM2

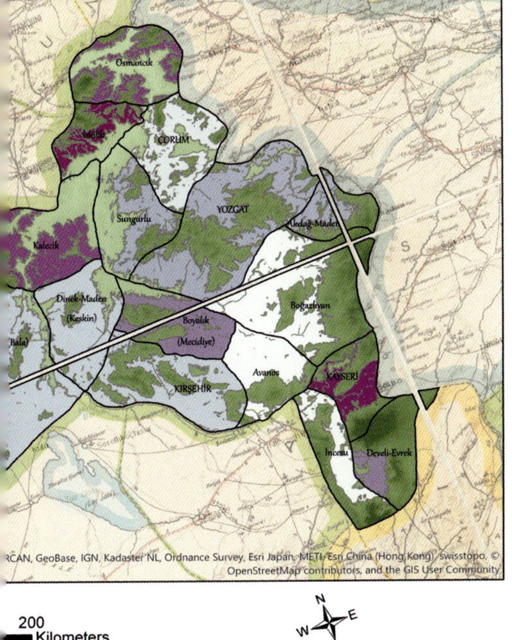

ANKARA KEÇISI YAŞAM ALANLARINDA ANKARA KEÇISI YOĞUNLUĞU
1893 SENESI - KAZA BAZINDA - ADET/KM2

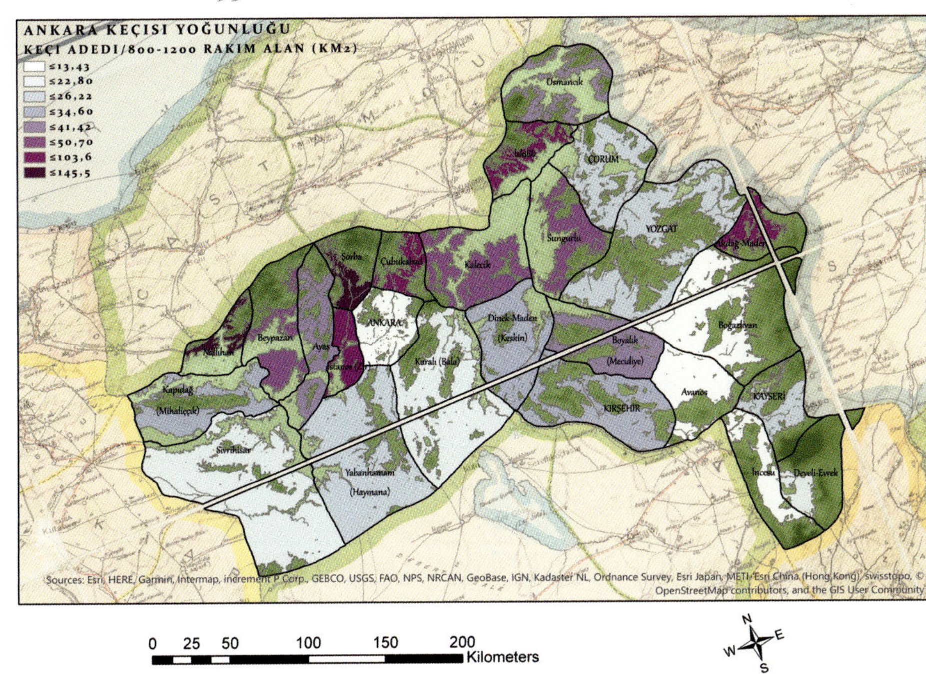

RINDA ANKARA KEÇISI YOĞUNLUĞU
A BAZINDA - ADET/KM2

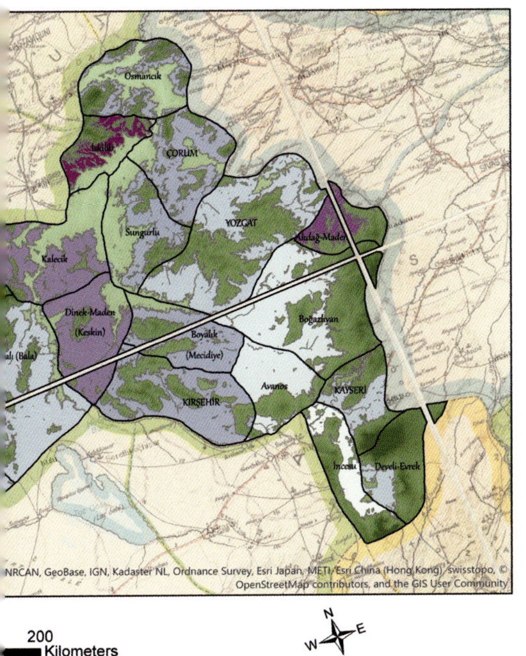

ANKARA KEÇISI YAŞAM ALANLARINDA ANKARA KEÇISI YOĞUNLUĞU
1901 SENESI - KAZA BAZINDA - ADET/KM2

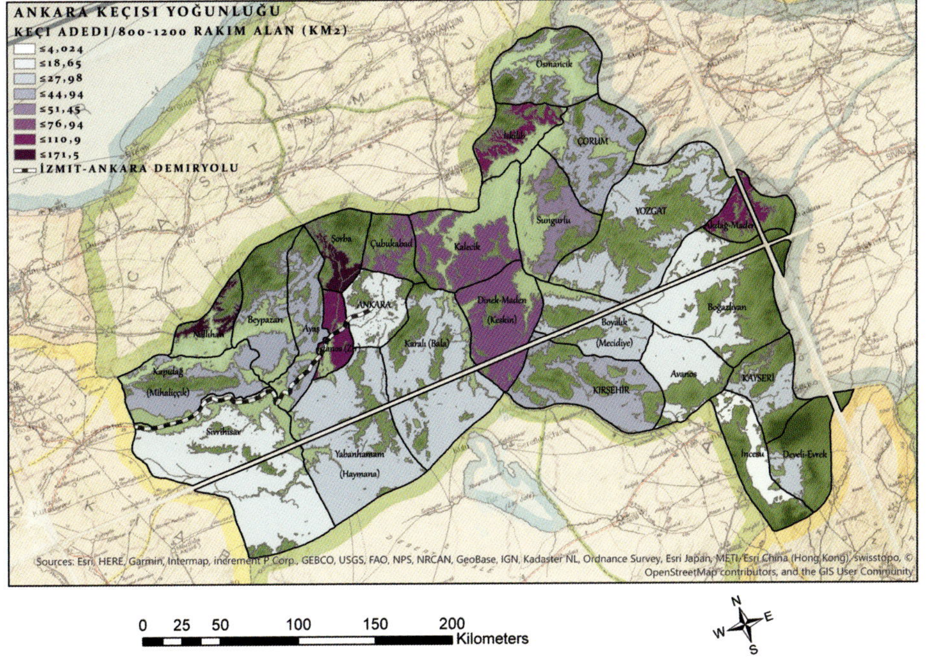

The Black Sea: Navigating Turkey The Angora Goat navigates ports in Europe with an Exhibition Boat

In the 3rd year of the Republic, on the proposal of Trade Minister Ali Cenani Bey and the support of Mustafa Kemal Atatürk, a mobile exhibition was projected to promote the young Republic and Turkish export goods to Europe. It was decided that the exhibition would be installed on a ship that would visit European ports. A renovated Steamship Karadeniz [Black Sea] would be decked out in fabrics with exhibition halls filled with all valuables and products, from Kütahya tiles to paintings and sculptures that can be installed in a boat, to promote our country in Europe. The exhibit team long discussed the exigency of shipping live Angora goats, eventually decided in favour of mounted goats, due to the difficulty of transporting living animals in such a journey. Thus, the Angora Goat was not forgotten in departing from Karaköy in June 1926, when the Karadeniz, which cruised away to promote this young republic, with its 285 passengers of contemporary artists, journalists, members of parliament and writers, and weighed anchor in 16 harbours in 12 countries, including Spain, the Netherlands, France, England, Germany and Russia.

The documentary Karadeniz: Seyr-i Türkiye [The Black Sea: Navigating Turkey], was directed by Soner Sevgili, and featuring Nedim Olgun, Eray Ergeç, Müge Demir and Aytac Yıldız in its research team. It sheds light into this journey from Karaköy to Leningrad, of the Karadeniz, which was commissioned to introduce Turkey's new identity and promote the modernization process of the Turkish society, as well as showing off the significant products of the period.

Still Image from the The Black Sea: Navigating Turkey documentary
2006
Director: Soner Sevgili
Colour, Turkish film

Still image is taken from 6.30'-6.54' interval.

Inside the Exhibition Boat
1926
Black & White Photograph
Eray Ergeç Archive

The Angora Goats' Global Journey

Today Angora goats are farmed in various regions of the world. Among these mohair producing and processing countries are South Africa, the United States, Australia and New Zealand. The Ottoman state continued to be the world's sole quality producer of the mohair goat until mid-19th century. However, this advantageous starting was bound to be lost with the advent of Angora goat farming in different regions.

As a source of important raw material due to luxurious fabrics produced from its mohair, the Angora goat has been in demand since the 16th century and many attempts made by other countries such as Holland (1541), Cyprus (1598), Sweden (1740), France (1776) and Italy (1788) failed due to climatic and geographical conditions (Akman, 1994).

From the 18th century onwards, French wanted to breed the Angora goats in France. Hitzel (2018, pp. 89-91) puts forward that the first initiatives were taken by Louis Ternaux (1763-1833) who was a French producer, tradesman and a political figure. Due to the prohibition of the export of mohair of the Angora goat in the Ottoman Empire, French wondered about the other places to obtain this valuable product. In 1818, P. Amédée Jaubert who went to Astrakhan, facing Caucasia, purchased 1289 goats from Cossacs. However, due to the climatic conditions and the disadvantages of the long returning journey over Volga and Crimea, most of the animals were destroyed and only 400 goats could arive to the port of Toulon. In the following period the cashmere goats and the Angora goats that had been taken from Anatolia and have been brought to France over Italy, were crossed and a crossbred was obtained. In the period of Napoléon III (1852-1870), initiatives were started to acclimatize Angora goats to France. Abd el-Kader (1808-1883) an Algerian military and religious leader and a prestigious member and donator of the Zoological Acclimatization Society, established in Paris, sends a herd of Angora goats composed of 15 goats to Paris from Bursa, where he stayed for two years (1853-1855) in exile. Besides this, by means of French Consul in Bursa, Baron Rousseau, 72 Angora goats were purchased. These goats were transported to Algeria. The herd was sent to a farm in Chéraga in Sahel region then deported to Ben-Chicao farm located in the southern Atlas Mountain. Although the Angora goats adapted the climatic and geographical conditions of Algeria, French gave up the idea of breeding the Angora goats due to their nutrition habits of eating bushes and leafy plants that thought to harm forests.

With the advent of textiles and industrial developments, England, diverted to importing mohair yarn rather than luxurious woollen fabrics, and now diverting further to raw mohair, was searching for a new location for farming the Angora goat, which made it possible for the Angora goat to arrive in South Africa in the mid-19th century. While some sources (Kinghorn, 1972, pp. 3-4) note that 12 bucks and one nanny were taken to Port Elizabeth through purchases, other sources in South African Republic have recorded the adventure of the Angora goat as it began 1838, when Sultan II. Mahmud (1808-1839), who was keen on his protecting his country's advantage, sent neutered goats to South Africa. The reason for this was that the said nanny bore kids were regarded good luck (Mohair Story, 2018). Thus,

Map shows the Angora goats' global journey
2018

shipment of goats from Ankara to South Africa persisted for many years, and mohair farming began, especially in the Reinet and Jansenville regions (Tamur, 2003, pp. 151-172).

The transport of the Angora goat to South Africa resounded in the Ottoman era because the goats had perished on their long sea voyage to the Cape of Good Hope by long-standing sea voyages (Eyice, 1972). Turkish supporters appeared to regret tearing Ankara away goats from their homeland and transporting them over London away on a journey to the Cape and to Port Elizabeth (Üstar, 1940, pp. 20-21). However, in South Africa, where it bred successfully, the Angora goat thrived, and the mohair industry developed accordingly.

Angora goats were taken to the United States in the nineteenth century. James B. Davis (1807-1859), who was appointed by American President James K. Polk to contribute to the development of cotton production in the Ottoman Empire, upon completion of his work, succeeded in obtaining permission from Sultan Abdülmecid to ship live animals and took nine Angora goats to the US (Barnett, 1987, p. 351). Davis's goats are exhibited in trade fairs. Although parties of Angora goat continued to be sent, long travel conditions and other problems, such as the Asian scabies epidemic, some of the goats died on the way (Tamur, 2003, pp. 151-172).

Angora goat farming came to be successful with American entrepreneur Richard Peters's investments in careful farming methods in the US and by the end of the century, spread to regions such as California, Texas, New Mexico, Arizona and Oregon (Barnett, 1987, ss. 347-372). Today, besides Turkey, South Africa and Argentina are, along with the US, Australia, New Zealand and Lesotho engaged in breeding Angora goats and processing mohair (Mohair Report, 2016).

280 THE ILLUSTRATED LONDON NEWS [SEPT. 12, 1857

ELEPHANT-HUNTING IN AFRICA.

THE LATE PROFESSOR WAHLBERG, FELLOW OF THE ROYAL SWEDISH ACADEMY OF SCIENCES.

HOUSES OF THE ENGLISH AND FRENCH CONSULS AT RABAT, IN MOROCCO.

THE LATE PROFESSOR WAHLBERG.

ANGORA GOAT.

SALE OF ANGORA RAMS AT GRAAFF REINET, CAPE OF GOOD HOPE.

SALE OF ANGORA RAMS AT GRAAFF REINET.

THE ILLUSTRATED LONDON NEWS, SEPT. 25, 1880

GOATS EXHIBITED AT THE ALEXANDRA PALACE GOAT SHOW.—SEE NEXT PAGE.

A MONTENEGRIN WEDDING.—SEE NEXT PAGE.

A news item in *The Illustrated London News*
12.09.1857
40,3x28,2 cm
Newspaper
Erman Tamur Archive

A news item published in the Illustrated London News on September 12, 1857, related to the public auction of male Angora goats in Graaff Reinet, South Africa. An Angora goat engraving, and illustrations of the auction accompany the news report.

A news item in *The Illustrated London News*
25.09.1880
40,3x27,7cm
Newspaper
Erman Tamur Archive

A story in The Illustrated London News relates to an exhibition of goats, to be held at Alexandra Palace, one of London's major congregation centres during the end of the 19th century. The picture of the Angora goat included in the accompanying illustrations belongs to a nanny brought from the Cape of Good Hope.

La Chévre d'Angora
The second half of the 19th century
S. C. Sargent
21,6x18,6 cm
Engraving
Erman Tamur Archive

The engraving features an inscription in French Muséum *d'histoire naturel - Chévres d'Angora, d'après une photographie* [Natural History Museum – Angora goats, from a photograph]. Below the engraving is the signature of the American photographer and print artist S.C. Sargent.

Angora Goats
1880
R. Vandusen
18x26 cm
Engraving
Erman Tamur Archive

An English inscription appears on top of the engraving reads *Angora Goats Bred by Col. Robert W. Scott, Frankfort, Ky.*, and has been signed below by the Weedsport-New York artist R. Vandusen. The engraving was published in 1880, in a book titled *The American Farmer's Handbook.*

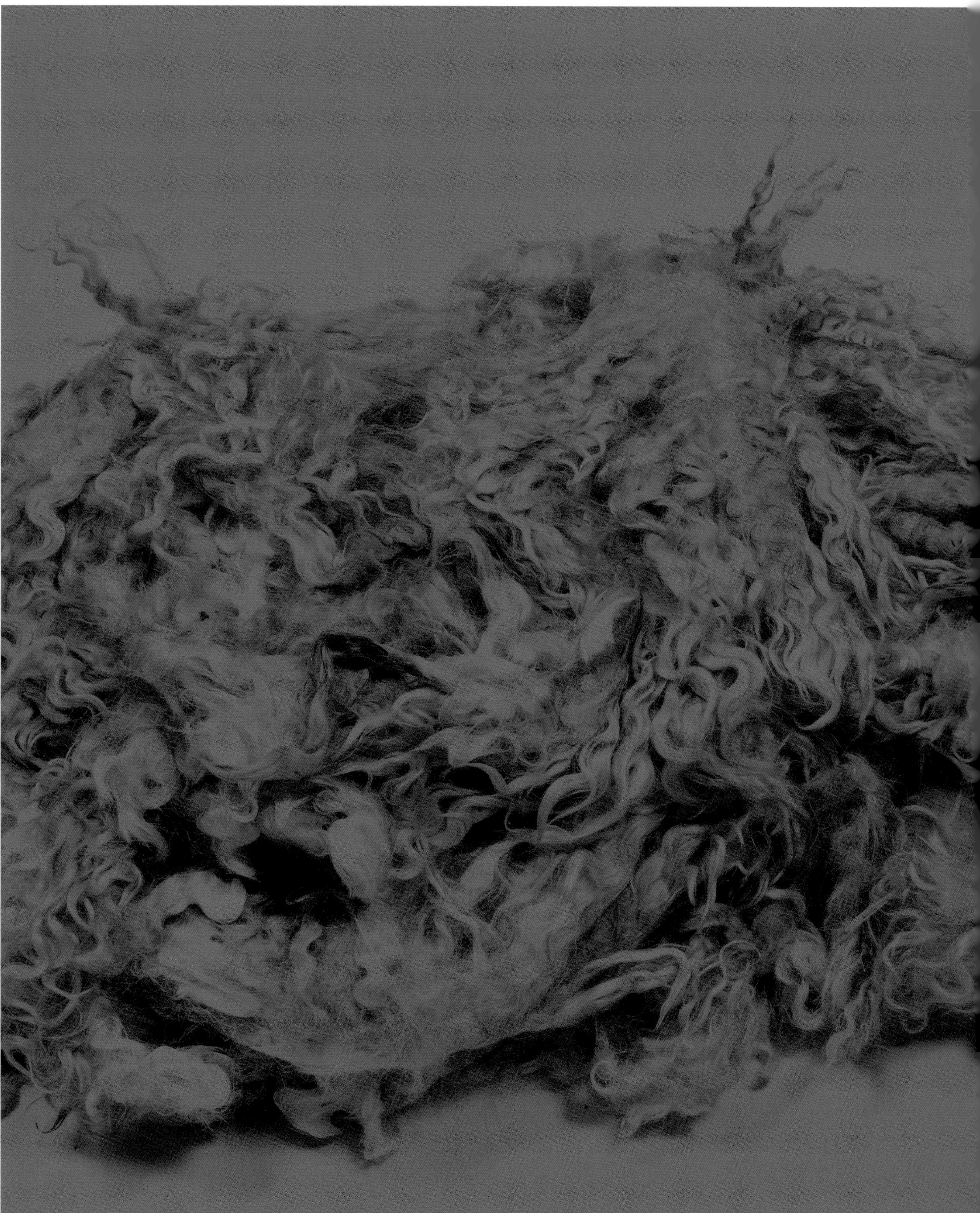

Mohair

Mohair: Soft like Silk, Brilliant like Diamond...

The Ankara sof was a kind of fabric obtained from Angora goats, woven from mohair, which held an important place with its length, its strength, and its brightness. The reason for its preference by elites throughout history, and the global awareness of its worth was due to the fact that it had been spun out of this very special animal and that the thinner the mohair was twisted for *sof*, the fabric would be considered all the better in its soft, shiny and silky appearance.

The use of the best quality of mohair to produce *sof* fabrics and the exports of the final product, the *sof*, being replaced first by the exports of mohair fibres, and then by fleece all have led to the depreciation of mohair over time.

Mohair is a valuable textile raw material and natural fibre that is durable, shiny, elastic, resistant to harmful solar rays, moisture proof, heat resistant, highly insulator and easily dyeable and resistant to contamination, due to its smooth and slippery structure. Thanks to its properties of keeping cool in summer and warm in winter, mohair has been a sought-after commodity not only in Turkey, since the earliest Ottoman times, but also in the UK, Netherlands, Poland, France, and in Russia. The use of mohair yarn in England, an important buyer in the Ottoman mohair yarn trade, was quite extensive since the 18th century; research has shown that the mohair yarn imported from the Ottomans was used in a variety of industries, including the military, as well as the production of upholstery fabrics, wigs, buttons, buttonholes and sash strips (Webb Yıldırmak, 2011, pp.58-162). It is also known that the mohair yarn exported from the Ottomans was used in the manufacturing of mohair fabrics in the Netherlands in the 17th and 18th centuries (Faroqhi, 2017, p.280).

While luxurious fabrics like mohair in the form of *sof* were the preference of higher echelons in Ottoman times; caftans, feraces and kerrakes were also made of *sof*; and mohair was used for military needs, too. It was also used in the manufacture of products such as sailcloth, due to its waterproofing and water-shifting nature (Ankara Vilayeti Salnamesi, 1325/ 1907, p.296).

Mohair was either used, especially in our country's textile industry during the Republican period, directly or mixed with silk fabrics in the production of fabrics. It is very valuable as a decorative fabric with excellent resistance against fire and high absorbing capacity. It is ideal for use in concert halls, theatres, hotel lobbies, offices and houses; and continues to be an upholstery fabric of choice for railway wagons, automobiles and curtains. It has been utilised in the production of carpets, blankets, shawls, mantles, wigs, gunpowder sacks, automobile upholstery, bedspreads, underwear as well as exterior clothing, knitwear, automobile accessories, stage sets, toy hairs, shoe linings, gloves, paintbrushes, paint rollers, tablecloths, pouches and belts (Üstar, 1940, p.2 and Mohair Ferla).

Iı is an imperative that the Angora goat, sheared once a year in Turkey, is shorn with great care to ensure the mohair is not dispersed (Açıl, 1961, p.43) and comes out in distinct shapes called a

Mohair Workers and Mohair Traders
1901-1905
9x13 cm
Black & White photograph
VEKAM Library and Archive. Inv. No: 0984

The inscription *Angora, Travailleurs de tiftik - Poils de chèvre* in French (Ankara, Mohair Workers, mohair) appears on the top right corner of this photograph.

Armenian Women Spinning Mohair
Early 20th century
8x14 cm
Black & White photograph
VEKAM Library and Archive. Inv. No: 2003

Inscriptions in Ottoman appears on the photograph. The inscription *Milli Talim Terbiye Kartları; Ankara'da Ermeni kadınları tiftik eğirirken* (National Education and Training Cards; Armenian women spinning mohair in Ankara) appears on the front side of the photograph while on the back side, Memalik-i Osmaniye Kartpostal (Ottoman lands postcard) can be read.

dulup, and two dulups are obtained from each goat (Tamur, 2003, p.244).

There are separate breeds of mohair. Mohair yields of billys, nannies and kids are collected in separate groups. There are differences in quality and area of usage, and therefore different prices among these breeds. The most favoured is the mohair obtained from animals 1-2 years old. Good mohair is usually soft, fine, and shiny with long tresses, and feels like a silk handkerchief when squeezed in one's palms (Örkiz, 1980, p.32).

A Lost Value...

The Angora goat and mohair used to be considered Ankara's lucky story, but they came to be regarded over the years as fading into oblivion, a worthy but "lost" value. Many writers in Turkey researching the topic has raised this issue, and offered prescriptions for preventing this value from being wiped out.

Factors such as inadequate nutrition, prevalence of primitive conditions from farming to marketing, a lack of global competitiveness in the existing export system, an undesirable "kemp-fibre ratio", the belief that the Angora goat should not be evaluated separately from other goats in harming forests, and declining mohair prices all combined to drag Turkey's mohair production and exports further down (İmeryüz, 1968, pp.353-355).

White *Dulup*
2017
Özbahar Family Collection
Produced in Ayaş, Gökçebağ village, Ankara.

Black *Dulup*
2017
Özbahar Family Collection
Produced in Ayaş, Gökçebağ village, Ankara.

Blue Mohair
2013-2018
Emine Kıraç Collection
This was hand-produced in Anatolia within the scope of the "Mohair Weaving in Anatolia" project.

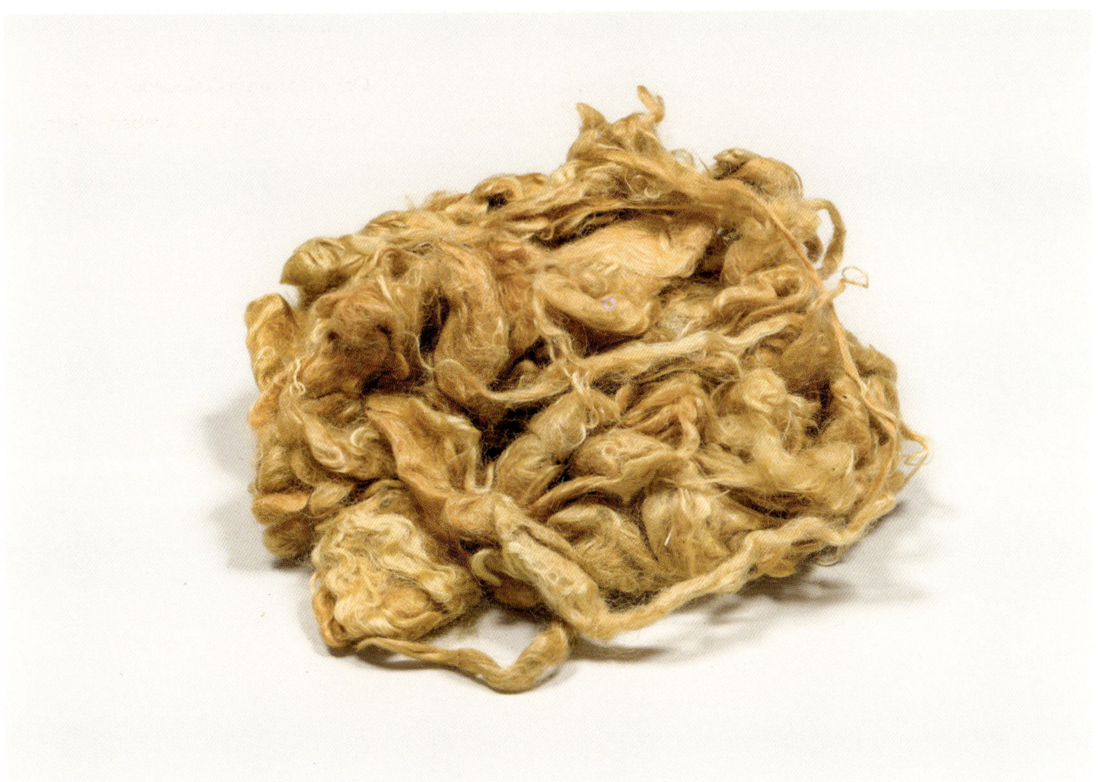

Tan Mohair
2013-2018
Emine Kıraç Collection
This was hand-produced in Anatolia within the scope of the "Mohair Weaving in Anatolia" project.

Mohair Yarn Preparation Tools

The production of Ankara *sof* consisted of myriad troublesome sequence of processes. The production stages of *the Ankara sof*, from unadulterated mohair yarn to market-ready fabric, begins with the obtaining of the mohair from the Angora goat. These operations can be classified as shearing, collecting, aeration, cleaning, and sorting the mohair by type. Tools used have changed over time. The mohair that used to be obtained by handpicking in the 17th century as told by Evliya Çelebi, has graduated to shears over time, and nowadays, to electric shears. This is a pair of scissors employed in shearing. Shearing is the cutting off the Angora goat's mohair clean of the bottom, in accordance with procedure and without harming it. However, the mohair needs to be free from the dirt and straws off the goat's back, so they are combed according to types and length. During the combing process, some mohair separated from the waste, dirt and short fibres are picked out and put side by side. Long and smooth mohair bunches are called *sümek* (Tamur, 2003, p.65). The separated short and coarse fibre is called küreğit and it is not used for weaving (Turkish Cultural Foundation, 2018).

Spinning the mohair yarn is the next important stage. Spinning is the twisting together of drawn-out strands of mohair fibres to form yarn. As the thickness of the curved yarn depends on the number of hairs thus elongated, yarn may be spun in various thicknesses. Although the thi-ckness of the yarn depends on the purpose of use, thin spun yarn is favoured for *the Ankara sof*. Wooden tools used for fine spinning include a *iğ*, a *kirmen* and *öreke*. The *iğ* is a spindle made of a simple rod of 15-20 cm., and a piece that creates some weight at one end of this rod is a kirmen used for spinning mohair and wool, and the four-winged wooden contraption that spins the wool or mohair into yarn is known as an öreke, a distaff, a stick or spindle, on to which wool or flax is wound for spinning. Examples of woodcarving workmanship can be seen on the weights attached to these tools made of trees such as pine, plane, hornbeam, boxwood (Tamur, 2003, pp.65-68). In stories about *the Ankara sof*, it is often said that women do all the spinning work. Today, mohair is spun in the villages of Ankara, although not too commonly. In the village of Ayaş, a district of Ankara, kirmen is used in spinning mohair yarn and there it is called *fengere*.

Spindle (detail)
20th century
30,1x4,8 cm
Wood, iron
Erman Tamur Collection

Spindle
20th century
30,1x4,8 cm
Wood, iron
Erman Tamur Collection

Spindle
20th century
47,3x5,1 cm
Wood, iron
Erman Tamur Collection

Distaff
20th century
35,2 cmx7,2 cm
Wood
Özbahar Family Collection

Distaff
20th century
40,5x8,4 cm
Wood
Özbahar Family Collection

Kirmen
20th century
22,2x14,6 cm
Wood
Özbahar Family Collection

Kirmen
20th century
20,1x10,1 cm
Wood
Erman Tamur Collection

Kirmen
20th century
34x114 cm
Wood
Erman Tamur Collection

Metal Shears
20th century
32,7 cm
Iron
Erman Tamur Collection

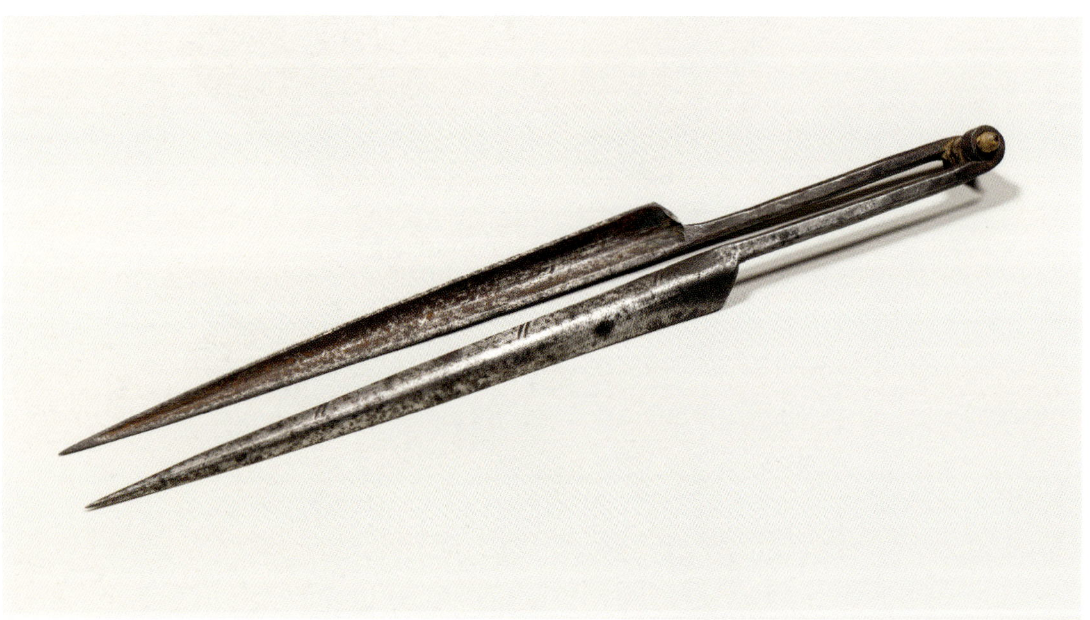

Metal Shears
20th century
32,2 cm
Iron
Erman Tamur Collection

Wooden Mohair Comb with Reed Teeth
20th century
68,6x10,5 cm
Wood, reed
Erman Tamur Collection

Wooden Mohair Comb with Iron Teeth
25x57x17 cm
Wood, iron
Özbahar Family Collection

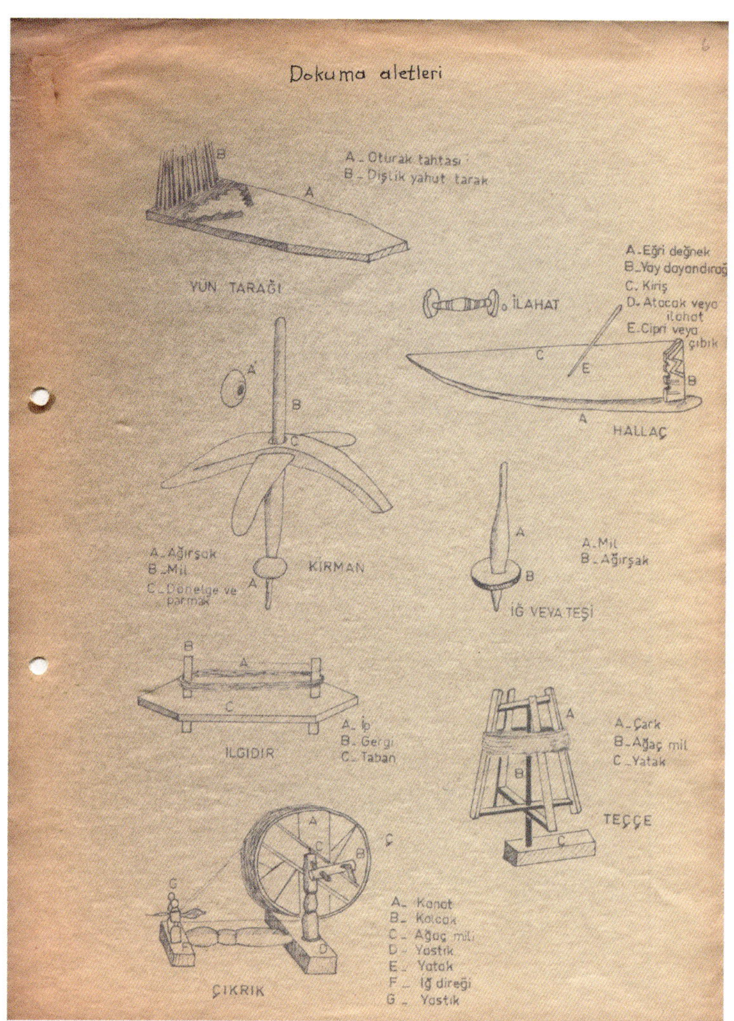

Drawings of Weaving Tools
Anonymous
Republican Era
31x21,7 cm
Blueprint on paper
Erman Tamur Archive

Drawings of wool card, *Kirmen* (a type of spinner), fluffer, *iğ* (splindler), twister, windlass, pulley. These are used for gathering and spinning mohair.

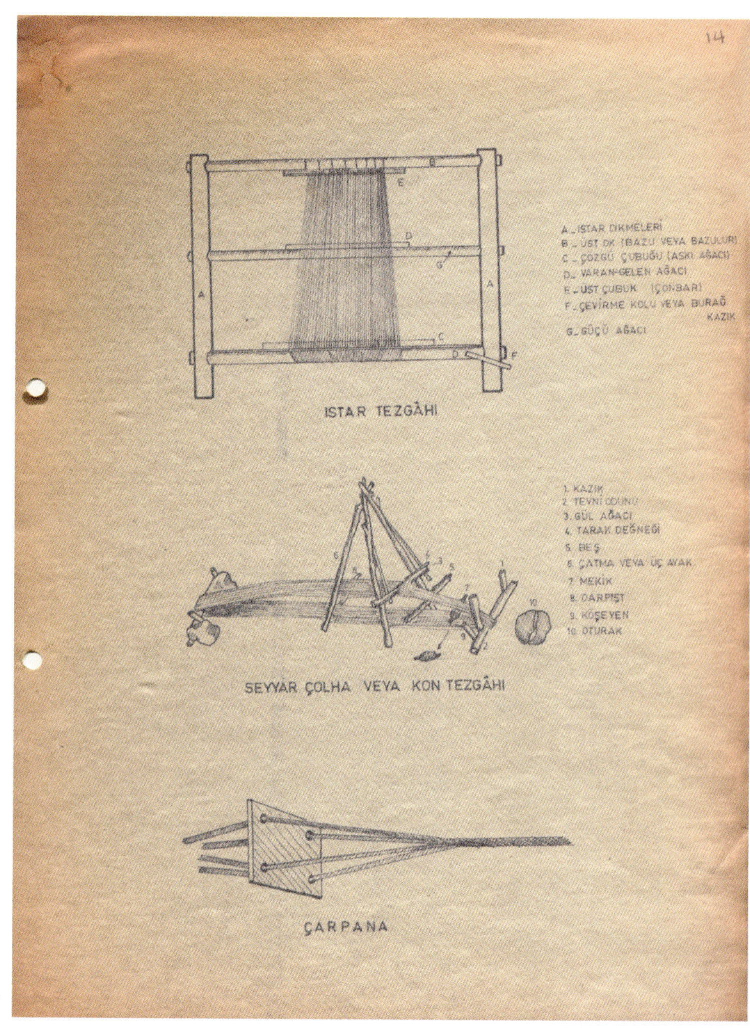

Drawings of Weaving Tools
Anonymous
Republican Era
31x21,7 cm
Blueprint on paper
Erman Tamur Archive

Drawings of weaving bench, hand loom (tent bench), simple nomadic loom. These are used for weaving. The parts of the tools are indicated with letters.

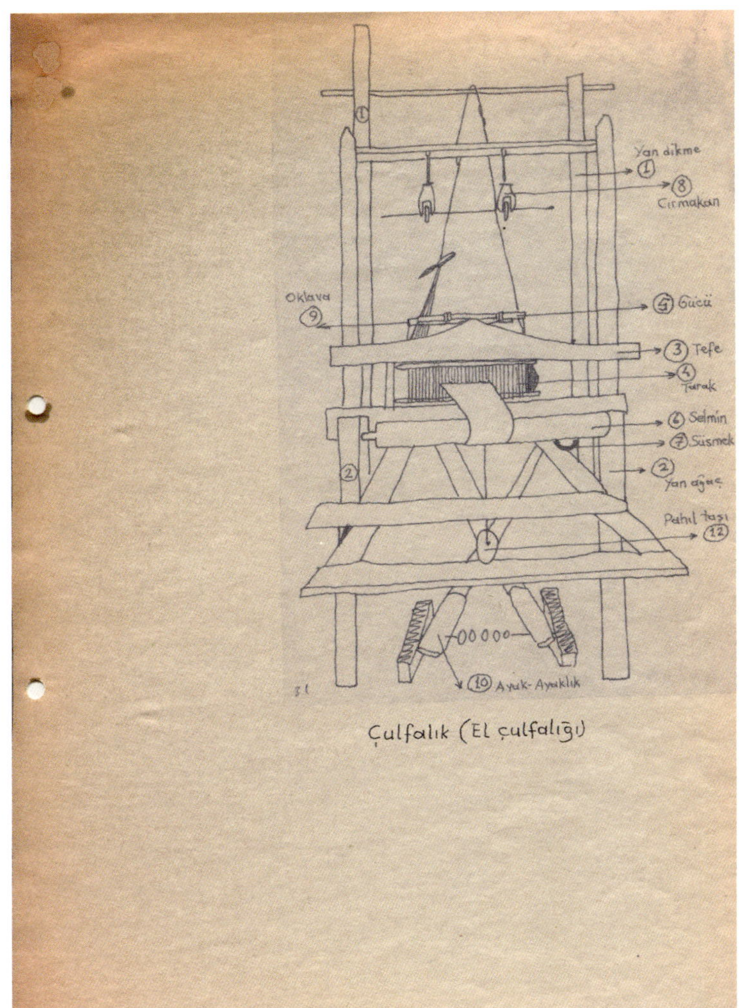

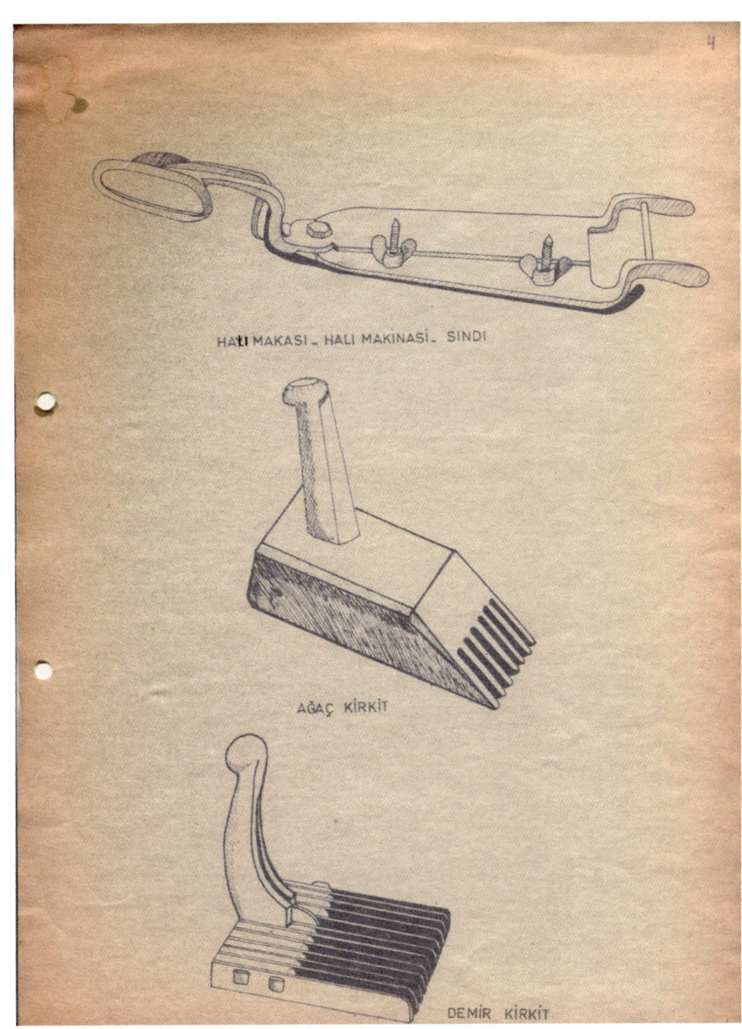

Drawing of Hand Loom
Anonymous
Republican Era
31x21,7 cm
Blueprint on paper
Erman Tamur Archive

Drawings of Weaving Tools
Anonymous
Republican Era
31x21,7 cm
Blueprint on paper
Erman Tamur Archive

Drawings of carpet shears (carpet machine, shears), wooden comb, iron comb which are used in weaving.

Weaving the History: Ayaş

The documentary Weaving the History: Ayaş, prepared specially for the exhibition and directed by Kerime Senyücel, and shot between January 29 and February 2, 2018, in Ankara's Ayaş district, in Gökçebağ Village and Yağmurdede Neighbourhood, focuses specifically on the Angora goat breeders Özbahar Family Farm and also on Kezban Yıldız, who produces knitwear using the mohair yarn of the local goats.

In this, members of the Özbahar Family, one of the largest Angora goat farmers who have worked with this special creature for at least four generations, share the characteristics, difficulties and experiences of the fast-dwindling Angora goat husbandry. Bekir Özbahar, the family patriarch at over 90 years of age, presents his personal knowledge and experiences about the history of this profession in the city.

At the same time, we have Kezban Yıldız, who was born in the Yağmurdede Neighbourhood of Ayaş and learned how to spin mohair from her family, contributes with her knowledge of creating mohair. These include preparing the dye, using natural materials such as tomatoes, walnuts and onion peel, and cleaning and washing the mohair with increasingly endangered natural methods, such as scribbling, flocking, and spinning, sharing with the hope that this thoroughly arduous process will help contribute to its documentation before it disappears from Ankara and environs.

Weaving the History: Ayaş
2018
Director: Kerime Senyücel
15'38"

Mohair Yarn

Natural Coloured Mohair Yarn
2013-2018
Emine Kıraç Collection

Produced within the scope of "Mohair Weaving in Anatolia" Project.

Unadultarated Mohair Yarn
2013-2018
Emine Kıraç Collection

Produced within the scope of "Mohair Weaving in Anatolia" Project.

Cream-Coloured Mohair Yarn Bobbin
Mohair Ferla Collection

Black Mohair Yarn Bobbin
Mohair Ferla Collection

Yarn Mounted on a Cord Knitter
1990
6,4 cm (length), 4 cm (diameter)
Hatice Doğruol Collection

It was handspun by Hatice Doğruol with kirmen and dyed with a textile dye. It was mounted on the cord knitter by four nails.

Natural Coloured Mohair Yarn
1950-2000
Hatice Doğruol Collection

It was spun by Makbule Doğruol with an *öreke* (distaff).

Ultramarine Mohair Yarn
1995
Hatice Doğruol Collection

It was handspun by Makbule Doğruol and dyed with a textile dye.

Brown Mohair Yarn
Hatice Doğruol Collection

It was handspun by Makbule Doğruol and dyed with walnut shell.

Brown Mohair Yarn with Sock-Knitting Needles
1990-2000
Hatice Doğruol Collection

It was handspun by Makbule Doğruol and dyed with walnut shell.

Natural Coloured Mohair Yarn
1950-2000
Hatice Doğruol Collection

The naturally milky-brown mohair was handspun with an *öreke* (distaff) to make a double coat.

Natural Coloured Mohair Yarn
1995-2000
Hatice Doğruol Collection

Dyeing Mohair and *The Sof*

Turkish Cultural Foundation Cultural Heritage Preservation and Natural Dyes Laboratory

The Cultural Heritage Preservation and Natural Dyes Laboratory (DATU), established by TCF[1] in Istanbul in 2010, maintains the world's most extensive collection of natural dyes. The inventory consists of 680 dye plants, dye insects, seashells, and natural organic lake pigments.

Natural Dyeing

Natural dyestuffs are created from pigments obtained from natural vegetal or animal sources such as plants, insects, seashells and lichens. Throughout history, these dyes have been applied to various materials and most commonly used to colour textile fibres, such as cotton, linen, wool, mohair, and silk. Colouring these fibre types using natural dyes is called natural dyeing.

Three varying methods are employed in natural dyeing: these are direct, mordant and vat-dyeing methods. In the direct dyeing process, fibres are treated directly with natural dyes. In the mordant dyeing method, fibre is processed with a type of alum called a mordant, of iron, tin, etc., after which the material is dyed with natural dye(s). Another method, the vat-dyeing technique, is used to obtain blue pigment from indigo dyestuffs extracted from specific plants. In this method, because dyestuffs in indigo plants are not water-soluble, extraction is accomplished by reduction using ancillary substances. The fibre is dipped into a prepared dyeing liquor, allowing the reduced indigo to combine with the oxygen in the air, thus facilitating the dyeing process. Dyeing with this method is usually carried out for blue pigments and for the blue constituents of green pigments. However, some historical textiles show that it has also been used as the blue constituent of purple pigments.

Today, many natural dye projects have been started with the aim of supporting the use of natural dyes, and their numbers are increasing day by day. Natural dye projects are supported especially in countries like France, Spain and Italy. In Turkey, the Turkish Cultural Foundation (TCF) and ARMAGGAN Inc. have partnered in a pioneering effort for nearly a decade to improve natural dyes and reintroduce them into textile production. Studies show that natural dyes can be sustainable in the textile industry. Standard

1 This part is provided by the Turkish Cultural Foundation (TCF), Cultural Heritage Preservation And Natural Dyes Laboratory (DATU). The Turkish Cultural Foundation (TCF) was established in 2000 by Drs. Yalçın and Serpil Ayaslı. The mission of TCF is to support the preservation and promotion of Turkish culture and heritage worldwide. TCF is a U.S. tax-exempt public charitable organization supported by a Trust established by the Ayaslı family and private donations. It has offices in Boston, Washington, D.C. and Istanbul, Turkey. The mission of TCF is to increase knowledge of Turkey's cultural heritage and to highlight Anatolia's contributions to world culture and humanity while building people-to-people cultural exchanges across the world. TCF has been accepted into official relations with UNESCO in 2015.

Turkish Cultural Foundation Cultural Heritage Preservation and Natural Dyes Laboratory- Natural Dyeing of the Mohair
2018
9.06'
This video footage shows the natural dyeing of the mohair yarn and dyeing of mohair tops in ten different colours in the laboratory environment.

dyeing methods are determined at the DATU laboratory within the scope of these studies and applied at the industrial scale.

Dyeing *The Ankara Sof*

Firstly, the mohair collected from Angora goats is purified of straw and other contaminants. Next, the mixed breeds and lengths of the mohair are sorted. Mohair fibres are separated by breed, height and variety. Usually particular care is taken to separate coarse fibres from the fine. This mohair is then combed with long-toothed special iron combs. The fibres are straightened and separated from each other. These are then placed in parallel arrays. The combing process helps separate short strands, waste and dirt. The separated short and coarse mohair is called küreğit and not used in weaving fabric. Long mohair is formed into mohair hanks.

After this stage, next comes the process of dyeing the combed and sorted mohair in various colours. Dyeing is performed using two different methods. Mohair is dyed either directly before or after washing. Usually, however, dyeing takes place in great boilers before washing. Historically, *the Ankara sof* was dyed mostly with vegetable dye sources, with annual or biennial plants grown in and around Ankara. The most commonly used plant sources are walnut shells, oak acorns, madder, buckthorn, weld, dyer's sumac, dyer's woad, and safflower plants. Mohair is boiled according to the desired colours in boilers with adequate water, with little or a lot of mixing. All dyed mohair is then taken out of the boilers and washed in cold water. Next, it is dried by spreading it on the ground, or hanging it from ropes and poles. Thus, the mohair is dyed to the desired colour. *The Ankara sof* may be dyed after weaving or in the form of yarn, too. The most important stage in the *sof* process is the dyeing. The role of a competent dyeing master is vital at this point, and it is said that there were only five mohair masters in Ankara in 1707. Another important element in dyeing is the quality of water. The water used for dyeing must be very clear and pure. The dyed *sof* is washed thoroughly in cold water and dried. The mohair, prior to being dyed, is washed thoroughly in large boilers with lukewarm water and soapwort. Thus, all of the impurities are washed out of the mohair, leaving it a lighter colour and as bright as silk. As the dyed and washed mohair is now mixed together, they are subjected to a second combing; the strands are disentangled and smoothened. After completion of the dyeing and all other processes, *the Ankara sof* is ready for use.

Identification of *The Ankara Sof* and Other Historical/Archaeological Textiles

Although there are different analytical methods adopted for the determination of the dyes present in *the Ankara sof* and other historical and archaeological textile artefacts, the most preferred method is liquid chromatography. The device used for this purpose is High-Performance Liquid Chromatography HPLC. A sample of between 0.5 to 3.0 mg is adequate for analysis. The dyes in the sample, following hydrolysis and solubilisation, are loaded on the HPLC apparatus in the form of a clear liquid. The obtained results are compared to the preloaded pure certified dyestuff standards on the device to determine dyestuff source(s) and colouring compounds. The result reveals the identity of both the work and the type of dyeing material to be used in restoration. Another analysis technique in textiles is fibre analysis. This technique may be used to determine the type of plant or animal fibre by conducting simple spot tests, as well as precise detection of the fibre used for the artefact with the aid of advanced devices such as electron microscopes. If the material features other elements such as wire, gold thread, sequin, bead, etc., electron microscopy and a linked EDX detector system detects components of these materials. The CIELAB spectrophotometer is used for measuring colours on the artefact's surface. Colour values are expressed numerically as Lab, CMK or RGB. Finally, technical analyses reveal data on the weave types of textile works, warp and weft density, yarn twist direction, number of twists etc.

Saffron *(Crocus sativus L.)*
Used for yellow and orange colours.

Saffron *(Crocus sativus L.)*
November, 2012
Collected from Safranbolu, Karabük.
TCF DATU Natural Dyes Collection
Used for yellow and orange colours.

Anatolian Buckthorn
(Rhamnus petiolaris L.)
July, 2013
Collected from Nevşehir.
TCF DATU Natural Dyes Collection
Used for yellow colour.

Madder *(Rubia tinctorum L.)*
September, 2011
Collected from Ankara, Ayaş.
TCF DATU Natural Dyes Collection
Used for red colour.

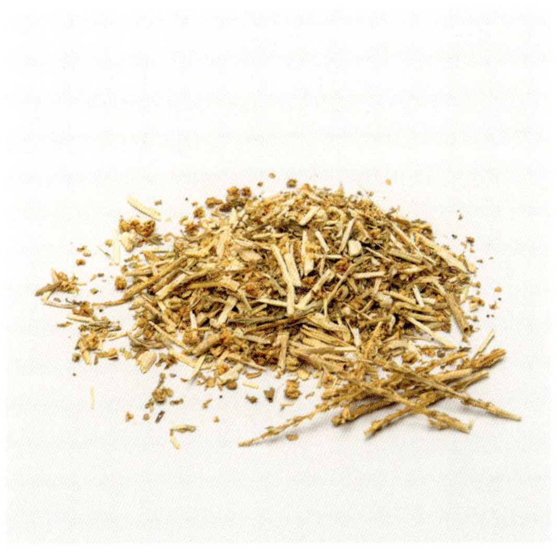

Weld *(Reseda luteola L.)*
June, 2012
Collected from Ankara, Ayaş.
TCF DATU Natural Dyes Collection
Used for khaki and olive green colours.

Kermes *(Kermes vermilio Planchon L.)*
June, 2011
Collected from Çanakkale, Güzelyalı.
TCF DATU Natural Dyes Collection
Used for red colour.

Safflower *(Carthamus tinctorius L.)*
July, 2013
Collected from Ankara, Beypazarı.
TCF DATU Natural Dyes Collection
Used for yellow and red colours.

Valonia Oak *(Quercus ithaburensis Decaisne L.)*
September, 2014
Collected from Çanakkale, Kepez.
TCF DATU Natural Dyes Collection
Used for grey and black colours.

Cochineal *(Dactylopius coccus Costa L.)*
2014
Collected from Mexico.
TCF DATU Natural Dyes Collection
Used for red colour.

Dyer's Sumac
(Cotinus coggygria scop Rhus cotinus L.)
June, 2012
Collected from Bolu, Mudurnu.
TCF DATU Natural Dyes Collection
Used for yellow colour.

Woad *(Isatis tinctoria L.)*
September, 2011
Collected from Ankara, Nallıhan.
TCF DATU Natural Dyes Collection
Used for blue colour.

Walnut Shell *(Juglans regia L.)*
August, 2017
Collected from Çanakkale, Dardanos.
TCF DATU Natural Dyes Collection
Used for brown colour.

Alum *(Alumen)*
Used for fixing colours.

Dyed Samples

Mohair Yarn and Mohair Tops Dyed Ultramarine with Natural Indigo Plant
2018
46,7x2,5 cm
VEKAM/Ankara Orchard House Collection

Mohair Yarn and Mohair Tops Dyed Light Blue with Natural Indigo Plant
2018
48x3 cm
VEKAM/Ankara Orchard House Collection

Mohair Yarn and Mohair Tops Dyed Red with Dyer's Madder and Oak Acorn
2018
48x3 cm
VEKAM/Ankara Orchard House Collection

Mohair Yarn and Mohair Tops Dyed Purple with Cochineal and Oak Acorn
2018
44,5x3 cm
VEKAM/Ankara Orchard House Collection

Mohair Yarn and Mohair Tops Dyed Maroon with Dyer's Madder, Walnut Shell and Oak Acorn
2018
48,5x3 cm
VEKAM/Ankara Orchard House Collection

Mohair Yarn and Mohair Tops Dyed Brown with Walnut Shell and Oak Acorns
2018
46x2,5 cm
VEKAM/Ankara Orchard House Collection

Mohair Yarn and Mohair Tops Dyed Dark Pink with Cochineal Beetle and Oak Acorn
2018
44x2,5 cm
VEKAM/Ankara Orchard House Collection

Mohair Yarn and Mohair Tops Dyed Pink with Cochineal and Oak Acorn
2018
46x2,5 cm
VEKAM/Ankara Orchard House Collection

Mohair Yarn and Mohair Tops Dyed Green with Natural Indigo, Dyer's Weed (*Reseda luteola L.*) and Oak Acorn
2018
45,5x2,5 cm
VEKAM/Ankara Orchard House Collection

Mohair Yarn and Mohair Tops Dyed Yellow with Dyer's Weed, Dyer's rocket and Oak Acorn
2018
46x2,5 cm
VEKAM/Ankara Orchard House Collection

Mohair Society of Turkey 1937 Assembly Photo
1937
29x34 cm
Black & White Photograph
VEKAM Library and Archive. Inv. No: LF022

The Mohair Society of Turkey

In 1924, unlike the thousand looms functioning around in the Ankara region in 1867, only a handful of mohair benches remained in Zir (Istanos) in the region known today as Yenikent (Batu, 1951, p. 40). The number of goats that stood at 1,500,000 in 1863 had been greatly reduced by the First World War (Batu, 1951, s. 35).

The Republic wanted to take up the matter in the Angora goat and mohair weaving industry; Ankara was attempting to increase the goat population and revitalise the mohair weaving industry. Establishing a Mohair Society of Turkey to improve Angora goat breeding, for the acquisition of high quality mohair for processing and exporting came on the agenda in 1929, the Society actually began work in 1930 (Gürler, 2006, s. 40). The Society's charter was published in the Official Gazette on April 10, 1932, to the effect that the Mohair Society of Turkey, established under the auspices of the Ministry of Economy, with headquarters in Ankara, and branches in other provinces that farmed mohair (Kastamonu, Konya, Eskisehir, Afyon, Çankırı, Çorum, Yozgat, Bolu, Kütahya, Kırşehir, Aksaray, Mardin, Sinop, Niğde, Zonguldak and Bilecik) (Source: T.C. Resmi Gazete, 10 Nisan 1932).

The Mohair Society of Turkey was founded by MPs of the period, especially Yozgat MP Süleyman Sırrı İçöz, veterinarians, and mohair farmers and traders. It has contributed greatly to the modernization of husbandry techniques, the maintenance of the species, and the revitalization of *sof* weaving (Gürler, 2006).

The Mohair Society created a husbandry facility/exemplary pen near Ankara, Lalahan; and providing brood stocks for villagers; forming a highbred herd selected from the best Angora goats in Anatolia, and thus launching the Lalahan Livestock Central Research Institute.

The Society was housed at the *Sof* Weaving House by the old Çakırlar Bridge over the Bentderesi, at the tannery district. It is known that the fabrics produced in the *Sof* Weaving House were presented to Mustafa Kemal Atatürk, and that he encouraged *sof* weaving by wearing it at the time (Source: Cumhuriyet Gazetesi, 23 Ağustos 1932).

The Mohair Society of Turkey continued its activities until 1951, having served over the 1930s and 1940s as a model organization that demonstrated the importance the Republic attached to the Angora goat and mohair weaving. The land and buildings used by the society was transferred to the Ministry of Agriculture; and it was shut down due to factors such as rescinding of the Ministry of Agriculture, and the aging of Süleyman Sırrı İçöz, who had been foundation chairperson for many years. , has occasionally been closed as the Ministry of Agriculture cuts off the aid. In 1960, Congress decreed that the Mohair Society's Headquarters in Turkey Bentderesi also was transferred to the Child Protection Agency (Gürler, 2006, pp. 44-45).

Süleyman Sırrı İçöz (1878-1963)

Süleyman Sırrı İçöz was a graduate of Civil High school. He was employed as a clerk and teller at the School of Industry, township director at Mucur, Zir, Hacıbektaş, Salmanlı, and district governor of Halce, Koyulhisar and Darende. During his Bozok deputyship at the First Parliamentary Assembly, he applied to be conscripted as a private soldier and he was granted his wish on August 22, 1921, upon which he fought in the Çekirdeksiz Köy and Doğatepesi battles on the Western Front. Afterwards he was Bozok deputy in the Second term and Yozgat deputy in the Third, Fourth, Fifth, Sixth and Seventh consecutive terms. He was the holder of a red-green Independence Medal (Source: TBMM Web Site).

One of the founders of the Mohair Society of Turkey, Süleyman Sırrı İçöz was a pioneer in the efforts to renew interest in the Angora goat in the Republican era and the development of mohair research scientifically. The Society gained this status in 1939, thanks to the efforts Mr. İçöz (Gürler, 2006, p.44).

With the incitement of the Republican People's Party, who deems as it does in all such cases that this matter needs to be improved, and with the initiative of a number of citizens who believe that this charming creature with its unique and historical presence in our country, and a commodity of great worth, does not deserve to be neglected thus, and therefore have established this Society (Mohair Society of Turkey), for the reinstating of mohair goat husbandry. Its headquarters in Ankara and its branches located in the provinces and jurisdictions of Yozgat, Ayaş, Beypazarı, Kızılcahamam, Koçhisar, Balâ, Çubukabat started to operate as of 1930. (İçöz, 1938, p.349)

Portrait of Süleyman Sırrı İçöz,
one of the founders of
The Mohair Society of Turkey (1878-1963)
1920
71,6x81,1 cm
Black & White Photograph
Erman Tamur Archive

Süleyman Sırrı İçöz and the Angora Goats
1932-1951
33,4x37,7 cm
Black & White Photograph
Erman Tamur Archive

Mohair Society of Turkey 1937 Assembly Photo
1937
29x34 cm
Black & White Photograph
VEKAM Library and Archive. Inv. No: LF022

Angora Goats grazing in the Mohair Society's Lalahan Farm
1932-1951
26x34 cm
Black & White Photograph
VEKAM Library and Archive. Inv. No: 3080

The inscription in Turkish "*sürülerden bir güruh*" (flock) appears on this photograph.

Goats being shorn in front of Lalahan pen
1932-1951
26x34 cm
Black & White Photograph
VEKAM Library and Archive. Inv. No: 3079

The inscription in Turkish "*ağılların önünde keçiler kırkılırken*" (goats being short in front of pens) appears on this photograph.

Mohair Society of Turkey, Lalahan Scientific Bath
1932-1951
26x34 cm
Black & White Photograph
VEKAM Library and Archive. Inv. No: 5320

The inscription in Turkish "fenni banyo heyeti muayenesi" (Scientific Bath Committee's Examination) appears on this photograph. In the assembly that was held on 21 April 1935, it was stated that the bath was constructed for the goats which's population reached 875. (Gürler, 2006, s. 43).

Mohair Society of Turkey, Lalahan Model Pens
1932-1951
26x34 cm
Black & White Photograph
VEKAM Library and Archive. Inv. No: 3081

Mohair Society of Turkey, Lalahan Model Pens
1932-1951
26x34 cm
Black & White Photograph
VEKAM Library and Archive. Inv. No: 3075

The inscription in Turkish "*numune ağıllarından birisi*" (one of the model pens) appears on this photograph.

Mohair Society of Turkey – Lalahan, Shepherds and Sheepdogs
1932-1951
26x34 cm
Black & White Photograph
VEKAM Library and Archive. Inv. No: 3076

The inscription in Turkish "*çobanlar ve çoban köpekleri*" (Shepherds and sheepdogs) appears on this photograph. A committee from the Ministry of Agriculture visited the Mohair Society on August 25, 1935 and stated in their expedition report that the Society considers establishing a "shepherds' school" (Gürler, 2006, s. 43).

Mohair Society of Turkey – Lalahan Production Farm, Peach Meadow Pasture and Guard House
1932-1951
26x34 cm
Black & White Photograph
VEKAM Library and Archive.
Inv. No: LF016

March 2, 1932 meeting report of the Mohair Society of Turkey reveals that the Society purchased the land, located 27 km from Ankara, in the area of Lalahan Station which was known as Odabaşı Çiftliği (Odabaşı Farm) (Gürler, 2006, p.42). This land, will become the most known production farm of the Society called as Lalahan Production Farm.

Mohair Society of Turkey *Sof* Weaving House at the Bentderesi Valley
1934-1951
18x24 cm
Black & White Photograph
VEKAM Library and Archive. Inv. No: 0014

The 300 metersquared land that was located at the Bentderesi Valley and belonged to the Treasury, was allocated to the use of the Mohair Society of Turkey by decree number 12151 on January 13, 1932 by the Cabinet of Ministers. However, it was later understood that the land was actually 690 metersquare and it was assigned to the Society by a second decree that was issued on February 27, 1934. The headoffice building and *sof* weaving house were built on this land (Gürler, 2006, pp.41-42).

Album commemorating the visit to the Lalahan Model Farm and Pens of the Mohair Society of Turkey of Minister of Agriculture the Honourable Mr Şevket Hatipoğlu and Ministry Veterinarian and Dignitaries of Agriculture with Deans and Associates of the Higher Institute of Agriculture

May 11, 1944

29,5x21 cm

Album that consists of 59 Black & White photographs.

VEKAM Library and Archive. Inv. No: ALB_13

Under the Microscope: Fiber Analysis

An interactive table is designed for visitors to observe mohair under a basic microscope. On this table, microscopic images of the mohair are also displayed.

An electron microscope is used to determine the nature of fibre is used in historical textiles and to perform dye analyses. The microscope used in the analyses is called a SEM-EDX or SEM-EDS. This device is able to magnify the analysed sample surface by one million. Turkish Cultural Foundation (TCF), Cultural Heritage Preservation and Natural Dyes Laboratory also use this device for identification of the fiber type.

Microscopic Image of a Relic of woven material made from goat's wool unearthed at the King's Grave at Arslantepe Malatya, Arslantepe Plate VI B1 (3000-2750 BC).
20.05.2008

University of Rome Sapienza, Italian Expedition in Eastern Anatolia (MAIAO) Archives

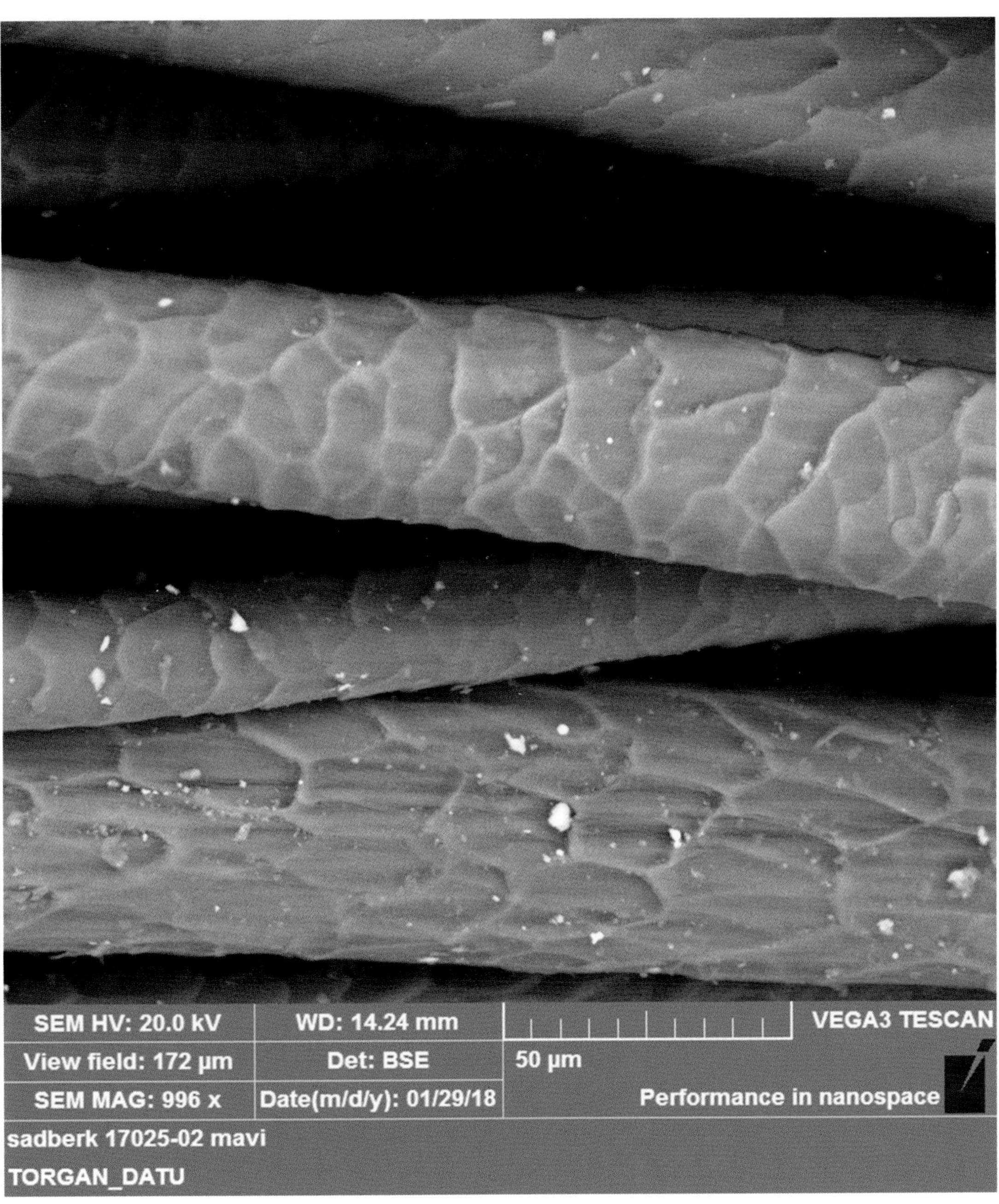

SEM Image of the sample from a cloth from Sadberk Hanım Museum (Inv. No: 14006-K.732)
29.01.2018

Image produced at TCF DATU Laboratory using high resolution electron microscope (SEM-EDX). Sample surface was magnified 996 times. The analysis regarding the identification of the fiber revealed that the fiber is mohair in the animal structure. When the thickness of the analyzed yarn is examined it is highly probable that the sample belongs to *Ankara sof*.

The Ankara Sof

Sof weaving, was a handicraft peculiar to Ankara and its environs. Given the best quality mohair obtained in the region, the best quality *sof* were woven in Ankara. It is thought that the historic *sof* fabric was woven with the plain-weave technique. The reason for its fine appearance is that although the mohair yarn is hand-spun, it is woven with a minimum of warping, without twisting weft and warp threads and only folding once (İmer, 1994, pp. 85-86). It is thought that the moiré and shiny appearance, which is considered the most vital feature of the *sof* fabric, is formed by the process of pressing and glazing (İmer, 1994, pp. 85-86). The knowledge of these processes, which gave the fabric its softness, shine and moiré appearance, disappeared over time.

In the Ottoman period, how and where the *sof* are to be woven, the dimensions and techniques of weaving, the techniques of weaving, and who may weave and dye how and where, were always proscribed by law and strict supervision. *Sof* weavers were tasked with weaving fabrics in certain dimensions, within the boundaries certain trade guilds, under the control of the sheikh, steward, and guild masters, providing the *sof* yarns according to needs. The *sofs* were exhibited at the Mahmutpaşa Bedesten, or sold through brokers (Ergenç, 1995, p. 101). Decrees on weaving dimensions were communicated to local judges in places such as Ankara, Ayaş, Sivrihisar, Kalecik and Tosya, and weavers that cheat in *sof* production, such as those who attempt to sell deficient work or use sheep's fleece instead of mohair, would be warned or punished (Ongan, 1954-1955, p.73).

In the 16th century heyday of *sof*, *sof* producers were the stars. The Avancıklar district, located to the east of the city, was the most densely populated part of the city for *sof* weavers. *Sof* would be woven in home workshops at various neighbourhoods; and all family members took a part in the production process. In Istanos (later called Zir and Yenikent, today), Erkeksu and Miranos villages near the city, rather that farming, the major activity was *sof* weaving (Ergenç, 1984, p. 54). The *sof* produced in these villages, the great majority of which population consisted of weaver Armenians, were specially celebrated(Tamur, 2003, pp. 173,175).

In the 17th century, travelers Simeon of Poland and Evliya Çelebi, pooint at these villages as Armenian villages and their effectiveness in *sof* weaving in their travelogues. Evliya Çelebi describes Zir as the town whereby beautiful *sof* and muhayyer were woven in thousand looms. (Kurşun, Kahraman ve Dağlı, 1999, p. 229; Tamur, 2003, p. 175).

Research reveals that of the 343 houses around the year 1600, 30 of them were *sof* weaving workshops, at the end of the century there were 290 households, 28 of which were workshops. The average number of looms in the houses was around 2.4 in 1600, while this increased to 2.5, and up to 2.9 around 1690 (Faroqhi, 1985, p.243).

Dyeing of The *Sof* Fabric

There are two divergent opinions on dyeing *sof*. One opinion holds that *sof* was woven using dyed yarn, while the other claims the opposite, i.e. is that it was dyed after it has been woven. Özer Ergenç, who has studied 16th century Ankara through Ottoman archival documents, court records and tax records, supports the opinion that the *sof* were dyed after they were woven. The dyer and polisher (presser) artisans in Ankara dyed, alongside the local product, the *sof* woven in regions such as Tosya, Kastamonu, Sivrihisar and Çankırı; and completed their polishing and finishing processes, too (Ergenç, 1995, p.100).

Taxation of the dyeing and pressing of the *sof* necessitated that these process be kept under strict supervision (Ergenç, 1995). Records showing that there was a serious taxation system also provide information about the fees payable for washing, dyeing, pressing and finishing services, and thus about the *sof* weaving industry.

Sof, in addition to being produced in the natural colour of the mohair, was also produced in various colours, as evidenced by historical documents. These colours included deep red, vermilion, deep purple, violet, purple, hyacinth, sky blue, pistachio green, rose, bright red, light mauve, cornelian cherry, wine, grass green, orange, Egyptian purple, light violet, black and ruddy(Ongan, 1954-1955).

The *Sof* Trade

The Ankara sof was a well-known fabric in the West, and especially famous in Venice because it was a foreign trade product. Therefore, it was not just Western fabric traders visiting Ankara to purchase *sof*. Anatolian traders were also travelling to foreign markets, especially to Venice (Kafadar, 2009, p.100). During Ottoman times, various names were used for the *sof* fabric where this trade was conducted, in places such as Venice, England, France, Poland, and Holland.

Mohair: denotes mohair, and the fine, luxurious fabric weaved with mohair yarn. It was adapted from the Arabic word mukhayyar, literally "choice".

Camlet: is a water-resistant and durable fabric made from goat's wool, used primarily for capes/raincoats. It was also used as a synonym for *sof*. This word may also derive from the Arabic khaml/khamlat. This is from the Arabic seil al kemel i.e. "Angora goat." There is a variety of uses such as camelot in French, czamlet in Polish, as well as chamlyt, chamelet (t), chamlett, cham (e) lot, chambelot, chamblet (t), chamlet camblet, chamolet, camelott, and camlott.

Ciambellotti: is the word used for *sof* in Italian. There are different pronunciations such as Zambelotti in Venetian dialect.

In 16th century England, *sof* and mohair fabrics produced in Ankara were well known and highly preferred. This is well-documented by William Harborne, appointed British ambassador to the Ottomans on November 26, 1582, and who was involved in the business of the Levant Company, which provided commercial relations between the Ottomans and the UK, in a letter instructing British merchant James Towerson to purchase various fabrics from Ankara (French, 1972, pp. 241-247).

The fabric and colours mentioned in this letter, besides revealing much about the British fashion of the period, enumerates the wool products, and particularly the mohair fabrics created in Ankara. The words water chamblets; mockados and grogerin used by Harborne are terms used by the British to describe the different types of mohair fabrics woven in Ankara.

In the 18th and 19th centuries, the mohair yarn exported from the Ottoman to the West replaced the *sof* trade. Mohair yarn was needed by various industries, such as the button manufacturers of France, clothiers and wigmakers in the UK, and used in wool production in the Netherlands, where a special fabric called greinen was manufactured in Leiden. There was significant trade of mohair yarn between the Netherlands and the Ottomans during this period (Faroqhi,2017, p.280 and Wilson, 1960,pp.215-217). Fabrics produced from Turkish mohair gain importance.

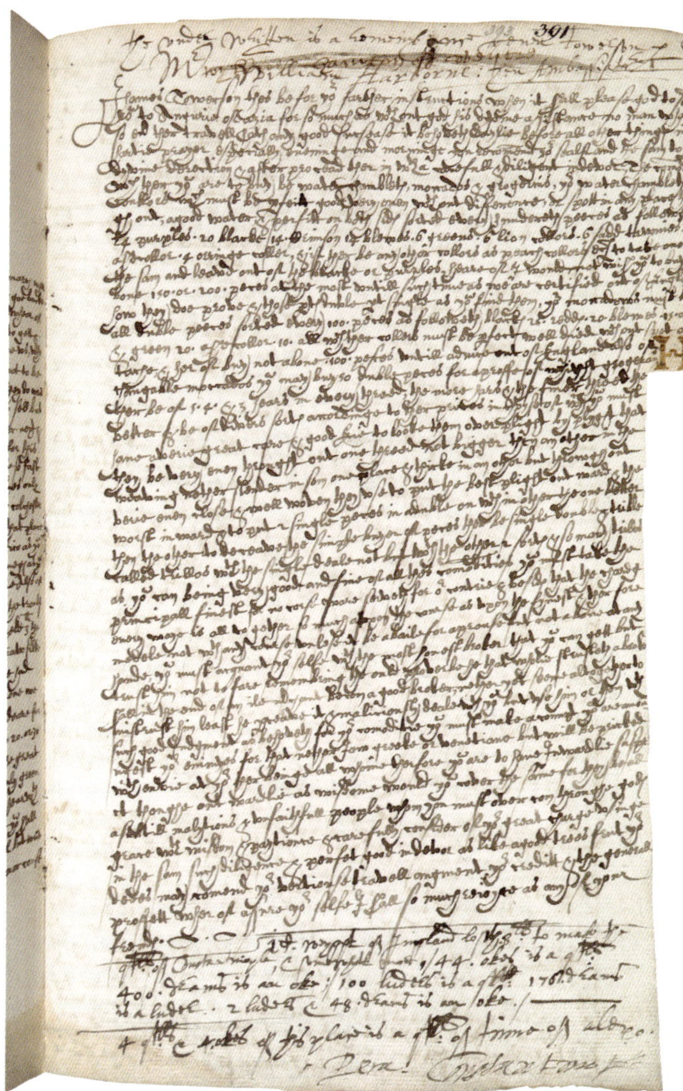

Copy of instructions (undated) from William Harborne to James Towerson, for the purchase of goods at 'Angurie of Azia' (i.e. Angora)
1538 (According to David French)

Inv. No: MS241,f393a

"... water chamblets, moccados & grogerins, yor water chamblets in coullors which must be pfeit good, very even without difference, or spott in any place throu ghout, a good water, & perfitt on both sids sorted every hundereth peeces as followeth 24 purples. 20 blacke. 14. crimson 14 blewes. 6 greens. 6 lion collors. 6 sadd tawnies. 6. asie colour. 4 orringe collor, & if ther be any other collors as peach collors ect to take one of the sam and leave out of the blacke or purples ... moccadows must be all duble peeces sorted every 100. peces as followeth blacks 25. redds. 20. blewes. 15. oring.& green 20. ashe collor. 10 ... also of thorngalle moccados you may buy 50 duble peces for aproffe of whight grogeran ther be of 5.4. & 3 hears in every threed, the more hars & the finer threed the better & be of divers sorts accordinge to ther prices." (French, 1972, p.245)

Portefeuille met stalen van 'Camelot' of Turks laken, uit Leiden (Portfolio with samples of Camlet or Turkish cloth from Leiden)
Circa 1800
25x11,8x2,5cm (closed), 25x24,5x1 cm (opened)
Museum De Lakenhal Collection, Leiden, Netherlands, Inv. No: 1671

The portfolio includes a red Moroccan leather cover printed with "ECHANTILLONS DE LA FABRIQUE DES CAMELOTS & C. A LEIDE". The portfolio consists of ten flaps and samples are numbered from 1 to 77. The samples include plush, camelots, moiré, polemite and broché. On the back is a French description of the samples written with the title "Explication de la Carte des Echantillon", with two wax stamps.

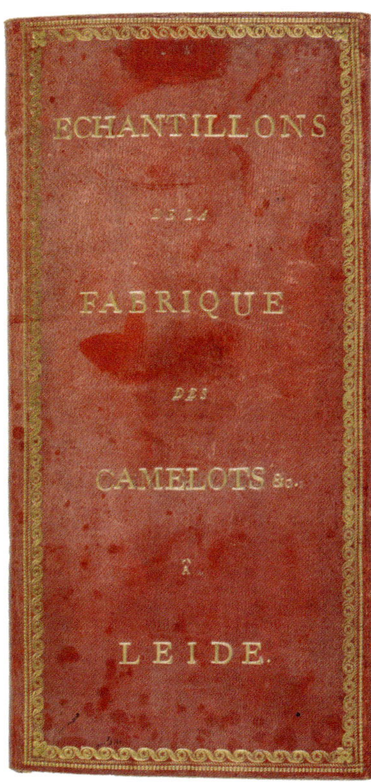

Portfolio with samples of 'Camelot' or Turkish cloth at the Museum De Lakenhal in Leiden stands evidence of the significance of the role of the Turks in woollen fabric production in the West.

Places Where The *Sof* Trade Took Place

In the 16th century, the bedestens and inns in Ankara were the places where *sof* trade took place. Production and trade at that time in Ankara were conducted in the Atpazarı neighbourhood and vicinity, where foundation hans and civil hans drove a significant part of the region's trade. The hans not only provided lodgings for foreigners who came to the city, the passengers and the *sof* traders, but also served as their warehouses (Ergenç, 1995, pp.17-21). This was considered a secure area due to its proximity to the Citadel, therefore towards the end of the 15th century, Mahmut Pasha, Fatih Sultan Mehmed's Grand Vizier, built the Bedesten at its centre (Öney, 1971, pp. 135-136). In the area, besides the Bedesten, were the Pembe Han, Kapan Han, Kurşunlu Han, Hasan Paşa Han, Zağfirancı Han, Tuz Han, Çengel Han, and Bakır Han (Ergenç, 1995, pp. 17-18). *Sof* traders lodged and stored their goods at the Kurşunlu Han, which today hosts the Museum of Anatolian Civilizations, and the mohair trade was conducted from the Çengel Han.

Atpazarı Meydanı
(The Horse Market)
1925
18x25 cm
Black & White Photograph
VEKAM Library and Archive,
Inv. No: 0016

Atpazarı Meydanı (The Horse Market Square) is the square that is located at the center of Ankara hans' region.

Mahmut Pasha Bedesten
Republican Era
18x26 cm
Black & White Photograph
VEKAM Library and Archive,
Inv. No: 0590

Mahmut Pasha Bedesten was constructed towards the end of 15th century by Mahmut Pasha, the Grand Vizier of Fatih Sultan Mehmed and it has no inscription. It was abondened until 1932 in the aftermath of the fire that took place in 1881. In 1933 it was used as Eti Museum and in 1946 it was restored and has been used as the Museum of Anatolian Civilizations since then (Öney, 1971, pp. 135-136).

Kurşunlu Han
Before 1938
18x24 cm
Black & White Photograph
VEKAM Library and Archive,
Inv. No: 1618

It was constructed by Mahmut Pasha, the Grand by Vizier of Fatih Sultan Mehmed towards the end of the 15th century. It is adjacent to the Mahmut Pasha Bedesten. Today, it serves as the office and warehouse of the Museum of Anatolian Civilizations (Öney, 1971, s. 136).

Kurşunlu Han
03.05.1954
18x24 cm
Black & White Photograph
VEKAM Library and Archive,
Inv. No: 0591

Çengel Han
1978-1979
8,8x12,2 cm
Black & White Photograph
VEKAM Library and Archive, Inv. No: TKV0190.1

Çengel Han was built in the Sultan Suleiman I period in 1522-1523 (929 Hijri) in affiliation with the Grand Vizier Rüstem Pasha's waqf. Before being abondened towards the end of the 20th century it had been used as a wool warehouse and a tanyard whereby mohair, fleece and unprocessed leather trade took place. In the aftermath of the renovation between 2003 and 2005, Çengelhan was opened to the public as an affiliate of the Rahmi M. Koç Foundation for Museology and Culture.

Çengel Han
1978-1979
11x9 cm
Black & White Photograph
VEKAM Library and Archive, Inv. No: TKV0190.2

Safran Han
Republican Era
8,8x11,5 cm
Black & White Photograph
VEKAM Library and Archive,
Inv. No: TKV0192

The Safran Han, without an inscription, thought to be constructed in the 16th century. Han, has been renovated many times throughout the history therefore it is believed that its historical characteristics might have been lost (Öney, 1971, p.141).

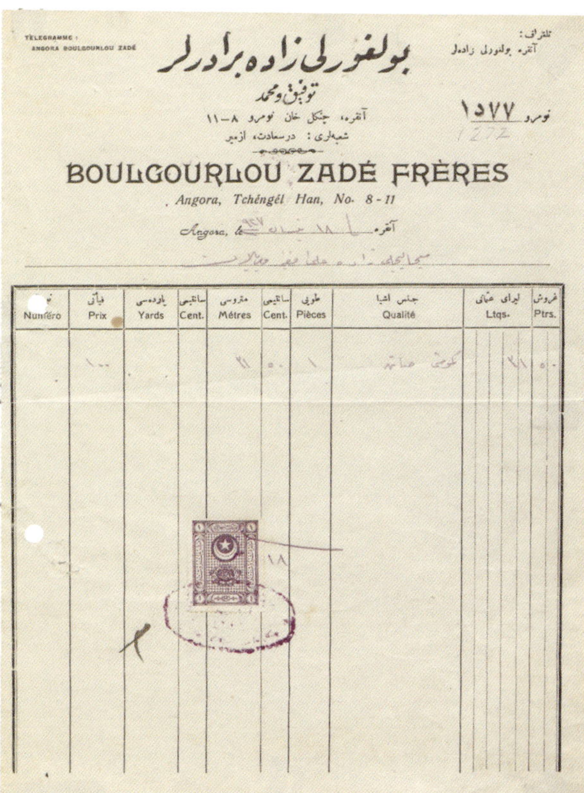

TÉLEGRAMME :
ANGORA BOULGOURLOU ZADÉ

تلغراف :
آنقره بولغورلی زاده‌لر

بولغورلی زاده برادرلر
توفیق و محمد
آنقره، چنگل خان نومرو ٨-١١
شعبه‌لری : درسعادت، ازمیر

نومرو ١٥٧٧

BOULGOURLOU ZADÉ FRÈRES
Angora, Tchéngél Han, No. 8 - 11

Angora, le .... آنقره

Numéro	قیأتی Prix	یاردەسی Yards	سانتیمی Cent.	متروسی Métres	سانتیمی Cent.	طوپی Pièces	جنس اشیا Qualité	لیرای عثمانی Ltqs.	غروش Ptrs.
	١٠٠			٢١	٥٠	١	[illegible]	٢١	٥٠

Invoice for Brothers Bulgurluzade Operating in Çengel Han
10.04.1905
20x27,7 cm
VEKAM Library and Archive,
Inv. No: A388

Examples From Topkapı Palace Museum Collection

Velense (Ground cloth)
Ottoman, 16th century
216x145 cm
Mohair, felt
Topkapı Palace Museum, Inv. No: 13/148

This ground cloth is a unique example from Topkapı Palace Museum collection. On a felt surface, it has long mohair fringes. According to the museum's records it belonged to Sultan Süleyman I (1520-1566). The centre was dyed green with luteolin, apigenin, indigotine obtained from dyer's rocket (*Reseda luteola L.*) and indigo (*Indigofera tinctoria L.*) or dyer's woad (*Isatis tinctoria L.*). The fringes and edges were dyed with dyestuffs Laccain acid, A, B, C, and flavokermesic acid obtained from the lac bug (*Kerria lacca*). (Source: Sibel A. Arça, TPM)

Velense (Prayer Rug)
Ottoman, 17th century
193x102 cm
Mohair
Topkapı Palace Museum, Inv. No: 13/1191

It is one of the two velense prayer rugs from the Topkapı Palace Museum collection. The sides and mihrab niche of the natural mohair-coloured prayer rug were dyed an orange/brown yellow using Brazilin obtained from the brazilwood tree (*Caesalpinia brasiliensis*) and dyer's sumac (*Cotinius coggygria SCOP*). (Source: Sibel A. Arça, TPM)

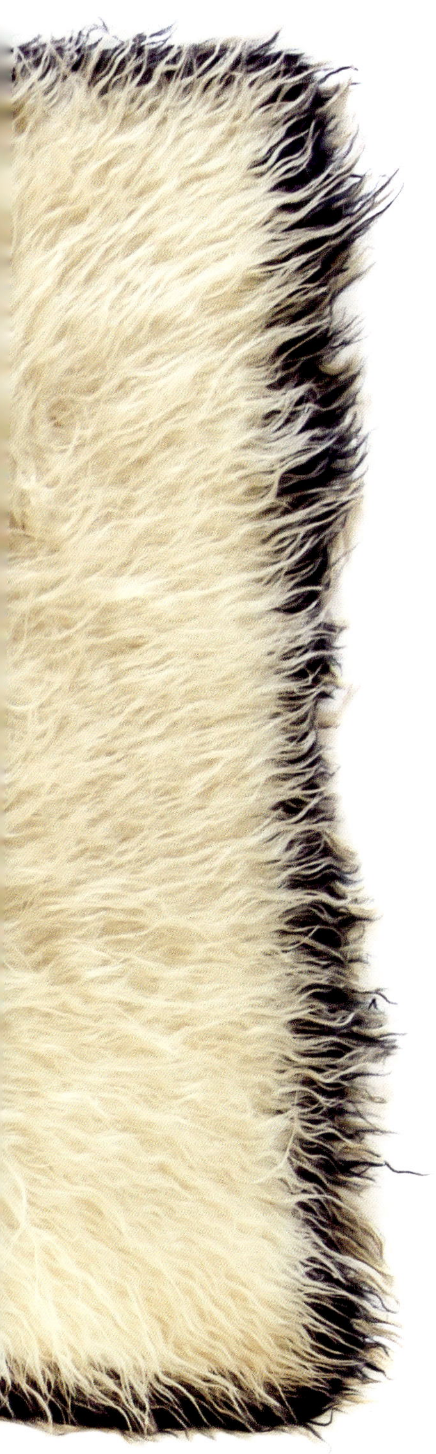

Velense Spread/Blanket
Ottoman, 17th century
200x138 cm
Mohair
Topkapı Palace Museum, Inv. No: 13/1193

Ottoman documents from the mid 16th century registers these spreads as *velençe* and in the early 17th century official Ottoman price lists (*narh defterleri*) it appears as *velense* and they were used as blanket and prayer rug in the palace. The warp yarn of the *velense* woven with the plain weave is from wool, while the weft yarn is from mohair and the thick mohair weft yarn fibers are used as fringes. There are four velense blankets in the Topkapı Palace Museum collection and all are in natural colour. According to museum's records one of the velense blankets (Inv. No: 13/455) belonged to Sultan Murad IV (1623-1640). The border of this velense was dyed ultramarine using indigotine and indirubin obtained from indigo plant (*Indigofera tinctoria L.*) or dyer's woad plant. (Source: Sibel A. Arça, TPM)

Angora Goat's Hide
Ottoman, 17th century
126x107 cm
Mohair
Topkapı Palace Museum, Inv. No: 13/482

There are six Angora goat's hides in the Topkapı Palace Museum collection. According to museum's records, these hides belonged to Sultan Murad IV (1623-1640). Four of the hides (Inv. No: 13/480, 13/481, 13/482, 13/484) including this one, were dyed ultramarine using indigotine and indirubin obtained from the indigo plant (*Indigofera tinctoria L.*) or the dyer's woad plant (*Isatis tinctoria L.*).
(Source: Sibel A. Arça, TPM)

Angora Goat's Hide
Ottoman, 17th century
116x98 cm
Mohair
Topkapı Palace Museum, Inv. No: 13/483

It belonged to Sultan Murad IV (1623-1640). It is one of the two bright yellow-dyed hides in the Topkapı Palace Museum collection and it was dyed using luteolin and apigenin, obtained from weld (*Reseda luteola L.*). (Source: Sibel A. Arça, TPM)

Examples From Sadberk Hanım Museum Collection

Sof Ferace **(Light overcoat)**
Ottoman, Early 20th century
133 cm (length), 60 cm (sleeve length), 15 cm (shoulder), 13,5 cm (back collar length)
Sadberk Hanım Museum, Inv. No: SHM 14006-K.732

This *ferace* is made of dark blue *sof*. It is wide cut and has a wide collar and fitted shirred sleeves. It fastens down the front with black velvet buttons, button loops and hidden snap fasteners. There are large decorative cuffs on the sleeve hems and each cuff is decorated with two buttons. On both sides of the collar there are black buttons as decorative items. There are black velvet bindings on all sides. Under the collar is supported by pasted cloth. (Source: Lale Görünür, SHM)

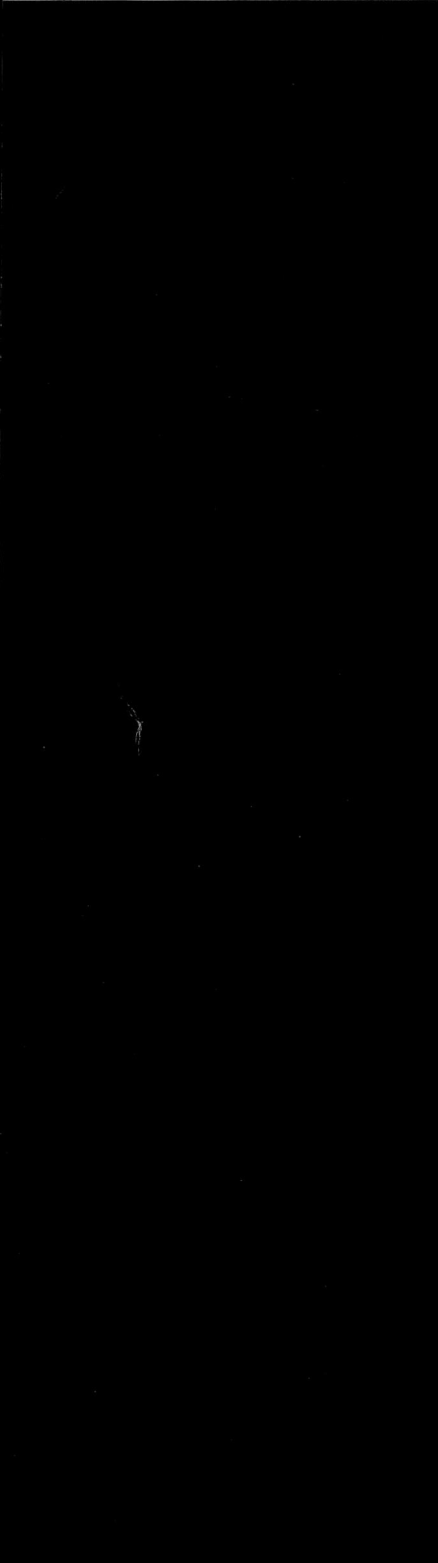

Sof Cardigan
Ottoman, Early 20th century
132 cm (length), 62 cm (sleeve length), 14 cm (shoulder)
Sadberk Hanım Museum, Inv. No: SHM 15312-K969

This cardigan was sewn from mustard-coloured woolen fabric. This long, slightly fitting cardigan has long fitted sleeves and wide cuffs. It has a small v-neck and open down the front. It fastens down with snap fasteners. The sides of the opening on the front, around the collar and cuffs' edges were trimmed with cream-coloured cord. It is unlined and machine-sewn.

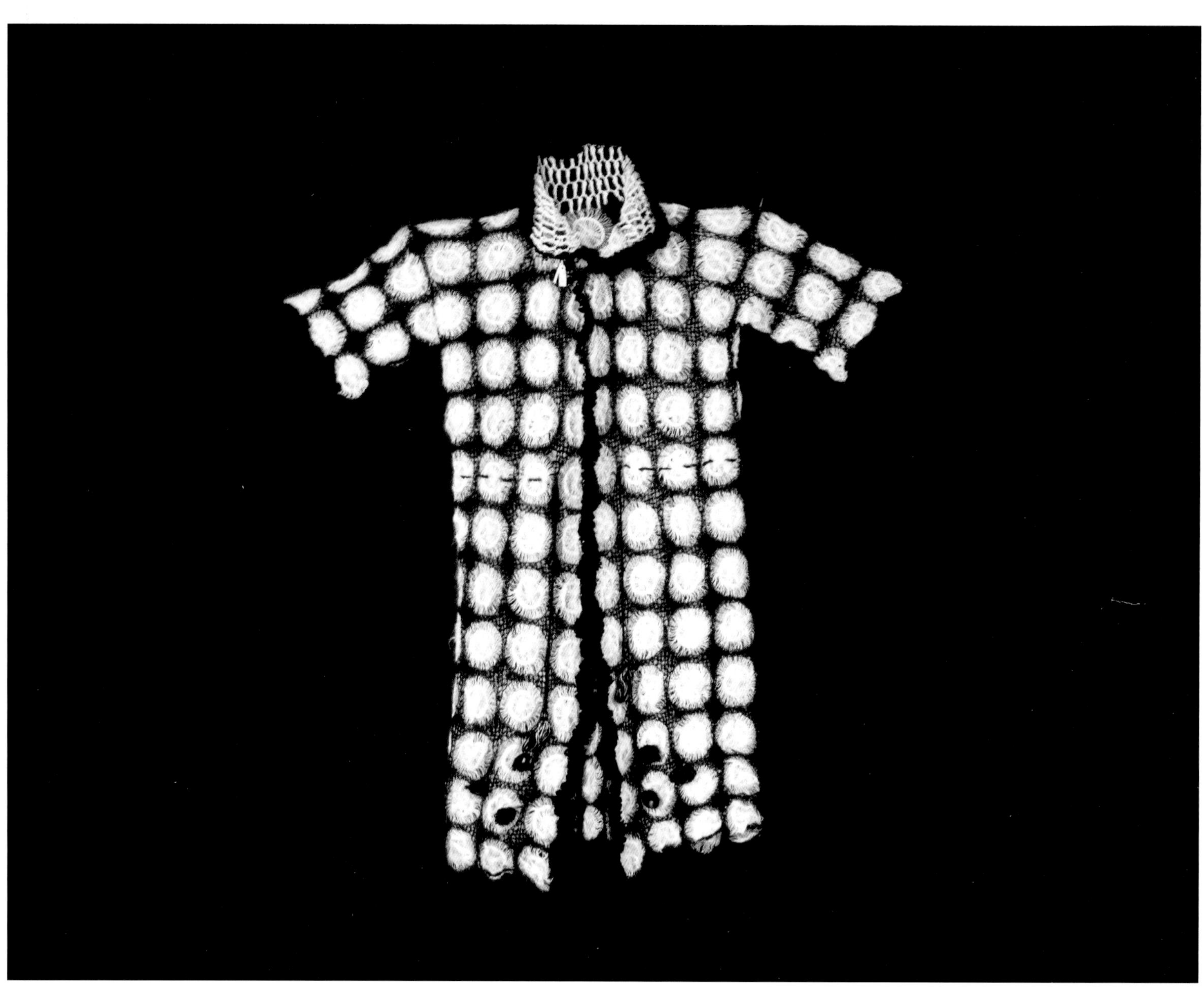

Mohair Cardigan
1925-1930
88 cm (length), 38 cm (sleeve length)
Sadberk Hanım Museum, Inv. No: SHM 18008-K121

This short-sleeved, black and cream-coloured mohair hairpin-work cardigan has a shawl collar. It was prepared by gathering round motifs and hand-made wool cords were inserted to the edges. It is tied by a string spinned from wool. Black and cream-coloured wool pompoms were sewn on various places. (Source: Lale Görünür, SHM)

Sof Skirt
Ottoman, Early 20th century
101 cm (length)
Sadberk Hanım Museum, Inv. No: SHM 2614-K.32

This flared skirt, was sewn from almond green sof and it is composed of lengthwise five pieces. It fits the waits with a drawstring. Four green satin bands of 3 cm width and three machine-made lace bands were sewn alternatively, under the knee level, circulating the skirt. Under these, there is a furbelow from the skirts' fabric. This skirt is machine-sewn and is unlined. (Source: Lale Görünür, SHM)

Sof Skirt
Ottoman, Early 20th century
88 cm (length)
Sadberk Hanım Museum, Inv. No: SHM 11508-K.173

This flared long skirt is sewn from ecru *sof*. There is a furbelow in the hemline. The front panel of the skirt is made of a single piece in width of the loom, and the back panel is made of three narrow pieces. It has a loosely gathered waistline. The hemline of the skirt is decorated with a wide furbelow and lace and ribbon bands. The ribbon is threaded to the edges of the furbelow and on its above ribbon is trimmed in zigzag shape and machine sewing is applied. (Source: Lale Görünür, SHM)

Sof Skirt
Ottoman, Early 20th century
93 cm (length)
Sadberk Hanım Museum, Inv. No: SHM 11935-K.502

This flared skirt is made of ecru *sof*. It fits the waist by a drawstring. The skirt is decorated with two wide rows. Diagonal trimmed silk lace and satin ribbon bands circles around the skirt. Lace borders are trimmed both from below and above. Beneath it, there is a double layered frill and the upper layer is scalloped. The edges are trimmed with a row of lace and a row of satin ribbons. The lower layer is plain ruffled, and a satin ribbon is trimmed to its edge. The skirt is unlined, and machine sewn.

Sof Skirt
Ottoman, Early 20th century
91 cm (length)
Sadberk Hanım Museum, Inv. No: SHM 13835-K.708

This full-length skirt is made of light blue *sof*. It is composed of four pieces in flared cut. It has a drawstring in the waistline and tied in the middle at the back. There is a wide band at the hem which is decorated with silky fabric and various materials and at the edge there is a ruffle from its own fabric. Beneath the ruffle two bands of silky ribbons are trimmed. The skirt is unlined and machine-sewn. (Source: Lale Görünür, SHM)

Sof Skirt
Ottoman, Early 20th century
95 cm (length)
Sadberk Hanım Museum, Inv. No: SHM 14172-K.830

This flared, full-length skirt is made of light lilac-coloured *sof*. The hem is pleated and from below the knees to the hem, it is trimmed with machine made lace appliqué work. The skirt is unlined and machine-sewn. (Source: Lale Görünür, SHM)

Sof Skirt
Ottoman, Early 20th century
94 cm (length)
Sadberk Hanım Museum, Inv. No: SHM 17523-K.1078

This light pink *sof* skirt is slightly flared and is composed of four pieces. There is a wide frill at the hemline and there is a small opening at the middle of the back side. The waistline fits with a drawstring. The hem is trimmed with lace and silky ribbon bands and has a pleated frill. The skirt is unlined and machine-sewn. (Source: Lale Görünür, SHM)

Sof Shalvar
Ottoman, Late 19th century-Early 20th century
136 cm (length)
Sadberk Hanım Museum, Inv. No: SHM 13392-K.655

This bright pink shalwar is a baggy pantaloon and has hems which enclose drawstrings at the waist and at calves sewn from lining fabric. The outer sides of the calves are embroidered in *dival* technique- a type of couched supported embroidery. The embroidery is made with metal-wrapped thread, sequin and twisted wire. A scattered composition is made with flower bouqets whereby, a large bouqet is embroidered at the center and four mid-size and four small bouqets are placed around. It is hand-sewn and undercoated with an ecru lining. (Source: Lale Görünür, SHM)

Mohair Bed Cardigan
1905-1908
55 cm (length), 18 cm (sleeve length)
Sadberk Hanım Museum, Inv. No: SHM 17630-K.1120

This cream and light blue coloured mohair cardigan was short-sleeved and shawl-collared and knitted with a hairpin. It is prepared with joining circular motifs and inserting a hand-knitted border. It has a string twisted from the mohair of the Angora goat. (Source: Lale Görünür, SHM).

Mohair Cape
Early 20th century
70 cm (length), 150 cm (skirt circumference)
Sadberk Hanım Museum, Inv. No: SHM 18357-K.1313

This double layered cape is prepared by gathering round motifs with a hairpin work. It has a fitted collar composed of round motifs. It is decorated by mini pompoms in all edges. (Source: Lale Görünür, SHM)

Mohair Shawl
Early 20th century
176x63 cm
Sadberk Hanım Museum, Inv. No: SHM 2714-K.130

This shawl is made of mohair with a crochet needle. It is rectangular and knitted with a star-shaped knit and it has a six-row border from triangles and fringes on its three sides. On the single side without the fringe, a knitted band like a ruffle is sewn in waves. Around it, there are roses and leaves knitted from mohair. (Source: Lale Görünür, SHM)

Mohair Shawl
Early 20th century
200x200 cm (including fringes)
Sadberk Hanım Museum, Inv. No: SHM 2722-K.138

This mohair shawl is a work of hairpin lace crochet. Crochet round motifs gathered to form a square and fringes added to the edges. (Source: Lale Görünür)

Examples of *Sof*

Sof Sample
1890-1900
28,1x20,2 cm
Mohair
Prof. Dr. Zahide İmer Collection

This sample was collected during Prof. İmer's (1992) study on *the Ankara sof*. It is an important sample exemplifying 19th century *sof* weaving in Ankara.

Sof Fabric
Ottoman, Late 19th century-Early 20th century
68x103 cm
Sadberk Hanım Museum, Inv. No: SHM 10568-D.127

This plain, woven firm fabric from undyed goat's hair, is woven with a plain weaving technique (*bezayağı tekniği*) whereby there are 31 warp yarn and 14 weft yarn. The weft yarn was not spun rather a single strand is composed of fourfold thread. Sixfold thread is used in edges. (Source: Lale Görünür, SHM)

Blue *Sof* Sample
1934-1951
107x73,5 cm
Ethnography Museum of Ankara,
Inv. No: 14194

It is the product of Turkish Mohair Society.
(Ç. Yücel, 2018, pp. 32-34)

White *Sof* Sample
1934-1951
73x63 cm
Ethnography Museum of Ankara,
Inv. No: 14193

It is the product of Turkish Mohair Society.
(Ç. Yücel, 2018, pp. 32-34)

Brown *Sof* Sample
1934-1951
348x73 cm
Ethnography Museum of Ankara,
Inv. No: 14195

It is the product of Turkish Mohair Society.
(Ç. Yücel, 2018, pp. 32-34)

Sof Sample
1934-1951
103,5x67 cm
Ethnography Museum of Ankara,
Inv. No: 14207

It is the product of Turkish Mohair Society.
(Ç. Yücel, 2018, pp. 32-34)

Sof Sample
Date Unknown
86x65 cm
Ethnography Museum of Ankara,
Inv. No: 23600

Received as a gift from Saadet Ayyakın in 1978.

Maroon *Sof* Sample
Date Unknown
282x31 cm
Ethnography Museum of Ankara,
Inv. No: 23601

Received as a gift from Saadet Ayyakın in 1978.

A Continued Tradition: Tosya Mohair Weaving

Weaving The History: Tosya

In Ottoman times, Tosya was one of the places where *sof* was woven. Nowadays, this cultural legacy continues in Tosya with the production of bath gloves and waist-clothes, woven by very few mohair weavers. Examining the past and present of Ankara *sof* through examples, Prof. Dr. Zahide İmer (1994) notes that today more stiff and thick fabrics in mohair's natural colour can be produced whereas elegant, thinner *sof* fabric could be woven in various colours in the past to produce clothing such as ferace (light overcoat) and caftans.

This documentary, produced specifically for the exhibition and directed by Kerime Senyücel, was filmed between January 29 and February 2, 2018, in the town of Tosya in Kastamonu. This is the only place today where mohair weaving continues on hand looms, and the film focuses on the weavers of the special health products known as the Tosya bath glove and the Tosya waistcloth.

Although the number of weavers of mohair yarn has declined in Tosya, there are still those who continue this profession and keep it alive. The documentary interviews Mahmut Salman, and wife Melahat Salman, the son and daughter-in-law of the now-deceased Nedim Salman, who used to be one of the oldest mohair weavers, İsmail Koyuncugil, who produced a lot of dress fabric for politicians and bureaucrats in the 1950s, and who continues to weave bath gloves and waistcloths despite his advanced age, and Seyfi Bektaş, the President of the Tosya Chamber of Bath Glove and Waistcloth Producers, which has very few members today.

Weaving the History: Tosya
2018
Director: Kerime Senyücel
9′8″

Tosya Bath Glove
Date Unknown
20,8x14,2 cm
Mohair
Mustafa Kürşat Bazlamatçı Collection

Tosya Waistcloth
Date Unknown
380,9x25,7 cm
Mohair
Mustafa Kürşat Bazlamatçı Collection

Fabric Sample
1990-1995
20,4x92,5 cm
Mohair
Prof. Dr. Zahide İmer Collection

Tosya Bath Glove Fabric Sample
1995
19,3x21,1 cm
Mohair
Prof. Dr. Zahide İmer Collection

Tosya Bath Glove Fabric Sample
1995
20x29,2 cm
Mohair
Prof. Dr. Zahide İmer Collection
The stamp on the fabric reads: *Keseci Hasan Çamur Tosya.*

Spinning Wheel
Early 20th century
70x69x100 cm
Rahmi M. Koç Museum Ankara Collection
It is used for spinning thread or yarn from natural or synthetic fibres.

Sley
Late 19th century-Early 20th century
115x103cm
Rahmi M. Koç Museum Ankara Collection
It is the part of a hand-loom whereby comb is inserted. It helps the interlacement of the weft with the warp threads to form cloth.

Nedim Salman was weaving waistcloth on the traditional hand loom in Tosya
1999
Photograph: Prof. Dr. Yavuz Sabuncu
12,6x8,9 cm
Colour Photograph
Erman Tamur Archive
It is the photograph of late Nedim Salman weaving waistcloth, referred as the mohair weaver in Weaving the History: Tosya documentary.

Design, Representation and Current Production Samples

In addition to being a symbol of a city, the Angora goat is a value that plays a decisive role in the economic and social life of a city with its unique mohair. Nevertheless, unfortunately it is a forgotten value. It is important to maintain this tradition in Ankara, which used to be a world-renowned weaving centre, with the *sof* woven with the finest mohair. It is imperative to encourage the presence of the Angora goats and breeders of mohair production in Turkey, and support enterprises to revitalizing historic *sof* weaving, to transfer this cultural heritage to future generations.

Today, one of the most important establishments for Angora goat breeding and the mohair trade is the Tiftikbirlik, the Union of Agricultural Cooperatives for Mohair and Fleece. Founded in 1969 by cooperatives in Nallıhan, Ayaş, Çamlıdere and Akçakent Çamlıdere, the headquarters of Tiftikbirlik is in Ankara. Today, there are 12 cooperatives affiliated to the union; Aksaray, Ayaş, Beypazarı, Çankırı, Eskişehir, Güdül, Karaman, Kırıkkale, Kızılcahamam, Nallıhan, Polatlı, Seben. Tiftikbirlik buys the products of the joint cooperatives and sells them to its domestic and foreign markets by operating in its own business facility. (Tiftikbirlik Official Website, Kuruluş, 2018).

Weaving *Sof* Once Again...

In recent years and nowadays, there are various initiatives and projects to revive *sof* weaving. The "Reintroduction of Ankara's Historical *Sof* Fabric to the Cultural and Economic Life of the City" is one such project, designed by the by the Mohair and *Sof* Research and Development Society (TIFSOF). This project was deemed worthy of the support of the Ankara Development Agency's "2012 Rural Development Financial Support Program" and greenlit at the Kahraman Kazan district. (Ankara Development Agency Official Web Site, Padişahların Kumaşı *Sof*, Kazan'da Dokunacak, 2013). Administered by Süreyya Zile, a workshop was set up in Kahraman Kazan within the scope of the project, where trainees were overseen by specialists in mohair yarn with handlooms. The project has been concluded (Source: Bünyamin Zile, 2018).

Emine Kıraç, a retired director of the Advanced Technical Institute for Girls, personally continues the projects she devised to reproduce the *sof* weaving efforts she had started in this institution. Emine Kıraç has worked with master and experts in Adana, Erzurum, Gaziantep, Cizre and Eruh, and especially in Ankara, to produce woven fabrics and apparel from mohair yarn (Source: Emine Kıraç, 2018).

Some of the problems that the contemporary projects have experienced in the production of historical Ankara sofa fabric were the lack of information in preparing the mohair yarn properly, which culminates with the destruction of the yarn, and the lack of pressing and burnishing knowledge, which should impart the silky feels, brightness and moiré patterning it is known for. With today's technology, it is important that laboratory analyses are applied to historical sofa fabrics and evaluating these scientific data to be able to reproduce *sof*.

Mohair Yarn and Knitting

Production of knitwear such as socks, vests, cardigans, shawls is widespread in Anatolia. In Ankara and its vicinity, this has been reduced to knitting products from mohair yarn, which is mostly hand-woven by women, because the processing of the mohair and the spinning of the yarn are troublesome tasks. The mohair knitting is a continuing occupation in Ankara's Ayaş town. Hatice Doğruol, Makbule Doğruol, Dicle Vural, Günsel Özyörük and Kezban Yıldız are examples of this. In Ayaş county and its villages, very few craftspeople are spending effort on processing mohair into yarn, dyeing it with natural methods and finally, transferring it to commodities such as socks, shawls, sweaters, cardigans and vests.

Altınyıldız

Textiles and Garment Factory, Inc. was founded in 1952 by Ali Osman Boyner, Ahmet Sadıkoğlu, Hasan Boyner and Fazıl Boyner, members of the Boyner family who in the Tosya mohair trade at the province of Kastamonu (Öğüt, 2013).

The company started exporting in 1956 to introduce Turkish fabrics to the world. At one time among the biggest buyers of mohair in Turkey, exported the high luxury mohair products and contributed much to the establishment of the term "Turkish Mohair" across the globe. A fabric titled "Mohair Super Kid" produced by this company reached many buyers in countries such as Britain, Switzerland and Italy.

Altınyıldız continues to produce woollen fabrics under Boyner Holding and operates in the ready-to-wear sector (Altınyıldız Classics, 2018).

Tuxedo, Osman Boyner
After 1952
80x57 cm
Mohair
Altınyıldız Collection

Altınyıldız Advertorial
12.08.1963
Cumhuriyet Newspaper
Altınyıldız Archive

The Angora goats and the goatherd appears on the advertisement. Below the image, it asks, "Did you know that "domestic or foreign, best "alpaca" cloth is made of Turkish mohair?". Below this question appears an information regarding the production of Altınyıldız company. The advertorial emphasizes the global importance of the local mohair production in Anatolia.

Altınyıldız Advertorial
21.08.1963
Milliyet Newspaper
Altınyıldız Archive

The inscription on the advertorial reads: *Mohair, Alpaka, Altınyıldız* ve *Tiftik* (Mohair, Alpaca, Altınyıldız and Mohair) and "*Bu isimler arasındaki irtibat nedir?*" (What is the relationship between these names?). The following inscription is a detailed reply to the question.

Altınyıldız Advertorial
15.06.1963
Cumhuriyet Newspaper
Altınyıldız Archive

This advertorial introduces "Superfine Turkish Kid Mohair" which is a fabric produced from Turkish mohair and the advertorial emphasizes the "Turkish" aspect of the product and announces that Altınyıldız added the word "Turkish" to the new mohair fabric produced by the company.

Altınyıldız Advertorial
15.12.1964
Milliyet Newspaper
Altınyıldız Archive

In this advertorial the Altınyıldız company introduces fabrics produced within its facility. The inscription in Turkish appears within the frame. It reads: "*Memleket içinde ve dışında büyük şöhret yapmış çeşitlerini iftiharla takdim eder*" (Proudly presents [Altınyıldız] the varieties that acquired fame both in country and abroad).

Mohair Ferla

Ferla Foreign Trade & Marketing Limited Company was established in 1988. Today it produces mohair that has been washed, combed, and formed into skeins called tops, which are used in various fields. The company, which specializes in the production of mohair and wool tops, is one of the leading companies in this field in Turkey and targets to grow on the global stage.

Ferla Foreign Trade, which has a management office in Istanbul, today has an annual production capacity of 1,000 tons of mohair tops with an indoor production area of 8,000 m2 at the Kütahya 2nd OSB.

Mohair Tops
2017
Mohair
Mohair Ferla Collection

Mohair Ferla Production Plant
2018
Mohair Ferla Archive

Mohair & Angora

Mohair & Angora is a knitwear production company based in Ankara. It targets to combine the 45-year tradition of mohair yarn work with contemporary designs. Mohair & Angora has helped brandization of mohair with their women's and men's shawls, scarves, gloves, socks, etc., often blended with silk.

Angora Goat Figurine
Date Unknown
Anonymous
10x9,8 cm
Ceramic and mohair tops.

Mohair tops is placed inside the Angora goat figurine.

Shawl
2018
172,3x44,2cm
Mohair, silk
Mohair & Angora Collection

It is produced by Mohair & Angora and it is made of mohair thread and silk.

Shawl
2018
170x47cm
Mohair, silk
Mohair & Angora Collection

It is produced by Mohair & Angora and it is made of mohair thread and silk.

Mens Brown Vest
Kezban Yıldız
2016
Mohair yarn dyed with walnut shell.
Kezban Yıldız Collection

Kezban Yıldız is a crafter from Yağmurdede district of Ayaş, Ankara. She obtains mohair from the Angora goat farms in Ayaş and cleans, washes and prepares mohair for knitting. She also uses natural dyes such as walnut shell, tomato plant, onionskin for dyeing the mohair and spins mohair yarn. This vest was knitted by using mohair yarn and dyed with walnut shell.

Gloves
1990
Hatice Doğruol
25,6cm (length), 6,5cm (wrist)
Mohair
Hatice Doğruol Collection

It is made of natural-coloured mohair and Ayaş local patterns were used.

Gloves
1995-2000
Makbule Doğruol
28,7cm (length), 7,5cm (wrist)
Hatice Doğruol Collection

Ayaş patterns were used to knit the gloves. The pattern is called "rat-tooth" in Ayaş.

Socks
1990-2000
Hatice Doğruol
25,5 cm (length), 10,2 cm (around the ankle)
Factory-made mohair yarn
Hatice Doğruol Collection

These socks have coloured patterns. They were designed by using Ayaş socks' models.

Leggings
2005
Dicle Vural
24,3 cm (length), 15cm (width)
Mohair yarn, beads
Ayaş Culture House Collection

These leggings were made by using five knitting needles from mohair yarn and beads. The pattern that is used to shape these leggings was called as "rat-tooth" in Ayaş.

Collar
2005
Günsel Özyörük
43 cm (length)
Factory-made mohair yarn
Ayaş Culture House Collection

It was made with the crochet needle and the form of the collar was given by gathering six motifs.

Socks
1950-2000
Makbule Doğruol
33,5cm (length), 10cm (width)
Mohair yarn dyed with walnut shell.
Hatice Doğruol Collection

The local, Ayaş pattern called as midye (mussel) was used to form these socks.

Knee-high Socks
1947
Makbule Doğruol
41,9cm (length), 8,6cm (calf width)
Mohair
Hatice Doğruol Collection

These knee-high socks are formed with Ayaş socks' pattern called *bıçak burnu* (knife edge).

Men's socks
1950-1960
Makbule Doğruol
52,8cm (length), 11,3cm (calf width)
Mohair
Hatice Doğruol Collection

These men's socks were knitted for dowry with local patterns with two strands of yarn. Ayaş locals call these socks as *Eğri şemsiyeli, şapka kenerli* (crooked umbrella and hat-shaped edges).

Women's Socks
1950-1990
Makbule Doğruol
34,6 cm (length), 9,1 cm (calf width)
Mohair
Hatice Doğruol Collection

It is made of natural-coloured mohair with a Ayaş pattern.

Socks Knitted with Two Layers of Mohair Yarn
1950-1960
Hatice Doğruol
39 cm (length), 11,1 cm (calf width)
Mohair
Hatice Doğruol Collection

These socks were knitted with two layers of mohair yarn as a special gift for dowry.

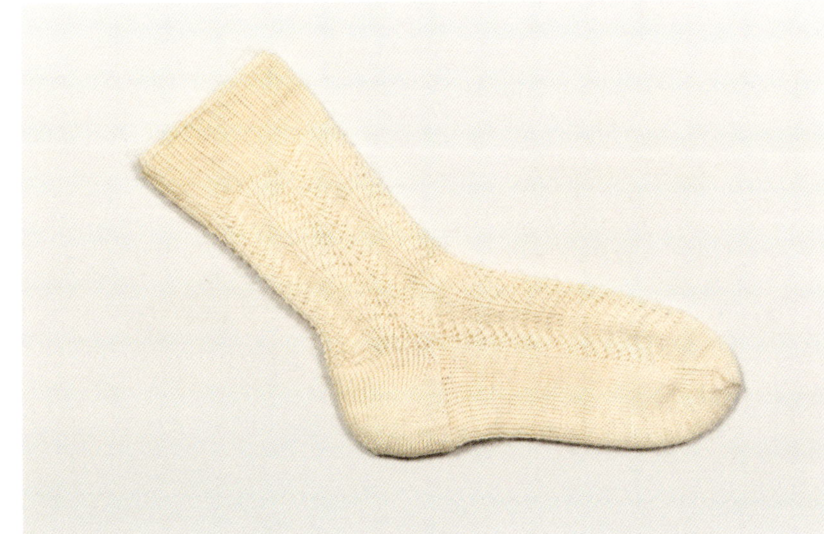

Socks
1950-1960
Makbule Doğruol
33,5 cm (length), 8,5 cm (calf width)
Mohair
Hatice Doğruol Collection

These socks are natural in colour and they were designed with local Ayaş patterns.

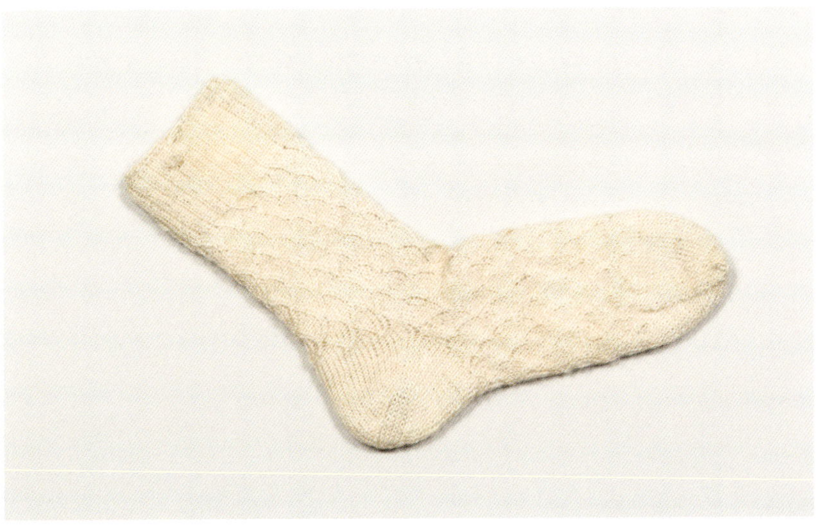

Bed Cardigan with Belt
1910-1920
Anonymous
62x56 cm (bed cardigan), 95,7x5,5 cm (belt)
Mohair
Ayaş Culture House Collection

This bed cardigan belonged to the mother of Mehmet Savaş from Ayaş. The crafter is unknown. This bed cardigan was made with a hairpin and decorated with crochet work.

Mohair Woven Jacket
2013-2018
65x57,5 cm
Emine Kıraç Collection

This was produced within the scope of Emine Kıraç's "Mohair Weaving in Anatolia" project.

Gray Mohair Two-piece Dress
2000
Makbule Doğruol
68,3x59 cm (jacket), 73,4x43,4 cm (skirt)
Natural-coloured mohair
Hatice Doğruol Collection

Handspun gray mohair yarn (as known as purple mohair in Ayaş) was knitted in two strands with moss stitch technique and formed as skirt and jacket.

Cream Mohair Shawl
2017
Kezban Yıldız
Kezban Yıldız Collection

This shawl was made with natural coloured mohair yarn.

Gray Mohair Shawl
2017
Kezban Yıldız
Kezban Yıldız Collection

This shawl was made with natural coloured mohair yarn.

White Mohair Shawl
Date Unknown
Hatice Doğruol
88,8x148,3 cm
Hatice Doğruol Collection

This shawl was made with natural coloured mohair yarn.

Shoulder Bag
2014
Design, sewing and embroidery:
Süreyya Zile
Weaving: TİFSOF *Sof* Fabric Workshop
25,5x37,5 cm
Mohair
Süreyya Zile Collection

It was produced within the scope of Reintroduction of Ankara's Historical *Sof* Fabric to the Cultural and Economic Life of the City project, prepared by the Tiftik and *Sof* Research and Development Association (TİFSOF).

Shoulder Bag
2014
Design, sewing and embroidery:
Süreyya Zile
Weaving: TİFSOF *Sof* Fabric Workshop
20,1x29 cm
Mohair
Süreyya Zile Collection

It was produced within the scope of Reintroduction of Ankara's Historical *Sof* Fabric to the Cultural and Economic Life of the City project, prepared by the Tiftik and *Sof* Research and Development Association (TİFSOF).

Hooded Jacket
2014
Design, sewing: Süreyya Zile
Weaving: TİFSOF *Sof* Fabric Workshop
90x54 cm
Mohair
Süreyya Zile Collection

It was produced within the scope of Reintroduction of Ankara's Historical *Sof* Fabric to the Cultural and Economic Life of the City project, prepared by the Tiftik and *Sof* Research and Development Association (TİFSOF).

Jacket with Buttons
2014
Design, sewing: Süreyya Zile
Weaving: TİFSOF *Sof* Fabric Workshop
57,5x51,5 cm
Tiftik
Süreyya Zile Collection

It was produced within the scope of Reintroduction of Ankara's Historical *Sof* Fabric to the Cultural and Economic Life of the City project, prepared by the Tiftik and *Sof* Research and Development Association (TİFSOF).

Vest
2014
Design, sewing: Süreyya Zile
Weaving: TİFSOF *Sof* Fabric Workshop
65,5x47,5 cm
Mohair
Süreyya Zile Collection

It was produced within the scope of Reintroduction of Ankara's Historical *Sof* Fabric to the Cultural and Economic Life of the City project, prepared by the Tiftik and *Sof* Research and Development Association (TİFSOF).

Tie
2014
Design, sewing and embroidery: Süreyya Zile
Weaving: TİFSOF *Sof* Fabric Workshop
151,5x9.5 cm
Mohair
Süreyya Zile Collection

It was produced within the scope of Reintroduction of Ankara's Historical *Sof* Fabric to the Cultural and Economic Life of the City project, prepared by the Tiftik and *Sof* Research and Development Association (TİFSOF).

Brown Fabric Sample
2013-2018
Emine Kıraç
125x30cm
Mohair
Emine Kıraç Collection

This was produced within the scope of Emine Kıraç's "Mohair Weaving in Anatolia" project.

Blue Fabric Sample
Emine Kıraç
2013-2018
100x30 cm
Mohair
Emine Kıraç Collection

This was produced within the scope of Emine Kıraç's "Mohair Weaving in Anatolia" project.

Cream Coloured Closely Woven Fabric Sample
Emine Kıraç
2013-2018
48x30,5 cm
Mohair
Emine Kıraç Collection

This was produced within the scope of Emine Kıraç's "Mohair Weaving in Anatolia" project.

Tan Coloured Closely Woven Fabric Sample
Emine Kıraç
2013-2018
62,5x30,5 cm
Mohair
Emine Kıraç Collection

This was produced within the scope of Emine Kıraç's "Mohair Weaving in Anatolia" project.

Beige Coloured Loose Woven Fabric Sample
Emine Kıraç
2013-2018
218x30 cm
Mohair
Emine Kıraç Collection

This was produced within the scope of Emine Kıraç's "Mohair Weaving in Anatolia" project.

Cream Coloured Loose Woven Fabric Sample
Emine Kıraç
2013-2018
329x88 cm
Mohair
Emine Kıraç Collection

This was produced within the scope of Emine Kıraç's "Mohair Weaving in Anatolia" project.

Şal-Sepik **Fabric Sample**

1990
30,9x70,3 cm
Mohair
Zahide İmer Collection

Şal-Şepik is an ancient local fabric woven with mohair in the Southern Eastern Turkey. This piece was collected within the scope of Prof. Dr. Zahide İmer's studies on the Ankara *sof* and mohair weaving.

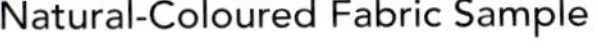
Natural-Coloured Fabric Sample
2014
310,3x42,5 cm
Mohair
Süreyya Zile Collection

This fabric was hand-woven within the scope of Reintroduction of Ankara's Historical *Sof* Fabric into the Cultural and Economic Life of the City project, prepared by the Tiftik and *Sof* Research and Development Association (TİFSOF).

Angora Goat as a Symbol: Designs with Angora Goat

The Republic regarded the Angora goat as a value to be protected in the 1930s and hoped to improve husbandry with modern methods and thus increase the goat's economic value. Therefore, it is not surprising that in parallel to the establishing of the Mohair Society with this purpose, that the goat would appear, in their modern pen, on the 50-lira notes issued in 1938.

The Angora goat also figured in the Fifty Turkish Lira notes, issued in 1942. This time, the Angora goats are at the centre of the banknote. The same figure was also used in the stamp called "Mohair Goat," published in 1943

Emmision Group: E-2
Denomination: 50 Turkish Lira
Series: 1
Printed in: England
Printed in pieces: 1.550.000
Printed in value: TRL 77.500.000
Printed in series: A, B, C, D
Issued on: 01.04.1938
Withdrawn from circulation on: 02.6.1952
Legal circulation period ended on: 02.06.1953
Redemption period ended on: 02.06.1962
Signatures/General Manager: Selahattin Çam
Signatures/Assistant General Manager: Said Erda
Dimensions: 8x17,5 cm
Design/Obverse: A Portrait of Atatürk
Design/Reverse: Angora goats
(Source: Central Bank of the Republic of Turkey, The Banknotes of the Republic of Turkey, 2014)

Emmision Group: E-3
Denomination: 50 Turkish Lira
Series: 1
Printed in: USA
Printed in pieces: 6.000.000
Printed in value: TRL 300.000.000
Printed in series: N, O, P, R, S, Ş, T, U, V, Y, Z, Z'
Issued on: 25.4.1942
Withdrawn from circulation on: 01.12.1951
Legal circulation period ended on: 01.12.1952
Redemption period ended on: 01.12.1961
Signatures/General Manager: Kemal Zaim Sunel
Signatures/Assistant General Manager: Nedim Ersun
Dimensions: 8x17,5 cm
Design/Obverse: A Portrait of İsmet İnönü
Design/Reverse: Angora goats
(Source: Central Bank of the Republic of Turkey, The Banknotes of the Republic of Turkey, 2014)

Stamps

During the Republican period, the figure of the Angora goat entered the state's official images by appearing on stamps and banknotes. Mohair, obtained from Angora goats, was shown in the top ten of foreign trade agriculture until the 1970s. The Angora goat, on the other hand, is one of the capital's symbols due its special historic significance in Ankara.

Mohair Goats
1943
3,3x2,5 cm
VEKAM Library and Archive, Inv. No: A032_38

Angora goat themed 30+5 *Kuruş* Postal Stamps
1964
3,6x2,6 cm
VEKAM Library and Archive, Inv. No: A032_05

Anki

Murat Karayalçın was nominated by the Social Democratic People's Party (SHP) for the Ankara Metropolitan Municipality in the municipal elections of 26 March 1989. Graphic designer Sadık Karamustafa and his team were invited to create visual designs for Mr Karayalçın's promotion campaign. In this process, the Angora goat was chosen as an icon for its important role in the city's economic and social history. This symbol was named "Anki". Anki needed to be a young, cheerful animated figure and continued to be an important symbol in designs during Murat Karayalçın's tenure as mayor of the Ankara Metropolitan Municipality until 1993.

Anki Emblem
1990
Sadık Karamustafa
Sadık Karamustafa Archive

Drawing for Anki figure
1990
Sadık Karamustafa
Sadık Karamustafa Archive

Poster for Ankara Metropolitan Municipality
1990
60x42 cm
Sadık Karamustafa
Sadık Karamustafa Archive

Postcards for Ankara Metropolitan Municipality
1990
16,5x11,5cm
Sadık Karamustafa
Sadık Karamustafa Archive

Ankara Potholes' Illustration
1989-1993
İbrahim Keleş Archive

Ankara Potholes' illustration was used in Kızılay subway construction panels' billboards. Afterwards, it was used as a visual for desk calendars.

Sources

Açıl, A. F. (1961). *Ankara keçisi ve tiftiğin memleket bünyesindeki ekonomik önemi.* Ankara: Ankara Üniversitesi Ziraat Fakültesi Yayınları.

Akder, F. (2018). View of Ankara: The story of a painting. In F. Yenişehirlioğlu ve G. Çerçioğlu Yüce (Prep. by), *Weaving the History: Mystery of a City, Sof* (pp. 107-128).

Akder, H. (2018). Angora goat and mohair supply chain. In F. Yenişehirlioğlu ve G. Çerçioğlu Yücel (Prep. by), *Weaving the History: Mystery of a City, Sof* (pp. 137-149).

Akman, N. ve Düzgüneş, O. (1988). Türkiye'de tiftik keçisi yetiştiriciliğinin problemleri. *Ziraat Mühendisliği, 209,* 16-19.

Akman, N. (1994). Ankara keçisi, *Ankara Dergisi, 2*(6), 516.

Aktan, S. (1983). Ankara sofu. *Türk Folkloru Araştırmaları Yıllığı-1982, 44,* 7-20.

Akyüz, Y. (1999). Ankara keçisi ve insan psikolojisi üzerine bir halk hikâyesi. *Kebikeç Dergisi, 9,* 123-124.

Altınyıldız Classics (2018). Retrieved from https://www.altinyildizclassics.com/content/hakkimizda Angora Goat. (2018, Şubat 2). https://global.britannica.com/animal/Angora-goat.

Angora Goat. (2018, February 2). Retrieved from http://www.turkishculture.org/nature/animal-breeds/angora-goat-185.htm?type=1.

Ankara'da Geleneksel Sanatlar, Meslekler. (2018, February 2). Retrieved from http://www.envanter.gov.tr/belge/halk-kulturu/detay/34850.

Ankara Development Agency (2013, November 4). *Padişahların kumaşı sof, Kazan'da dokunacak.* Retrieved from http://www.ankaraka.org.tr/tr/padisahlarin-kumasi-sof-kazanda-dokunacak_1822.html.

Ankara Keçisi Üçlemesi: Sanat, Tarih ve Gelenek: Sergi Kataloğu. (2010). Ankara: VEKAM.

Ankara Keçisi ve Sof Kumaşı Çalıştayı. (2013, December 22). Retrieved from http://www.haberler.com/ankara-kecisi-ve-sof-kumasi-calistayi-5454131-haberi/.

Ankara Vilayet Salnamesi. (1325/1907). K. Emiroğlu, A. Yüksel, Ö. Türkoğlu ve E. Coşkun (Eds.). (1995). Ankara: Ankara Enstitüsü Vakfı Yayınları.

Annual Report of the Bureau of Animal Industry for the year. (1901). United States: Congress House.

Arseven, C. E. (1965). *Sanat ansiklopedisi, fasikül VI.* İstanbul: Milli Eğitim Basımevi.

Ateş, H. (1968). Tiftiğin kullanıldığı yerler ve eski sof kumaş. *İstanbul Ticaret Dergisi, 11*(519), 5.

Barnett, D.E. (1987). Angora goats in Texas: agricultural innovation on the Edwards Plateau, 1858-1900. *The Southwestern Historical Quarterly, 90* (4), 347-372.

Barnett, R. D. (1974). European Merchants in Angora. *Anatolian Studies, 24,* 135-141.

Batu, S. (1951). *Türkiye keçi ırkı ve keçi yetiştirme bilgisi.* Ankara: Ankara Üniversitesi Veteriner Fakültesi.

Batu, S. ve Okaner, H. (1946). Ankara keçisinin Ankara bölgesindeki yetişme, bakım, beslenme şartları ve beden yapısı üstüne araştırmalar. *Ankara Yüksek Ziraat Enstitüsü 2*(5), 444-475.

Batur, E. (Ed.). (1994). *Ankara Ankara.* İstanbul: Yapı Kredi Yayınları.

Black, D. (1978). *Islemeler: Ottoman domestic embroideries.* Londra.

Bostan, A. ve Özsaraç, N. (2011, 5 Mart). Ankara keçisinin kendi gitti heykeli kaldı. *Ankara-Zaman Eki,* 8.

Braude, B. (1979). International competiton and domestic cloth in the Ottoman Empire, 1500-1650: a study in undevelopment. *Review, 2*(3), 437-451.

British Library. (2018). Retrieved from https://www.bl.uk/collection-guides/lansdowne-manuscripts.

Conolly, A. (1841). On the white-haired Angora goat, and on another species of goat found in the same province, resembling the Thibet shawl goat. *The Journal of the Royal Asiatic Society of Great Britain and Ireland, C. 6, 1*(1841), 159-172.

Cronwright-Schreiner, S. (1898). *The Angora goat.* Londra: Longsman.

Çerçioğlu Yücel, G. (2018). Weaving the History: Mystery of a City, Sof Exhibition. In F. Yenişehirlioğlu ve G. Çerçioğlu Yücel (Prep. by), *Weaving the History: Mystery of a City, Sof* (pp. 9-41)

Çınar Kul, B. (2018). A precious creature that adorns the Anatolian highlands: The Angora goat. In F. Yenişehirlioğlu ve G. Çerçioğlu Yücel (Prep. by), *Weaving the History: Mystery of a City, Sof* (pp. 65-70)

Dağlı, Y. and Kahraman, S. A. (Eds.). (2003). *Günümüz Türkçesiyle Evliya Çelebi seyahatnamesi.* İstanbul: Yapı Kredi Yayınları.

Davaslıgil, Ş. (1965). *Tiftik mamülleri, tiftikten yapılabilecek mamüller, tiftiğin dış memleketlerde ve memleketimizde kullanılış yerleri.* Sümerbank Merinos Yünlü Sanayii Müessesesi Eğitim Bürosu Yayınları.

Denny, W.B. (1972). *'Ottoman Turkish Textiles' in Washington.* Textile Museum, Washington DC.

Dinç, Z. *Osmanlı Devleti'nde Yabancı Tüccarlar: Ankara Örneği.* Retrieved from http://www.academia.edu/3861387/Osmanlı_Devletinde_Yabancı_Tüccarlar_Ankara_Örneği.

Dinçer, N. (1948, February). Ankara tiftiği. *Ülkü Halkevi Dergisi, 2*(14), 28-29.

Dinçer, N. (1948, April). Ankara sofu I. *Ülkü Halkevi Dergisi, 2*(16), 31-33.

Dinçer, N. (1948, July). Ankara sofu II. *Ülkü Halkevi Dergisi, 2*(21), 40-41.

Dinçer, N. (1948). Ankara milli tiftik ve sof sanayimiz. *Karınca Dergisi, 6*(135), 22-25.

Doğal Boyamacılıkta Mordanlama ve Boyama Yöntemleri. (2018). Retrieved from http://www.turkelhalilari.gov.tr/sayfalar.php?language=tur&icerik=dogalboyamacilik/dogal-boyamacilikta-mordanlama

Dün, bugün ve daima: tiftik ve kültürel zenginlikleriyle Ayaş (Ora e Sempre: Ayaş, its Angora Wool Products and Cultural Riches). (2005). Ankara: VEKAM.

Ekdoğan, M. (1955, April). Ankara sofçuluğu. *Türk Folklor Araştırmaları Dergisi, 3*(69),1091-1092.

Erdoğan, Z. and Jirousek, C. A. (2005). Ankara (Angora) goat hair: the Turkish mohair tradition. *The Fabric of Life: Cultural Transformations in Turkish Society.*

Ergenç, Ö. (1975). 1600-1615 yılları arasında Ankara iktisadi tarihine ait araştırmalar. *Türkiye İktisat Tarihi Semineri 8-10 Haziran 1973,* 145-168.

Ergenç, Ö. (1980). XVII. yüzyıl başlarında Ankara'nın yerleşim durumu üzerine bazı bilgiler. In H. İnalcık, N. Göyünç and H. W. Lowry (Eds.) *Osmanlı Araştırmaları I.* (pp. 85-106).

Ergenç, Ö. (1982). Osmanlı klasik dönemindeki "Eşraf ve A'yan" üzerine bazı bilgiler. In H. İnalcık, N. Göyünç and H. W. Lowry (Eds.) *Osmanlı Araştırmaları III.* (pp. 85-106).

Ergenç, Ö. (1984). 16. yüzyıl Ankara'sı: ekonomik, sosyal yapısı ve kentsel özellikleri. In E. Yavuz and N. Uğurel (Der.). *Tarih İçinde Ankara (Eylül 1981 Seminer Bildirileri)* (pp. 49-59).

Ergenç, Ö. (1995). *XVI. yüzyılda Ankara ve Konya: Osmanlı klasik döneminde kent tarihçiliğine katkı.* Ankara: Ankara Enstitüsü Vakfı Yayınları.

Ergenç, Ö. (2012). *XVI. yüzyılda Ankara ve Konya.* İstanbul: Tarih Vakfı Yurt Yayınları.

Ertuğ, A., Baker,P., Tezcan, H. And Wearden, J. (1996). *Silks for the Sultans: Ottoman imperial garments from the Topkapı Palace.* İstanbul: Ertuğ & Kocabıyık.

Eyice, S. (1972). *Ankara'nın eski bir resmi: tarihi vesika olarak resimler – Ankara'dan bahseden seyyahlar – eski bir Ankara resmi.* Ankara: Türk Tarih Kurumu.

Faroqhi, S. (1985). Onyedinci yüzyıl Ankara'sında sof imalatı ve sof atölyeleri. *İktisat Fakültesi Mecmuası,* (41), 1-4.

Faroqhi, S. (2017). *Osmanlı zanaatkârları.* İstanbul: Alfa Basım Yayım Dağıtım.

Frangakis, E. (1985). The Ottoman port of Izmir in the eighteenth and early nineteenth centuries. 1695-1820. *R. O. M. M.,* (39), 149-162.

Fransa'nın Tiftik İthalatı. (1952*). Mensucat Meslek Dergisi, 5*(8), 322-324.

French, D. (1972). A sixteenth century English merchant in Ankara? *Anatolian Studies,* (22), 241-247.

Gezicht op Ankara [Painting]. (1700-1709). Retrieved from https://www.rijksmuseum.nl/nl/collectie/SK-A-2055.

Güneş, H. (2017, March 13). *Ankara keçisi yünü.* Retrieved from http://tekstilmuhendisleri.blogspot.com.tr/2009/12/ankara-kecisi-yunu.html.

Gür, N. (2014). *1900 yılı uluslararası Paris sergisinde Osmanlı Devleti* (Yayımlanmamış doktora tezi). Marmara Üniversitesi Türkiyat Araştırmaları Enstitüsü, İstanbul.

Gürcan, H. A. (1980). Tiftik iplikçiliğinde İngiliz ve Fransız sistemlerinin iplik özellikleri yönünden karşılaştırılması üzerinde araştırma. *Ege Üniversitesi Tekstil Fakültesi Dergisi, 1*(2), 131-139.

Gürler Menteş, A. (2006). Türkiye tiftik cemiyeti tarihçesi. *Lalahan Hayvancılık Araştırma Enstitüsü Dergisi, 46*(2), 39-46.

Hacıgökmen, M. A. (2005). Ankara Ahilerinin ticarî faaliyetleri ve Bacıyân-ı Rûm hakkında bir araştırma. *A.Ü. Osmanlı Tarihi Araştırma ve Uygulama Merkezi Dergisi (OTAM),* (18), 185-213.

Hayes, J. L. (1880). *Origin and growth of sheep husbandry in the United States with some remarks on Angora fleece.* Washington: Government Printing Office.

Hayes, J. L. (1882). *The Angora goat: it's origin culture and products.* New York: Orange Judd.

History of Angora Goats. (2018, February 2). Retrieved from http://www.angoragoats-mohair.org.uk/angora-goats/history-of-angora-goats/.

Hitzel, F. (2018). L'acclimatation de la chèvre angora en France et en Afrique du Sud. In F. Yenişehirlioğlu ve G. Çerçioğlu Yücel (Prep. by), *Weaving the History: Mystery of a City, Sof* (pp. 87-94)

İçöz, S. S. (1938). Türkiye tiftik cemiyetinin gayesi ve tarihi teşekkülünden Cumhuriyetin on beşinci yıl dönümüne kadar sarf ettiği mesai. *Türk Veterinerler Birliği Dergisi, 8*(5-6), 347-353.

İhsan Abidin [Akıncı]. (1924/1340). *Ankara keçisinin hâli ve ıslahı.* İstanbul: Vatan Matbaası.

İhsan Abidin [Akıncı]. (1932). *Tiftik: istihsalden istihlake kadar.* İstanbul: Kader Matbaası.

İmer, Z. (1992). *Ankara sofunun dünü ve bugünü* (Master thesis). Gazi Üniversitesi Sosyal Bilimler Enstitüsü, Ankara.

İmer, Z. (1994, March). Ankara sofunun geçmişi ve bugünü. *Ankara Dergisi, 2*(6), 85-86.

İmeryüz, F. (1965). *Bazı Ankara keçisi yetiştirme bölgesinden elde edilen Türk tiftiklerinin ve yabancı memleket tiftiklerinin özellikleri.* Sümerbank Merinos Yünlü Sanayii Müessesesi Eğitim Bürosu Yayınları.

İmeryüz, F. (1968). Kaybettiğimiz değer tiftik. *Prodüktivite Verimlilik Dergisi, 2*(6), 352-355.

İnalcık, H. (2011). *Studies in the history of textiles in Turkey.* İstanbul: Türkiye İş Bankası Yayınları.

İşcen, Y. (1993, Mart). Ankiler- sof ve Ankara. *Anfora Dergisi, 1*(11), 6-7.

İvgin, H. (2012), Ankara'nın somut olmayan bir kültürel mirası: Ankara sofu. *Kültür Evreni Dergisi,* 14, 86-93.

Jirousek, C. A. (2008). Rediscovering camlet: traditional mohair cloth weaving in southeastern Turkey. *Textile Society of America Symposium Proceedings,* 267-282.

Kafadar, C. (2009). *Kim var imiş biz burada yoğ iken: dört Osmanlı: Yeniçeri, tüccar, derviş, hatun. İstanbul: Metis Yayınları.*

Kantürk Yiğit, G. (2011). Angora goat and mohair production in Turkey. *Archives of Applied Science Research, 3*(3), 145-153.

Karababa, E. (2012). Investigating early modern Ottoman consumer culture in the light of Bursa probate inventories. *Economic History Review, 65(1), 194-219.*

Karadağ, R. (2007). *Doğal boyamacılık.* Ankara: Geleneksel El Sanatları ve Mağazalar İşletme Müdürlüğü (DÖSİM).

Kılıçbay, M. A. (1994). Sof şehri Ankara. E.

Batur. (Ed.). In *Ankara Ankara* (pp. 65-72). İstanbul: Yapı Kredi Yayınları.

Kınacı, B. (1979, 30 March). Ankara tiftik keçisi, *İstanbul Ticaret Gazetesi, 21*(1049), 4.

Kinghorn, P. M. (1972). *Angora goat husbandry.* Jansenville: S.A. Mohair Growers Association.

Konyalı, İ. H. (1951, February). Ankara keçisinin tarihi. *Tarih Hazinesi Dergisi, 7*(28-02), 360-362.

Koyuncu, M. (1994). Dünya'da ve ülkemizde Ankara keçisi ile tiftik üretimi. *Tekstil & Teknik Dergisi, 10*(110), 26-30.

Köseoğlu, Ü. (2000). Dünya'da ve Türkiye'de Ankara keçisi yetiştiriciliği ve tiftik üretimi. *Tarım ve Köy Dergisi,* (134), 39-40.

Kurşun, Z, Kahraman, S. ve Dağlı, Y. (1998). *Evliyâ Çelebi seyahatnâmesi II. kitap Topkapı Sarayı kütüphanesi Bağdat 304 numaralı yazmanın transkripsiyonu-dizini.* İstanbul: Yapı Kredi Yayınları.

Jardinet, J. G. (1985, Julliet 4). Le voleur illustre. *La Gazette De Lorraine,* 1983, 417-422.

Leiser, G. (1994). Travellers' accounts of mohair production in Ankara from the fifteenth through the nineteenth century. *The Textile Museum Journal,* 5-34.

Namikawa, B., Rogers, J. M. ve Tezcan, H. (1986). *The Topkapı Saray Museum: costumes, embroideries and other textiles.[1], the albums and illustrated manuscripts.* Boston: New York Graphic Soc. Book, Little, Brown.

Mackie, L. W. (1973). *The splendour of Turkish weaving.* Textile Museum, Washington DC.

Manners, I. (2007). *European cartographers and the Ottoman world 1500-1750: maps from the collection of O. J. Sopranos.* Chicago: The Oriental Institute of The University of Chicago.

Miras Üretimde. (2013, December 23). Retrieved from http://www.ankaraka.org.tr/tr/data.asp?id=1942.

Mohair. (2018, February 1). Retrieved from https://en.oxforddictionaries.com/definition/mohair.

Mohair. (2018, February 2). Retrieved from https://en.wikipedia.org/wiki/Mohair.

Mohair Story. (2018, January 29). Retrieved from http://www.mohair.co.za/page/mohair_story.

Museum de Lakenhal. (2018). http://www.lakenhal.nl/en adresinden edinilmiştir.

Müftüoğlu, Ş. and Öznacar, K. (1972). *Ankara keçisi yetiştiriciliği ve tiftik.* Ankara: Veteriner İşleri Genel Müdürlüğü Zootekni Araştırma Enstitüsü.

Ongan, H. (1954-1955). Ankara sofçuluğu ile ilgili bazı vesikalar. *Ankara Belediyesi Dergisi,* 9/13.

Ongan, H. (1958). *Ankara'nın 1 numaralı şer'iye sicili: 21 Rebiülâhır – 991 – Evahir-i Muharrem – 992 (14 Mayıs 1583 – 12 Şubat 1584).* Ankara: Ankara Üniversitesi Dil ve Tarih Coğrafya Fakültesi.

Ongan, H. (1974). *Ankara'nın 2 numaralı şer'iye sicili: 1 Muharrem 997 –8 Ramazan 998 (20 Kasım 1588 – 11 Temmuz 1590).* Ankara: Türk Tarih Kurumu.

Öğüt, G. (2013, Octıber 8). *Boyner ailesinin 150 yıllık aile geleneği.* Retrieved from http://www.hurriyet.com.tr/boyner-ailesinin-150-yillik-aile-gelenegi-24845155.

Öney, G. (1971). *Ankara'da Türk devri yapıları/ Turkish period buildings in Ankara.* Ankara: Ankara Üniversitesi Dil ve Tarih, Coğrafya Fakültesi Yayınları.

Örkiz, M. (1980). *Ankara keçisi yetiştirme ve tiftik pazarlaması.* Ankara: Gıda Tarım ve Hayvancılık Bakanlığı Lalahan Zooteknik Araştırma Enstitüsü.

Özdemir, R. (1986). Ankara esnaf teşkilatı. *Ondokuz Mayıs Üniversitesi Eğitim Fakültesi Dergisi, 1*(1), 156-181.

Özdemir, R. (1998). *XIX. Yüzyılın ilk yarısında Ankara (fiziki, demografik, idari ve sosyo-ekonomik yapısı): 1785-1840.* Ankara: Kültür ve Turizm Bakanlığı.

Özkan Tağı, S. and Erdoğan, Z. (2014). The adventure of mohair in Anatolia. *Folk Life, 52*(1), 49-61.

Öztuncay, H. (1960). Tiftik lüks hammaddedir. *Mensucat Meslek Dergisi, 13*(1), 20-22.

Öztürk, İ. (1982) Bitki boyaları üzerine birkaç not ve Yenikent köyünden boyama örnekleri. *Türk Etnografya Dergisi,* (17), 49-58.

Porter, H. G., and Hornbeck, M. B. (1964). Wool and other animal fibers. *The Yearbook of Agriculture,* (224), 251-257.

Ryder, M. (1993). The use of goat hair an introductory historical review. *Anthropozoolog,* (17), 37-46.

Speake, J. (Ed.). (2013). *Literature of travel and exploration: an encyclopedia.* Oxford: Routledge Publishing.

Su, K. (1982). Tiftik ve sofçuluk. *Türk Etnografya Dergisi, 8,* 59-77.

Sunley, D. (1971). *The Lesotho mohair industry: history and evaluation 1970, and five more years.* Port Elizabeth, South Africa: Mohair Board.

Sunley, D. (1988). *Cinderella to princess: the story of mohair in South Africa, 1838 to 1988.* Port Elizabeth, South Africa: Mohair Board.

Sülüner, H. S. (2014). Yabancı seyyahların gözlemleriyle Roma ve Bizans dönemi'nde Ankara. *Ankara Araştırmaları Dergisi, 2*(1), 11-21.

Şahin, G. (2013a). Türkiye'de Ankara keçisi (Capra hircus ancryrensis) yetiştiriciliğinin dünü bugünü ve yarını. *Celal Bayar Üniversitesi Sosyal Bilimler Dergisi, 11*(2), 338-352.

Şahin, G. (2013b). Coğrafi bir simge olarak Ankara keçisinin Türkiye'deki mevcut durumu. *Milli Folklor Dergisi,* 195-209.

Tamur, E. (2003). *Ankara keçisi ve Ankara tiftik dokumacılığı: tükenen bir zenginliğin ve çöken bir sanayinin tarihsel öyküsünden kesitler.* Ankara: Ankara Ticaret Odası.

Tamur, E. (2008). Amsterdam'da bir Türk resmi. *Kebikeç, 13*(25), 385-409.

Tan, S. (2014). XIX. yüzyılda Anadolu'dan Güney Afrika'ya tiftik keçisinin yasal ve kaçak sevkiyatı. *Osmanlı Tarihi Araştırma ve Uygulama Merkezi Dergisi (OTAM),* (35), 137-152.

Tarih Boyunca Ankara'nın Simgesi Ankara Keçisi. (2002). *Tarım İl Müdürlüğü Yayınları, 10.*

TDK Güncel Türkçe Sözlük. (2018). Retrieved from http://tdk.gov.tr/index.php?option=com_gts&view=gts.

TDK Derleme Sözlüğü. (2018). Retrieved from http://tdk.gov.tr/index.php?option=com_ttas&view=ttas.

The Origins of the Angora Goat.(2005, May). *British Angora Goat Society.* Retrieved from https://www.angoragoats-mohair.org.

uk/angora-goats/history-of-angora-goats/.

Thompson, G. F. (1903). *A manual of Angora goat raising*. Chicago: American Sheep Breederco Press.

Thompson, G. F. (1906). *Information concerning the Angora goat.* Washington: Government Printing Office.

Tiftikbirlik. (2018). Tiftik [Mohair]. Retrieved from http://tiftikbirlik.com.tr/sayfa.aspx?ID=3.

Tiftikbirlik. (2018, February 2). Retrieved from http://www.tiftikbirlik.com.tr/sayfa.aspx?ID=1.

Tiftik Raporu [Mohair Report]. (2016). Retrieved from http://koop.gtb.gov.tr/data/58e5f6ac1a79f54dd851b460/2016%20Tiftik%20Raporu.pdf.

Tiftik: Türkiye ve Diğer Memleketlerde Tiftik Keçisi ve Yetiştirilmesi Hakkında Düşünce ve Tavsiyeler. (1964). İstanbul: Yenilik Basımevi.

Topkapi Sarayı Museum. (1983) *The Anatolian Civilizations,* (3).

Tournefort, J. P. (1741). *A voyage into the levant*. Londra: D. Midwinter.

Tournefort Seyahatnamesi. (2013). S. Yerasimos (Ed.), A. Berktay (Çev.). İstanbul: Kitap Yayınevi.

İstanbul'dan Anadolu'ya Seyahat Günlüğü. (1992). H. Dernschwam (Yaz.), Y. Önen (Çev.). Ankara: Kültür Bakanlığı.

Tunçer, M. (2015). Angora'nın merkezi: Hacıdoğan mahallesi. *Kadriye Zaim Kütüphanesi Yansı Dergisi*, (39), 27-43.

Turhan, S. (2016, Nisan 6). *Ankara'nın altını: sof.* Retrieved from http://www.tarihhaber.net/ankaranin-altini-sof/.

Turkish Cultural Foundation. (2018). Retrieved from tcfdatu.org.

Türkiye Ticaret Odaları ve Ticaret Borsaları Birliği. (1969). *Tiftik semineri, 25-27 kasım 1968*. Ankara: Türkiye Ticaret Odaları ve Ticaret Borsaları Birliği.

Türkoğlu, Ömer. (2010, Mayıs-Haziran). Ankara'nın unuttuğumuz değerlerinden sof. *Ankara Eğitim, Kültür ve Sanat Dergisi, 12*(67), 22.

Türk Mektupları (2011). O.G. Busbecq (Author), D. Türkömer (Tran.). İstanbul:Türkiye İş Bankası Yayınları.

Utkanlar, N. (1965). *Dünya'da Ankara keçisi yetiştirciliği ve tiftikçiliğimizin milli ekonomideki yeri.* Sümerbank Merinos Yünlü Sanayii Müessesesi Eğitim Bürosu.

Üstar, M. F. (1940). *Tiftik ve tiftikçiliğimiz.* İstanbul: Üniversite Kitabevi.

Vajanto, K. (2014). Finnish shipwreck textiles from the 13th–18th centuries. In AD. S. Lipkin and K. Vajanto (Eds.). *Monographs of the Archaeological Society of Finland 3: Focus on Archaeological Textiles: Multidisclipinary* (pp. 116–131). Helsinki: Archaeological Society of Finland.

Varlık, M. B. (2014). Ankara milli mensucat (Türk) anonim şirketi (1916-1930). *Ankara Araştırmaları Dergisi, 2*(1), 74-92.

V&A Museum. (2018). Retrieved from https://www.vam.ac.uk/.

VEKAM. (2018). Retrieved from https://vekam.ku.edu.tr/tr/vekam.

Webb Yıldırmak, G. (2006). *XVIII. yüzyılda tiftik ipliğinin Osmanlı-İngiliz ticaretindeki yeri/ the place of mohair yarn in XVIIIth century Anglo-Ottoman trade* (Unpublished doctoral dissertation). Ankara Üniversitesi Sosyal Bilimler Enstitüsü, Ankara.

Webb Yıldırmak, G. (2011). *XVIII. yüzyılda Osmanlı-İngiliz tiftik ticareti.* Türk Tarih Kurumu Yayınları.

Wilson, S. (1873). *The Angora goat: with an account of its introduction into Victoria and a report on the flock.* Melbourne: Stillwell and Knight.

Yanar, A. and Akpınarlı, F. (2016). Geleneksel Ankara sof dokumaları. *Ankara Araştırmaları Dergisi, 4*(2), 170-179.

Yaman, B. (2014). *Sarayın terzileri: 16-18. yüzyıl Osmanlı hâssa kıyafet birimleri.* M. Kocaaslan (Ed.). Isparta: Nokta Digital Yayınları.

Yavuz, E., and Uğurel, Ü. N. (Eds.). (1984). *Tarih içinde Ankara (Eylül 1981 Seminer Bildirileri).* Ankara: Orta Doğu Teknik Üniversitesi.

Yazıcıoğlu, G. (1994). Tiftik keçisinin kökeni ve Türkiye'de tiftik. *Tekstil ve Mühendis, 8*(43-44), 21-23.

Acknowledgements

Ahmet Kaymaz | Tosya

Alev Ayaokur | Koç University, VEKAM

Ayşe Erdoğdu | Topkapı Palace Museum

Ayşegül Ertan | Mohair & Angora

Begüm Akkoyunlu Ersöz | Pera Museum

Bengi Çınar Kul | Ankara University

Ceyda Cüceloğlu | Koç University, VEKAM

Clare Brown | Victoria & Albert Museum

Damla Çinici | Hacettepe University

E. Gökhan Bozkurtlar | T.R. Ministry of Culture and Tourism, General Directorate of Cultural Heritage and Museums

Elif Turgut | Hacettepe University

Elif Yıldırım | Mohair Ferla

Emine Kıraç | Retired Director of the Advanced Technical Institute for Girls

Emine Torgan Güzel | DATU

Eray Ergeç | Netherlands Embassy in Ankara

Erik Weststrate | Netherlands Embassy in Ankara

Erman Tamur | Researcher and writer

Feyza Akder | Koç University

Gizem Gün | Hacettepe University

Güldane Oğuz | Tiftikbirlik

Güler Köknar | TCF

Hannah Kauffman | Victoria & Albert Museum

Hatice Doğruol | Gazi University

Hatice Ildıroyuk | Ethnography Museum of Ankara

Hülya Bilgi | Sadberk Hanım Museum

İbrahim Keleş | Graphic Designer

İlkay Türkdoğan | T.R. Ministry of Culture and Tourism, General Directorate of Cultural Heritage and Museums

İsmail Koyucugil | Tosya, weaver

İsmi Kazkayası

Janneke Martens | Rijksmuseum, Amsterdam

Jori Zijlmans | Museum de Lakenhal

Kerime Senyücel | Director

Kezban Yıldız

Koray Olşen | AFSAD

Lale Avşar| Selçuk University

Lale Görünür | Sadberk Hanım Museum

M. Öcal Oğuz | UNESCO

Mehtap Türkyılmaz | Koç University, VEKAM

Melahat-Mahmut Salman | Tosya, weavers

Mine Sofuoğlu | Rahmi M. Koç Museum Ankara

Mustafa Kürşat Bazlamatçı | Tosya Municipality

Nilüfer Aykar | Altınyıldız

Nilüfer Ertan | T.R. Ministry of Culture and Tourism, General Directorate of Cultural Heritage and Museums

Onur Bal

Osman Boyner | Boyner Holding

Özbahar Family

Recep Karadağ | DATU

Sadık Karamustafa | Karamustafa Design

Semih Yolaçan

Seyfi Bektaş | Tosya Chamber of Bath Glove and Waistcloth Producers

Sibel Alpaslan Arça | Topkapı Palace Museum

Suat Alp | Hacettepe University

Süreyya-Bünyamin Zile

Taco Dibbits | Rijksmuseum, Amsterdam

The State Art and Sculpture Museum, Ankara

Türkiye İş Bankası

Utku Can Akın

Veysel Tiryaki | Altındağ Municipality Mayor

Yavuz Sökün | Altınyıldız

Yücel Kumandaş | Ethnography Museum of Ankara

Zahide İmer | KTO Karatay University

STRÖER • KENTVİZYON